THE IDEOLOGIC
OF THE BRITIS

MW00810189

The Ideological Origins of the British Empire presents the first comprehensive history of British conceptions of empire for more than half a century. David Armitage traces the emergence of British imperial ideology from the middle of the sixteenth to the middle of the eighteenth century, using a full range of manuscript and printed sources. By linking the histories of England, Scotland and Ireland with the history of the British Empire, he demonstrates the importance of ideology as an essential linking between the processes of state-formation and empire-building. This book sheds new light on major British political thinkers, from Sir Thomas Smith to David Hume, by providing novel accounts of the 'British problem' in the early-modern period, of the relationship between Protestantism and empire, of theories of property, liberty and political economy in imperial perspective, and of the imperial contribution to the emergence of British 'identities' in the Atlantic world.

DAVID ARMITAGE is Associate Professor of History at Columbia University. He is the editor of *Bolingbroke: Political Writings* for Cambridge Texts in the History of Political Thought (1997) and *Theories of Empire 1450–1800* (1998), and co-editor (with Armand Himy and Quentin Skinner) of *Milton and Republicanism* (1995).

IDEAS IN CONTEXT

Edited by QUENTIN SKINNER (*General Editor*), LORRAINE DASTON,
DOROTHY ROSS and JAMES TULLY

The books in this series will discuss the emergence of intellectual traditions and of related new disciplines. The procedures, aims and vocabularies that were generated will be set in the context of the alternatives available within the contemporary frameworks of ideas and institutions. Through detailed studies of the evolution of such traditions, and their modification by different audiences, it is hoped that a new picture will form of the development of ideas in their concrete contexts. By this means, artificial distinctions between the history of philosophy, of the various sciences, of society and politics, and of literature may be seen to dissolve.

The series is published with the support of the Exxon Foundation.

A list of books in the series will be found at the end of the volume.

IDEAS IN CONTEXT 59

THE IDEOLOGICAL ORIGINS
OF THE BRITISH EMPIRE

THE
IDEOLOGICAL ORIGINS
OF THE
BRITISH EMPIRE

DAVID ARMITAGE

Columbia University

PUBLISHED BY THE PRESS SYNDICATE OF THE UNIVERSITY OF CAMBRIDGE
The Pitt Building, Trumpington Street, Cambridge, United Kingdom

CAMBRIDGE UNIVERSITY PRESS
The Edinburgh Building, Cambridge CB2 2RU, UK
40 West 20th Street, New York NY 10011-4211, USA
477 Williamstown Road, Port Melbourne, VIC 3207, Australia
Ruiz de Alarcón 13, 28014 Madrid, Spain
Dock House, The Waterfront, Cape Town 8001, South Africa

http://www.cambridge.org

© David Armitage 2000

First published 2000
Fourth printing 2004

Printed in Great Britain at the University Press, Cambridge

Typeset in Baskerville 11/12.5 pt [VN]

A catalogue record for this book is available from the British Library

Armitage, David, 1965–
The ideological origins of the British Empire / David Armitage.
p. cm. – (Ideas in context; 59)
Includes bibliographical references and index.
ISBN 0 521 59081 7 (hb)
1. Great Britain–Colonies–History. 2. Political science–Great Britain–History. I. Title. II. Series.

JV1011 .A75 2000   325'.341–dc21   99-087438

ISBN 0 521 59081 7 hardback
ISBN 0 521 78978 8 paperback

For
DH, MRA, BGA and CFLA

Contents

Acknowledgements

The origins of this book are tangled and extend back over a decade. I have been very fortunate to receive material and moral assistance for it from many generous institutions. For financial support, I am grateful to the British Academy; the Commonwealth Fund of New York; the John Carter Brown Library; Emmanuel College, Cambridge; and the Columbia University Council on Research and Faculty Development in the Humanities. For providing ideal conditions in which to work on the book and a series of associated projects, I thank particularly the staff and Librarian of the John Carter Brown Library; the Master and Fellows of Emmanuel College; the staff and Director of the Institute for Advanced Studies in the Humanities, Edinburgh University; the staff and Director of the National Humanities Center; and the members of the History Department at Columbia University.

Institutional obligations mask a host of personal debts. During my tenure of a Harkness Fellowship at Princeton University, Sir John Elliott, Peter Lake, John Pocock, David Quint and the late Lawrence Stone offered crucial and lasting inspiration; back in Cambridge, Chris Bayly, Peter Burke, Patrick Collinson, Istvan Hont and Anthony Pagden asked essential and abiding questions; later, John Robertson and Blair Worden examined the doctoral dissertation from which this study sprang. All have since provided indispensable support, for which I am deeply grateful.

As the scope of the study, and of my other work, has expanded over subsequent years, I have particularly appreciated the encouragement and assistance of Richard Bushman, Nicholas Canny, Linda Colley, Martin Dzelzainis, Andrew Fitzmaurice, Lige Gould, Jack Greene, John Headley, Karen Kupperman, Elizabeth Mancke, Peter Marshall, Roger Mason, Karen O'Brien, Jane Ohlmeyer and Jenny Wormald. For vital support and confidence at crucial moments, I owe special debts to David Kastan, Darrin McMahon, Nigel Smith and Dror Wahrman.

For their friendship and hospitality, over many years and in many places, I cannot adequately thank Catharine Macleod and Frank Salmon, Jennifer McCullough and Peter McCullough or Melissa Calaresu and Joan Pau Rubiés.

For their comments, I am happy to be able to thank a variety of audiences on both sides of the Atlantic who have heard earlier versions of parts of my argument. I must express particular appreciation to the University Seminars at Columbia University for assistance in the preparation of the manuscript for publication. Material drawn from the book was presented to the University Seminars on Early American History and Culture, Irish History and Culture, the Renaissance, Eighteenth-Century European Culture, and Social and Political Thought. For permission to reproduce and revise material which has appeared elsewhere in print, I am also grateful to the editors of *The Historical Journal* and *The American Historical Review*; the Past and Present Society; Cambridge University Press; the University of North Carolina Press; Oxford University Press; and K. G. Saur Verlag. Most of all, I must thank the staff at Cambridge University Press for their patience and care at every stage of writing and publishing this book. Richard Fisher has exemplified these virtues, along with generosity and confidence well beyond the reasonable expectations of any author; my thanks also to Nancy Hynes for her excellent copy-editing and to Auriol Griffith-Jones for compiling the index so efficiently.

It is a special pleasure to be able to acknowledge enduring debts to Nick Henshall, without whose example, I should never have become an historian, and to Ruth Smith, without whose lasting confidence, I could not have remained one; her remarkable vigilance also greatly improved this book at a very late stage. More recently, and no less importantly, David Cannadine has been a model of collegiality, commitment and comradeship.

Finally, my greatest debts are to Quentin Skinner and Joyce Chaplin. Quentin has throughout been a reader, critic and interlocutor without peer; many have had cause to thank him, but few can be as grateful as I. Joyce has seen everything of this book and of its author but has not flinched or faltered; for this faith and love, much thanks.

CHAPTER I

Introduction: state and empire in British history

> ... the word, *empire*, conveys an idea of a vast territory, composed of
> various people; whereas that of *kingdom*, implies, one more
> bounded; and intimates the unity of that nation, of which it is
> formed.[1]

By the second quarter of the eighteenth century, the British Empire
comprehended the United Kingdom of Great Britain, Ireland, the
islands of the Caribbean and the British mainland colonies of North
America.[2] The frontiers of that extensive monarchy were guarded by a
common religion and by the Royal Navy. The gentle, but powerful
influence of laws and manners had gradually cemented the union of the
provinces. Their free, white inhabitants enjoyed and produced the
advantages of wealth and luxury. The image of a free constitution was
preserved with a decent reverence. The Hanoverian kings appeared to
possess the sovereign authority, and devolved on their parliaments all
the executive powers of government. During a crucial period of almost
fourscore years (1688–1760), the public administration was conducted
by a succession of Whig politicians. It is the design of this, and of the
succeeding chapters, to describe the ideological origins of their empire,
though not to deduce the most important circumstances of its decline
and fall: the American Revolution, which dismembered the British
Atlantic Empire, lies beyond the immediate scope of this book.

The history of the rise, decline and fall of the British Empire has most
often been told as the story of an empire whose foundations lay in India
during the second half of the eighteenth century.[3] That empire formally

---

[1] John Trusler, *The Difference, Between Words, Esteemed Synonymous, in the English Language*, 2 vols.
(London, 1766), II, 15.

[2] C. H. Firth, '"The British Empire"', *Scottish Historical Review*, 15 (1918), 185–9; James Truslow
Adams, 'On the Term "British Empire"', *American Historical Review*, 27 (1922), 485–9.

[3] From J. Holland Rose, A. P. Newton and E. A. Benians (gen. eds.), *The Cambridge History of the
British Empire*, 9 vols. (Cambridge, 1929–61) to Wm. Roger Louis (gen. ed.), *The Oxford History of the
British Empire*, 5 vols. (Oxford, 1998–99).

encompassed parts of South Asia, Australasia, Africa and the Americas. Its ascent began with British victory at the battle of Plassey in 1757, continued almost unabated in South Asia and the Pacific until the end of the Napoleonic Wars, resumed momentum in the latter half of the nineteenth century during the European 'scramble for Africa', and then unravelled definitively during and after the Second World War. William Pitt was its midwife, Lord Mountbatten its sexton and Winston Churchill its chief mourner in Britain. Its ghost lives on in the form of the Commonwealth; its sole remains are the handful of United Kingdom Overseas Territories, from Bermuda to the Pitcairn Islands.[4] In this account, the American Revolution and its aftermath divided the two (supposedly distinct) Empires, chronologically, geographically and institutionally. The Peace of Paris that ended the Seven Years War in 1763 marked the end of French imperial power in North America and South Asia. Twenty years later, in 1783, the Peace of Paris by which Britain acknowledged the independence of the United States of America marked the beginnings of a newly configured British Atlantic Empire, still including the Caribbean islands and the remaining parts of British North America; it also signalled the British Empire's decisive 'swing to the east' into the Indian and Pacific oceans.[5] Historians of the eighteenth-century British Empire have protested against any easy separation between the 'First' and 'Second' British Empires on the grounds that the two overlapped in time, that they shared common purposes and personnel, and that the differences between the maritime, commercial colonies of settlement in North America and the military, territorial colonies of conquest in India have been crudely overdrawn.[6] Nevertheless, among historians, and more generally in the popular imagination, the British Empire still denotes that 'Second' Empire, which was founded in the late eighteenth century and whose character distinguished it decisively from the 'Old Colonial System' of the British Atlantic world that had gone before it.[7]

[4] For instance, most recently, in Lawrence James, *The Rise and Fall of the British Empire* (London, 1994), Denis Judd, *Empire: The British Imperial Experience, From 1765 to the Present* (London, 1996) and P. J. Marshall (ed.), *The Cambridge Illustrated History of the British Empire* (Cambridge, 1996); exceptions are Angus Calder, *Revolutionary Empire: The Rise of the English-Speaking Peoples from the Fifteenth Century to the 1780s* (London, 1981) and T. O. Lloyd, *The British Empire 1558–1983* (Oxford, 1984).

[5] V. T. Harlow, *The Founding of the Second British Empire, 1763–1793*, 2 vols. (London, 1952–64).

[6] Peter Marshall, 'The First and Second British Empires: A Question of Demarcation', *History*, 49 (1964), 13–23; Philip Lawson, 'The Missing Link: The Imperial Dimension in Understanding Hanoverian Britain', *The Historical Journal*, 29 (1986), 747–51; P. J. Marshall, 'Britain and the World in the Eighteenth Century: 1, Reshaping the Empire', *Transactions of the Royal Historical Society*, 6th ser., 8 (1998), 1–18.

[7] G. L. Beer, *The Origins of the British Colonial System 1578–1660* (London, 1908).

The conflation of British Imperial history with the history of the Second British Empire has encouraged the separation of the history of Britain and Ireland from the history of the Empire itself.[8] 'British' history is assumed to mean 'domestic' history; Imperial history implies extra-territorial history. This distinction was at least understandable, if not defensible, as long as the Empire was assumed to be divided from the metropole by vast physical distances, to be overwhelmingly distinct in its racial composition, and to be dependent upon, rather than formally equal with, Britain itself. The attributed character of the Second British Empire – as an empire founded on military conquest, racial subjection, economic exploitation and territorial expansion – rendered it incompatible with metropolitan norms of liberty, equality and the rule of law, and demanded that the Empire be exoticised and further differentiated from domestic history. The purported character of the First British Empire – as 'for the most part a maritime empire, an oceanic empire of trade and settlement, not an empire of conquest; an empire defended by ships, not troops'[9] – assimilated it more closely to the domestic histories of the Three Kingdoms by making it the outgrowth of British norms, exported and fostered by metropolitan migrants. The revolutionary crisis in the British Atlantic world, between 1763 and 1783, revealed the practical and theoretical limits of any such assimilation. Thereafter, the former colonies became part of the history of the United States. This in turn facilitated the identification of the history of the British Empire with the history of the Second Empire and fostered the continuing disjuncture between 'British' and 'Imperial' histories.

The Ideological Origins of the British Empire attempts to reintegrate the history of the British Empire with the history of early-modern Britain on the ground of intellectual history. This approach faces its own difficulties, in that the history of political thought has more often treated the history of ideas of the state than it has the concepts of empire, at least as that term has been vulgarly understood.[10] Political thought is, by definition, the

[8] A note on terminology: 'Britain' is used either as a geographical expression, to refer to the island encompassing England, Wales and Scotland, or as a shorthand political term, to denote the United Kingdom of Great Britain created by the Anglo-Scottish union of 1707; 'Britain and Ireland' is taken to be synonymous with the 'Three Kingdoms' of England, Scotland and Ireland throughout the period before 1707. 'British Isles' is only used when it expresses the vision of a particular author – for example, Edmund Spenser; 'British' is likewise not held to include 'Irish', except when particular authors employed it otherwise.
[9] Thomas R. Metcalf, *Ideologies of the Raj, The New Cambridge History of India*, III.4 (Cambridge, 1994), 4.
[10] For the emergence of concepts of the state in competition with ideologies of empire see Quentin Skinner, *The Foundations of Modern Political Thought*, 2 vols. (Cambridge, 1978), I, 8–12; James Tully, *Strange Multiplicity: Constitutionalism in an Age of Diversity* (Cambridge, 1995), 15–17.

history of the *polis*, the self-contained, firmly bounded, sovereign and integrated community that preceded and sometimes shadowed the history of empire and that paralleled and ultimately overtook that history during the age of the great nation-states. For this reason, the British Empire has not been an actor in the history of political thought, any more than political thought has generally been hospitable to considering the ideologies of empire. The very pursuit of an intellectual history for the British Empire has been dismissed by historians who have described seventeenth-century arguments regarding the British Empire as 'intellectually of no … commanding calibre', and have counselled that '[t]o look for any significant intellectual or ideological contribution to the ordering of empire in the first two decades of George III's reign would seem at first sight to be a barren task'.[11] This is symptomatic of a more lasting unwillingness to consider ideologies of empire as part of political theory or the history of political thought.[12] However, the study of imperial ideologies can clarify the limits of political theory studied on the unexamined principle that it encompasses solely the theory of the state and its ideological predecessors.[13] It is therefore essential to recover the intellectual history of the British Empire from the 'fit of absence of mind' into which it has fallen.[14]

    This study understands the term 'ideology' in two senses: first, in the programmatic sense of a systematic model of how society functions and second, as a world-view which is perceived as contestable by those who do not share it.[15] This latter sense does not imply that such an ideology should necessarily be exposed as irrational because it can be identified as simply the expression of sectional interests; rather, it implies that contemporaries may have seen such an interconnected set of beliefs as both

---

[11] Klaus E. Knorr, *British Colonial Theories 1570–1850* (Toronto, 1944), 62; P. J. Marshall, 'Empire and Authority in the Later Eighteenth Century', *Journal of Imperial and Commonwealth History*, 15 (1987), 105.

[12] Though for early attempts to consider this problem, from the dying decades of the British Empire, see Sir Ernest Barker, *The Ideas and Ideals of the British Empire* (Cambridge, 1941), George Bennett (ed.), *The Concept of Empire: Burke to Attlee, 1774–1947* (London, 1953) and Eric Stokes, *The Political Ideas of English Imperialism: An Inaugural Lecture Given in the University College of Rhodesia and Nyasaland* (Oxford, 1960).

[13] Tully, *Strange Multiplicity*, 58–98.

[14] Compare Peter N. Miller, *Defining the Common Good. Empire, Religion and Philosophy in Eighteenth-Century Britain* (Cambridge, 1994); Anthony Pagden, *Lords of All the World: Ideologies of Empire in Spain, Britain and France c. 1500 – c. 1800* (New Haven, 1995); David Armitage (ed.), *Theories of Empire, 1450–1800* (Aldershot, 1998).

[15] Raymond Geuss, *The Idea of a Critical Theory: Habermas and the Frankfurt School* (Cambridge, 1981), 10; Keith Michael Baker, 'On the Problem of the Ideological Origins of the French Revolution', in Baker, *Inventing the French Revolution: Essays on French Political Culture in the Eighteenth Century* (Cambridge, 1990), 17–18.

argumentatively flawed and compromised by needs which they did not
share. This spirit of ideological critique could see such beliefs as ra-
tionally indefensible, or even false, just because they answered to a
particular set of needs; more importantly, rational disagreement about
the status of those beliefs rendered them the product of contemporary
political and philosophical argument. The purpose of this study is
therefore not to expose beliefs about the British Empire as either true or
false, but rather to show the ways in which the constitutive elements of
various conceptions of the British Empire arose in the competitive
context of political argument. It deploys resources from a wider tradition
of political thought, stretching back to classical sources in ancient Greece
and, especially, Rome, but also encompassing contemporary Spain and
the United Provinces, as part of a wider European dialogue within which
the various empires were defined and defended.[16] Its purpose is therefore
not to claim that the origins of the British Empire can be found only in
ideology; rather, it seeks to locate the origins of the ideological definition
of empire in Britain, Ireland and the wider Atlantic world.

Any search for origins is, of course, fraught with a basic conceptual
ambiguity. An origin can be either a beginning or a cause, a logical and
chronological *terminus a quo*, or the starting-point from which a chain of
consequences derives. 'In popular usage, an origin is a beginning which
explains', warned Marc Bloch. 'Worse still, a beginning which is a
complete explanation. There lies the ambiguity, there the danger!' To
discover the etymology of a word does nothing to explain its present
meaning, though the gap between its etymological root and its current
usage can be historically revealing, but only if approached contextually.
'In a word, a historical phenomenon can never be understood apart
from its moment in time.'[17] Similarly, the context within which a
concept emerges does not determine its future usage, though the history
of its usage across time will reveal a great deal about the history of the
later contexts within which it was deployed. The origins of a concept, as
of any other object of historical inquiry, are not necessarily connected to
any later outcome, causally or otherwise: aetiology is not simply teleology in reverse. Conversely, present usage or practice offers no sure
guide to the origins of a concept or activity.

No matter how perfectly you have understood the *usefulness* of any physiological
organ (or legal institution, social custom, political usage, art form or religious

---

[16] On which see generally Pagden, *Lords of All the World*.
[17] Marc Bloch, *The Historian's Craft*, trans. Peter Putnam (New York, 1953), 30, 32–3, 35.

rite) you have not yet thereby grasped how it emerged ... the whole history of a 'thing,' an organ, a tradition, can to this extent be a continuous chain of signs, continually revealing new interpretations and adaptations, the causes of which need not be connected even amongst themselves, but rather sometimes just follow and replace one another at random.

Meaning cannot therefore be identified with purpose, least of all in the case of a concept, of which '[t]he form is fluid, the "meaning" even more so'.[18]

Confusion between origins as beginnings and origins as causes has bedevilled the history of the British Empire at least since the eighteenth century. The chronological origins of the British Empire have most often been traced back to the reign of Elizabeth I, and hence to the maritime exploits of her English sailors. This chronology defined the Empire as Protestant, *Anglo*-British, benign and extra-European, because it originated in post-Reformation, specifically English activities, was the product of navies not armies, and was conducted across vast oceanic expanses, far from the metropolis.[19] This was the vision of imperial origins emblematised in Millais's 'The Boyhood of Raleigh' (1870), itself inspired by the painter's reading of J. A. Froude's essay on the Elizabethan sea-dogs, 'England's Forgotten Worthies' (1852).[20] More recent historians have espoused a similar chronology but for different reasons, by finding the origins of British imperialism in English colonialism on the Celtic crescent surrounding the English core-state. This was still an Anglo-British imperialism, though it was neither benign nor exotic. External 'imperialism' was the offspring of 'internal colonialism', as the English developed their ideologies of racial supremacy, political hegemony, cultural superiority and divinely appointed civilising mission in their relations with a 'Celtic fringe', beginning in Ireland in the sixteenth century.[21] Maintaining the content, but disputing the chronology, an alternative aetiology for English imperialism – defined by its supremacist racism, its crusading national identity and its ideology of conquest – has instead been traced to the twelfth century, and the

[18] Friedrich Nietzsche, *On the Genealogy of Morality* (1887), ed. Keith Ansell-Pearson, trans. Carol Diethe (Cambridge, 1994), 55.
[19] Cynthia Fansler Behrman, *Victorian Myths of the Sea* (Athens, Ohio, 1977), 30–7, 113–16.
[20] [J. A. Froude,] 'England's Forgotten Worthies', *The Westminster Review*, n.s. 2, 1 (July 1852), 29; M. H. Spielman, *Millais and His Works* (Edinburgh, 1898), 124; John Burrow, *A Liberal Descent: Victorian Historians and the English Past* (Cambridge, 1981), 231–2.
[21] Michael Hechter, *Internal Colonialism: The Celtic Fringe in British National Development* (London, 1975); Philip Corrigan and Derek Sayer, *The Great Arch: English State Formation as Cultural Revolution* (Oxford, 1985); Hugh Kearney, *The British Isles: A History of Four Nations* (Cambridge, 1989), 106–27.

attempted anglicisation of Ireland, Scotland and Wales chronicled in the works of William of Malmesbury and Gerald of Wales.[22] This thesis in turn disrupts any continuity between state-formation and empire-building by making English imperialism a solely archipelagic phenomenon whose continuities with extra-British empire-building were tenuous and analogical. In reaction, other historians, attempting to save the chronology of origins but extend its scope forward from the sixteenth century, have 'unearthed in protestant religious consciousness a root, perhaps even the taproot, of English imperialism';[23] even more precisely, the 'origins of Anglo-British imperialism' have been located in the Anglo-Scottish propaganda wars of the mid-sixteenth century.[24]

This study reconsiders both the traditional and more recent accounts of the ideological origins of the British Empire by tracing the histories both of the concept of the British Empire and of the different conceptions of that empire from the mid-sixteenth century to the mid-eighteenth century.[25] The 'concept' of the British Empire means the idea that an identifiable political community existed to which the term 'empire' could be fittingly applied and which was recognisably British, rather than, for example, Roman, French or English. It will be argued that the emergence of the concept of the 'British Empire' as a political community encompassing England and Wales, Scotland, Protestant Ireland, the British islands of the Caribbean and the mainland colonies of North America, was long drawn out, and only achieved by the late seventeenth century at the earliest. This was not because the conceptual language of Britishness was lacking; rather, it had been used in the sixteenth and seventeenth centuries to describe less expansive communities within the Three Kingdoms of Britain and Ireland. Nor was it because the language of 'empire' was absent from British political discourse: it too was used in more restricted senses. Only in the first half of the eighteenth century, it will be argued, did the two languages coincide to provide the conception of that larger community within

---

[22] John Gillingham, 'Images of Ireland 1170–1600: The Origins of English Imperialism', *History Today*, 37, 2 (Feb. 1987), 16–22; Gillingham, 'The Beginnings of English Imperialism', *Journal of Historical Sociology*, 5 (1992), 392–409; Rees Davies, 'The English State and the "Celtic" Peoples 1100–1400', *Journal of Historical Sociology*, 6 (1993), 1–14.

[23] Patrick Collinson, *The Birthpangs of Protestant England: Religious and Cultural Change in the Sixteenth and Seventeenth Centuries* (London, 1988), 5.

[24] Roger A. Mason, 'The Scottish Reformation and the Origins of Anglo-British Imperialism', in Mason (ed.), *Scots and Britons: Scottish Political Thought and the Union of 1603* (Cambridge, 1994), 161–86.

[25] For the distinction between 'concepts' and 'conceptions' see, for example, Ronald Dworkin, *Taking Rights Seriously*, rev. edn (Cambridge, Mass., 1978), 134–6.

which the Three Kingdoms of Britain and Ireland and the English-speaking islands, colonies, plantations and territories of the western hemisphere were all members – albeit, unequal members – of a single political body known as the 'British Empire'.

The unifying concept of the British Empire left generous room for different conceptions of that Empire. By the 1730s, an integrated concept of the British Empire could be found in the political writings of creole elites and imperial officials throughout the British Atlantic world. It was yoked to a particular conception of the Empire, espoused in particular by oppositional politicians within Britain, that became dominant (though it did not remain unchallenged). According to this conception, the British Empire had certain characteristics which distinguished it both from past empires and from contemporary imperial polities such as the Spanish Monarchy. Its inhabitants believed it to be primarily Protestant, despite the variety even of Protestant denominations that could be found within the Three Kingdoms and among the islands and colonies; most importantly, it was not Catholic, despite the obvious presence of a persistent Catholic majority in Ireland and of other pockets of Roman Catholicism, for instance in Maryland.

The British Empire was an arena of hemispheric and international trade. Its character was therefore commercial. The attachment to commerce – and the means by which commerce connected the various parts of the Empire to one another – made the British Empire different from its predecessors or its rivals, most of which (it was believed) had been integrated by force, or had been operated more for reasons of power (often over subject peoples) than plenty. For the far-flung British Empire to be successful in its commerce, it had also to be maritime. The British dominions were not all contiguous, and the richest parts of the Empire, such as Barbados and Jamaica, were separated both from the Three Kingdoms and from the mainland colonies by vast oceanic expanses. The waters around Britain itself had always been defended by the Royal Navy, and a series of naval myths provided the legendary foundations for such maritime supremacy. Protestantism, oceanic commerce and mastery of the seas provided bastions to protect the freedom of inhabitants of the British Empire. That freedom found its institutional expression in Parliament, the law, property and rights, all of which were exported throughout the British Atlantic world. Such freedom also allowed the British, uniquely, to combine the classically incompatible ideals of liberty and empire. In sum, the British Empire was, above all and beyond all other such polities, Protestant, commercial, maritime and free.

The concept of a British Empire had its roots within the Three Kingdoms of Britain and Ireland; however, to become elaborated in its later, more expansive form, it had to overcome some formidable conceptual and practical obstacles. The collision between an Erastian English church and a Presbyterian Scottish kirk obviated the emergence of a pan-British ecclesiology and exacerbated the denominational diversity of the British Atlantic world. The British Empire therefore had no unitary theological foundation, though the common Protestantism of the majority of its inhabitants distinguished it sufficiently from the Spanish and French monarchies. Secular political thought defined the community in terms that could accommodate the contiguous territories of a composite monarchy and even encompass an ethnic definition of community that extended to Ireland, but nonetheless proved resistant to imagining colonies and factories as members of the polity before the rise of mercantilist thought in the period after the Restoration. Political economy in turn redefined the nature of British maritime dominion, which under the Stuarts had implied exclusive British *imperium* solely over home waters; this was replaced by a conception of *mare liberum* on the oceans which underpinned arguments for the free circulation of trade around the Atlantic world.

The British Atlantic world could therefore only be conceived of as a single political community once the intellectual limits to its growth had been overcome in an era of expanding commerce and reform in colonial government. The impetus of political contention helped to generate a distinctive ideology for the Empire, but only once a pan-Atlantic conception of the British Empire had been generated by a cadre of provincials and imperial officials beyond the metropolis itself in the second quarter of the eighteenth century. That conception sprang initially from Britain's imperial provinces; when metropolitans took it up later, theirs would be the derivative discourse, not the colonists'. The ideological definition of the British state, and the conceptualisation of its relationship with its dependencies, was therefore neither a solely metropolitan nor an exclusively provincial achievement: it was a shared conception of the British Empire that could describe a community and provide a distinguishable character for it. However, the instabilities which marked both the concept and the conception from their origins in debates within the Three Kingdoms would ultimately create the ideological conditions for the debate preceding and surrounding the American Revolution. The ideological origins of the British Empire also constituted the ideological origins of the American

Revolution;[26] the decline, fall and reconstruction of the British Atlantic Empire can therefore be traced back to the limitations and instabilities of the British state.

'[H]istory devises reason why the lessons of past empire do not apply to ours', remarked J. A. Hobson in 1902.[27] The objects of his criticism were those nineteenth-century English historians who denied the British Empire any origins or antecedents at all and thereby left it suspended, statically, outside history and beyond the reach of the conventional compulsions of imperial decline and fall (or expansion and overstretch). Hobson accurately diagnosed the fact that most of the major modes within which British history has been written since the nineteenth century had been inhospitable to Imperial history. This was partly the result of the hegemony of English history and historians, for whom England stood proxy for the United Kingdom, and who maintained a willed forgetfulness about the rest of Britain, Ireland and the Empire.[28] Their grand narratives produced an English exceptionalism that sustained an insular account of national history and proved increasingly impregnable to the history of the Empire. For example, the historiography of English religion told the history of the Church *in* England as the story of the Church *of* England, a story that might begin with St Augustine of Canterbury, Bede, or at least Wycliffe, but that found its lasting incarnation in the Erastian Church founded under Henry VIII at the English Reformation.[29] That Church had, of course, expanded across the globe to create a worldwide communion, but so had the Dissenting and Nonconformist denominations. The Church of England never became a unified imperial Church, least of all in the seventeenth and eighteenth centuries, and the existence of discrete Church establishments in Scotland, Ireland and Wales meant that the English Church remained but one ecclesiastical body within a more extensive Anglo-British state (as constituted by the Anglo-Scottish Union of 1707). English ecclesiastical history could thus claim a lengthy pedigree, and even a providential charter for insularity, but it did little to encourage an ampler imperial perspective.

[26] Bernard Bailyn, *The Ideological Origins of the American Revolution*, 2nd edn (Cambridge, Mass., 1992).
[27] J. A. Hobson, *Imperialism: A Study*, 3rd edn. (London, 1938), 221.
[28] J. G. A. Pocock, 'The Limits and Divisions of British History: In Search of the Unknown Subject', *American Historical Review*, 87 (1982), 311–14.
[29] Michael Bentley, 'The British State and its Historiography', in Wim Blockmans and Jean-Philippe Genet (eds.), *Visions sur le développement des états européens: théories et historiographies de l'état moderne* (Rome, 1993), 154, 162–4.

The Whig history of the constitution proved similarly resistant to the incorporation of Imperial history. That resistance can be traced back in part to the Henrician Reformation, when the English Parliament had declared in the preamble to the Act in Restraint of Appeals (1533) that 'this realm of England is an empire, entire of itself', independent of all external authority and free of any entanglements, whether in Europe or further abroad. Though the exact import of those words has been much debated,[30] they were held to 'assert that our king is equally sovereign and independent within these his dominions, as any emperor is in his empire', in the words of William Blackstone.[31] Regal independence represented national independence, and therefore associated the constitutional, statutory language of 'empire' with isolation and insularity. From the era of the Huguenot historian Paul de Rapin-Thoyras, a generation after the Glorious Revolution, until the age of Macaulay in the mid-nineteenth century and beyond, the constitution was of greater interest to Whig historians than expansion.[32]

Constitutional liberty and imperial expansion seemed to be necessarily incompatible to many Whigs and to their ideological heirs. The collision between empire and liberty lay at the heart of the debate surrounding the American Revolutionary crisis, both for the Whiggish supporters of American independence and for their sympathisers in Britain.[33] Yet even that was only one moment in a seemingly eternal drama of the contention between *imperium* and *libertas* that was sure to be played out again in the Second British Empire.[34] 'Is it not just possible that we may become corrupted at home by the reaction of arbitrary political maxims in the East upon our domestic politics, just as Greece and Rome were demoralised by their contact with Asia?' asked Richard Cobden in 1860.[35] 'Not merely is the reaction possible, it is inevitable', replied Hobson: 'the spirit, the policy, and the methods of Imperialism are hostile to the institutions of popular

[30] G. L. Harriss, 'Medieval Government and Statecraft', *Past and Present*, 25 (July 1963), 9–12; G. R. Elton, 'The Tudor Revolution: A Reply', *Past and Present*, 29 (Dec. 1964), 30–6; Harriss, 'A Revolution in Tudor History?' *Past and Present*, 31 (July 1965), 87–8; G. D. Nicholson, 'The Nature and Function of Historical Argument in the Henrician Reformation' (Ph.D. dissertation, Cambridge, 1977), 171–80; John Guy, *Tudor England* (Oxford, 1988), 369–76.
[31] William Blackstone, *Commentaries on the Laws of England*, 4 vols. (London, 1765–9), I, 235.
[32] Burrow, *A Liberal Descent*, 233, 247–8.
[33] H. Trevor Colbourn, *The Lamp of Experience: Whig History and the Intellectual Origins of the American Revolution* (Chapel Hill, 1965).
[34] Miles Taylor, 'Imperium et Libertas? Rethinking the Radical Critique of Imperialism during the Nineteenth Century', *Journal of Imperial and Commonwealth History*, 19 (1991), 1–23.
[35] Richard Cobden to William Hargreaves, 4 August 1860, in John Morley, *The Life of Richard Cobden*, 2 vols. (London, 1881), II, 361.

self-government'.[36] Though most nineteenth-century Liberals and even Radicals might not have shared these fundamentally classicising fears of Asiatic luxury, such anxieties were symptomatic of a wider unwillingness to admit the Empire within the history of the metropolitan state itself, for fear of corrupting 'domestic politics'.[37] The potential for the incompatibility of empire and liberty was one of the great legacies of the First British Empire to the Second; the genesis and afterlife of the argument between these two values forms one of the central strands of this study.

Whiggish indifference to the history of the Empire, and Radical critiques of the threat posed by empire to the very fabric of English liberty, might have rendered 'the story of British expansion overseas . . . the real tory alternative to the organization of English history on the basis of the growth of liberty', as Herbert Butterfield thought in 1944. Butterfield argued that 'the shock of 1940' had shown that the Whig history of liberty and the Tory history of Empire were inseparable;[38] what he could not foresee in 1944 was that the war itself would become a major solvent of the Empire. Decolonisation rapidly rendered implausible any attempt retrospectively to write the history of the British Empire as the history of liberty: Winston Churchill's *History of the English-Speaking Peoples* (1956–58), which he had first conceived in the mid-1930s, and Arthur Bryant's even more belated *History of Britain and the British Peoples* (1984–90), remained the monuments to hopes of effecting such an historiographical reconciliation.[39] The futility of this Tory rapprochement was accompanied by the silence of the heirs of Whig history. Historians on the Left were suspicious of the benign claims made on behalf of the British Empire by paternalists, yet were also embarrassed by the part played by the Empire in creating a conservative strain of patriotism.[40] Accordingly, they perpetuated the separation of domestic and Imperial history by overlooking the Empire almost entirely, as the works of Christopher Hill, E. P. Thompson and Lawrence Stone, for

[36] Hobson, *Imperialism: A Study*, 150.
[37] Compare Uday Singh Mehta, *Liberalism and Empire: A Study in Nineteenth-Century British Liberal Thought* (Chicago, 1999), 4–8.
[38] Herbert Butterfield, *The Englishman and His History* (Cambridge, 1944), 81–2.
[39] Winston Churchill, *A History of the English-Speaking Peoples*, 4 vols. (London, 1956–8); Arthur Bryant, *The History of Britain and the British Peoples*, 3 vols. (London, 1984–90).
[40] Stephen Howe, 'Labour Patriotism, 1939–83', in Raphael Samuel (ed.), *Patriotism: The Making and Unmaking of British National Identity*, 1: *History and Politics* (London, 1989), 127–39. Robert Gregg and Madhavi Kale, 'The Empire and Mr Thompson: Making of Indian Princes and English Working Class', *Economic and Political Weekly*, 33, 36 (6–12 September 1997), 2273–88, offers an excellent case-study of such historical amnesia on the historiographical Left.

instance, mutely testify.[41] The history of the Empire – by which is still meant, overwhelmingly, the 'Second' British Empire – has been left to Imperial historians, who have followed their own trajectory from post-Imperial diffidence to a measured confidence in the prospects for their own subfield. Only belatedly have they acknowledged that their purview should also include the history of the metropolis, and hence that 'British imperial history should be firmly rooted in the history of Britain'.[42]

The persistent reluctance of British historians to incorporate the Empire into the history of Britain is symptomatic of a more general indifference towards the Empire detected by those same historians. 'British historians may have some grounds for their neglect of empire', it has been argued, because in the modern period it only intermittently intruded into British politics; the British state itself was little shaped by imperial experiences; there was no single imperial 'project'; rather, 'empire performed a reflexive rather than a transforming role for the British people'.[43] The question of 'Who cared about the colonies?' in the eighteenth century has been answered equally scrupulously: 'A lot of people did, though they were very unevenly distributed geographically and socially and quite diverse in their approach to American questions.' Few benefited directly from colonial patronage; merchants took an abiding interest in the Atlantic trade but they, of course, were concentrated in mercantile centres; lobbying groups on behalf of American interests had little impact upon British politics, while handfuls of Britons visited or corresponded with the colonies, whether as traders, soldiers, sailors or professionals.[44] If the Empire had so little impact upon the

[41] Each found some belated interest in the Empire: Thompson, for familial reasons in Thompson, *'Alien Homage': Edward Thompson and Rabindranath Tagore* (Delhi, 1993), and the others more generally, for example in Christopher Hill, *Liberty Against the Law: Some Seventeenth-Century Controversies* (London, 1996), pt III, 'Imperial Problems', and Lawrence Stone, 'Introduction', in Stone (ed.), *An Imperial State at War: Britain from 1689 to 1815* (London, 1994), 1–32. The works of Eric Hobsbawm and V. G. Kiernan are, of course, notable exceptions to this caveat, though neither has been solely concerned with Britain.

[42] P. J. Marshall, *'A Free Though Conquering People': Britain and Asia in the Eighteenth Century*, Inaugural Lecture, King's College London, 5 March 1981 (London, 1981), 2 (quoted); David Fieldhouse, 'Can Humpty-Dumpty Be Put Together Again? Imperial History in the 1980s', *Journal of Imperial and Commonwealth History*, 12 (1984), 9–10, 17; John M. MacKenzie, *Propaganda and Empire: The Manipulation of British Public Opinion, 1880–1960* (Manchester, 1984); MacKenzie (ed.), *Imperialism and Popular Culture* (Manchester, 1988); A. G. Hopkins, *The Future of the Imperial Past*, Inaugural Lecture, 12 March 1997 (Cambridge, 1997), 8–9.

[43] P. J. Marshall, 'Imperial Britain', *Journal of Imperial and Commonwealth History*, 23 (1995), 380, 382, 386, 392.

[44] Jacob M. Price, 'Who Cared About the Colonies? The Impact of the Thirteen Colonies on British Society and Politics, circa 1714–1775', in Bernard Bailyn and Philip D. Morgan (eds.), *Strangers within the Realm: Cultural Margins of the First British Empire* (Chapel Hill, 1991), 395–436.

historical experience of metropolitan Britons, why would it be necessary to integrate the history of the Empire with the history of the metropolis?

This division between domestic history and extraterritorial history was not unique to the history of Britain. The rise of nationalist historiography in the nineteenth century had placed the history of the nation-state at the centre of European historical enquiry, and distinguished the state from the territorial empires that had preceded it, and in turn from the extra-European empires strung across the globe. The classic nation-state united popular sovereignty, territorial integrity and ethnic homogeneity into a single definition; it therefore stood as the opposite of empire, in so far as that was defined as a hierarchical structure of domination, encompassing diverse territories and ethnically diverse populations. The nation-state as it had been precipitated out of a system of aggressively competing nations nonetheless functioned as 'the empire *manqué*', which always aimed at conquest and expansion within Europe, but which often had to seek its territorial destiny in the world beyond Europe.[45] 'Nowadays', as Max Weber put it, 'we have to say that a state is that human community which (successfully) lays claim to the *monopoly of legitimate physical violence* within a certain territory, this "territory" being another of the defining characteristics of the state.'[46] That association of the state with territoriality – and hence, implicitly, with contiguity – deliberately dissociated integral, legally bounded states from the less well-demarcated empires, which could be defined either formally or informally, which were separated by sometimes vast oceanic distances from their metropoles, and within which legitimacy was incomplete and physical violence more unevenly distributed.

The distinction between the 'internal' histories of (mostly) European states and the 'external' histories of (exclusively) European empires obscured the fact that those European states had themselves been created by processes of 'conquest, colonization and cultural change' in the Middle Ages.[47] Outside the conventional heartland of Europe, the westward expansion both of medieval Russia and of the nineteenth-century United States, for example, proceeded by many of the same

---

[45] Istvan Hont, 'The Permanent Crisis of a Divided Mankind: "Contemporary Crisis of the Nation State" in Historical Perspective', *Political Studies*, 42 (1994), 172–3; V. G. Kiernan, 'State and Nation in Western Europe', *Past and Present*, 31 (July 1965), 35.

[46] Max Weber, 'The Profession and Vocation of Politics' (1919), in *Weber: Political Writings*, ed. Peter Lassman and Ronald Speirs (Cambridge, 1994), 310–11.

[47] Robert Bartlett, *The Making of Europe: Conquest, Colonization and Cultural Change 950–1350* (New Haven, 1993).

methods, yet the history of territorial 'extension' has been rigorously distinguished from the history of maritime 'expansion': 'sea space is supposed to constitute the difference between the former, which is part of the national question, and the colonial question as such'.[48] This would be true of the histories of Portugal, the Dutch Republic, France and even Sweden, the bulk of whose empire lay close to home, around the shores of the Baltic Sea.[49] Sea-space lay between Aragon and Naples, between Castile and the Spanish Netherlands, and between Britain and Ireland. The sea could be a bridge or a barrier, whether within states, or between European states and their possessions *outre-mer*.

The distinction between states and empires has rarely been a clear one, least of all in the early-modern period. As Fernand Braudel observed of the fifteenth and sixteenth centuries, 'a formidable newcomer confronted the mere territorial or nation-state': the new composite monarchies of early-modern Europe, 'what by a convenient though anachronistic term one could call empires in the modern sense – for how else is one to describe these giants?'[50] In this context, it is notable that those European countries that accumulated the earliest overseas empires were also those that earliest consolidated their states; conversely, those weaker states that had not attempted extensive colonisation outside Europe – most obviously, Germany and Italy – only pursued imperial designs after they had acquired the marks of statehood in the later nineteenth or early twentieth centuries. Empires gave birth to states, and states stood at the heart of empires. Accordingly, the most precocious nation-states of early-modern Europe were the great empire-states: the Spanish Monarchy, Portugal, the Dutch Republic, France and England (later, Britain).

The United Kingdom of Great Britain (and, after 1801, Ireland) would become the most powerful among the composite states of Europe, and would command the greatest of all the European overseas empires. However – perhaps because of this conspicuous success in both state-formation and empire-building – the disjuncture between British history and the history of the British Empire has been peculiarly abrupt and enduring. Even when the Empire has been construed more widely than just the Thirteen Colonies, and its potential sphere of influence broadened to encompass cultural, as well as political and economic,

[48] Marc Ferro, *Colonization: A Global History*, trans. K. D. Prithipaul (London, 1997), 2.
[49] Michael Roberts, *The Swedish Imperial Experience, 1560–1718* (Cambridge, 1979), 16–18, 83–6, though see also C. A. Weslager, *New Sweden on the Delaware 1638–1655* (Wilmington, Del., 1988).
[50] Fernand Braudel, *The Mediterranean and the Mediterranean World in the Age of Philip II*, trans. Siân Reynolds, 2 vols. (London, 1973), II, 659.

concerns, even the most modest assessment of who cared concludes in a paradox. Though empire 'was all-pervasive' – as the far-fetched paraphernalia on every tea-table in Britain could demonstrate by the late eighteenth century – it 'often went strangely unacknowledged – even by those who benefited from it most'. In Britain, as in Italy, Germany or France, for much of the time 'empire simply did not loom all that large in the minds of most men and women back in Europe'.[51] Such a paradox may make it easier to incorporate the fruits of empire into social history,[52] but it still encourages the belief that the Empire took place in a world elsewhere, beyond the domestic horizons of Britons, and hence outside the confines of British history.

Imperial amnesia has of course been diagnosed before. 'We seem, as it were, to have conquered and peopled half the world in a fit of absence of mind', J. R. Seeley told his Cambridge audience in 1881. 'While we were doing it, that is in the eighteenth century, we did not allow it to affect our imaginations or in any degree to change our ways of thinking.'[53] Seeley hoped to provoke in his audience the realisation that they were, and long had been, inhabitants not of little England but rather of a 'Greater Britain' that encompassed the colonies of white settlement in North America, the Caribbean, the Cape Colony and Australasia, all bound together into an 'ethnological unity' by the common ties of 'race', religion and 'interest'. Yet his aims were also more specifically historiographical, as he partook in the first stirrings of the reaction against insular Whig constitutionalism which would culminate in Butterfield's *The Whig Interpretation of History* (1931) half a century later. The grounds for Seeley's attack were not, like those of later Whig revisionists, anti-teleological, for he wished to substitute the expansion of the Empire for the growth of the constitution as the backbone of 'English' history since the eighteenth century. Just as he wished to recall his Cambridge audience to their responsibilities as members of a global community, so he wanted to remind fellow-historians, who were transfixed by 'mere parliamentary wrangle and the agitations about liberty', that in the eighteenth century 'the history of England is not in England but in America and Asia'.[54]

[51] Linda Colley, 'The Imperial Embrace', *Yale Review*, 81, 4 (1993), 92, 98–9.
[52] James Walvin, *Fruits of Empire: Exotic Produce and British Taste, 1660–1800* (Basingstoke, 1997); Philip Lawson, *A Taste for Empire and Glory: Studies in British Overseas Expansion, 1660–1800* (Aldershot, 1997), chs. XIV–XV.
[53] J. R. Seeley, *The Expansion of England* (London, 1883), 8.
[54] Seeley, *The Expansion of England*, 10, 50, 9; P. B. M. Blaas, *Continuity and Anachronism: Parliamentary and Constitutional Development in Whig Historiography and in the Anti-Whig Reaction between 1890 and 1930* (The Hague, 1978), 36–40.

Seeley's *Expansion of England* became one of the best-sellers of late Victorian Britain, and remained in print until 1956, the year of the Suez crisis. Its very popularity ensured that its effects would be widespread and enduring, even if they were not necessarily those sought by Seeley himself. The work certainly failed in its positive agendas. The Imperial Federation movement of the 1880s, to which the lectures gave succour, did not achieve its aim of bringing institutional union to the 'ethnological' entity he had described. Nor did the writing of domestic history become any more noticeably hospitable to the matter of Greater Britain, despite the brief vogue enjoyed by the term.[55] Seeley himself retreated from the imperial perspective he had encouraged in *The Expansion of England*. His next major work, *The Growth of British Policy* (1895), despite its title, chronicled the diplomatic history of England alone from 1588 to 1713, but in this work the only empire in that period was the Holy Roman Empire. It thereby confirmed the assumption of his earlier book that England's expansion to become a global 'Commercial State' was the creation of the eighteenth century: hence the British Empire, in its classic and enduring form, had not encompassed the Atlantic empire of the seventeenth and early eighteenth centuries.[56]

Instead of promoting a new imperial synthesis among British historians, Seeley's work inspired the creation of the new and separate subfield of Imperial history.[57] This created a novel area of historical inquiry, but it institutionalised the very separation between British history and Imperial history that Seeley had deplored; it also identified Imperial history almost exclusively as the history of the 'Second' British Empire. Though Seeley had reserved particular scorn for those historians of eighteenth-century Britain who had failed to recognise the true direction of British history in that century, and who overlooked the Empire at the expense of the Whiggish history of liberty, even in *The Expansion of England* the eighteenth century was important only as a prelude to the Imperial grandeur of the nineteenth. It marked the prologue to the Second British Empire, while the American Revolution

---

[55] C. W. Dilke, *Greater Britain: A Record of Travel in the English-Speaking Countries during 1866 and '67*, 3 vols. (London, 1868); E. A. Freeman, *Greater Greece and Greater Britain; and, George Washington, The Expander of England* (London, 1886); Dilke, *Problems of Greater Britain* (London, 1890); David Armitage, 'Greater Britain: A Useful Category of Historical Analysis?', *American Historical Review*, 104 (1999), 427–45.

[56] J. R. Seeley, *The Growth of British Policy*, 2 vols. (Cambridge, 1895), II, 349–81.

[57] Peter Burroughs, 'John Robert Seeley and British Imperial History', *Journal of Imperial and Commonwealth History*, 1 (1972), 191–211; J. G. Greenlee, 'A "Succession of Seeleys": The "Old School" Re-examined', *Journal of Imperial and Commonwealth History*, 4 (1976), 266–82.

('an event', Seeley thought, '... on an altogether higher level of importance than almost any other in modern English history') was the regrettable but instructive entr'acte between two largely distinct empires.[58]

Seeley elsewhere remarked on the fragility of the First Empire, and its
failure to produce the kind of organic community united by strong ties
of nationality, religion and interest that he believed characterised
Greater Britain in the nineteenth century: 'We had seen on the other
side of the Atlantic only tobacco and fisheries and sugar, not English
communities', a 'materialist' (or mercantilist) empire created for the
benefit of the metropolis, but thereby doomed to dissolution as '[t]he
fabric of materialism crumbled away'.[59] Some among Seeley's contemporaries disagreed strongly with that verdict, most notably the man soon
to be his counterpart as Regius Professor at Oxford, E. A. Freeman, an
opponent of the Imperial Federation movement but a proponent of an
expansive community of the Anglo-Saxon and anglophone peoples,
including the United States, rather than the narrower Imperial community of Greater Britain.[60] Freeman effectively forgave the Americans for
their Revolution and pronounced them to be brethren sprung from the
same Anglo-Saxon stock, speakers of the same language, and inheritors
of the same patrimony of freedom as the English. His proselytising
Anglo-Saxonism, spread on a lecture-tour of the eastern United States
in 1881–82 just as Seeley was delivering his lectures in Cambridge, had
an equal but opposite effect: as Seeley planted the seeds for Imperial
History, so Freeman helped to prepare the ground for the 'Imperial
School' of early – or colonial – American history.[61] However, the
different premises on which the two syntheses rested, their almost
entirely exclusive chronologies, and their competing orientations – one
eastward, the other, westward from Britain – effectively confirmed the
divorce between the histories of the First and Second British Empires for
much of the following century.

For Seeley, 'history has to do with the State', just as the study of
history should be a 'school of statesmanship' for its practitioners and

---

[58] Seeley, *The Expansion of England*, 147.
[59] Seeley, *The Expansion of England*, 147; Seeley, 'Introduction', in A. J. R. Trendell, *The Colonial Year Book for the Year 1890* (London, 1890), xx.
[60] E. A. Freeman, 'Imperial Federation' (1885), in Freeman, *Greater Greece and Greater Britain*, 104–43. For an instructive comparison of Seeley and Freeman, see Stefan Collini, Donald Winch and John Burrow, *That Noble Science of Politics: A Study in Nineteenth-Century Intellectual History* (Cambridge, 1983), 219–34.
[61] E. A. Freeman, *Lectures to American Audiences* (Philadelphia, 1882); Freeman, *Greater Greece and Greater Britain*, 38–48; Peter Novick, *That Noble Dream: The 'Objectivity Question' and the American Historical Profession* (Cambridge, 1988), 80–4.

their pupils.[62] The state in his sense was defined functionally, by its monopoly of force and its duty to uphold justice and defend its inhabitants; more importantly, it was constituted as a community ethnically, religiously and by commonality of interest. On these grounds, Seeley argued, Greater Britain had as much of a claim to be called a state as 'England' itself: both were organic communities, united by common interests, and not merely 'composed of voluntary shareholders' or formed by force into 'inorganic quasi-state[s]'. The British Empire was therefore not an empire in the ordinary sense at all, since it was not held together by force (India of course excluded); it was simply 'an enlargement of the English State'. Yet, if the British Empire was in fact the 'English' state writ large, many of the nation-states of Europe were in fact empires in minuscule, since they had come into being by incorporating diverse peoples and scattered territories by conquest, annexation and force. Indeed, in so far as most modern states contained huge expanses of territory, and were inevitably divided by region and locality, they all exhibited the kind of federal 'double-government', in the centre and at the localities, that was a feature of imperial governance. In this sense, all contemporary states – the United States, with its individual states; England, with its counties; France, with its *départements* – were to a greater or lesser degree federal and composite. In their structures of governance, they approximated modern empires far more than they did classical city-states; similarly, modern empires like 'Greater Britain' could be called states, if states were defined by the 'ethnological' unity they displayed.[63]

Seeley's attention to the common features of state and empire led him to consider as convergent and similar processes which later historians have tended to treat as parallel or distinct. States had once had the characteristics of empires; empires were now the enlarged versions of states. State-building and empire-formation did not have to be treated as if one were a centrifugal process, drawing everything inwards to a governmental centre, and the other centripetal, extending metropolitan governance into new territories and over new peoples. Seeley's conflation of state and empire of course had its limitations. The greatest of these was the necessary omission of India from the community of Greater Britain. This masked the fact that the British Empire in South

---

[62] Seeley, *The Expansion of England*, 6; Seeley, 'The Teaching of Politics' (1870), in Seeley, *Lectures and Essays* (London, 1870), 296.

[63] Seeley, *Introduction to Political Science: Two Series of Lectures* (London, 1896), 35, 68, 70, 92–4; Seeley, *The Expansion of England*, 43, 50.

Asia was precisely the kind of 'inorganic quasi-state' Seeley deplored in his *Introduction to Political Science* (1896).[64] Nonetheless, it enabled him to see continuities between the First and Second British Empires that other historians had overlooked; more fruitfully, it allowed him to discern a relationship between state-formation and empire-building that historians have yet to investigate comprehensively.

Seeley argued that two movements defined the history of Britain after 1603: 'the internal union of the three kingdoms', and 'the creation of a still larger Britain comprehending vast possessions beyond the sea'.[65] The recent construction of a 'New British History' by historians of England, Scotland and Ireland has made it possible to perceive connections between these two processes that were invisible to Seeley, who remained more concerned with the expansion of 'England' than with the creation of Britain. This 'New British History' has taken its inspiration from J. G. A. Pocock's exhortations that the contraction of Greater Britain should be the reason to rewrite the history of Britain in its widest sense.[66] Pocock initially called for a 'new subject' of British history in New Zealand in 1973, just after Britain's decision to enter the European Economic Community, and with it, the Common Agricultural Policy, which had potentially devastating consequences for economies like New Zealand's, which had for over a century been the beneficiaries of imperial preferences.[67] This 'New British History' would not simply treat the histories of the Three Kingdoms and four nations that had variously interacted within 'the Atlantic Archipelago' of Britain, Ireland and their attendant islands and continental neighbours. Those histories would be central to its agenda, but Pocock's inclusion of British America before 1783, and British North America (later, Canada) thereafter, as well as the histories of Australia and New Zealand (and, presumably, of other white settler communities of primarily British descent), 'obliges us to conceive of "British history" no longer as an archipelagic or even an Atlantic-American phenomenon, but as having occurred on a planetary scale'.[68] Pocock therefore offered a vision of Greater Britain in light of the contraction of 'England' rather than its expansion, and from the

---

[64] Freeman, *Greater Greece and Greater Britain*, 41–2; Deborah Wormell, *Sir John Seeley and the Uses of History* (Cambridge, 1980), 142.

[65] Seeley, *The Expansion of England*, 9–10.

[66] J. G. A. Pocock, 'British History: A Plea for a New Subject', *New Zealand Historical Journal*, 8 (1974), 3–21, rptd in *Journal of Modern History*, 4 (1975), 601–24; Pocock, 'The Limits and Divisions of British History'.

[67] J. G. A. Pocock, 'History and Sovereignty: The Historiographical Response to Europeanization in Two British Cultures', *Journal of British Studies*, 31 (1991), 361–4, 380–9.

[68] Pocock, 'The Limits and Divisions of British History', 317–19.

vantage point of a former imperial province rather than from that of the metropole. The post-Imperial anxiety behind Pocock's historiographical agenda is as obvious as the high-Imperial confidence behind Seeley's. These equal yet opposite motives nonetheless produce the same historiographical conclusion: that it is essential to integrate the history of state and empire if British history, not least in the early modern period, is to be properly understood.

The New British History has concentrated on the 'British problem', the recurrent puzzle faced especially by the political elites of England, Wales, Scotland and Ireland of how to integrate four (or more nations) into three (or, at times, fewer) kingdoms, or to resist absorption or conquest by one or other of the competing states within Britain and Ireland. It has become clear that some points in the histories of Britain and Ireland were more 'British' than others. During these moments, the problem of Britain – whether within Anglo-Scottish, Anglo-Irish, Hiberno-Scottish or pan-archipelagic relations – came to the forefront of political debate, and profoundly affected the interrelations between the Three Kingdoms. These were all stages in a process of state-formation construed teleologically as the history of political union within the 'British Isles', from the Statute of Wales (1536), via the Irish Kingship Act (1541), the attempted dynastic union between England and Scotland under Henry VIII and Edward VI (1542, 1548–49), to the personal union of England and Scotland under James VI and I and Charles I (1603–49), the creation of a British Commonwealth (1651–60), the Stuart Restoration, the Glorious Revolution and the Williamite Wars in Ireland (1688–91), the Anglo-Scottish Union (1707) and on to the Union of Great Britain and Ireland (1801–1922).

Concentration on the history of the British state has reproduced many of the features of the whiggish histories of the Three Kingdoms that preceded it. Above all, it has perpetuated the separation between the history of Britain and the history of the British Empire. For all of its avowed intentions to supersede the national historiographies of England, Scotland, Ireland and Wales, the New British History has not encompassed the settlements, provinces and dependencies of Greater Britain, whether in the nineteenth century or, especially, earlier.[69]

---

[69] Almost none of the major collections of essays on the New British History covers any British territories, populations, or influences outside Britain and Ireland: Ronald Asch (ed.), *Three Nations – A Common History? England, Scotland, Ireland and British History c. 1600–1920* (Bochum, 1993); Alexander Grant and Keith Stringer (eds.), *Uniting the Kingdom? The Making of British History* (London, 1995); Steven G. Ellis and Sarah Barber (eds.), *Conquest and Union: Fashioning a British State 1485–1725* (London, 1995); Brendan Bradshaw and John Morrill (eds.), *The British Problem:*

Meanwhile, the history of the British Empire has remained in the hands of Imperial historians. As a result, neither Seeley's suggestive juxtaposition of the creation of the 'English' state and the expansion of 'England', nor Pocock's more comprehensive agenda for British history written on a global scale, has yet been pursued to its logical conclusion by treating the histories of Britain and Ireland and of the British Empire as necessarily conjoined rather than inevitably distinct.

The adoption of early-modern European models of state-formation by practitioners of the New British History has had the effect of further separating metropolitan from Imperial history. These historians have rediscovered what J. R. Seeley realised a century ago: that England, like France, was a composite monarchy, just as Britain, like the Spanish Monarchy, was a multiple kingdom.[70] In the former, a diversity of territories, peoples, institutions and legal jurisdictions is cemented under a single, recognised sovereign authority; in the latter, various kingdoms were ruled by a single sovereign, while they maintained varying degrees of autonomy. 'All multiple kingdoms are composite monarchies, but not all composite monarchies are multiple kingdoms', as Conrad Russell has put it.[71] The various moments in the British – or British-and-Irish – problem registered the tensions between these two predecessors of the classically defined nation-state, but in doing so they also exemplified pan-European processes whose consequences were felt in Burgundy, Béarn, the Spanish Netherlands, Catalonia, Naples, the Pyrenees, Bohemia and elsewhere during the sixteenth and seventeenth centuries. The divisive consequences of these processes were sharpened when one partner in a composite state successfully attempted overseas expansion: 'imperialism and composite monarchy made uncomfortable bedfellows'.[72] Yet this assertion that 'imperialism' was somehow distinct from state-formation, rather than continuous with it, further entrenches the

State-Formation in the Atlantic Archipelago c. 1534–1707 (Basingstoke, 1996); Laurence Brockliss and David Eastwood (eds.), *A Union of Multiple Identities: The British Isles c. 1750–c. 1850* (Manchester, 1997); Brendan Bradshaw and Peter Roberts (eds.), *British Consciousness and Identity: The Making of Britain, 1533–1707* (Cambridge, 1998); S. J. Connolly (ed.), *United Kingdoms? Ireland and Great Britain from 1500 – Integration and Diversity* (Dublin, 1998); Glenn Burgess (ed.), *The New British History: Founding a Modern State, 1603–1715* (London, 1999). Tony Claydon and Ian McBride (eds.), *Protestantism and National Identity: Britain and Ireland, c. 1650–c. 1850* (Cambridge, 1998), is the sole exception.

[70] H. G. Koenigsberger, '*Dominium Regale* or *Dominium Politicum et Regale*: Monarchies and Parliaments in Early Modern Europe', in Koenigsberger, *Politicians and Virtuosi: Essays in Early Modern History* (London, 1986), 1–25.

[71] Conrad Russell, 'Composite Monarchies in Early Modern Europe: The British and Irish Example', in Grant and Stringer (eds.), *Uniting the Kingdom?*, 133.

[72] J. H. Elliott, 'A Europe of Composite Monarchies', *Past and Present*, 137 (Nov. 1992), 59–60.

assumption that states – even composite states – and empires – even largely intra-European empires, like Sweden's – belong to different areas of historical inquiry because they were distinguishable, even competing, historical processes.

The model of composite monarchy offers fruitful analogies with the history of the European empires. Monarchies were compounded by the same means that empires were acquired: by conquest, annexation, inheritance and secession. The rulers of composite monarchies faced problems that would be familiar to the administrators of any empire: the need to govern distant dependencies from a powerful centre; collisions between metropolitan and provincial legislatures; the necessity of imposing common norms of law and culture over diverse and often resistant populations; and the consequent reliance of the central government on the co-optation of local elites.[73] It is important not to overstate the similarities: after all, the extra-European empires were often acquired and governed without any recognition of the political standing of their inhabitants; composite monarchies and multiple kingdoms tended to have a bias towards uniformity rather than an acceptance of diversity; and the provinces of composite monarchies were not usually treated both as economic and as political dependencies. However, it is equally important not to underestimate the continuities between the creation of composite states and the formation of the European overseas empires. As the succeeding chapters of this study will show, ideology provided just such a link between the processes of empire-building and state-formation in the early-modern period.

[73] H. G. Koenigsberger, 'Composite States, Representative Institutions and the American Revolution', *Historical Research*, 62 (1989), 135–54; Michael J. Braddick, 'The English Government, War, Trade, and Settlement, 1625–1688', in Nicholas Canny (ed.), *The Oxford History of the British Empire*, I: *The Origins of Empire* (Oxford, 1998), 286–308.

CHAPTER 2

The empire of Great Britain: England, Scotland and Ireland c. 1542–1612

… realmis ar nocht conquest be buikis bot rather be bluid.[1]

The ideological history of the relations between the Three Kingdoms of England, Scotland and Ireland in the sixteenth century reveals the inseparability of – and, in many ways, the identity between – state-formation and empire-building in the early modern period. For the last half-century, historians have argued that the origins of English (and, later, British) imperial ideology can be found in English policy towards Ireland under the Tudors.[2] The governing assumptions of the English official mind, according to this argument, were that Ireland, though a kingdom after 1541, should be treated as if it were a colony, especially during the 'New English' period of settlement beginning in the 1560s; that the Irish were barbarians, comparable to the inhabitants of the western hemisphere encountered by the Spanish; and that the English had a duty to civilise and to Christianise (that is, to Protestantise) both the Gaelic Irish and the Catholic 'Old English' descendants of the Anglo-Norman settlers of the twelfth century. The continuity of person-nel, similarity of methods and justifications, and parallel relations be-tween Ireland and the new settlements of the late Elizabethan and early Jacobean periods together created a narrative of English colonialism that runs in a straight line from England, through Ireland, to the Caribbean and thence the eastern seaboard of North America. In this account, maritime enterprise transformed state-formation into empire-building in the British Atlantic world along a path running from east to

---

[1] [Robert Wedderburn,] *The Complaynt of Scotland (c. 1550)*, ed. A. M. Stewart (Edinburgh, 1979), 64.
[2] Howard Mumford Jones, 'Origins of the Colonial Idea in England', *Proceedings of the American Philosophical Society*, 85 (1942), 448–65; D. B. Quinn, 'Sir Thomas Smith (1513–1577) and the Beginnings of English Colonial Theory', *Proceedings of the American Philosophical Society*, 89 (1945), 543–60; Nicholas Canny, 'The Ideology of English Colonization: From Ireland to America', *William and Mary Quarterly*, 3rd ser., 30 (1973), 575–98.

west, and from England to America, with Ireland as the crux of a comprehensive English 'westward enterprise'.[3]

Historians of early-modern Ireland have been both the most vigorous proponents and the most sophisticated critics of this argument. In some versions, it can be reduced to a crudely teleological narrative which renders Ireland perpetually a colonial dependency of England and its non-Protestant inhabitants the subdued 'natives' within an imperfectly anglicised colony. However, the most persuasive critique of the argument for the Irish origins of English colonial ideology situates Ireland not within the history of early-modern colonialism but within the paradigm of composite monarchy. Ireland thereby appears as a province of a composite state, comparable to Bohemia or Naples, for example, rather than as a colony of an emergent hemispheric empire. It possessed powerful elites on whom the English often needed to rely; even when those elites had been rejected as partners in English government after the Geraldine rebellion of 1534–35, they were sufficiently powerful to pose major threats to the success of attempted English hegemony. Ireland also had its own sovereign parliament, admittedly constrained by the operation of Poynings' Law (which since 1495 had subjected all of its decisions to the scrutiny of the English Privy Council), and in that way it offered a parallel to the provincial estates of other early-modern European composite monarchies. To capture the ambiguity of Ireland's position – as juridically a kingdom, though treated practically by the English as if it were a colony – demands seeing it 'as a mid-Atlantic polity having some of the features of both the Old World and the New'.[4] This allows the comparisons with the European overseas empires to remain, but also links them more closely to the processes of state-building that characterised the early-modern composite monarchies. Ireland can therefore still provide a crucial test case for any attempt to link the histories of states and empires in the early-modern period, without making any teleological assumptions about either its later unwilling dependency or its ultimate independence.

The origins of British imperial ideology are therefore to be found in

---

[3] D. B. Quinn, 'Ireland and Sixteenth Century European Expansion', in T. Desmond Williams (ed.), *Historical Studies*, 1 (London, 1958), 21–32; Quinn, *The Elizabethans and the Irish* (Ithaca, 1966); K. R. Andrews, N. P. Canny and P. E. H. Hair (eds.), *The Westward Enterprise: English Activities in Ireland, the Atlantic, and America 1480–1650* (Liverpool, 1978); Canny, *Kingdom and Colony: Ireland in the Atlantic World 1560–1800* (Baltimore, 1988); Canny, *Making Ireland British, 1580–1650* (Oxford, forthcoming).

[4] Hiram Morgan, 'Mid-Atlantic Blues', *Irish Review*, 11 (1991–92), 50–5; Raymond Gillespie, 'Explorers, Exploiters and Entrepreneurs: Early Modern Ireland and its Context 1500–1700', in B. J. Graham and L. J. Proudfoot (eds.), *An Historical Geography of Ireland* (London, 1993), 152.

the problematics of composite monarchy. Both England and Scotland were typical early-modern monarchies in that each was a composite territorial state before it became a maritime and colonial power overseas.[5] Each combined diverse territories acquired by inheritance, conquest, cession or incorporation under the rule of a single sovereign. Such territories could either be absorbed juridically into the state or they could remain more or less distinct from it by retaining their own laws, claiming various immunities, possessing separate ecclesiastical establishments or maintaining representative institutions within a federal or confederal structure. These early-modern states were not always nations, if nations are defined by their ethnic or cultural homogeneity. Distinct peoples inhabited diverse territories, so that the problems raised by composite states, though primarily juridical, were often also cultural. Similar legal, political and cultural dilemmas lay at the origins of all the states of medieval Europe, each of which was the product of warfare, colonisation and cultural aggression. The early-modern manifestations of these problems were distinctive only in that they arose simultaneously within the process of European state-building and in the activity of expansion beyond Europe. In Britain and Ireland they were continuous with half-a-millennium of activity by both the English and the Scottish monarchies since at least the twelfth century.

If the origins of a specifically *British* ideology of empire are to be understood, it is necessary to construct an account that incorporates the history of Scotland as well as the histories of England and Ireland. Scotland, like England, was a composite monarchy; also, like the English monarchy, it could be described anachronistically as 'colonialist' in that it used settlement, acculturation and economic dependency as a means to 'civilise' its territorial margins and their inhabitants.[6] It would also be colonialist in that it chartered and encouraged overseas ventures and settlements in the Atlantic world during the early seventeenth century.[7] Moreover, after 1608, the Stuart composite monarchy created in 1603 by the accession of King James VI of Scotland to the English throne as King James I became, for the first time, the agent of collective-

---

[5] Conrad Russell, *The Fall of the British Monarchies 1637–1642* (Oxford, 1991); Michael Perceval-Maxwell, 'Ireland and the Monarchy in the Early Stuart Multiple Kingdom', *The Historical Journal*, 34 (1991), 279–95; Jenny Wormald, 'The Creation of Britain: Multiple Kingdoms or Core and Colonies?', *Transactions of the Royal Historical Society*, 6th ser., 2 (1992), 175–94.

[6] Jane H. Ohlmeyer, '"Civilizinge of Those Rude Partes": Colonization within Britain and Ireland, 1580s–1640s', in Nicholas Canny (ed.), *The Oxford History of the British Empire*, I: *The Origins of Empire* (Oxford, 1998), 124–47.

[7] G. P. Insh, *Scottish Colonial Schemes, 1620–1686* (Glasgow, 1922).

ly British (that is, Anglo-Scottish) colonisation in the escheated lands of Ulster. The process of transforming English state-building into British empire-formation was therefore not solely linear, passing through Ireland on its passage eastwards to America. Instead, it was triangular, encompassing Anglo-Scottish, Anglo-Irish, and Hiberno-Scottish relations from the 1540s to the 1620s.[8]

The problems of composite monarchies had distinguished the connections between the British monarchs and their dominions since the early Middle Ages. The English Crown, for example, at various times claimed or held Ireland, Wales, Scotland, Normandy, Gascony, Aquitaine, the Isle of Man and the Channel Islands among its possessions, while the Scottish Crown incorporated the Western Isles, the Orkneys and the Shetlands, and challenged English claims to land in the Anglo-Scottish borders well into the sixteenth century. The assertion of these claims in practice raised a host of problems that were to supply precedents for the constitutional relations between metropolis and colonies in the early-modern period.[9] Chief among these were questions about the property rights which the Crown (or the king, in his capacity as duke of Normandy, for example) had in its various territories; what jurisdiction it held over them; what capacity it might have to legislate for its overseas dominions; and how subject peoples should be treated. In dealing with their possessions, both the English and the Scottish Crowns experienced the dilemma of reconciling uniformity with diversity that would plague later relations between the British state and the British Empire.

The first 'British' empire, in the thirteenth and fourteenth centuries, imposed England's rule over a diverse collection of territories, some geographically contiguous, others joined to the metropolis by navigable seas. The various peoples who inhabited those territories were not all treated alike by English colonists, who extended their power by military aggression. At first, a commission to evangelise pagan populations had legitimated English expansion; subsequently, a cultural mission to civilise the barbarian maintained the momentum of conquest; later still,

---

[8] Compare Jane E. A. Dawson, 'Two Kingdoms or Three? Ireland in Anglo-Scottish Relations in the Middle of the Sixteenth Century', in Roger A. Mason (ed.), *Scotland and England, 1286–1815* (Edinburgh, 1987), 113–38.

[9] On which see Julius Goebel, Jr, 'The Matrix of Empire', in Joseph Henry Smith, *Appeals from the Privy Council from the American Plantations* (New York, 1950), xiii–lxi; John T. Juricek, 'English Claims in North America to 1660: A Study in Legal and Constitutional History' (Ph.D. dissertation, University of Chicago, 1970), II, 'The Constitutional Status of Outlying Dominions: King and Crown'; A. F. McC. Madden, '1066, 1776 and All That: The Relevance of the English Medieval Experience of "Empire" to Later Imperial Constitutional Issues', in John E. Flint and Glyndwr Williams (eds.), *Perspectives of Empire: Essays Presented to Gerald S. Graham* (London, 1973), 9–26.

an ideology of domination and an historical mythology together encouraged further English migration and the resettlement of native peoples on the conquered lands.[10] Though the English did export their governing institutions, the exigencies of colonial rule demanded that control of the outlying territories be left in the hands of absentee proprietors or entrusted to a creolised governing elite. That elite in time grew to demand its independence, and appropriated legislative institutions to affirm its autonomy. The English nonetheless remained the cultural arbiters and commercial masters of what was formally an Anglo-British empire over which they steadfastly asserted their sovereignty. They had acquired this empire haphazardly and with little determining forethought. Within two centuries of its inception, it had disintegrated, apparently for good. Failure to enforce institutional uniformity, incomplete assimilation of subject peoples, the cultural estrangement of the English settlers from metropolitan norms and monarchical indifference together conspired to bring about its collapse.

This 'British' empire reached its apogee in the reign of Edward I (1272–1307), not under George III. Its dependencies were not the colonies of British North America, the western Atlantic and the Caribbean, but rather Ireland, Wales and Scotland, the constituent kingdoms and principalities of the north-west European archipelago.[11] It extended the claims of an even earlier empire within Britain, the *Imperium Anglorum* of the Anglo-Saxon kings. Athelstan (924–40) occasionally used the title of *Imperator*, meaning a supreme ruler over the diverse territories he ruled within what are now the boundaries of England; more fulsomely, Edgar I (959–75), 'King of the Angles' (*Anglorum Basileus*), proclaimed himself 'Emperor and Lord' (*Imperator et Dominus*) of the islands and the ocean around Britain, including all of the kings and all of the nations within its borders.[12]

The 'empire' of the Anglo-Saxon monarchs was long remembered, and its memory partly inspired the aggressive posture of the Angevin

---

[10] James Muldoon, 'Spiritual Conquests Compared: *Laudabiliter* and the Conquest of the Americas', in Steven B. Bowman and Blanche E. Cody (eds.), *In Iure Veritas: Studies in Canon Law in Memory of Schafer Williams* (Cincinnati, 1991), 174–86; John Gillingham, 'The English Invasion of Ireland', in Brendan Bradshaw, Andrew Hadfield and Willy Maley (eds.), *Representing Ireland: Literature and the Origins of Conflict, 1534–1660* (Cambridge, 1993), 24–42.

[11] R. R. Davies, 'The Failure of the First British Empire? England's Relations with Ireland, Scotland and Wales 1066–1500', in Nigel Saul (ed.), *England in Europe 1066–1453* (London, 1994), 121–32.

[12] James Campbell, 'The United Kingdom of England: The Anglo-Saxon Achievement', in Alexander Grant and Keith J. Stringer (eds.), *Uniting the Kingdom? The Making of British History* (London, 1995), 38; compare John Dee, 'ΘΑΛΛΑΤΟΚΡΑΤΙΑ ΒΡΕΤΤΑΝΙΚΗ' (1597), BL Harl. MS 249, ff. 95v–96r.

and Plantagenet kings towards Wales, Ireland and Scotland. Despite the Anglo-Saxons' success in creating a unified English kingdom between the seventh and the eleventh centuries, they were unable to absorb the bordering territories of Scotland and Wales, which were left as potential prizes for future rulers. The Scottish Crown similarly used the language of empire to claim its independence and supremacy in the fifteenth century, and for similar reasons. The collision between these two imperial monarchies in the mid-sixteenth century would give rise to the first claims (by the English Crown) to an 'Empire of Great Britain', and would evoke the counterclaim, by defenders of Scottish autonomy, that to become part of such an 'empire' would make Scotland into little more than a 'colony' of England. These appeals to *imperium* and *coloniae*, throughout the Three Kingdoms in the late medieval and early-modern period, indicated the Roman roots of British imperial ideology. From those neo-Roman origins sprang the continuity between the creation of a unitary, legally-bounded, independent conception of the state and the later process of forming a multinational, extensive empire in the Atlantic world.

Empire was always a language of power. In its original Roman sense, *imperium* denoted the authority of a magistrate to act on behalf of Rome and its citizens, whether at home (*domi*), in the city of Rome, or abroad (*militiae*). The people donated *imperium* to their magistrates; they, in turn, acted only in so far as they represented the people collectively. No one but a magistrate could command such authority, and such authority could only be vested in a magistrate. *Imperium* was thus formally restricted, even though it was potentially unlimited in its extent outside the city itself. In the early years of the Roman Republic, the exclusivity of *imperium* was strengthened by the absolute distinction between *imperium domi* and *imperium militiae*. Though each was temporary, and vested in a particular agent, the latter was even more tightly restricted because it was much more expansive in its powers. The boundary between *imperium domi* and *imperium militiae* was the outer limit of the city of Rome itself, whether defined (in the earliest days) as the walls of the city or (in later years) as the furthest reach of Roman government. The barrier between the two was absolute; to cross it meant the reversion of theoretically limitless power over soldiers and subjects to the sphere of Romans and free people.[13]

[13] Andrew Lintott, 'What was the "Imperium Romanum"?' *Greece and Rome*, 28 (1981), 53–67; P. A. Brunt, '*Laus Imperii*', in Brunt, *Roman Imperial Themes* (Oxford, 1990), 288–323; J. S. Richardson, '*Imperium Romanum*: Empire and the Language of Power', *Journal of Roman Studies*, 81 (1991), 1–9.

The scope of *imperium* expanded with Rome's growth beyond the bounds of the city and outward from the heartlands of northern Italy. It gradually came to mean authority in any form, detached from any particular holder of it; when it no longer applied solely to the strictly defined authority of a magistrate, it also lost the restrictions that magistratical authority had borne. This relaxation of the limits on *imperium* accompanied the dissolution of the boundary between *imperium domi* and *imperium militiae*. As the distinction between domestic and military authority was no longer recognised, *imperium* came to mean unlimited authority in any sphere. That dissolution of the boundary between the city and the lands beyond it also allowed the two areas to become confounded. No longer was Rome itself distinct from the territory ruled in the name of Rome by its magistrates wielding *imperium*. The city, its colonies and its provinces now became a single territorial unit. This was the *Imperium Romanum* or, at times, the *Imperium Romanorum* – the Roman Empire, or the Empire of the Romans. By the time of the Principate, the emperors carried the supreme authority over all of the peoples and territories of that *Imperium Romanum*. Their authority did not go unchallenged in practice, but in theory it could not be legitimately supplemented, diluted or replaced. *Imperium* now denoted ultimate, self-sufficient, indivisible authority over a territorial expanse formally known as the Empire itself.

The Roman legacy of *imperium* to medieval and early modern Europe was threefold. It denoted independent authority; it described a territorial unit; and it offered an historical foundation for claims to both the authority and the territory ruled by the Roman emperors. *Imperium* in the sense of independent and self-sufficient authority offered a more generally applicable precedent for later polities and, especially, their rulers. To claim *imperium* was to assert independence, whether from external powers or from internal competitors. The revival of the concept of *imperium* as a conception of sovereignty has been traced to the twelfth-century recovery of Roman law. According to this reformulation, the sovereign – whether collective, or individual – within each polity could claim the same independence of authority that had been enjoyed by the Roman emperors at the height of their power. Sovereignty could not be divided within the polity; neither could it be overridden from without. Each ruler therefore claimed the same powers within his own domain as the emperors had asserted over the *Imperium Romanum*; each *rex* therefore *in regno suo erat imperator*.[14]

All of these conceptions of *imperium* were territorially static. None of them necessarily encouraged any ruler to expand the boundaries of his dominions or implied any spatial dimension of rule. The history of the Roman Empire presented an obvious example of a polity whose rulers possessed both independent and universal *imperium*, and whose territories expanded by alliance, inheritance and conquest. The Roman example could inspire future rulers to extend their own territories, but it did not inevitably do so. *Imperium* in the sense of unlimited authority demanded the fastening of boundaries and clarification of the limits of authority within and beyond those boundaries; similarly, *imperium* as composite monarchy denoted diversity within unity, but did not imply that such diversity had to be multiplied by the acquisition of further dependencies.

The formula of particular sovereignty emerged from competing claims to *imperium*. One result of the recovery of Roman law was the reassertion of the universalist claims of the emperor to be *dominus mundi*, as the *Digest* (XIV. 2. 9) had it. Since the *Imperium Romanum* at its height had encompassed the whole of the world known to the Romans, the authority of the emperor was *ipso facto* universal. Undeterred by the tautology at the root of this claim, the emperor and his successors continued to assert the universality of their *imperium*. The barbarian invasions, the sack of Rome in 410 and the end of the Western Empire in 476 had extinguished the *Imperium Romanum*. Out of its ruins rose two empires – Eastern and Western – as well as the Papacy. Unabashed by the diversity of claimants to the imperial succession, the Holy Roman emperors, the Byzantine emperors and the popes all at times demanded recognition of their universal authority. Though the tradition of Roman universalism remained intact, albeit controversial, particular claims to *imperium* more successfully challenged papal and Imperial pretensions to universality.

Late medieval and early modern rulers made increasingly frequent claims to independent *imperium*. Such claims were particular, rather than universal; they did not suggest any intention to compete with the emperor or the pope for supremacy, but asserted both independence from external interference and ascendancy over internal competitors. For example, lawyers for the French monarchy asserted that the king of France was an *imperator in regno suo* from the fourteenth century on-wards.[15] This was not to claim parity with the pope or the emperor,

[14] Walter Ullmann, 'The Development of the Medieval Idea of Sovereignty', *English Historical Review*, 64 (1949), 1–33.
[15] André Bossuat, 'La Formule "Le Roi est empereur en son royaume": son emploi au XVᵉ siècle devant le parlement de Paris', *Revue Historique de Droit Français et Etranger*, 4th ser., 39 (1961), 371–

since the French kings had long since abandoned their candidacy for the headship of the Holy Roman Empire.[16] Instead, it was an assertion of the French kings' power over the clergy and the nobility within France itself, derived from the Roman law principle of *plenitudo potestatis*. This was a claim to internal authority rather than external power, an assertion of royal supremacy not national self-determination, and therefore a statement not of independence from outside authority but rather of predominance over internal competitors. For this reason, the French crown's imperial claims have been associated more with the origins of French absolutism than with the beginnings of French national sovereignty.[17] This would not always be true of other monarchical claims to imperial status in the following centuries; nevertheless, the French case does illustrate well the Janus face of *imperium*, as an authority which could either be used to ensure the dependency of internal competitors or to assert independence from external powers.

For those European rulers who claimed independent *imperium* for their particular realms or cities, the greatest external threat came from those supranational polities that claimed both universal authority in the present and descent from the Roman Empire in the past. This was true, in varying degrees, of both the Holy Roman Empire and the Papacy. The headship of the Empire remained the most prestigious attribute of secular kingship in the early modern period. Though it was clearly no longer the emblem of universal rulership, the multinational character of the Empire endowed its holder with greater authority than any that could be held by any particular ruler of a single realm. When Charles V of Spain became Holy Roman Emperor in 1519, the Empire was united with the Spanish Monarchy under his rule to become the most far-flung monarchy the world had ever known. Charles's dominions could not encompass all of the realms of Europe, but they did include territories unknown even to the Romans, in the New World beyond the Pillars of Hercules. This was the nearest the post-classical world would come to seeing a truly worldwide monarchy, and hence the closest approximation to universal *imperium* since the last days of the *Imperium Romanum* itself.[18]

81.

[16] Gaston Zeller, 'Les Rois de France, candidats à l'empire: essai sur l'idéologie impériale en France', *Revue Historique*, 173 (1934): 273–311, 497–543.

[17] Jacques Krynen, *L'Empire du roi: idées et croyances politiques en France XIIIe–XVe siècle* (Paris, 1993), 388–414.

[18] Ramón Menendez Pidal, *El Idea Imperial de Carlos V* (Buenos Aires, 1941); Frances A. Yates, 'Charles V and the Idea of the Empire', in Yates, *Astraea: The Imperial Theme in the Sixteenth Century* (London, 1975), 1–28; Earl Rosenthal, '*Plus Ultra, Non Plus Ultra*, and the Columnar Device of the Emperor Charles V', *Journal of the Warburg and Courtauld Institutes*, 34 (1971), 204–28.

The Papacy could not make such widespread territorial claims, but its authority was deemed to be more truly universal, because unconstrained by territoriality. The spiritual authority of the popes theoretically united the whole of Christendom into a single flock with a single shepherd. The Papacy could lay equal claim to historical continuity from the Roman Empire because the Empire itself had become a vehicle for the propagation of Christianity with the conversion of Constantine, notwithstanding the shock of the Sack of Rome by the Goths and Augustine's meditation thereon in the *City of God*. Particularist claims to *imperium* made by other European monarchs could therefore have two universalist antagonists outside their own realms, the Empire or the Papacy. Each was a supranational body, claiming descent from the Roman Empire, and asserting its universality as the legatee of Rome's extension. In the struggle for *imperium*, all roads led back to Rome, though they did not necessarily lead back to the same conception of Rome. Few polities could legitimately claim direct descent from the Roman Empire; only the emperor and the pope could plausibly claim even a restricted form of universal rulership. However, the powerful language of *imperium* could and did sustain many rulers in their battles, both internal and external, for independence and supremacy.

Yet even when there was no competition for *imperium*, rulers could claim imperial status on the grounds that they possessed a number of distinct territories which were united only under their headship. This conception of *imperium* as a compound of territories could, like the other meanings of the term, be traced back to the Roman Empire. As later commentators were aware, the Roman Empire at its greatest extent had been composed of distinct provinces bound to the Empire by the emperor himself, as the representative of the *Populum Romanorum*. Once these provinces dissolved their allegiance and became barbarian kingdoms in the latter days of the Western Empire, the federative structure of the Empire became clear, when previously it had been obscured by the ever-expanding ambit of Roman law and citizenship. As Isidore of Seville defined it in the seventh century, it had become 'a Roman Empire, of which other kingdoms are dependencies': no longer a unitary and integrative territorial *imperium*, but rather an *imperium* in the form of a composite monarchy, linking disparate realms and territories under a single, supreme head.[19] This federal conception of *imperium*, and of the emperor as the head of such a federation, began to be imitated

---

[19] Isidore of Seville, *Etymologiæ* (c. 622–33), quoted in Robert Folz, *The Concept of Empire in Western Europe from the Fifth to the Fourteenth Century*, trans. Sheila Ann Ogilvie (London, 1969), 7.

beyond the boundaries of the contracted Empire itself from the tenth century, as the king of Castile-Léon proclaimed himself an emperor in this sense, as did Athelstan and Edgar. Any ruler of multiple territories could therefore be an *Imperator*, whether or not it was necessary for him to claim independence from other such rulers.

The language and symbolism of empire provided early-modern monarchies with the resources for the legitimation of their independence, just as it had originally allowed Italian city-states in the fourteenth century to assert their juridical independence from the Empire.[20] Such resources encompassed regal symbols, legislative enactments and the increasingly widespread and self-conscious use of the language of empire in statements of national purpose. Since the late fourteenth century, English kings had been represented as wearing the 'closed' crown of a circlet topped by two crossed bands, though it seems not to have been called an 'imperial crown' until the reign of Henry V in the 1420s.[21] The image of a monarch wearing such a crown first appeared on Scottish coinage *circa* 1485, three years before the English king Henry VII issued a gold sovereign which showed him wearing the closed, imperial crown.[22]

The regal appurtenance of the closed crown symbolised the 'imperial' status of the monarch who wore it. The crown worn by the Holy Roman Emperor himself in fact had only one band atop it; the closed crowns of other monarchs did not seek to usurp the status of the emperor within their own jurisdictions, but rather to assert a claim of independence and superiority within a specific territory that was equivalent to the emperor's within his. For this reason, the physical crown came to be identified with the authority implied by the claim to imperial status. For instance, when Cuthbert Tunstall advised Henry VIII in 1517 that the king could not be proposed as a candidate to be emperor, because he was not a prince of the Empire, he soothed the monarch with the observation that 'the Crown of England is an Empire of hitselff, mych better then now the Empire of Rome: for which cause your Grace werith a close crown'.[23]

[20] Quentin Skinner, *The Foundations of Modern Political Thought*, 2 vols. (Cambridge, 1978), I, 8–12; J. P. Canning, 'Ideas of the State in 13th- and 14th-Century Commentators on the Roman Law', *Transactions of the Royal Historical Society*, 5th ser., 33 (1983), 1–27.

[21] Philip Grierson, 'The Origins of the English Sovereign and the Symbolism of the Closed Crown', *British Numismatic Journal*, 33 (1964), 127–34; Dale Hoak, 'The Iconography of the Crown Imperial', in Hoak (ed.), *Tudor Political Culture* (Cambridge, 1995), 56–60.

[22] Roger A. Mason, '*Regnum et Imperium*: Humanism and the Political Culture of Renaissance Scotland', in Mason, *Kingship and the Commonweal: Political Thought in Renaissance and Reformation Scotland* (East Linton, 1998), 130; Grierson, 'The Origins of the English Sovereign', 118.

[23] Cuthbert Tunstall to Henry VIII, 12 February 1517, in *Original Letters Illustrative of English History*, ed. Henry Ellis, 1st ser., 3 vols. (London, 1824), I, 136.

This statement of the English Crown's imperial status anticipated the language of the declaration in the preamble to the 1533 Act of Appeals that 'this realm of England is an empire'; however, such language was not otherwise unprecedented, even in England. Thomas Cromwell's claim, made on behalf of Henry VIII, implied that the king possessed the same power over temporal and ecclesiastical (if not necessarily spiritual) matters as the later Roman emperors, particularly (though this can be exaggerated) the British Roman emperor, Constantine.[24] The implied territorial definition of empire, the inclusion of all members of the community of England within its territorial bounds, and the independent superiority of the monarch over his subjects, without any jurisdictional interference from outside, had also been asserted after Henry's conquest of the French town of Tournai in 1513. Coins for Tournai bearing the closed imperial crown hammered the point home.[25] The Act of Appeals may have 'inaugurated names and concepts destined to be symbolic of political realities vastly outshining the king's authority in England';[26] it did so by providing a convenient statutory statement of an attribute of English kingship that had been recognised, theorised and supplemented for almost a century.

The fifteenth-century French arguments that the *rex Christianissimus* was *in regno suo imperator* had travelled to Scotland (by way of Scottish civilians trained in French law-schools) as they would, two generations later, to England (by way of French legal sources).[27] Looking back from the 1760s, William Blackstone distinguished the language of the Act in Restraint of Appeals from the 'ridiculous notion, propagated by the German and Italian civilians, that an emperor could do many things which a king could not (as the creation of notaries and the like)'.[28] Such a notion would not have seemed quite so ridiculous to either the English or the Scottish Crown in the fifteenth or sixteenth centuries. Indeed, it was precisely a dispute regarding notaries in 1469 that provoked the Scottish Parliament to declare that James III possessed

[24] Hoak, 'The Iconography of the Crown Imperial', in Hoak (ed.), *Tudor Political Culture*, 101; Richard Koebner, ' "The Imperial Crown of this Realm": Henry VIII, Constantine the Great, and Polydore Vergil', *Bulletin of the Institute of Historical Research*, 26 (1953), 29–52; Walter Ullmann, ' "This Realm of England is an Empire" ', *Journal of Ecclesiastical History*, 30 (1979), 175–203.

[25] Thomas F. Mayer, 'On the Road to 1534: The Occupation of Tournai and Henry VIII's Theory of Sovereignty', in Hoak (ed.), *Tudor Political Culture*, 25–9.

[26] Koebner, ' "The Imperial Crown of this Realm" ', 29.

[27] Mason, '*Regnum et Imperium*: Humanism and the Political Culture of Renaissance Scotland', in Mason, *Kingship and the Commonweal*, 129; Mayer, 'On the Road to 1534', in Hoak (ed.), *Tudor Political Culture*, 21–2.

[28] William Blackstone, *Commentaries on the Laws of England*, 4 vols. (London, 1765–69), I, 235.

'ful Jurisdictioune and fre Impire within his realm', some sixty years
before the English Parliament made any similar enactment.[29] These
claims may also have been related to the acquisition of the Orkney and
Shetland Islands after the marriage of James III to Margaret of Denmark in 1468, to claims to territories in France (such as Saintonge), as
well as to James IV's attempts to bring the Western Isles under the
control of the crown.[30] The Scottish assertion of *imperium* was both
jurisdictional and territorial; it at once proclaimed the independence of
the Scottish monarchy and projected its authority throughout the diverse dominions that made up the kingdom of the Scots. Similarly,
Henry VIII's parliamentary claim to empire in the 1530s had territorial
as well as caesaropapal implications, and was intended not only to assert
the independent ecclesiastical authority of the Crown but also England's
overlordship of its neighbours in Wales, Ireland and ultimately Scotland. Accordingly, it can be linked conceptually to the two Acts of
Union that incorporated Wales to the English Crown between 1536 and
1543, to the Irish Parliament's declaration in 1541 that Henry VIII was
'King of Ireland', rather than merely its 'lord', and, finally, to English
aggression against the Scots in the 1540s.[31]

The vernacular language of British imperial ideology – of 'Great Britain', 'empire' and 'colony' – was forged in the context of Anglo-Scottish
relations in the 1540s. Beginning in 1542, and then again in 1547–49, a
group of English and Scottish writers associated with Henry VIII and
Protector Somerset offered a series of arguments in favour of Scottish
submission to England. Under Henry, and in the early stages of Edward's reign, these arguments reinforced the necessity of a dynastic
marriage between the infant Mary, Queen of Scots, and the English
prince (later, king) Edward; when such a marriage became impossible,
they appeared to justify military invasion of Scotland by England. 'The
idea of Henry the imperialist bent on the union of the British Isles is no
longer supportable',[32] though that idea was accepted by contemporary
Scots who responded in kind with arguments against English designs,

---

[29] *Acts of the Parliaments of Scotland*, ed. Thomas Thomson and Cosmo Innes, 12 vols. (Edinburgh, 1814–75), I, 95.
[30] Norman Macdougall, *James III: A Political Study* (Edinburgh, 1982), 78, 90–1. My thanks to Roger Mason for advice on this point.
[31] Graham Nicholson, 'The Act of Appeals and the English Reformation', in Claire Cross, David Loades and J. J. Scarisbrick (eds.), *Law and Government under the Tudors* (Cambridge, 1988), 23–5.
[32] David M. Head, 'Henry VIII's Scottish Policy: A Reassessment', *Scottish Historical Review*, 61 (1982), 2.

especially when they were revived under Edward VI. Somerset saw the subjection of Scotland as a means to increase English power within Britain and to effect the spread of Protestantism by solving the long-standing 'British' problem of two adjacent and hostile monarchies inhabiting a single island. Somerset's announced aim was not to create a new monarchy within Britain, but to restore the ancient one called 'Great Britain', 'which is no new name but the old name to them both'.[33] However, English claims to feudal overlordship, the use of Geoffrey of Monmouth's 'British' history to justify those claims and the prominence of 'imperial' language in the English propaganda of the 1540s, lent credibility to Scottish fears of English intentions.[34]

Proponents of the English cause in the Anglo-Scottish wars of 1543–46 and 1547–50 located the origins of the British Empire in the early history of Britain as it had been told by Geoffrey of Monmouth in the twelfth century. That empire was 'British' because it had been founded by Brutus, a refugee from the Trojan wars; it was an empire because it became a composite monarchy after Brutus's death, when it was ruled by his three sons, Locrine, Albanact and Camber. Geoffrey's *Historia Regum Britanniæ* (1136) enshrined a vision of English dominance over Britain within his legendary history. Brutus's eldest son, Locrine, ruled England; the younger sons paid homage to him on account of his seniority, just as their respective kingdoms of Scotland and Wales were held to owe homage to England: seniority implied superiority within the post-Brutan feudal composite monarchy.[35]

Supporters of England's claims over Scotland also used early British history to affirm the longevity of an English civilising mission within Britain. The Galfridian history of early Britain provided the basis for the English assertion in 1542 of feudal superiority over the Scottish Crown. The *Declaration, Conteyning the Just Causes and Consyderations of This Present Warre with the Scottis* (1542) issued by Henry VIII before his invasion of Scotland argued that such feudal submission had been affirmed uninter-

[33] Public Record Office, SP 50/3/60, quoted in M. L. Bush, *The Government Policy of Protector Somerset* (London, 1975), 10, n. 21; S. T. Bindoff, 'The Stuarts and their Style', *English Historical Review*, 60 (1945), 200–1. The earlier history of the term is treated in Denys Hay, 'The Use of the Term "Great Britain" in the Middle Ages', *Transactions of the Society of Antiquaries of Great Britain*, 89 (1955–56), 55–66.

[34] See generally Marcus Merriman, 'War and Propaganda during the "Rough Wooing"', *Scottish Tradition*, 9/10 (1979–80), 20–30, and, more specifically, Roger A. Mason, 'The Scottish Reformation and the Origins of Anglo-British Imperialism,' in Mason (ed.), *Scots and Britons: Scottish Political Thought and the Union of 1603* (Cambridge, 1994), 168–78.

[35] Roger A. Mason, 'Scotching the Brute: Politics, History and National Myth in Sixteenth-Century Britain', in Mason (ed.), *Scotland and England*, 60–84.

ruptedly from the earliest times until the reign of the English king Henry
VI. Before the arrival of Brutus, the author of the *Declaration* argued,
Britain had been inhabited by a race of giants, 'people without order or
civilitie'; Brutus and his sons had brought order to the 'rude' inhabitants, and ensured the continuing administration of justice by the appointment of a single superior over the three kingdoms 'of whom the
sayd astates should depend'. Justice and peace replaced disorder and
incivility as Scotland and Wales became dependent states within a
multiple monarchy headed by England.[36] John Elder, a Highlander and
supporter of Henry VIII's dynastic policies in 'Scotland, a part of your
Highnes empyre of England', appealed to Henry's treatment of the
Gaelic lords of Ireland as a precedent for bringing civility to his own
'rude and barbarous' people in the Highlands of Scotland. Just as the
'gyauntes and wilde people, without ordour, civilite, or maners' were
brought to 'ordour and civilitie' by Albanact's rule in Scotland, so
Henry could bring civility to Scotland's Gaelic lords, and the true,
Protestant, religion in place of 'the papistical, curside spiritualitie of
Scotland'.[37] As would later be the case in Ireland, and in North America, civility and Christianity were closely associated as the foundations of
order within a 'British' empire. However, in Elder's case, at least, the
association between civility and Protestantism was not enduring: in
1555, he looked forward to the return of the true, Catholic, religion to
'this moste noble and holy yle of Britayn' as he celebrated the marriage
of the English Queen Mary to the Spanish Prince Philip, a ruler for
whom God had foreordained a worldwide empire (*Cui Deus imperium
totius destinat orbis*), and who would 'enriche [Mary's] empyre of Englande'.[38]

The renewed attempts between 1547–50 by the Edwardian regimes to
enforce Anglo-Scottish dynastic union, whether by persuasion or by fire
and sword, generated a conception of a British empire that was Protestant, commercially expansive, bounded by the sea, and inhabited by the
subjects of two free and independent kingdoms united under one head.
This monarchy could be called 'British' because it traced its origins back

[36] *A Declaration, Conteyning the Just Causes and Consyderations of this Present Warre with the Scottis* (5
November 1542), in *The Complaynt of Scotlande wyth an Exortatione to the Thre Estaits to be Vigilante in
Deffens of Their Public Veil*, ed. J. A. H. Murray (London, 1872), 199.
[37] John Elder, 'A Proposal for Uniting Scotland with England, Addressed to King Henry VIII. By
John Elder, Clerke, a Reddshanke' (*c.* 1542), BL MS Royal 18. A. xxxvIII, in *The Bannatyne
Miscellany*, I, ed. Sir Walter Scott and David Laing (Edinburgh, 1827), 9, 11, 14.
[38] [John Elder,] *The Copie of a Letter Sent in to Scotlande, of the Arivall and Landynge, and Moste Noble
Marryage of the Moste Illustre Prynce Philippe, Prynce of Spaine, to the Moste Excellente Princes Marye Quene of
England* (1555), in *The Chronicle of Queen Jane, and of Two Years of Queen Mary, and Especially of the
Rebellion of Sir Thomas Wyat*, ed. John Gough Nichols (London, 1850), 146, 163, 165.

to its first king, Brutus, and reunited the isle of Britain under a single ruler. The inhabitants of the island over which Brutus had ruled were the original, ethnic Britons, though in due course they became mingled with the Scots and the English. The 'one sole Monarchie, shalbee called Britayn', and its subjects would 'take the indifferent old name of Britaynes again'. It could also be called an empire for good historical reasons. Though the earliest Britons had 'lost their name and Empire' through sin and discord, their English and Scottish descendants had been reunited when Britain became a province of the Roman Empire, and when the British-born Christian Constantine had become emperor, 'al Britayn, was under one Emperor, and beeyng under one Emperor, then was Scotlande and Englande but one Empire'. The symbols of that British empire remained as emblems of the English monarchy: the red cross, originally borne by Constantine, and 'a close crowne Emperiall, in token that the lande is an empire free in it selfe, & subject to no superior but GOD'.[39]

The most elaborate exposition of the Tudor claim to the Scots throne, Nicholas Bodrugan's *Epitome of the Title That the Kynges Majestie of Englande, Hath to the Sovereigntie of Scotlande* (1548), recalled that Somerset's supposed ancestor, Eldulph de Samour, had repelled a Saxon invasion whereby 'this Realme was delivered from the tyrany of Saxons, and restored to the whole *Empire* & name *of great Briteigne*'. That empire had its origins in Brutus's monarchy, and had been affirmed later by the Scots' reception of English law, the ecclesiastical supremacy of the archbishop of York over the Scottish bishops and the feudal submission of Scotland, a nation 'from the begynnyng inseparably appendaunt to the crowne of this realm'.[40] The centuries of civil strife between the kingdoms of England and Scotland had renewed the divisions within Britain. It would be the task of the English to restore unity to the island, as they had done in the past. As the French ambassador reported, the different kingdoms of England and Scotland would then be abolished, and 'les deux royaumes unys et réduictz en ung empire quy sera dict et nommé tousjours *l'empire de la Grande Bretaigne* et le prince dominateur d'icelluy empereur de la Grande Bretaigne'.[41]

[39] James Henrisoun, *An Exhortacion to the Scottes to Conforme Themselves to the Honourable, Expedient, and Godly Union Betweene the Two Realmes of Englande and Scotland* (1547), in *The Complaynt of Scotlande* (ed.) Murray, 218–19.
[40] Nicholas Bodrugan, *An Epitome of the Title That the Kynges Majestie of Englande, Hath to the Sovereigntie of Scotlande* (London, 1548), sigs. aiiiᵛ, [av]ᵛ, giiiᵛ–gvᵛ (my emphasis).
[41] 'Mémoire contenant les articles proposés au Comte de Huntley' (January 1548), in *Correspondance Politique de Odet de Selve, Ambassadeur de France en Angleterre (1546–1549)*, ed. Germain Lefèvre-Pontalis (Paris, 1888), 269 (my emphasis).

The 'Edwardian Moment' of the 1540s saw the birth of the concept of the 'empire of Great Britain' (or 'l'empire de la Grande Bretaigne'); it also saw the beginnings of a Protestant conception of that empire. Henry VIII's *Declaration* did not specify any particular religious settlement for the proposed union of England and Scotland, though sometime Protestants like John Elder did see English hegemony as a means to accelerate reformation in Scotland. The return to the reformist programme of Protestantising England under Somerset offered new hope for Scots sympathisers of the English like the Edinburgh merchant James Henrisoun that 'as these two Realmes should grow into one, so should thei also agre in the concorde & unite of one religion, & the same *the* pure, syncere & incorrupt religion of Christ'.[42] William Patten, the militantly Protestant judge of the Marshalsea Court who accompanied Somerset's expedition of 1547, similarly promised the Scots deliverance 'from the most servile thraldom and bondage under that hideous monster, that venemous *aspis* and very ANTICHRIST, the bishop of Rome'. The Greeks, the Russians and other members of the Eastern Church would not submit to his 'insolent Impery': why then should the Scots?[43] English intervention in 1560 would in due course help to secure the Scottish Reformation, and ensure the existence of Britain as a Protestant island; however, the enduring differences in theology and church government between the English and the Scottish Churches would render Protestantism more of a bone of contention than a bond of union between the two kingdoms.

A more immediate bond between the two kingdoms would be trade, according to Somerset's partisans, who tentatively conceived the empire of Great Britain as a commercial, as well as a political and religious, union. Henrisoun, the Edinburgh merchant, hoped to persuade his countryfolk that union with England would increase national security and that 'the marchaunt might without feare goo abrode, and bryng in forreine commodities, into the realme' and offered a set of economic proposals, embracing wage-labour, the grain-trade, fishing, mining, and poor relief to cement the union and benefit the 'commonwealth'.[44]

[42] Henrisoun, *Exhortacion to the Scottes*, in *The Complaynt of Scotlande*, ed. Murray, 234; on Henrisoun see Marcus Merriman, 'James Henrisoun and "Great Britain": British Union and the Scottish Commonweal', in Mason (ed.), *Scotland and England*, 85–112.
[43] William Patten, *The Expedition into Scotland of the Most Worthily Fortunate Prince Edward, Duke of Somerset* (1548), in *Tudor Tracts 1532–1588*, ed. A. F. Pollard (London, 1903), 70, 72.
[44] Henrisoun, *Exhortacion to the Scottes*, in *The Complaynt of Scotlande*, ed. Murray, 230; Henrisoun, 'The Godly and Golden Booke for Concorde of England and Scotland' (9 July 1549), in *Calendar of State Papers Relating to Scotland and Mary Queen of Scots 1547–1603*, ed. Joseph Bain et al., 13 vols. (Edinburgh, 1898–1969), I, 143–5.

Somerset's *Epistle or Exhortacion, to Unitie and Peace* (1548), the regime's most widely-circulated piece of propaganda, concluded its appeal with a promise to allow all Scots free access to English ports, and permission to trade with England 'as liberally and frely, & with the same, & no other custome or paimentes therefore then Englishmen, & the Kynges subjectes'.[45] The Scots would demand such freedom of trade after James VI's accession to the English throne, in the early 1640s, and repeatedly throughout the seventeenth century as a precondition for union with England, but they would only receive it – and access to the English colonial trade – under the terms of the Treaty of Union of 1707.[46]

As in the debate preceding the Union of 1707, proponents of Anglo-Scottish union appealed to geographical determinism. A single religion, and a unified commercial system, were the necessary complements of the natural unity of England and Scotland within the island of Britain. Together, the Scots and the English were dwellers within a single land, 'severed . . . from the reste of the worlde, with a large sea', 'separate by seas from other nations', and 'of one nature tonge and bredd in one ile compased with the sea'.[47] Such arguments echoed Virgil's first *Eclogue*, in which the Britons appeared as the furthest-flung inhabitants of the known world, cut-off from the rest of civilised humanity (*penitus toto divisos orbe Britannos*, *Eclogues*, I. 36). This Virgilian trope of Britain's isolation would be used later in the sixteenth century as an explanation for the British kingdoms' lack of overseas territorial possessions, and a means whereby the English and the Scots alike could congratulate themselves on their indifference to the demeaning scramble for trade and land that the powers of continental Europe pursued.[48] In the context of the 'Rough Wooing', however, it offered an argument in favour of a union to create a British empire conceived as an insular composite monarchy. The conception of this British empire in the 1540s was therefore only maritime in so far as it was bounded by the sea; it was

---

[45] [Edward Seymour, Duke of Somerset,] *An Epistle or Exhortacion, to Unitie and Peace, Sent from the Lord Protector . . . To the Nobilitie, Gentlemen, and Commons, and Al Others the Inhabitauntes of the Realme of Scotlande* (5 February 1548), in *The Complaynt of Scotlande*, ed. Murray, 246.

[46] Brian P. Levack, *The Formation of the British State: England, Scotland, and the Union 1603–1707* (Oxford, 1987), 138–47, 163–8.

[47] Henrisoun, *Exhortacion to the Scottes*, in *The Complaynt of Scotlande*, ed. Murray, 232; Patten, *Expedition into Scotland*, in *Tudor Tracts*, ed. Pollard, 66; Henrisoun, 'Godly and Golden Booke', in *Calendar of State Papers Relating to Scotland*, ed. Bain, I, 144.

[48] Josephine Waters Bennett, 'Britain Among the Fortunate Isles', *Studies in Philology*, 53 (1956), 114–17; Jeffrey Knapp, *An Empire Nowhere: England, America, and Literature from Utopia to the Tempest* (Berkeley, 1992), 4, 12, 64–5, 87.

insular, rather than expansionist; and nature set its limits, which the empire of Great Britain would naturally fill but not overflow.

A Protestant union would bring with it independence from the Papacy; a commercial union would be based on freedom of trade between the two kingdoms. These advantages provided an English promise to the Scots that even feudal dependency within a composite monarchy would not imply their own personal dependency within the new empire of Great Britain. All appearances to the contrary, the English did not intend to secure Anglo-Scottish union by force or right of conquest, but rather by dynastic union, 'which title enduceth no servitude, but fredome, libertie, concord and quietnesse'. The French towns of Thérouanne and Tournai had indeed been conquered by force of English arms in the reign of Henry VIII, argued Henrisoun, but the Scots should instead be persuaded peaceably to join a union of equals. There had historically been two methods by which two nations could be joined under a single ruler, Somerset's *Epistle* recalled: 'Either by force & superioritie whiche is conquest, or by equalitie & love, whiche is parentage and mariyng'. William Patten told the Scots, echoing Cicero, that England sought 'not the Mastership of you, but the Fellowship!' Anglo-Scottish union would restore the historic unity of Britain, and bring to Scotland the clear advantages of peace, prosperity and Protestantism. The Scots should therefore 'laie doune their weapons, thus rashly received, to fight against the mother of their awne nacion: I mean this realm now called Englande the onely supreme seat of the*m*pire of greate Briteigne'.[49]

The empire of Great Britain was therefore the invention of the unionist pamphleteers who wrote on behalf of Henry VIII and Protector Somerset. Those English writers conceived of a composite monarchy (and hence, an empire) that would include both England and Scotland. It would be British not only because it encompassed the whole island of Britain, but also because it would restore the integrity of the monarchy founded by Brutus, whose subjects had been named 'Britons' in his honour. The supporters of this new British monarchy, in both England and Scotland, were overwhelmingly Protestants who envisaged Anglo-Scottish union as the means to create a Protestant island. The political and religious unity of Britain would render it secure from the

---

[49] Henrisoun, *Exhortacion to the Scottes*, in *The Complaynt of Scotlande* (ed.) Murray, 227; [Somerset,] *Epistle*, in *The Complaynt of Scotlande* (ed.) Murray, 241, 244; Patten, *Expedition into Scotland*, in *Tudor Tracts* (ed.) Pollard, 69 (compare Cicero, *De Officiis*, ii.27); Bodrugan, *Epitome of the Title*, sig. [av]ᵛ (my emphasis).

designs of the French, and increase the British monarchy's standing within Europe. This would guarantee stability and prosperity, and secure the religious and political freedom of the two British nations.

Though many Scots, especially in the Lowlands, signed assurances of compliance with the English,[50] the Scottish monarchy and the Scottish Church resisted the pressure towards union, and in due course affirmed their French allegiance with the betrothal of Queen Mary to the French dauphin rather than the English king. The Scottish Crown produced no official responses to Henry VIII's *Declaration*, Somerset's *Epistle*, or the associated English propaganda. Two unofficial Scottish responses to the English arguments did emerge from the intersection of courtly and ecclesiastical circles. William Lamb, the author of 'Ane Resonyng of Ane Scottis and Inglis Merchand Betuix Rowand and Lionis' (1549), was a parson, a senator of James V's College of Justice, and later a member of Mary of Guise's administration. Robert Wedderburn, the presumed author of *The Complaynt of Scotland* (c. 1550), was a vicar in the Scottish Church whose residence at Dundee had been burned by the English army after their victory at the battle of Pinkie in 1547.[51] The two authors evidently knew each other, and Lamb seems to have drawn upon the *Complaynt* for elements of his counterargument to the English claims. Though their rhetorical procedures and the emphases of their arguments differed, Lamb and Wedderburn together provided a reasoned case against the English conception of an Anglo-Scottish empire within Britain that would be Protestant, commercial, insular, and free.

Lamb brought the techniques of humanist source-criticism to bear upon the historical arguments for Scottish allegiance to England arrayed in Henry VIII's *Declaration*. As the English merchant in his dialogue paraphrased the *Declaration*'s arguments for English suzerainty, the Scottish merchant refuted them at even greater length with material taken from the Scots historian, Hector Boece, but most often from the Italian humanist, Polydore Vergil, 'your awin liturate, autentik historiciane'. Polydore had shown in his *Anglica Historia* (1534) that there was no good evidence for the existence of Brutus, let alone for the division of the British monarchy after his death. The Romans, not Brutus, had brought 'literatoure and ... civiliteis' to Britain, as Tacitus

[50] Marcus Merriman, 'The Assured Scots: Scottish Collaborators with England during the Rough Wooing', *Scottish Historical Review*, 47 (1968), 10–35.
[51] William Lamb, *Ane Resonyng of Ane Scottis and Inglis Merchand Betuix Rowand and Lionis* (1549), BL Cotton MS Caligula B. vii, ff. 354ʳ–81ᵛ, ed. Roderick J. Lyall (Aberdeen, 1985), x–xvii; [Wedderburn,] *Complaynt of Scotland* (ed.) Stewart, xi–xvi.

had shown in the *Agricola*. Later historians gave no credence to the argument that the Scots had been vassals of the English crown. The first king to have ruled '*totius Anglie imperium*' was Athelstan, but he had never held '*totius Britanie imperium*; be quhilk word *Britanie* wes than and also now is conte*n*it bay*th* Ingland and Scotland'. There had therefore never been a British empire within Britain, and certainly none over which the English monarch had ruled as a feudal superior. In the absence of any good historical evidence, there could be no foundation for English claims to suzerainty over Scotland. English arguments from history could not be trusted any more than English intentions in the present. As the merchants' audience of three Catholic victims of Henry VIII (Sir Thomas More, Bishop John Fisher, and 'the Good Man of Sion', a Brigittine monk) pointed out, Henry had been a good king until 'the new leirnyng of Germanie' had entered his court. The English attempt to recover their specious British empire would bring with it persecutory Protestantism; the refutation of claims to the former would be one means of preventing the latter.[52]

The Complaynt of Scotland placed Anglo-Scottish relations within the larger context of universal history, told as the rise and fall of empires and the consequent *translatio imperii* from Assyria to Rome and from Rome to the multiplicity of contemporary polities. Lucan had foretold that the weight of Rome would bring its downfall, 'quhilk is the cause that the monarche of it, is dividit amang mony diverse princis', just as all such 'dominions altris dechaeis ande cummis to subversione'. This was not the effect of fortune, but of divine judgment. Just as God had used the Assyrians as a scourge for Israel, so he had given victory to the English at Pinkie to punish the Scots for their apostasy. The Scots had now 'to deffende the liberte and save the dominione' of their homeland or fall under the mastery of the English king: 'fra the tyme that he get dominione of the cuntre ye sal be his sklavis in extreme servitude', like the inhabitants of Ireland. Any Scot who did not adopt a precisely Ciceronian conception of patriotism as the defence of 'ther public veil, & ther native cu*n*tre, to perreis al to gyddir ... ar mair brutal nor brutal beystus'. Wedderburn therefore rejected any natural, historical or ethnic arguments for the unity of Great Britain which, he witheringly pointed out, 'is nou callit ingland'. Least convincing of all were English appeals to ancient prophesies of British unity or to the history of Brutus. Such fables were easily disproved, and the English only used them 'to

---

[52] Lamb, *Ane Resonyng* (ed.) Lyall, 57, 63 (citing Tacitus, *Agricola*, 21), 75 (citing Polydore Vergil, *Anglica Historia* (Basel, 1534), 146), 169.

preve that Scotland vas ane *colone* of ingland quhe*n* it vas fyrst inhabit'.⁵³ This was the first vernacular use of the Latin *colonia* to mean a settlement from a metropole in a foreign territory, but Wedderburn adopted the term in the course of rebutting, rather than asserting, an imperial claim derived from supposed ethnic homogeneity.⁵⁴

Both sides recognised that the debate of the 1540s regarding Anglo-Scottish union and Scottish independence was a dispute between exponents of the classical art of rhetoric, the 'oratours of our scottis nation' ranging themselves against the 'oratours of ingland'.⁵⁵ With calculated rhetorical irony, John Elder had called himself 'a wretch destitute of all good lernynge and eloquence', James Henrisoun asserted that 'there needeth no subtile perswasions or finesse of woordes' to convince the Scots of the need for union, and Nicholas Bodrugan stated that 'it was not my mynde to trifle with the fine flowers of Rethorike but to bryng rather faithfull, then painted gliteryng overture, unto thinges afflicted'.⁵⁶ All of the defences of the English stance towards Scotland were, in fact, examples of deliberative oratory, fashioned to state the case in favour of English sovereignty over the Scots, and for the restitution of the historic 'empire of Great Britain'. In response, William Lamb adopted the techniques of forensic oratory to refute the English *Declaration* of 1542 point by point, while Robert Wedderburn arrayed the Ciceronian conception of patriotism as loyalty to the *res publica* as a defence against English imperial claims; 'the eloquent Cicero' was the most frequently cited source named in the *Complaynt*.⁵⁷

The Anglo-Scottish debate of the 1540s introduced the concept of an empire of Great Britain into British political thought, and associated it for the first time with the Roman conception of a colony. Its sources lay, on the English side, in the British history of Geoffrey of Monmouth and,

---

⁵³ [Wedderburn,] *Complaynt of Scotland* (ed.) Stewart, 16–17, 21–2, 57, 72–3, 56–7 (citing Cicero, *De Officiis*, 1.57; *De Finibus*, 1.15), 67, 83–4, 64 (my emphasis).

⁵⁴ *OED*, s.v. 'colony', II. 4; Jones, 'Origins of the Colonial Idea in England', 449; compare [Wedderburn,] *Complaynt of Scotland*, ed. Stewart, 13: 'it is necessair at sum tyme, til myxt oure langage vitht part of termis drevyn fra lateen be rason that oure scottis to*n*g is nocht sa cope*us* as is the lateen to*n*g'.

⁵⁵ [Wedderburn,] *Complaynt of Scotland*, ed. Stewart, 13, 64.

⁵⁶ Elder, 'Proposal for Uniting Scotland with England', in *Bannatyne Miscellany*, I, ed. Scott and Laing, 10; Henrisoun, *Exhortacion to the Scottes*, in *The Complaynt of Scotlande*, ed. Murray, 211; Bodrugan, *Epitome of the Title*, sig. [aii]ᵛ.

⁵⁷ Lamb, *Ane Resonyng* (ed.) Lyall, xxxiii; [Wedderburn,] *Complaynt of Scotland*, ed. Stewart, xxxiv, 24. On the educational importance of Cicero in early sixteenth-century Scotland see John Durkan, 'Education: The Laying of Fresh Foundations', in John MacQueen (ed.), *Humanism in Renaissance Scotland* (Edinburgh, 1990), 125–6.

in the Scottish rebuttals, the humanist historiography of Polydore Vergil. The use by both sides of the techniques of classical rhetoric foreshadowed the prominence of the *ars rhetorica* in the promotional literature later produced to encourage migration and settlement in the Caribbean and North America, though in this debate neo-classical conceptions of patriotism and the *res publica* were deployed in opposition to the creation of a novel commonwealth cast in the form of a composite monarchy, rather than as the inducements to create a multitude of new commonwealths across the Atlantic Ocean.[58] 'The long struggle, intellectual as well as military, against English territorial ambitions, had ensured that the Scots were already the historical nation', especially in their use of the Roman historians begun by John Bellenden's translation of Livy's first five books in the early 1530s. Wedderburn had reinforced his moral appeals to Ciceronian patriotism with a battery of historical examples drawn from 'Crisp Salust' and Livy's *Histories*, as well as from other classical historians such as Valerius Maximus and Thucydides.[59] This was a response to the pro-English deployment of classical exempla, as when Nicholas Bodrugan had appealed to Sallust to show the ill effects of disunity, 'as by the civill warres between *Silla* and *Marius* the ruine of Rome is sufficient example to all the worlde'. He had argued that the Scots should embrace true patriotism, '*the* love that *Plato* & *Cicero* require in you to be borne to your countrey', and follow the English into the creation of that new *res publica*, the empire of Great Britain.[60]

The Edwardian conception of an 'empire of Great Britain' did live on among Welsh and Scots antiquaries. The Welsh antiquary, Humphrey Llwyd, in 1572 described King Arthur's pan-Britannic monarchy in its declining years under the last British kings as the '*Britannicum imperium*'; when his work appeared in English the following year, the translation referred to 'the BRITISH Empyre' and its decadence.[61] This Galfridian

[58] Andrew Fitzmaurice, 'Classical Rhetoric and the Promotion of the New World', *Journal of the History of Ideas*, 58 (1997), 221–44.
[59] John MacQueen, 'Aspects of Humanism in Sixteenth and Seventeenth Century Literature', in MacQueen (ed.), *Humanism in Renaissance Scotland*, 11–19; [Wedderburn,] *Complaynt of Scotland*, ed. Stewart, 20, 85–6 (Sallust); 73–4, 77–81, 89–90, 104, 137–40, 142–3 (Livy); 91 (Thucydides).
[60] Bodrugan, *Epitome of the Title*, sigs. [gviii]ᵛ, hivˣ–vⁱ.
[61] Humphrey Llwyd, *Commentarioli Britannicæ Descriptionis Fragmentum* (Cologne, 1572), f. 75a; Llwyd, *The Breviary of Britayne*, trans. Thomas Twyne (London, 1573), f. 92ʳ; Bruce Ward Henry, 'John Dee, Humphrey Llwyd, and the Name "British Empire"', *Huntington Library Quarterly*, 35 (1972), 189–90; Peter Roberts, 'Tudor Wales, National Identity and the British Inheritance', in Brendan Bradshaw and Peter Roberts (eds.), *British Consciousness and Identity: The Making of Britain, 1533–1707* (Cambridge, 1998), 23–7.

conception of an Arthurian British empire also lay at the heart of John Dee's appeals in the 1570s to 'this Incomparable Brytish Empire' and its inhabitants 'the true and naturall born subjects of this Brytish Empire'.[62] Dee's conception of the British Empire included among its dominions Ireland (which he claimed had been settled by Arthur's Britons), Iceland, Gotland, Orkney, Norway, Denmark and Gaul. Moreover, this British empire encompassed the seas around Britain even as far as the French and German coasts, and the recently rediscovered lands on the north-east coast of America. However, at the heart of this enormous monarchy lay '*the* Lawfull British, and English Jurisdiction over Scotland'; 'the Lawfull Possession as well as the Proprietie of the Supremacy over *Scotland*' had been vested in the English royal line from 900 CE until 1542, as Henry VIII's 'little Pamphlet', the *Declaration* of 1542, had sufficiently proved.[63] The Edwardian conception of the empire of Great Britain would also be revived in 1604, as proponents of Anglo-Scottish union under James VI and I recalled approvingly Somerset's arguments in favour of a 'perfect monarchie' under 'the comon name of Albion or Brytane'.[64]

The neo-Roman conception of Britain as a new *res publica* had been strongly promoted by Sir Thomas Smith and William Cecil, two of the prominent Cambridge humanists who had been drafted into Somerset's government in the 1540s.[65] Smith, the Regius Professor of Civil Law and Vice-Chancellor of Cambridge University, had been Cecil's tutor, and became Clerk of the Privy Council in March 1547. In that capacity, he was put in charge of searching for the evidence of English suzerainty over Scotland which would become the foundation of Bodrugan's argument in his *Epitome*, a work which the Imperial ambassador attributed to Smith himself. In the autumn of 1547, Smith, like Cecil, had accompanied Somerset's army as it marched northwards to meet the

---

[62] John Dee, *General and Rare Memorials Pertayning to the Perfect Arte of Navigation* (London, 1577), 8, 14; Gwyn A. Williams, *Welsh Wizard and British Empire: Dr. John Dee and a Welsh Identity* (Cardiff, 1980), 12–13, 17–19; William H. Sherman, *John Dee: The Politics of Reading and Writing in the English Renaissance* (Amherst, Mass., 1995), 182–92.

[63] John Dee, 'Brytanici Imperii Limites' (22 July 1576), BL Add. MS 59681, ff. 22ʳ, 28ᵛ.

[64] Robert Pont, 'Of the Union of Britayne' (1604), and Sir Henry Spelman, 'Of the Union' (1604), in *The Jacobean Union: Six Tracts of 1604*, ed. Bruce R. Galloway and Brian P. Levack (Edinburgh, 1985), 30, 167; for further references to the Edwardian tracts see *The Jacobean Union*, ed. Galloway and Levack, 29–31, 63, 102–3, 119–20, 166, 167–8; Sir Thomas Craig, *De Unione Regnorum Britanniæ Tractatus* (1605), ed. C. Sanford Terry (Edinburgh, 1909), 37 (Latin)/257 (English), 68/297, 96/336; *The Queen an Empress, and Her Three Kingdoms One Empire* (London, 1706), 6; Arthur H. Williamson, *Scottish National Consciousness in the Age of James VI* (Edinburgh, 1979), 152, n. 44.

[65] On the Cambridge 'Athenians' generally see Winthrop S. Hudson, *The Cambridge Connection and the Elizabethan Settlement of 1559* (Durham, NC, 1980), 43–86.

Scots, though he was taken ill and had to sit out the campaign at York.[66] Despite Smith's involvement with Somerset's ideological offensive against Scotland, the attempt to create an Anglo-Scottish union had little effect on his political thought: that other English security problem and territorial claim, Calais, absorbed more of his legal and historical attention, though he did show awareness of the Anglo-Scottish context within which the Treaty of Câteau–Cambrèsis had been concluded.[67] He made no reference to Scotland in either his *Discourse of the Commonweal of This Realm of England* (1549) or the *De Republica Anglorum* (1562–65), though he was instrumental in the attempt to break the Auld Alliance during his time as ambassador in France in 1571–72. Among his effects at his death was a painting of 'England, Scotland, and Ireland'.[68] Such a depiction of the 'British' isles was much closer to Cecil's own vision of Britain, which had grown initially from his involvement in Somerset's campaign. Cecil, like William Patten, was a judge of the Marshalsea Court who had fought at the battle of Pinkie. He maintained close and lasting relations with the Scots who wrote in support of Somerset's designs; he may also have been partly responsible for drafting the Protector's 'Proclamation' of September 1547 and the *Epistle* of 1548. His experience in Scotland, his interest in cartography, and his awareness of England's strategic weakness, especially after Mary, Queen of Scots' marriage to the French dauphin, and the consequent revival of French influence in Scotland, led him to form a uniquely wide-ranging vision of England as the centre of a Protestant British monarchy encompassing both Scotland and Ireland.[69]

Once the Scottish Reformation of 1559–60 had achieved Cecil's aim of creating a Protestant island, Smith and Cecil agreed on the necessity of drawing Ireland closer to England. 'In my mind', Smith wrote to Cecil in 1565, 'it needeth nothing more than to have colonies. To augment our tongue, our laws, and our religion in that Isle, which three

---

[66] Mary Dewar, *Sir Thomas Smith: A Tudor Intellectual in Office* (London, 1964), 28, 48; compare John Mason, 'Instrumentorum Quorundam Authenticorum Exemplaria Aliquot ... Ex quibus planum fit ... Reges Scociae in fide fuisse Regum Anglie, regnumque Scocie, Reges Anglie tanquam superiores dicti regni Dominos, per sacramentorum fidelititatis [*sic*] agnovisse' (1549), BL MS Add. 6128.

[67] [Sir Thomas Smith,] 'A Collection of Certain Reasons to Prove the Queen Majesty's Right to Have the Restitution of Calais' (3 April 1567), BL MS Harl. 36, ff. 74–90; Dewar, *Sir Thomas Smith*, 118–19.

[68] John Strype, *The Life of the Learned Sir Thomas Smith, Kt. D.C.L. Principal Secretary of State to King Edward the Sixth, and Queen Elizabeth* (London, 1820), 109–10, 112; Dewar, *Sir Thomas Smith*, 193–4.

[69] Jane E. A. Dawson, 'William Cecil and the British Dimension of Early Elizabethan Foreign Policy', *History*, 74 (1989), 197–9; Stephen Alford, *The Early Elizabethan Polity: William Cecil and the British Succession Crisis 1558–1569* (Cambridge, 1998), 44–51, 59–62.

be the true bands of the commonwealth whereby the Romans conquered and kept long time a great part of the world.'[70] A year later, Sir
Henry Sidney, the Lord Deputy of Ireland, also advised Cecil of the
necessity that 'persuasion woolde be used emonges the nobiletie, and
principal gentlemen of England, that there might ... be induced here
some Collany' at private expense.[71] The term 'colony' had first appeared in Scots in the *Complaynt of Scotland*, where it had indicated
Wedderburn's knowledge of early Roman history; it had appeared for
the first time in English in Smith's pupil Richard Eden's translation of
the *Decades* of Peter Martyr in 1555, though Smith popularised it as a
practical rather than an historical term.[72] In the *Discourse of the
Commonweal*, Smith affirmed that 'among all nations of the world, they
that be politic and civil do master the rest'. This equation between
civility and superiority informed Smith's own colonising ventures. Between 1572 and 1575, Smith and his son, Thomas, sent three abortive
expeditions to establish colonies in the north of Ireland, on the Ards
peninsula, 'to make the same civill and peopled with naturall Englishe
men borne'. Land would be wrested from the native Irish by the sword,
cultivated in parcels by the English *coloni*, with the help of those Irish
'churls' who could be persuaded to join the English, and defended by
the arms-bearing soldier-farmers. Fortified towns would be planted
amidst these agricultural settlements as retreats for merchants and
strongholds against attack. The precedents for this were once again
Roman: 'Mark Rome, Carthage, Venice and all other where notable
beginning hath been', Smith advised his son.[73]

Such appeals to the Roman model of colonisation through cultivation were not unprecedented in sixteenth-century England. In 1516,
Sir Thomas More had related that the Utopians settled colonies (*co-
loniam ... propagant*) of their people on the adjacent mainland at times

---

[70] Sir Thomas Smith to William Cecil, 7 November 1565, PRO SP 70/81/1654, f. 1302, quoted in
Dewar, *Sir Thomas Smith*, 157.
[71] Sir Henry Sidney to William Cecil, summer of 1566, PRO SP 63/26/18, quoted in Quinn, 'Sir
Thomas Smith (1513–1577) and the Beginnings of English Colonial Theory', 545.
[72] D. B. Quinn, 'Renaissance Influences in English Colonization', *Transactions of the Royal Historical
Society*, 5th ser., 26 (1976), 77–9; Peter Martyr, *The Decades of the Newe Worlde or West India*, trans.
Richard Eden (London, 1555), 56 ('This ryver is called *Darien*, upon the bankes whereof ... they
entended to playnte their newe colonie or habitacion').
[73] [Sir Thomas Smith,] *A Discourse of the Commonweal of This Realm of England* (1549), ed. Mary Dewar
(Charlottesville, Va. 1969), 24–5; 'The Petition of Thomas Smythe and his Associates' (c. 1570), in
*Historical Manuscripts Commission, Report on the Manuscripts of Lord de L'Isle and Dudley Preserved at
Penshurst Place*, ed. C. L. Kingsford, 5 vols. (London, 1934), II, 12–15; Smith to Thomas Smith, 18
May 1572, in *Calendar of State Papers, Foreign Series, of the Reign of Elizabeth January–June 1583 and
Addenda*, ed. Arthur John Butler and Sophie Crawford Lomas (London, 1913), 491.

of overpopulation. They justified them on the grounds that the colonists would make productive use of land that others had allowed to fall vacant: if the colonists could live peacefully with the mainlanders, it would be to the great advantage of both (*utriusque populi bono*); if not, the Utopians could legitimately make war upon them for leaving their land waste and uncultivated.[74] The Ulsterman Rowland White revived this agriculturalist argument in the 1560s when he proposed that four thousand English ploughmen should be sent to Ireland 'to take wast landes to inhabyte and tyll', thereby to 'profytt them selves muche and also provoke other to the furtherance of the comon welth'.[75] Smith may have read White's 'Discors', and, like More, argued that pressure of overpopulation necessitated the creation of colonies. As he and his son stated in their pioneering pamphlet to persuade English settlers to migrate, Ireland 'lacketh only inhabitants, manurance, and pollicie'; the English *coloni* would be prevented from degenerating into barbarousness because civility 'encreaseth more by keeping men occupyed in Tyllage, than by idle followyng of heards, as the Tartarians, Arabians, and Irishe men doo'. The settlers would be rewarded with their own 'peculiar gain', but there would be obvious advantages to the 'common profite' in having Ireland 'replenished with building civill inhabitantes, and traffique with lawe justice, and good order'. 'How say you now have I not set forth to you another Eutopia?' the Smiths asked.[76]

'We live in Smith's Commonwealth, not in More's Utopia', Smith's client Gabriel Harvey stated, as if in reply.[77] Harvey had been present in 1570 or 1571 at Hill House, Smith's home in Essex, when Smith, his son, Walter Haddon and Sir Humphrey Gilbert had debated the relative merits of ruthless militarism and peaceful persuasion, with examples drawn from Livy's *Histories*. Smith and Haddon had argued on behalf of Fabius's gradualism; Gilbert and the younger Smith, for Marcellus's use

[74] Sir Thomas More, *Utopia: Latin Text and English Translation*, ed. George M. Logan, Robert M. Adams and Clarence H. Miller (Cambridge, 1995), 134, 136 (Latin)/135, 137 (English); Quinn, 'Renaissance Influences in English Colonization', 75.
[75] Rowland White, 'Discors Touching Ireland' (*c.* 1569), PRO SP 63/31/32, ff. 73–117, ed. Nicholas Canny, *Irish Historical Studies*, 20 (1977), 457–8.
[76] [Sir Thomas Smith and Thomas Smith,] *A Letter Sent by I. B. Gentleman unto his Very Frende Mayster R. C. Esquire* (1572), in George Hill (ed.), *An Historical Account of the MacDonnells of Antrim* (Belfast, 1873), 409, 406, 413, 411; Hiram Morgan, 'The Colonial Venture of Sir Thomas Smith in Ulster, 1571–1575', *The Historical Journal*, 28 (1985), 269–70.
[77] 'Vivimus in Smithi Rep: non in Mori Utopia; aut Platonis Politeia; aut regno Xenophontis. Phantasticarum Rerum*publicarum* Usus tantummodò phantasticus': *Gabriel Harvey's Marginalia*, ed. G. C. Moore Smith (Stratford-upon-Avon, 1913), 197. On Harvey and Smith see Dewar, *Sir Thomas Smith*, 188–9.

of force.[78] Smith's advice to his son in 1572 to look to the examples of Rome, Carthage and Venice was evidently part of a series of lessons in which Smith had instructed his son in Roman history. His conception of colonies was also only one of his attempts to introduce Roman policy into the *respublica Anglorum*. He had hoped to create a college of civil law at Cambridge, and a 'College of Civilians' to advise the royal council. Smith the civilian and councillor may have been responsible for the notorious Vagrancy Act of 1547 (1 Edw. VI, c. 3) which imposed slavery for able-bodied indigents who refused to work, in imitation of the provision in the *Corpus Iuris Civilis* (XI. xxvi) condemning free-born beggars to the forced labour of a 'perpetual colonate' (*colonatu perpetuo*).[79] His *De Republica Anglorum* analysed the English commonwealth as a mixed monarchy with descriptive categories drawn from Aristotle, Cicero, and Roman civil law, in order to distinguish England from the countries of the civil law world. In the *Discourse of the Commonweal*, Smith had in passing called England 'this empire', and in *De Republica Anglorum* he referred to it as 'great Brittaine, which is nowe called England'. 'Edward College' came to naught; the Vagrancy Act was never enforced but rapidly repealed; Smith's colonies in the Ards collapsed in the face of resistance from the Irish and opposition from the Lord Deputy Sir William Fitzwilliam. Yet, despite his promotion of the Roman model of *coloni* in Ireland, and his conception of England as a new Rome for its civilising mission, Smith firmly portrayed England 'not in that sort as *Plato* made his common wealth ... nor as *Syr Thomas More* his *Utopia* feigned common wealths', but as it was on 28 March 1565: the *respublica Anglorum*, not an *Imperium Britannorum*.[80]

There was no necessary connection between humanism and humanitarianism.[81] However, classical humanism, of the kind practised by Smith, Cecil and many of the mid-sixteenth-century proponents of Anglo-Scottish union, did transmit important assumptions regarding the superiority of civility over barbarism and the necessity for civilised

[78] Lisa Jardine, 'Mastering the Uncouth: Gabriel Harvey, Edmund Spenser and the English Experience in Ireland', in John Henry and Sarah Hutton (eds.), *New Perspectives on Renaissance Thought: Essays in the History of Science, Education and Philosophy in Memory of Charles B. Schmitt* (London, 1990), 72–5.

[79] C. S. L. Davies, 'Slavery and Protector Somerset: The Vagrancy Act of 1547', *Economic History Review*, 2nd ser., 19 (1966), 543–5; *Corpus Iuris Civilis*, ed. Paul Krueger, 4 vols. (Berlin, 1892), II, 435.

[80] [Smith,] *Discourse of the Commonweal*, ed. Dewar, 82; Sir Thomas Smith, *De Republica Anglorum* (1562–65), ed. Mary Dewar (Cambridge, 1982), 63, 144.

[81] Anthony Pagden, 'The Humanism of Vasco de Quiroga's "Información en Derecho"', in Wolfgang Reinhard (ed.), *Humanismus und Neue Welt* (Bonn, 1987), 134–5, 142.

polities to carry their civility to those they deemed barbarous. Though it was true, as Robert Wedderburn noted in the *Complaynt of Scotland*, 'euere nations reputis vthers nations to be barbariens quhen there tua natours and complexions ar contrar til vtheris',[82] not all 'nations' derived a charter for a civilising mission from this imputation of barbarity, nor indeed did all humanists. Three major humanistic treatments of colonisation in the 1590s emerged from among the New English in Munster. Sir William Herbert, Richard Beacon and Edmund Spenser each produced a reform tract in the 1590s: one a Latin treatise cast in the idiom of classical moral philosophy (dedicated to a veteran of Somerset's Scottish wars, Sir James Croft); one an allegorical dialogue set in the Athens of Solon; and the third an English dialogue set firmly in the present of the 1590s.[83] Only Spenser provided an ethnological justification for conquest; likewise, only he offered a vision of a unified British monarchy within the Three Kingdoms, on ethnological as much as political grounds.[84]

Though Spenser made no explicit references to the British propaganda of the 1540s, he shared with the Edwardian proponents of Anglo-Scottish union an historical genealogy and an ethnology. In his *View of the Present State of Ireland* (*c.* 1596) and his uncompleted epic *The Færie Queene* (1590–96), Spenser adopted the conception of the British Empire found in the works of Humphrey Llwyd and John Dee, to show that the Protestant New English settlers were reviving the 'British' dominion in Ireland which had originally been established by King Arthur. The New English were therefore restoring 'British' rule over the Gaelic Irish and the Old English, rather than attempting to create a novel polity in Ireland. Yet it was also clear from Spenser's works that this would be but the first step towards the recreation of the Arthurian *imperium* in northern Europe and across the Atlantic. Accordingly, he dedicated *The Færie Queene* 'To the Most High, Mightie and Magnificent Empresse Elizabeth

---

[82] [Wedderburn,] *Complaynt of Scotland*, ed. Stewart, 84.

[83] Sir William Herbert, *Croftus sive De Hibernia Liber* (*c.* 1591), ed. Arthur Keaveney and John A. Madden (Dublin, 1992); Richard Beacon, *Solon His Follie* (1594), ed. Clare Carroll and Vincent Carey (Binghamton, 1996); [Edmund Spenser,] *A View of the Present State of Ireland* (*c.* 1596), ed. Rudolf Gottfried, in *The Works of Edmund Spenser: A Variorum Edition*, ed. Edwin Greenlaw, Charles Grosvenor Osgood, Frederick Morgan Padelford and Ray Heffner, 11 vols. (Baltimore, 1932–57), IX, 39–231.

[84] Brendan Bradshaw, 'Robe and Sword in the Conquest of Ireland', in Cross, Loades and Scarisbrick (eds.), *Law and Government in Tudor England*, 154–62, emphasises Spenser's differences from Herbert and Beacon in this respect, but exaggerates the differences between the three humanists, largely in response to the argument of Nicholas Canny, 'Edmund Spenser and the Development of Anglo-Irish Identity', *Yearbook of English Studies*, 13 (1983), 1–19.

by the Grace of God Queene of England Fraunce and Ireland and of
Virginia', a unique expansion of the royal style (in Elizabeth's lifetime, at
least) to incorporate the new English province in North America.[85]

The neo-Galfridian vision of the empire of Great Britain, when
combined with the Aristotelian foundations of classical moral philosophy, provided the substance of Spenser's *Færie Queene*. Spenser claimed
for his work the educational purpose of an 'historical fiction', and
compared it to Xenophon rather than Plato, 'for that the one in the
exquisite depth of his judgement formed a Commune welth such as it
should be, but the other in the person of Cyrus and the Persians
fashioned a government such as might best be'.[86] He envisaged a plan
for his poem that would carry his readers through a course of instruction
in the private ethical virtues and the public political virtues. No utopian
fiction, *The Færie Queene* would provide not only an example after which
'to fashion a gentleman' but, like More's *Utopia*, also offer a vision of the
best state of the commonwealth (*optimum status reipublicae*), which in
Spenser's case was the commonwealth of Britain, encompassing the
islands of both Britain and Ireland. Spenser's ethical purposes were
accordingly at one with the aims English humanists hoped to achieve
through the study of the *litteræ* humaniores, while his political vision of
English domination throughout the British Isles presented perhaps the
most ambitious and hardline British imperial vision of its time.[87]

Spenser's conception of the British Empire remained strictly confined
to Britain and Ireland, within the historical limits set by Geoffrey of
Monmouth's *Historia*, apart from that single flattering reference to the
new province across the Atlantic. The Galfridian history provided him
with the traditional genealogy underpinning the Tudor claim to the
British Isles which he presented in his epic poem. In Books II and III of *The
Færie Queene*, he traced the line of British kings from Brutus down to
Elizabeth I. In the beginning, 'The land, which warlike Britons now
possesse,/ And therein have their mightie empire raysd,/ In antique
times was salvage wildernesse,/ Unpeopled, unmanured, unprov'd,
unpraysd' until settled by Brutus and passed to his three sons (*FQ*, II. x. 5,

---

[85] Edmund Spenser, *The Færie Queene* (1590–96), 'Dedication', in *Works of Edmund Spenser*, ed.
Greenlaw, Osgood, Padelford and Heffner, I, 2; Andrew Hadfield, 'Briton and Scythian: Tudor
Representations of Irish Origins', *Irish Historical Studies*, 28 (1993), 390–2, 405–7.

[86] Edmund Spenser, 'A Letter of the Authors Expounding his Whole Intention in the Course of
this Work', in *Works of Edmund Spenser*, ed. Greenlaw, Osgood, Padelford and Heffner, I, 168.

[87] Compare the other political visions of Britain before 1603 described in Hiram Morgan, 'British
Policies Before the British State', in Brendan Bradshaw and John Morrill (eds.), *The British
Problem, c. 1534–1707: State Formation in the Atlantic Archipelago* (Basingstoke, 1996), 66–88.

13–14). According to Merlin's prophecy, 'a royall virgin' would restore the Arthurian empire in the British Isles, and 'Thenceforth eternall union shall be made/ Between the nations different afore' (*FQ*, III. iii. 49). There were ethnic Britons in England, Britons in Scotland and Britons in Ireland. All traced their ancestry back to Brutus himself, and all would be reunited into a unitary British monarchy under Elizabeth. The 'British' colonists of Ireland would be absorbed once more into their parent monarchy, and the kingdoms formerly ruled by Albanact and Camber would once again be rightly subdued to the senior kingdom of England.

Spenser's conception of the British Empire appeared most forcibly in his *View of the Present State of Ireland*, in which he used it to support his argument for the cultural suppression of the Gaelic Irish and the reform of the 'degenerated' Old English settlers. Spenser traced the common origin of both the native Irish and the Scots to the migrations of the Scythians, 'for Scotlande and Irelande are all one and the same' and moreover 'there are two Scottlandes', one inhabited by migrants from Ireland, the other peopled from England. Spenser saw the divisions within the British Isles as both ethnic and cultural, 'for the difference of manners and Customes dothe followe the difference of nacions and people'. The Old English could no longer be counted with the inhabitants of England itself, for they were 'now muche more Lawles and Licentious then the verie wilde Irishe', and would accordingly be subject to the same treatment from the New English as the native Irish. Spenser's remedy for the barbarousness of the natives and the degeneration of the Old English was 'the sworde', that is, 'the Royall power of the prince', in the form of garrison government.[88] In adopting this forcible solution to the problem of English government in Ireland, Spenser placed himself at a distance from those among his contemporaries who argued for more gradual forms of pacification, such as colonisation, legal reform and education alone. Spenser demanded all of these measures, too, but without fear of the sword, and even its exercise, they would not be enough to restore civility and the rule of law within Ireland. The extremity of some of his measures matched the uniformity of his imperial vision: there could be as little compromise with cultural difference as with administrative and legal incoherence.

A unified British monarchy of England, Scotland and Ireland remained unachieved during Spenser's lifetime, just as his epic of moral and political education lay abandoned and truncated long before his

---

[88] Spenser, *View of the Present State of Ireland*, ed. Gottfried, in *Works of Edmund Spenser*, ed. Greenlaw, Osgood, Padelford and Heffner, IX, 83, 97, 113, 148.

death. The failure of both Spenser's great designs was not coincidental. The worsening situation in Ireland in the opening years of Tyrone's rebellion may have convinced him that he should offer more pointedly practical advice to achieve the British pacification of Ireland than an Aristotelian programme of moral re-education could provide. He may also have lost faith in the effectiveness of such humanist ethical edification during the darkening years of Elizabeth's last decade, a desperate period of *Sturm und Drang* on both sides of the Irish Sea.[89] The political alternatives were becoming starker and more circumscribed, and Spenser handled them as directly as he could in the dialogic form of *A View of the Present State of Ireland*. The tension in his own political theory between civil-law arguments derived from rights of conquest and common-law conceptions of property rights challenged the very foundations of English policy in Ireland and rendered his moral justifications for a British empire unstable;[90] as a result, few would follow him in finding an ethnological, and neo-Galfridian, foundation for a monarchy to encompass 'all that bear the *British* Islands name' (*FQ*, VII. vi. 38).

Even as Spenser was reaching his desperate intellectual impasse in Munster, the Scottish Crown began to pursue its own programme of civilising the barbarian just across the North Channel. Like the English Crown in Ireland, it couched its claims to authority over its dependencies in the language of civility and barbarism, which was mapped onto the divide between Celtic and non-Celtic.[91] The origins of Scottish colonial policies lay in these attempts by the Crown to enforce Lowland norms of civility and legality onto its Gaelic provinces, and to consolidate its own monarchy. Scotland's premier colonial theorist, James VI, used just such language from the 1590s in relation both to the Western Islands and, later, to Ulster. James continued the attempts of his predecessors to bring the clan elite on the fringes of his realm within the pale of civility by means of pledges of security, military containment, and cultural aggression against his Gaelic subjects.[92] He echoed the recom-

---

[89] Hiram Morgan, *Tyrone's Rebellion: The Outbreak of the Nine Years' War in Ireland* (Woodbridge, 1993); John Guy (ed.), *The Reign of Elizabeth I: Court and Culture in the Last Decade* (Cambridge, 1995).

[90] Ciaran Brady, 'The Road to the *View*: On the Decline of Reform Thought in Tudor Ireland', in Patricia Coughlan (ed.), *Spenser and Ireland: An Interdisciplinary Perspective* (Cork, 1989), 40–4; Elizabeth Fowler, 'The Failure of Moral Philosophy in the Work of Edmund Spenser', *Representations*, 51 (1995), 47–76.

[91] Arthur H. Williamson, 'Scots, Indians and Empire: The Scottish Politics of Civilization, 1519–1609', *Past and Present*, 150 (Feb. 1996), 46–66.

[92] Allan I. Macinnes, *Clanship, Commerce and the House of Stuart, 1603–1788* (East Linton, 1996), 56–87; Ohlmeyer, '"Civilizinge of Those Rude Partes"', in Canny (ed.), *Oxford History of the British Empire*, I, 131–5.

mendations of New English theorists in Ireland when in 1599 he warned
his infant son, Henry, about those that 'dwelleth in the Iles, and are
alluterly barbares, without any sort or shew of civilitie' and recommended 'planting Colonies among them of answerable In-lands subjects,
that within short time may reforme and civilize the best inclined among
them; rooting out or transporting the barbarous and stubborne sort, and
planting civilitie in their roomes'.[93] Two attempts to settle the island of
Lewis with Lowland adventurers, in 1598–1600 and 1605–6, failed,
though ultimately more aggressive means were urged to pacify the
Islands by main force, and to suppress the 'wilde savaiges voide of Godis
feare and our obedience'.[94] Expeditions sent to the Islands in 1596, 1599,
1605, and 1607 culminated in two successive civilising missions, one
military, the other religious, in 1608–9, under the leadership of Andrew
Stewart, Lord Ochiltree (who had earlier operated a judicial commission in the Anglo-Scottish Borders), and Andrew Knox, the bishop of
the Isles. Ochiltree imprisoned Island chiefs, appointed outside commissioners, and demanded strategies to civilise the Islands.[95] The Statutes of
Icolmkill (1609) legislated for such strategies, which were designed to
restore decayed religion, encourage hospitality, discourage idleness,
begging, drunkenness and the keeping of firearms, and thereby to
remedy the 'grite crueltie and inhumane barbaritie', 'ignorance and
incivilitie' in the Islands, at the expense of the clans' traditions of
sociability and militarism.[96]

The origins of Scottish colonial theory and practice in the seventeenth century lay in internal colonisation within the Stewart realm as
James VI of Scotland, later James I of England, continued the pacification of Gaeldom initiated by his royal ancestors. His presumed succession to the English throne in the 1590s evidently impelled him to
greater efforts of 'civilising' than might otherwise have been the case, so
that internal colonisation provided an emulative bond of union between
the two kingdoms. The debate over James's proposals for closer union
between England and Scotland in 1604 provided an opportunity for

[93] James VI, *Basilikon Doron* (1598), in *King James VI and I: Political Writings*, ed. Johann P. Sommerville (Cambridge, 1994), 24; compare Craig, *De Unione Regnorum Britanniæ Tractatus*, ed. Terry,
62/289 ('in insulis Skia et Levissa . . . Colonia in eam deducta . . .').
[94] Donald Gregory, *The History of the Western Highlands and Isles of Scotland, From A.D. 1493 to A.D. 1625*,
2nd edn (London, 1881), 278–93; Maurice Lee, *Great Britain's Solomon: James VI and I in His Three
Kingdoms* (Urbana, 1990), 200, 213–15; James VI, 'Instructions to the Commission to Improve the
Isles' (8 December 1608), in *Collectanea de Rebus Albanicis* (Edinburgh, 1847), 115.
[95] Macinnes, *Clanship, Commerce and the House of Stuart*, 60.
[96] Statutes of Icolmkill, 23 August 1609, in *The Register of the Privy Council of Scotland: IX A.D.
1610–1613*, ed. David Masson (Edinburgh, 1889), 26–30.

theorists to redefine 'Britain' as an empire, and its monarch as a potential emperor. When the question of the royal style was debated in Parliament in 1604, the Welsh MP Sir William Maurice of Clenennau proposed that the king should proclaim himself 'emperor of Great Britain', but the motion was rejected on the grounds that 'The Name of Emperor is impossible: – No particular Kingdom can make their King an Emperor'.[97] Undaunted, the Scottish mathematician Robert Pont hailed the reduction of 'this our Great Brittaine, Ireland and the adjoyning Brittish isles ... to the monarchicall obedience of one emperor', 'a compacting of all the Brittish isles and reducing them within the circle of one diadem ... so that the savadg wildnes of the Irish, and the barbarous fiercenes of the other ilanders shall easily be tamed'.[98]

The Gaels of Ireland and of Scotland had originally been separate problems for their respective monarchs; once the regal union had created a new British multiple kingdom, they became a single target for that monarchy's policies of security and 'civility'. The fruit of this anxiety is evident in the colonisation of Ulster, which James promoted as a specifically British venture, an extension of his policies on the western seaboard of Scotland, to be sure, but one in which both his Scottish and his English subjects could participate as equal partners. Francis Bacon echoed James's aspirations when he reckoned the Ulster plantation 'a second brother to Union', the first cooperative British enterprise of James's newly proclaimed Kingdom of Great Britain.[99] The Ulster planters were to be the first of a new race of Britons, whose legal identities as Scots or English would be supplemented and, for their children, replaced by their attachment to a new ethnic Britishness. The revised articles of the plantation in 1610 called them the 'Brittish undertakers' and a survey of 1618–19 referred throughout to Ulster's 'British families', to the 'British undertakers' of '*Brittish* birth and descent' and to their 'British tenants'.[100] From the roots of James's

[97] *Historical Manuscripts Commission, Report on the Manuscripts of the Duke of Buccleuch and Queensberry K.G., K.T., Preserved at Montagu House, Whitehall*, ed. R. E. G. Kirk, 3 vols. (London, 1926), III, 83–4; *Journals of the House of Commons From November the 8th 1547 ... to March the 2d 1628* (London, n.d.), 183; Bindoff, 'The Stuarts and their Style', 193, 203–4; Roberts, 'Tudor Wales, National Identity and the British Inheritance,' in Bradshaw and Roberts (eds.), *British Consciousness and Identity*, 39–40.

[98] Pont, 'Of the Union of Britayne', in *The Jacobean Union*, eds. Galloway and Levack, 4, 17, 18 (cf. 22).

[99] Francis Bacon, *The Letters and Life of Francis Bacon*, ed. James Spedding, 7 vols. (London, 1862–74), IV, 114.

[100] *Conditions To Be Observed By the Brittish Undertakers, of the Escheated Lands in Ulster* (London, 1610); Nicholas Pynnar's survey (1618–19), Lambeth Palace Library MS Carew 630, printed in George Hill, *An Historical Account of the Plantation in Ulster at the Commencement of the Seventeenth Century, 1608–1620* (Belfast, 1877), 499–590.

civilising mission in Scotland grew the first 'British' plantations in his kingdoms.[101]

James intended the Ulster plantation to provide a buffer zone of civility and stability between the Gaels in Ireland and those in Scotland, 'the people [there] being so easily stirred, partly through their barbaritie, and want of civilitie, and partly through their corruption in Religion to breake foorth in rebellions'.[102] It was therefore continuous with the late Stewart monarchs' campaigns to tame Gaeldom within their own dominions. Community of personnel in the plantation revealed that continuity of aim as, for example, Lord Ochiltree became one of the major Scottish undertakers in the plantation, and Andrew Knox continued his campaign of 'civility' in Ulster as bishop of Raphoe in Donegal from 1610 to 1633.[103] The majority of the Scottish undertakers were Lowland gentry and aristocracy who brought followers with them to settle the lands escheated after the Flight of the Earls in 1607. As an emblem of the cooperative Britishness of the enterprise, the parcels of land offered to Scots and English alike were roughly equal in size, 81,000 acres in total for the Scots, 81,500 for the English. The Ulster plantation offered opportunity and profit to Lowland Scots, as the earlier informal plantation of East Ulster had to their southwestern compatriots,[104] and it had the backing of the Scottish Crown as a national enterprise, as well as the aspiration of the new British king to be an undertaking to unite all of his subjects under the name of Britain.

The Ulster plantation provided a middle ground for Scots and English alike to pursue common schemes of plantation and 'civilisation' in a potentially pan-British enterprise. It also provided James with a testing-ground for the creation of Britons. Before the uprising of 1641, it became the most successful fruit of James's determination to create a united British monarchy, with common British enterprises, in the interests of generating mutual recognition among his subjects as Britons. Nevertheless, the fact that such self-identification only seems to have flowered among a handful of his courtiers, and in colonial Ulster but not otherwise on the mainland, is an indication of the practical limitations of such

[101] On the process whereby this 'British' plantation was created on the ground see Nicholas Canny, 'Fashioning "British" Worlds in the Seventeenth Century', in Nicholas Canny, Joseph Illick and Gary Nash (eds.), *Empire, Society and Labor: Essays in Honor of Richard S. Dunn, Pennsylvania History*, 54, supplemental vol. (College Park, Pa., 1997), 31–42.

[102] James VI and I, speech to English Parliament, 21 March 1610, in *Political Writings*, ed. Sommerville, 196.

[103] Hill, *Historical Account of the Plantation in Ulster*, 286; Michael Perceval-Maxwell, *The Scottish Migration to Ulster in the Reign of James I* (London, 1973), 99, 107, 257–60.

[104] Raymond Gillespie, *Colonial Ulster: The Settlement of East Ulster 1600–1641* (Cork, 1985).

a vision, even if colonisation did provide the only means to promote it. Ulster provided the only serious prospects for emigration, profit and civility, in contrast to the contemporaneous plantation of Virginia, which English administrators looked upon as a wasteful folly. Writing in 1606, Francis Bacon expressed the widespread scepticism about Virginia in notably classical terms, calling it, 'an enterprise in my opinion differing as much from [Ulster], as *Amadis de Gaul* differs from Caesar's *Commentaries*'.[105]

Like Gaul before the Roman invasion, Britain and Ireland before 1603 had been divided into three parts. Thereafter, the Three Kingdoms of England, Scotland and Ireland were united under the kingship of James VI, I and I, a British Caesar in his determined advocacy of his civilising mission, though never (despite the hopes of some of his Welsh subjects) a British emperor ruling a united British empire. James's interest in creating British plantations in Ulster immediately succeeded his disappointment at failing to create a united kingdom of Great Britain. Only a handful of his most immediate courtiers, and all of them Scots, thought of themselves as Britons within Britain itself; otherwise, in the seventeenth century, Britons would only be found overseas, in Ireland and even in Virginia. In 1611, John Speed in his account of what 'The British Empire Containeth, and Hath Now in Actuall Possession', included England, Scotland, Wales, Ireland and the Isle of Man; though he made no mention of Virginia among the King's dominions, he did note that 'at this present in the *new World* of *America* a *Colonie* of BRITAINES is seated in that part now called VIRGINEA'.[106] When Samuel Purchas dedicated his *Pilgrimes* to Prince Charles in 1625, he recognised that the three British kingdoms (and even the principality of Wales) each participated independently in the process of empire-building when he foresaw '*Englands* out of *England* ... yea Royall *Scotland, Ireland,* and Princely *Wales*, multiplying of new Scepters to his Majestie and His Heires in a New World'.[107]

The creation of a British empire was the extension of the consolidation of the two British monarchies in Britain and Ireland, but it was as imperfect, contingent and various as the process of state-formation itself.

---

[105] Francis Bacon, 'Certain Considerations Touching the Plantation in Ireland, Presented to His Majesty, 1606,' in *Letters and the Life of Francis Bacon*, ed. Spedding, IV, 123; compare Sir Arthur Chichester, 'I had rather labour with my hands in the plantation of Ulster than dance or play in that of Virginia', quoted in Philip Robinson, *The Plantation of Ulster: British Settlement in an Irish Landscape 1600–1670* (Belfast, 1984), 1.

[106] John Speed, *The Theatre of the Empire of Great Britaine* (London, 1611), sig. [1]ʳ, 157.

[107] Samuel Purchas, *Purchas His Pilgrimes*, 4 vols. (London, 1625), I, sig. ¶ 3ʳ.

As Purchas realised, just as there was no unitary British monarchy (of the kind hoped for by the Anglo-Scottish unionists of the 1540s, and more expansively by Edmund Spenser in the 1590s, or by James VI and I in the early 1600s), so there would only be a federative British Empire. All of the parts of the Stuart composite monarchy would pursue ventures across the Atlantic – the English in New England, Virginia, the Caribbean and Newfoundland; the Scots in Newfoundland and Cape Breton; the Welsh also in Newfoundland, or '*Britanniol*'; the Irish on the Amazon[108] – but they could no more create a pan-British empire abroad than they could create a pan-British monarchy at home, for the same reasons, and with the same effects. British state-building and British empire-building were therefore continuous with one another in their origins as in their outcomes: out of continuity would come disaggregation, and with it an empire that retained the federative characteristics of a multiple kingdom more than the integrated features of a composite monarchy.

[108] On the Scots, the Welsh and the Irish, see John G. Reid, *Acadia, Maine, and New Scotland: Marginal Colonies in the Seventeenth Century* (Toronto, 1981), 13–33; [William Vaughan,] *The Golden Fleece . . . Transported from Cambrioll Colchos, Out of the Southermost Part of the Iland, Commonly Called the Newfoundland* (London, 1626), 81 (quoted); *English and Irish Settlements on the River Amazon 1550–1646*, ed. Joyce Lorimer (London, 1989).

CHAPTER 3

Protestantism and empire: Hakluyt,
Purchas and property

> To plant Christian religion without conquest, will bee hard.
> Trafficke easily followeth conquest: conquest is not easie.
> Trafficke without conquest seemeth possible, and not uneasie.
> What is to be done, is the question.[1]

Protestantism should have been the solvent of difference within the Three Kingdoms, and hence the solution to the problem of diversity within the empire of Great Britain. The English proponents of Anglo-Scottish union in the 1540s, and their Scottish agents, argued that together the two kingdoms of England and Scotland could be joined to create a single Protestant island. The imposition of a post-Reformation conception of an Anglo-British empire could thereby extend the process of the Anglo-Welsh union to join another partly Celtic dominion to the English state, and thus form an insular bulwark against Roman Catholicism. Similarly, the New English settlers in Ireland argued from the 1560s that the extension of Protestantism could secure Ireland against invasion and even bring the Kingdom of Ireland into an archipelagic Protestant triumvirate. The integrative force of Protestantism could potentially serve as the bond of union between the civilised inhabitants of the Three Kingdoms to create a uniquely post-Reformation territorial and jurisdictional empire.

The judgments of later historians have followed the contours of these arguments for Protestant integration, as the ideological origins of English nationalism, British nationhood and, in turn, British imperialism have all been traced back to the Protestant Reformations in England and Scotland.[2] According to one recent student of primordial English

---

[1] Richard Hakluyt the elder, 'Inducements to the Liking of the Voyage Intended Towards Virginia' (1585), in *The Original Writings and Correspondence of the Two Richard Hakluyts*, ed. E. G. R. Taylor, 2 vols. (London, 1935), II, 332.
[2] See, generally, Tony Claydon and Ian McBride (eds.), *Protestantism and National Identity: Britain and Ireland c. 1650 – c. 1850* (Cambridge, 1998).

nationalism, Protestantism in the sixteenth century was 'perhaps the most significant among the factors that furthered the development of English national consciousness'.[3] The obvious failure to unite the Three Kingdoms around a consensual version of Protestantism left the development of a broader British national identity as a task for the eighteenth century: in this period, 'Great Britain might be made up of three separate nations, but under God it could also be one, united nation ... Protestantism was the foundation that made the invention of Great Britain possible.'[4] Looking back from this period to discern the origins of the eighteenth-century British Empire, 'Christian providentialism' has been identified as 'the ideological taproot of British Imperialism'.[5] Protestantism therefore provided Englishness, Britishness and the British Empire with a common chronology and a history stretching from the English and Scottish Reformations, through the attempted religious unification of the Stuart monarchies during the seventeenth century, across the Anglo-Scottish Parliamentary Union of 1707 and on to the United Kingdom of Great Britain that sat at the heart of the expanding British empire-state of the eighteenth and nineteenth centuries. That chronology was hardly continuous, nor the history seamless and uninterrupted; nonetheless, Protestantism was the only thread joining these three mutually constitutive processes from state-formation to empire-building.

Despite the efflorescence of interest in post-Reformation religious history in recent years, little attempt has been made to relate the findings of that historiography to the question of the origins of the British Empire. Historians have investigated the effect of the New World experience upon the religion of colonists;[6] they have also inquired, 'What did anticipation of overseas expansion do *for* religion as seventeenth-century Englishmen understood it?'[7] Nonetheless, they have almost entirely failed to examine the question of the contribution made

3 Leah Greenfeld, *Nationalism: Five Roads to Modernity* (Cambridge, Mass., 1992), 51.
4 Linda Colley, *Britons: Forging the Nation, 1707–1837* (New Haven, 1992), 53–4.
5 Richard Drayton, 'Knowledge and Empire', in P. J. Marshall (ed.), *The Oxford History of the British Empire*, II: *The Eighteenth Century* (Oxford, 1998), 233; for a more sceptical assessment of the contribution of Christianity to the origins of the British Empire see Kenneth R. Andrews, *Trade, Plunder and Settlement: Maritime Enterprise and the Genesis of the British Empire, 1480–1630* (Cambridge, 1984), 31–2.
6 David B. Quinn, 'The First Pilgrims', *William and Mary Quarterly*, 3rd ser., 23 (1966), 359–90; Avihu Zakai, *Exile and Kingdom: History and Apocalypse in the Puritan Migration to America* (Cambridge, 1992).
7 David S. Lovejoy, *Religious Enthusiasm in the New World* (Cambridge, Mass., 1985), 10.

by Protestantism to the ideological origins of the British Empire.[8] This is a specific manifestation of the fact that the history of Protestant theories of empire more generally – in England, Scotland, the United Provinces, Sweden and France – remains largely unwritten.[9] The neglect of such conceptions of empire has allowed Catholic theories to appear normative and Protestant theories exceptional; this has in turn helped to confirm the impression that it was the Protestant empires like the British that were acquired absent-mindedly: 'what is there in English literature that can compare to the letters of Hernán Cortés or the "true history" of Bernal Díaz? . . . Where, in all the long centuries of European imperialism, was there a scene to equal the public debate staged at Valladolid between Juan Ginés de Sepúlveda and Las Casas?'[10]

To return British imperial ideology to the context of theological debate can help to answer such questions. The more one investigates the relationship between these two bodies of thought, the harder it becomes to trace any specifically and exclusively Protestant ideology of empire. The visceral anti-Catholicism to which a unifying British identity has been attributed in the eighteenth century was mostly negative in content, and hence could hardly be a source of positive arguments in favour of a particular mission or foundation for the British Empire. Least of all could it, or post-Reformation theology more generally, provide a solution to the problem of defining, justifying or correlating claims both to sovereignty (*imperium*) and property (*dominium*) as the ideological basis for the Empire. In light also of the fact that distinctions within Protestantism could divide confessed Protestants as much as it had the potential to unite them, and also that the national and international contexts within which Protestant theorists operated shifted so dramatically and subtly across the course of the late sixteenth and early seventeenth centuries, it

---

[8] For exceptions to this generalisation see Lovejoy, *Religious Enthusiasm in the New World*, ch. 1, 'The Finger of God: Religious Conceptions of the New World'; Alfred A. Cave, 'Canaanites in a Promised Land: The American Indian and the Providential Theory of Empire', *American Indian Quarterly*, 12 (1988), 277–97; Paul Stevens, '"Leviticus Thinking" and the Rhetoric of Early Modern Colonialism', *Criticism*, 35 (1993), 441–61. The omission of any sustained treatment of religion in Nicholas Canny (ed.), *British Empire*, 1; *The Origins of Empire* (Oxford, 1998) is striking.

[9] For hints of the possibilities see Arthur Williamson, 'Scots, Indians and Empire: The Scottish Politics of Civilization, 1519–1609', *Past and Present*, 150 (Feb. 1996), 46–83; Simon Schama, *The Embarrassment of Riches: An Interpretation of Dutch Culture in the Golden Age* (London, 1987); Frank Lestringant, *Le Huguenot et le sauvage: l'Amérique et la controverse coloniale, en France, au temps des Guerres de Religion (1555–1589)* (Paris, 1990); Michael Roberts, *The Swedish Imperial Experience 1560–1718* (Cambridge, 1979).

[10] D. A. Brading, *The First America: The Spanish Monarchy, Creole Patriots, and the Liberal State 1492–1867* (Cambridge, 1991), 1.

becomes almost impossible to discern any precise and undeniable Protestant contribution to the ideological origins of the British Empire.

The two greatest memorialists in English of overseas enterprise, Richard Hakluyt the younger and Samuel Purchas, provide ample material for testing the hypothetical relationship between Protestantism and the ideological origins of the British Empire. As the bishop of Peterborough, White Kennett, noted with pride in 1713, 'Mr. HAKLUYT and Mr. PURCHAS (both Clergymen of the Church of *England*)' were indispensable providers of information and inspiration for the library he had assembled under the auspices of the Society for the Propagation of the Gospel.[11] Hakluyt – the rector of Wetheringsett in Norfolk, prebendary of Bristol Cathedral and archdeacon of Westminster Abbey – and Purchas – vicar of Eastwood, chaplain to archbishop George Abbot, rector of St Martin's, Ludgate, and of All Hallows, Bread Street – were also not alone, of course, among the host of English Protestant clerics who chronicled and promoted trade, colonisation and conquest in the late sixteenth and early seventeenth centuries.[12] For example, George Benson, Patrick Copland, Richard Crakanthorpe, William Crashaw, John Donne, Robert Gray and William Symonds all wrote on behalf of the Virginia Company, and deployed sermons as one of the major genres of promotional literature for the company.[13] Moreover, the most penetrating treatments of the question of English property rights in North America came in the writings of the Rev. John White of Dorchester and the Puritan leader John Winthrop.[14] John Locke later expanded upon such arguments, as he carefully distinguished between scriptural

[11] [White Kennett,] *Bibliothecæ Americanæ Primordiæ* (London, 1713), xii.
[12] D. B. Quinn (ed.), *The Hakluyt Handbook*, 2 vols. (London, 1974); L. E. Pennington (ed.), *The Purchas Handbook: Studies of the Life, Times and Writings of Samuel Purchas 1577–1626*, 2 vols. (London, 1997).
[13] On the sermons preached for the Virginia Company see John Parker, 'Religion and the Virginia Colony 1609–10', in K. R. Andrews, N. P. Canny and P. E. H. Hair (eds.), *The Westward Enterprise: English Activities in Ireland, the Atlantic, and America 1480–1650* (Liverpool, 1979), 255–62; H. C. Porter, *The Inconstant Savage: England and the North American Indian 1500–1660* (London, 1979), 339–59; Zakai, *Exile and Kingdom*, 100–19; W. Moelwyn Merchant, 'Donne's Sermon to the Virginia Company, 13 November 1622', in A. J. Smith (ed.), *John Donne: Essays in Celebration* (London, 1972), 437–52; Andrew Fitzmaurice, 'Every Man That Prints Adventures: The Rhetoric of the Virginia Company Sermons', in Lori Anne Ferrell and Peter E. McCullough (eds.), *The English Sermon Revised: Religion, Literature and History 1600–1750* (Manchester, 2000), 24–42.
[14] Chester Eisinger, 'The Puritans' Justification for Taking the Land', *Essex Institute Historical Collections*, 84 (1948), 131–43; Wilcomb E. Washburn, 'The Moral and Legal Justification for Dispossessing the Indians', in James Morton Smith (ed.), *Seventeenth-Century America: Essays in Colonial History* (Chapel Hill, 1959), 15–32; Francis Jennings, *The Invasion of America: Indians, Colonialism, and the Cant of Conquest* (Chapel Hill, 1975), 128–45; Ruth Baynes Moynihan, 'The Patent and the Indians: The Problem of Jurisdiction in Seventeenth-Century New England', *American Indian Culture and Research Journal*, 2 (1977), 8–18.

justifications for possession and those derived from the presumed state
of the souls of the dispossessed. To trace these arguments from the 1580s
to the 1680s is to see just how small a part Protestant conceptions of the
millennium, of the church and of salvation played in the development of
Anglo-British conceptions of empire; it is also to realise that, though
Protestantism may not have been the only cause of imperial amnesia, it
was far from the well-spring of imperial identity some later historians
have discerned.

The British Empire was nevertheless obviously a post-Reformation
empire, even in the territorial and dynastic sense examined in the last
chapter. 'Between the opening ages of Spanish and British transatlantic
colonization', J. H. Elliott has noted, 'fell the great divide of the Protestant Reformation'.[15] In particular, the institutional structure of the later
British Empire embodied the English and Scottish Reformations' chal-
lenges to the universalist claims of the Roman Church. In the long run,
this made the British Empire institutionally weaker, more flexible, but
also finally more fragile than the Spanish Monarchy in the Indies, for
example. Ecclesiological dissension racked the Church of England and
doctrinal Protestantism penetrated unevenly throughout the English
territories. The English Crown recognised a Presbyterian established
Church in the Channel Islands after 1565, even when it was most
ferociously attacking Presbyterianism within the English Church.[16]
England after the Elizabethan Settlement and Scotland after its Reformation remained ecclesiologically distinct after 1558–60, the one Epis-
copalian, the other Presbyterian; the pluralism of the Stuart composite
monarchy after 1603 was likewise transmitted to its overseas possessions.
By the 1580s, the Elizabethan state also effectively tolerated a powerful
Catholic minority (so long as they remained quiescent). Such pluralism
and *de facto* toleration of diversity can help explain the entrenchment of
ecclesiological diversity that characterised the British Atlantic Empire,
especially since it was enshrined in fundamental law by the Treaty of
Union in 1707, which recognised the perpetual separation of the established Churches of England and Scotland. One major consequence for
the later British Empire of the Protestant Reformations was therefore

[15] J. H. Elliott, 'Empire and State in British and Spanish America,' in Serge Gruzinski and Nathan
Wachtel (eds.), *Le Nouveau Monde – mondes nouveaux: l'expérience américaine* (Paris, 1996), 373.
[16] A. F. McC. Madden, '1066, 1776 and All That: The Relevance of the English Medieval
Experience of "Empire" to Later Imperial Constitutional Issues', in John E. Flint and Glyndwr
Williams (eds.), *Perspectives of Empire: Essays Presented to Gerald S. Graham* (London, 1973), 25; C. S. L.
Davies, 'International Politics and the Establishment of Presbyterianism in the Channel Islands:
The Coutances Connection', *Journal of Ecclesiastical History*, 50 (1999), 498–522.

disunity rather than unity. The common Protestantism of the Empire was not based on any shared conception of doctrines of salvation, the church or of Jesus's divinity. Instead, and increasingly, it depended upon a common anti-Catholicism that was more negative in content than affirmative in structure.[17]

Despite these obvious cracks in the facade of a common Protestantism, history could be used to provide a continuous religious tradition for the Empire. The traditional genealogy of the British Empire located its beginnings in the reigns of Elizabeth I and James I of England (though not of James VI of Scotland). It was in this period that England – which was assumed to be the primary and only seat of empire in Britain – extended its commerce westwards across the Atlantic, began to send settlers across the ocean and planted its first colonies and, with them, laid the foundations of a British Empire. This chronology affirmed the defining Protestantism of the British Empire by aligning its origins with the period of the consolidation of the English Reformation in the wake of the Elizabethan Settlement. Yet it also tended to displace the Scottish contribution to the origins of a comprehensively British Empire by assuming that the driving force behind both Protestantism and empire came from England alone. Just as Scotland after 1707 had become subsumed into an Anglo-British state, this narrative implied, so it could have made no contribution to the formation of the British Empire, nor could there have been any relationship between the multiple monarchy of the regal union (1603–1707) and the British Empire. Richard Hakluyt, in particular, provided a useful resource for this simplifying narrative, not least because he betrayed no interest at all in the British problem of the relations between the Three Kingdoms. One reason for the oblivion into which Samuel Purchas fell may indeed have been his own commitment to the projects of British federalism and, later, British unionism in the reigns of James VI and I and Charles I. It was always easier to assume that Anglican Protestantism defined an Anglo-British Empire, centred on London and superintended by London's bishop. To accept the diversity of the British kingdoms, or even the United Kingdom after 1707, would have been to admit a crucial fissure in the religious character of the Empire. In this context, Hakluyt's merely English accounts served the ideological purposes of the later British Empire better than Purchas's.

---

[17] For a rather different view of the religious character of the Empire see J. C. D. Clark, *The Language of Liberty 1660–1832: Political Discourse and Social Dynamics in the Anglo-American World* (Cambridge, 1995).

The historical narrative of the Elizabethan, and hence English, origins of the British Empire necessarily effaced the ideological origins of that empire in the period between Reformations. As we have seen, the concept of an 'Empire of Great Britain' first emerged in the aftermath of the English Reformation, in the context of Anglo-Scottish relations. It therefore preceded the coincident crises of British Protestantism in 1558–60 that reaffirmed the Protestantism of the English state in the first year of Elizabeth's reign and asserted the Protestantism of the Scottish Church by means of insurrection and *coup d'état* during the Scottish Reformation of 1560. These crises created two unstable and potentially short-lived Protestant monarchies in Britain that with hindsight appeared as the harbingers of unification, as indeed some of the supporters of Reformation in both England and Scotland during this period hoped. As F. W. Maitland famously put it, '[a] new nation, a British nation, was in the making' in the aftermath of 1560. That nation was decidedly Protestant and incipiently British with a glorious, global destiny ahead of it: 'The fate of the Protestant Reformation was being decided, and the creed of unborn millions in undiscovered lands was being determined'.[18]

If Protestantism was the bond of Britishness, and out of British nationhood sprang British imperialism, the Reformation should logically have been the ideological forcing-house for the British Empire itself. The British religious crises of 1558–60 may have created two Protestant kingdoms, and hence a Protestant island of Britain; however, they did not produce a common Protestantism, nor could they thereby have provided a mutual foundation for a Protestant empire beyond the Three Kingdoms. 'The great success of Anglo-Scottish Protestant culture in promoting a measure of cultural integration between the two realms was deeply deceptive', because England and Scotland retained their particular religious and political institutions, and remained in more respects divided by Protestantism than united by it.[19] Even the contemporary perception that Protestantism united England and Scotland, and distinguished them from their Catholic neighbours and adversaries, was undercut by the persistent institutional divergence between the two kingdoms. As the versatile poet and governor of Newfoundland,

[18] F. W. Maitland, 'The Anglican Settlement and the Scottish Reformation', in A. W. Ward, G. W. Prothero and Stanley Leathes (eds.), *The Cambridge Modern History*, ii: *The Reformation* (London, 1904), 550.

[19] Jane Dawson, 'Anglo-Scottish Protestant Culture and Integration in Sixteenth-Century Britain', in Steven G. Ellis and Sarah Barber (eds.), *Conquest and Union: Fashioning a British State 1485–1725* (London, 1995), 114.

Robert Hayman, versified this problem when memorialising King James in 1628:

> Our Ministers in their Evangeling,
> Praying for thee, stile thee *Great Brittaines King*:
> Our Lawyers pleading in *Westminster* Hall,
> Of *England*, and of *Scotland King* thee call.
> For what great mystery, I cannot see,
> Why Law, and Gospell should thus disagree.[20]

The same would be true of the later British Empire erected upon these unstable foundations.

The narrative of the late sixteenth-century origins of the British Empire suppressed the fact that the post-Reformation Empire was also a post-Renaissance Empire. As we have also seen, both English proponents of Anglo-Scottish union and their Scottish opponents employed classical rhetoric in the dispute over the creation of an 'empire of Great Britain' in the 1540s. Both sides appealed to Roman precedents to support their respective positions, and both used the neo-Roman language of empire (*imperium*) and colony (*colonia*) to describe the territorial consolidation they envisaged or the jurisdictional subordination they feared. The Scots antagonists of English claims to suzerainty turned the weapons of critical humanism against the historical foundations of those claims in the multiple monarchy of Brutus, while an Anglo-Briton like Edmund Spenser could later unabashedly draw on the British history in tandem with a neo-Aristotelian scheme for his truncated epic.

Both Hakluyt and Purchas identified the sixteenth-century revival of classical literature as a factor in encouraging commerce, colonisation and English settlement overseas. In the preface to his *Principal Navigations* (1598–1600), Hakluyt attributed the precedence of the Spanish and the Portuguese in the process of discovery in the Indies to their intellectual advantages, not least 'those bright lampes of learning (I meane the most ancient and best Philosophers, Historiographers and Geographers)'.[21] A quarter of a century later, Purchas located the origins of English expansion in 'the late eruption of captived learning in the former age, and more especially in the glorious sunshine of Queene *Elizabeth*'.[22] Pur-

---

[20] Robert Hayman, *Quodlibets; Lately Come Over from New Britaniola, Old Newfound-Land* (London, 1628), 13; on Hayman see G. C. Moore Smith, 'Robert Hayman and the Plantation of Newfoundland', *English Historical Review*, 33 (1918), 21–36.

[21] Richard Hakluyt (ed.), *The Principal Navigations, Voyages, Traffiques and Discoveries of the English Nation*, 3 vols. (London, 1598–1600), I, sig. [*4]ᵛ.

[22] Samuel Purchas, *Hakluytus Posthumus, or Purchas His Pilgrimes*, 4 vols. (London, 1625), I, 12. To avert the almost unavoidable confusion between this work and Purchas's *Pilgrimage* (1613) and his *Pilgrim* (1619), it is hereafter cited as *Hakluytus Posthumus*.

chas's chronology of the origins of an Anglo-British empire in Elizabeth's reign would later become conventional, particularly when an emergent linguistic nationalism traced the origins of English literature to the vernacular poetry and prose of this period. This association of Englishness (transmitted through literature) and empire (rooted in Elizabethan expansion) served at once to identify the origins of empire with the late sixteenth century – and hence with activity outside the Three Kingdoms – but also to efface the contribution of classical, pre-Christian learning to the origins of an empire deemed Protestant because English, and Anglo-British by virtue of its Protestantism.[23]

However, an enduring northern European myth of modernity sustained the association between the discovery of 'new worlds' in the Indies and the recovery of the Greek and Latin classics. The peculiar English version of this myth added the Protestant Reformation to the revival of ancient learning and the discovery of new worlds as a marker of the modern era. It was of course hardly fortuitous that the Tudor dynasty had presided over this conjunction: as Samuel Daniel noted in 1612, the Tudor reigns were '[a] time wherein began a greater improvement of the Soveraigntie ... The opening of a new world, which strangely opened the manner of this ... Besides strange alterations in the State Ecclesiasticall: Religion brought forth to be an Actor in the greatest Designes of Ambition and Faction'.[24] Daniel's assessment of the conjunction was not entirely approving, but he did deem it decisive in settling England's place in the longer span of European history. Later in the seventeenth century, the double conjunction of European reconnaissance and the Reformation became a decisive event in hemispheric, and even global, history: 'the Reformation of Religion, and the Discovery of the West Indies ... two Great Revolutions, happening neer about the same time, did very much alter the State of Affairs in the World'.[25] The most famous formulation of this conjunction was Thomas Paine's in 1776: 'The Reformation was preceded by the discovery of America; As if the Almighty graciously meant to open a sanctuary to the persecuted in future years'.[26] Gradually, the association with the Renaissance was forgotten in Protestant thought. It thereby became possible to define the post-Reformation origins of the British

[23] David Armitage, 'Literature and Empire', in Canny (ed.), *Oxford History of the British Empire*, I, 99–123.
[24] Samuel Daniel, *The First Part of the Historie of England* (London, 1612), sig. A3ᵛ.
[25] *A Declaration of His Highness ... Setting Forth, On the Behalf of this Commonwealth, the Justice of their Cause against Spain* (London, 1655), 517.
[26] Thomas Paine, *Common Sense; Addressed to the Inhabitants of America* (Philadelphia, 1776), 39.

Empire as specifically Protestant, just as it became necessary to define those origins as exclusively English, rather than collectively British.

Richard Hakluyt the younger was the major beneficiary of the narrative that located the origins of the British Empire in the Elizabethan period. In due course he was dubbed the intellectual progenitor of the Empire, the person 'to whom England [*sic*] is more indebted for its American possessions than to any man of that age', according to William Robertson.[27] In the mid-nineteenth century, J. A. Froude succinctly combined a similarly high estimation of Hakluyt's place in the history of the British Empire with an assessment of his position in the history of literature in English, and hence in the history of Englishness itself: in these terms, Froude memorably judged Hakluyt's *Principal Navigations* to be nothing less than the 'Prose Epic of the modern English nation'.[28] Classical epic had been transformed into vernacular prose; colonial fact replaced imperial fiction; modernity, nationhood and Englishness could all be traced back to the reign of Elizabeth, where they had been plotted by the pen of Hakluyt.[29] Likewise, Hakluyt's first scholarly biographer argued that '[t]he history of Hakluyt's career is in large part the intellectual history of the beginnings of the British Empire': much therefore depends on an accurate assessment of that career in any understanding of the ideological origins of an empire which later took him to be its intellectual progenitor.[30]

Hakluyt located the origins of his own vocation as the memorialist of English overseas enterprise in the juxtaposition of theology and geography. While he was 'one of her Majesty's scholars at Westminster' in *c.* 1568, he recalled, he visited the rooms of his cousin, Richard Hakluyt the elder, at the Middle Temple,

at a time when I found lying upon his board certeine bookes of Cosmographie, with an universall Mappe: he seeing me somewhat curious in the view therof, began to instruct my ignorance, by shewing me the division of the earth into three parts after the olde account, and then according to the later & better distribution, into more: he pointed with his wand to all the knowen Seas, Gulfs, Bayes, Straights, Capes, Rivers, Empires, Kingdomes, Dukedomes and Territories of ech part, with declaration also of their speciall commodities, & particular wants, which by the benefit of traffike & entercourse of merchants,

[27] William Robertson, *The History of America*, 3 vols. (London, 1777–96), III, 32.
[28] [J. A. Froude,] 'England's Forgotten Worthies', *The Westminster Review*, n.s. 2, 1 (July 1852), 19; D. B. Quinn, 'Hakluyt's Reputation', in Quinn (ed.), *Hakluyt Handbook*, I, 144–8.
[29] Richard Helgerson, *Forms of Nationhood: The Elizabethan Writing of England* (Chicago, 1992), 151–5, 166–81.   [30] George Bruner Parks, *Richard Hakluyt and the English Voyages* (New York, 1928), 2.

are plentifully supplied. From the Mappe he brought me to the Bible, and turning to the 107th Psalme, directed mee to the 23rd & 24th verses, where I read, that they which go downe to the sea in ships, and occupy by the great waters, they see the works of the Lord, and his woonders in the deepe, &c.[31]

Hakluyt represented this event in idiomatically Protestant terms, as an encounter with a prophetic text, guided by a layman and applied to the life of an individual reader and believer. The elder Hakluyt's cosmographies revealed a world of discrete territories, each endowed with their natural products but also connected by their mutual need for one another's goods. This confirmed the natural jurisprudential argument that God had so disposed the world's commodities that the reciprocity of scarcity and abundance between states would promote 'the benefit of traffic and intercourse of merchants'. The Psalmists' verses of course offered no scriptural foundation for this principle of natural rather than revealed religion;[32] however, they did authorise Hakluyt's own later conception of his mission, both as an editor and as a cleric in the Elizabethan Church. Nevertheless, Hakluyt's account was somewhat disingenuous for, as we shall see, his intellectual projects owed more to his Oxonian Aristotelianism and Thomism than they did to any supposedly unmediated Protestant experience of scripture.

Religion shaped little, if any, of Hakluyt's corpus, either generically or rhetorically. All of Hakluyt's printed works derived from his self-appointed task as the compiler of the English 'voyages and discoveries' and none from his position as rector, chaplain or prebendary. He published no sermons, intervened directly in no religious polemics and wrote no Biblical commentary. The most direct institutional source of his commitments was not the Elizabethan Church but rather the Clothworkers' Company. The company paid Hakluyt an annual pension from 1578 to 1586 even when he was stationed in Paris as chaplain to the English ambassador, Sir Edward Stafford, on and off between 1585 and 1588. The company's interest lay in replacing short-range European and Mediterranean markets for English cloth with more expansive arenas of trade. The geographical range of Hakluyt's various histories certainly encouraged such a reorientation of English exports, both to the East Indies and increasingly across the Atlantic.[33] Such a programme

---

[31] Richard Hakluyt, 'Epistle Dedicatory to Sir Francis Walsingham', in Hakluyt (ed.), *The Principall Navigations of the English People* (London, 1589), sig. *2ʳ.
[32] Jacob Viner, *The Role of Providence in the Social Order: An Essay in Intellectual History* (Princeton, 1972), 32–40, 44–7.
[33] G. D. Ramsay, 'Clothworkers, Merchant Adventurers, and Richard Hakluyt', *English Historical Review*, 2nd ser., 92 (1977), 504–21.

may have been closer to Hakluyt's intentions than his theological commitments, but it is hardly sufficient to explain the shape and development of his intellectual projects, both in manuscript and in print.

The extent – and the limits – of Hakluyt's conception of England's national mission were most evident in his two longest and most closely linked works, one the fruit of his position as an advisor to Sir Francis Walsingham and Sir Walter Ralegh in the 1580s, the other of his tutorial responsibilities at Oxford. Since its first publication in the late nineteenth century, the so-called 'Discourse of Western Planting' has been the major source for discussions of Hakluyt's ideas and of Elizabethan colonial ideology more broadly. Hakluyt's own title for the work – 'A particuler discourse concerninge the greate necessitie and manifolde comodyties that are like to growe to this Realme of Englande by the Westerne discoveries lately attempted' – is usually forgotten, as are its genre and the context of its original reception. The 'Discourse' was a position-paper, written at Walsingham's request, and submitted to Queen Elizabeth in 1584. As such, it was simultaneously an act of counsel, a rhetorical intervention into conciliar debate on policy and a gift offered from suppliant to monarch in hopes of generating reciprocal reward.[34] Yet it is also forgotten that the 'Discourse' was not Hakluyt's only such work at this time. In September 1583, Hakluyt had presented 'a couple of bookes of myne in wryting, one in Latin upon Arystotles politicks, the other in English concerning Mr Rawley's voyage'. As an attempt to influence conciliar policy, and to gain the Crown's financial backing for Ralegh's Roanoke voyage, the 'Discourse' was clearly a failure. However, in tandem with Hakluyt's 'wryting ... in Latin upon Arystotles politicks', it was impressive enough to gain him 'the next vacation of a prebend in Bristol' in October 1584.[35]

The simultaneous presentation of the 'Discourse' and the Latin synopsis of the *Politics* – the 'Analysis, seu resolutio perpetua in octo libros Politicorum Aristotelis' – was an attempt to frame English overseas activity within the context of classical civil philosophy.[36] The 'Analysis' was prior to the 'Discourse', both logically and in the manner

---

[34] On the rhetorical culture of the Elizabethan council see Stephen Alford, *The Early Elizabethan Polity: William Cecil and the British Succession Crisis, 1558–1569* (Cambridge, 1998), 14–24.

[35] Hakluyt to Sir Francis Walsingham, 7 April 1585, in *Writings and Correspondence*, ed. Taylor, II, 343–4; D. B. Quinn, 'A Hakluyt Chronology', in Quinn (ed.), *Hakluyt Handbook*, I, 286.

[36] Richard Hakluyt, 'Analysis, seu resolutio perpetua in octo libros Politicorum Aristotelis', BL MS Royal 12. G. XIII. The only extended treatment of the 'Analysis' does not draw any intellectual connection between it and the 'Discourse': Lawrence V. Ryan, 'Richard Hakluyt's Voyage into Aristotle', *Sixteenth Century Journal*, 12 (1981), 73–83.

of its presentation to Elizabeth and her ministers. Like the 'Discourse', it was a bid for patronage, and in this it was clearly successful. Unlike the 'Discourse', it might be added, the 'Analysis' was a supreme example of its genre, '[p]erhaps the most significant of all the manuscript materials relating to Aristotle coming from Oxford in the [Elizabethan] period'.[37] It was a characteristic product of the late sixteenth-century Oxford curriculum, and of the 'humanistic, Aristotelian culture' it fostered.[38] It derived from Hakluyt's lectures on Aristotle at Christ Church in 1581, and he evidently continued to draw upon it beyond the time of his composition of the 'Discourse', through the editing of his earliest geographical works, and almost up to the moment when he published the first edition of the *Principall Navigations*, since he produced a second, almost identical, manuscript of it in 1588.[39] The exposition of the *Politics* was therefore the one consistent thread in Hakluyt's intellectual life from 1581 to 1588, a fact which confirms the importance of the 'Analysis' to elucidate the context of the 'Discourse' with which he paired it for presentation to Elizabeth in 1583.

The 'Analysis' presented a complete recension of the *Politics* into Latin, broken down into books, chapters and questions. For Hakluyt's Oxford students, it provided a pedagogical tool, adequate to their need to understand Aristotle's work and to debate its meaning; for Elizabeth and her counsellors, it functioned rather as an argument regarding the nature, capacities and purpose of the commonwealth, and in that form stood as a preface to the 'Discourse'. Hakluyt's summary of Aristotle's chapters entitled it 'Octo librum Aristotelis de Republica', and, as if to nudge his readers further in the direction of considering the work as a contribution to the Latin literature on the best state of the commonwealth, he entitled Book vii, 'De optima Republica'.[40] Central to the best state was Aristotle's conception of self-sufficiency, recast in Thomist terms as the defining feature of the *communitas perfecta*. In his synopsis of Book i of the *Politics*, Hakluyt translated Aristotle's definition of the *polis* into just such Thomist terms: 'Societas perfecta ... est civitas. Cuius finis est sufficientia omnium rerum necessarium & vita beata' ('the

[37] Charles B. Schmitt, *John Case and Aristotelianism in Renaissance England* (Kingston, Ontario, 1983), 57, n. 164.

[38] James B. McConica, 'Humanism and Aristotle in Tudor Oxford', *English Historical Review*, 94 (1979), 315; Schmitt, *John Case and Aristotelianism in Renaissance England*, 41–5, 52–8.

[39] BL MS Sloane 1982. This copy is in Hakluyt's own hand.

[40] Hakluyt, 'Analysis', BL MS Royal 12. G. xiii, ff. 3ʳ, 38ᵛ; on the literature *de optimo statu reipublicae*, see Quentin Skinner, 'Sir Thomas More's *Utopia* and the Language of Renaissance Humanism', in Anthony Pagden (ed.), *The Languages of Political Theory in Early Modern Europe* (Cambridge, 1987), 126–40.

city is the perfect society, whose end is a sufficiency of all necessities and the blessed life'). He reaffirmed it in his translation of the definition of the *civitas* in Book III as 'multitudo ... civium, ad vitae sufficientiam seipsa contenta' ('a mass of citizens, self-sufficient in the necessities of life').[41] The 'protestant scholasticism' of Hakluyt's thought is also evident in the fact that he cited Aquinas more often than any other modern commentator on Aristotle.[42] Though Hakluyt referred to himself as 'verbi Dei Minister' in his preface to Elizabeth, and dedicated the 'Analysis' on its closing leaf, 'Deo Opt. Max. Honor Laus et Gloria', he made only one explicit attempt to insert a Christian conception of religion into Aristotle's analysis when he added a marginal note to the discussion of rebellion in Book III: 'Religionem ad quam classem referas, tu videris.'[43]

Hakluyt's vocabulary elsewhere could be read as a gloss on the 'Discourse', as for example in the initial description of the building-block of the *polis*: 'Vicus est *colonia* quaedam domorum & familiarum: ergo et vicus naturalis est' ('the village is a *colony* of some households and families: therefore, the village is also the product of nature'). Such meanings would be obvious in conjunction with the 'Discourse'. To trained and committed humanists like Sir William Cecil or Elizabeth herself, the significance of the juxtaposition would have been clear: if England were to be a *civitas perfecta*, and its citizens capable of living the *vita beata*, they, like the citizens of the Aristotelian *polis*, would need to be supplied with virtue, a physical sufficiency and an abundance of fortune ('Vita beata ... est, quae cum virtute coniuncta, ea bonorum corporis et fortunæ copia habet').[44] One way to supply that, and to found a new commonwealth, would be through the 'natural' activity of founding villages or *coloniae*, composed of families.

The 'Discourse' presented an argument both for the 'necessitie' of planting colonies across the Atlantic and for the 'manifolde commodyties' that would arise from them.[45] The necessity of colonisation arose from simultaneous overpopulation at home, and the contraction

---

[41] Hakluyt, 'Analysis', BL MS Royal 12. G. XIII, ff. 4ʳ, 15ʳ; Anthony Pagden, *Lords of All the World: Ideologies of Empire in Spain, Britain and France c. 1500–1800* (New Haven, 1995), 18.

[42] Hakluyt, 'Analysis', BL MS Royal 12. G. XIII, ff. 36ʳ, 37ʳ, 42ʳ; Ryan, 'Richard Hakluyt's Voyage into Aristotle', 81, 82; Peter Lake, *Anglicans and Puritans? Presbyterianism and English Conformist Thought from Whitgift to Hooker* (London, 1988), 226.

[43] Hakluyt, 'Analysis', BL MS Royal 12. G. XIII, ff. 2ʳ, 47ᵛ, 28ᵛ.

[44] Hakluyt, 'Analysis', BL MS Royal 12. G. XIII, f. 39ʳ (my emphasis).

[45] Richard Hakluyt, *A Particuler Discourse Concerning the Greate Necessitie and Manifolde Commodyties that are Like to Growe to this Realme of Englande by the Westerne Discoveries Lately Attempted ... Known as Discourse of Western Planting* (1584), ed. David B. Quinn and Alison M. Quinn (London, 1993). The original manuscript, of which this edition contains a facsimile, is in the New York Public Library.

of English markets abroad. The manifold commodities would therefore be general and particular: general, in providing an outlet for surplus population and production, and relief from those 'very burdensome to the common wealthe'; and particular, in the provision of new materials and products for the English economy, 'the vent of the masse of our clothes and other commodities of England, and ... receavinge backe of the nedefull commodities that wee nowe receave from all other places of the worlde'.[46] The overall aim of the new colonies would be to return the economy of England itself to self-sufficiency by balancing its production, consumption and population. This could only be achieved by the export of people, and the institution of new markets, all of which would be conceived as parts of the commonwealth, albeit across an ocean, rather than new commonwealths in themselves.[47]

A solely economic reading of Hakluyt's 'Discourse' would not do justice to the connection of the good of the commonwealth with the demands of the *vita beata*, and hence of religion, in that document. In the preface to his collection of *Divers Voyages* (1582), Hakluyt condemned 'the preposterous desire of seeking rather gaine then God's glorie', and counselled that, 'lasting riches do wait upon them that are jealous for the advancement of the Kingdome of Christ, and the enlargement of his glorious Gospell'.[48] Like his elder cousin, therefore, he linked trade, religion and conquest as essential parts of the same enterprise,[49] and hence *teloi* towards which English action in the Americas should be directed. Just as the *Politics*, and hence Hakluyt's synopsis of it, ended with the necessity of education for the pursuit of the good life, whether defined as *eudaimonia* or *beatitudo*, so the 'Discourse' began with the question of 'the inlarginge the gospell of Christe, and reducinge of infinite multitudes of these simple people that are in errour into the righte and perfecte waye of their salvacion'.[50]

The 'Analysis' of Aristotle and the 'Discourse' on western planting therefore complemented each other, the 'Discourse' picking up in its first chapter where Book VIII of the 'Analysis' left off, in its consideration of the means necessary for promoting the good life, and the capacities of

---

[46] Hakluyt, *Particuler Discourse*, ed. Quinn and Quinn, 28, 32, 71.
[47] Hakluyt's conception was therefore distinct from that of the later promoters of the Virginia Company and its colony: Andrew Fitzmaurice, 'The Civic Solution to the Crisis of English Colonization, 1609–1625', *The Historical Journal*, 42 (1999), 25–51.
[48] Richard Hakluyt (ed.), *Divers Voyages Touching the Discoverie of America* (London, 1582), sig. ¶ 3ʳ.
[49] Richard Hakluyt the elder, 'Inducements to the Liking of the Voyage intended towards Virginia' (1585), in *Writings and Correspondence*, ed. Taylor, II, 332.
[50] Hakluyt, *Particuler Discourse*, ed. Quinn and Quinn, 8.

those in whom it might be encouraged. In the 'Discourse', Hakluyt moved between assessments of the native peoples of the Americas in terms of their civil and religious capacities, as 'Savages' or 'Infidells'. Yet, like so many of his contemporaries, he ultimately deemed the two conditions to be inseparable: without civilisation, and hence induction into the classically-defined conception of life in the *polis* or the *civitas*, Christianity could not be implanted. As Hakluyt assured Sir Walter Ralegh in 1587, '[n]ihil enim ad posteros gloriosius nec honorificentius transmitti potest, quàm Barbaros domare, rudes & paganos ad vitae civilis societatem revocare, ... hominésq; atheos & à Deo alienos divini numinis reverentia imbuere' ('for nothing more glorious or honourable can be handed down to the future than to tame the barbarian, to bring back the savage and the pagan to the fellowship of civil existence and to induce reverence for the Holy Spirit into atheists and others distant from God').[51] Civilisation, defined in Ciceronian terms as the life of the citizen, was therefore prior to, and indispensable for, Christian salvation. In just the same way Hakluyt's conception of the civil life was prior to his conception of Christianity, and sprang from it, just as one would expect from one of the most distinguished exponents of humanist Aristotelianism and Protestant scholasticism in late sixteenth-century Oxford.

This classical conception of the good life, and the conception of time as bound by the existence of the *polis*, has greater relevance for an understanding of Hakluyt's thought than any contemporary schemes of eschatological history. There is little indication that Hakluyt conceived of his own enterprise within the categories of sacred time, even though the first edition of his *Principall Navigations* appeared in 1589, in the immediate aftermath of the defeat of the Spanish Armada. Hakluyt celebrated the victory and understood it as evidence of God's judgment on the Spanish; however, his work shows none of the resurgent apocalypticism that characterised English Protestant thought in the years after 1588. Even at this highly-charged and significant moment in England's relationship with God, therefore, Hakluyt showed little sign that he believed 'England was indeed the New Israel, God's chosen nation'.[52] His sole reference to the Pope as 'the greate Antechryste of Rome' in 1584 was an entirely conventional expression of a Calvinist binary, and did not betoken any larger apocalyptic scheme in Hakluyt's

[51] Richard Hakluyt (ed.), *De Orbe Novo Peter Martyris* (Paris, 1587), sig. [av]ᵛ.
[52] *Pace* Zakai, *Exile and Kingdom*, 98–9; on the upsurge of English apocalypticism after 1588 see Richard Bauckham, *Tudor Apocalypse* (Abingdon, 1978), 173–80.

theology.[53] Nor did he distinguish true and false churches from one
another, except on the grounds of their saving mission. In the sixteenth
century, and in the Americas, he noted, the Spanish had had greater
evangelical success, and hence had pressed a more convincing claim for
the truth of their church: now, it was time for the 'Princes of the
Relligion' (Elizabeth I pre-eminent among them) to catch up, and
reveal the truth of the Protestant Church through the active conversion
of souls.[54] None of these passing references amounts to evidence that
Hakluyt reflected systematically upon eschatology, nor that the con-
clusions of his theology – regarding the nature of the true church, the
identity of the Antichrist or the divine economy of salvation and reprobation – provided the intellectual foundation for his historiography.

Hakluyt's English nationalism (if such it was) may therefore have
owed more to his classicism than to his Protestantism. The evangelical
success of the Catholic monarchies in the New World confirmed his
lack of confidence in God's particular favour for England, the most
belated of all European powers in its attempts at American colonisation. Hakluyt's solution to overcome such belatedness lay in information disseminated through editions. The inspiration and the technical
models for those editions came from classical and contemporary geography, particularly Ptolemy, Abraham Ortelius and the 'perfect'
history of Lancelot de la Popeliniére, whose *L'Amiral de France* (1584)
appeared while Hakluyt was in Paris. Ptolemy encouraged the history
of travel (*Peregrinationis historia*) as the alternative to 'universall cosmographie';[55] Ortelius urged the combination of time and space to create
geographical histories;[56] and La Popeliniére added exhortations for
national enterprise to such geographical history.[57] Hakluyt in turn
produced a Latin edition of Peter Martyr's *Decades de Orbe Novo* (1587) in
Paris, and experimented with adding chronology to geography in that
edition as the prelude to his two collections of travels in the *Principal
Navigations*.

[53] Hakluyt, *Particuler Discourse*, ed. Quinn and Quinn, 116; Peter Lake, 'The Significance of the Elizabethan Identification of the Pope as Antichrist', *Journal of Ecclesiastical History*, 31 (1980), 161–78; Bauckham, *Tudor Apocalypse*, 91–108.
[54] Hakluyt, *Particuler Discourse*, ed. Quinn and Quinn, 11.
[55] Hakluyt, *Principall Navigations* (1589), sig. *3ᵛ.
[56] Compare Abraham Ortelius, *Theatrum Orbis Terrarum* (Antwerp, 1570), sig. Aiiiⁱ, with Hakluyt (ed.), *De Orbe Novo Peter Martyris*, sig. aiiiᵛ–aiiiⁱ, and Hakluyt (ed.), *Principal Navigations* (1598–1600), III, sig. (A2)ᵛ.
[57] For Hakluyt and La Popeliniére see Hakluyt, *Principall Navigations* (1589), sig. *2ᵛ; *Writings and Correspondence*, ed. Taylor, II, 241 and note, 295, 398; Edward Arber (ed.), *A Transcript of the Registers of the Company of Stationers of London; 1554–1640 A.D.*, 3 vols. (London, 1875), II, 424.

The specific models Hakluyt did acknowledge as sources for his own historiography were three of 'our owne Historians': John Foxe, the martyrologist and compiler of the *Acts and Monuments*; John Bale, the apocalyptic historian, through his least apocalyptic work, the *Scriptorum Illustrium Majoris Britanniæ . . . Catalogus* (1557–59); and Richard Eden, the mid-sixteenth-century translator of early Spanish works relating to the Americas. Hakluyt also took material relating to northern Germany from the *Commentaries* (1555) of another notable European apocalyptic historian, John Sleidan.[58] However, his debts to these various works were not evidently theological. The two works by Bale and Sleidan from which he drew material were in each case the works of their authors least obviously shaped by their apocalypticism. Eden's translations had been produced mostly in the reign of the Catholic Queen Mary, to whom he dedicated his translation of Peter Martyr's *Decades of the New World* as a gift on the occasion of her marriage to the Spanish prince Philip, in celebration of the alliance of England with the Spanish Monarchy.[59] Finally, Hakluyt's most evident debt to Foxe was his treatment of personal narratives – of merchants and sailors in his case, of martyrs in Foxe's – rather than in any larger scheme of salvation or reprobation within which they might be placed. None of his major works therefore depended upon, or contributed to, theological debate about the structure of the English Church, the relationship between true and false churches, the doctrine of salvation or the status of the English as agents in apocalyptic time.

Hakluyt's *Principal Navigations* were in due course carried on board the ships of the East India Company, alongside Foxe's *Acts and Monuments* and the works of the orthodox Calvinist divine William Perkins.[60] Foxe has long been taken to be the exemplar of English Protestant particularism, the antiquarian martyrologist whose greatest vernacular work supposedly sustained the vision of England as the 'elect nation' from the 1560s into the eighteenth century, and beyond.[61] But recent scholars have challenged the idea that England could have been *the* elect nation, rather than *an* elect nation, because election, within the Calvinist scheme of double predestination, was no respecter of national boundaries, and the true church of the elect was invisible and eternal

---

[58] Hakluyt (ed.), *Principall Navigations* (1589), sig. *3ᵛ; Hakluyt, *Particuler Discourse*, ed. Quinn and Quinn, 31, 36, 39.

[59] Peter Martyr, *The Decades of the Newe Worlde of India*, trans. Richard Eden (London, 1555), sig. [Ai]ᵛ.

[60] Louis B. Wright, *Religion and Empire* (Chapel Hill, 1943), 53, 71.

[61] William Haller, *Foxe's Book of Martyrs and the Elect Nation* (London, 1963).

rather than visible and earthly. As a result, Foxe no longer stands as the avatar of English elect nationalism. He clearly placed the history of the English Church within a universal scheme of salvation and reprobation, the small, persecuted, elect leaven within the lump of unregenerate mass humanity being as unequally distributed within his own nation as anywhere else. Nor was he a millenarian, since he located the millennium firmly in the past and not in the future, for England or anywhere else.[62] The fact that Francis Drake carried a copy of Foxe's book of martyrs on his circumnavigation – and amazed a Spanish prisoner by colouring the woodcuts during the voyage – seems less fraught with particular apocalyptic significance once Foxe's universalism, and Drake's own instrumental, Machiavellian, approach to religion, are appreciated.[63] The consensus among historians that elect nationalism was a quite restricted, particular and contested argument within English Protestantism also confirms the unlikelihood that it would have been espoused by a writer like Hakluyt as a justification for the promotion of English overseas trade and settlement. If the conception of the 'elect nation' were a taproot – even *the* taproot – of English imperialism, then Hakluyt did not supply much nourishment for it to grow and flourish.

Far from exulting in God's special favour for England, Hakluyt pointed to God's greater care for the Catholic monarchies. The belatedness of the English in the competition for American colonies was a sign to sixteenth-century English Protestants, at least, that Providence had offered Protestants no privileges. It was often recalled – albeit mistakenly – that Bartolomé Colon, Christopher Columbus's brother, had offered Henry VII the chance to sponsor a voyage in search of the Indies; the English king rejected the opportunity, which was taken up instead by the Castilian Crown.[64] Hakluyt included two documents in the *Principal Navigations* recording Colon's proposal, but drew from the episode the unsettling conclusion that 'God had reserved the sayd offer

[62] Bauckham, *Tudor Apocalypse*, 85–7; Katherine R. Firth, *The Apocalyptic Tradition in Reformation Britain 1530–1645* (Oxford, 1979), 106–9; Jane Facey, 'John Foxe and the Defence of the English Church', in Peter Lake and Maria Dowling (eds.), *Protestantism and the National Church in Sixteenth Century England* (London, 1987), 183–5; Palle J. Olsen, 'Was John Foxe a Millenarian?' *Journal of Ecclesiastical History*, 45 (1994), 600–24.

[63] *New Light on Drake*, ed. Zelia Nuttall (London, 1914), 348, 354–8; Haller, *Foxe's Book of Martyrs*, 221; Harry Kelsey, *Sir Francis Drake: The Queen's Pirate* (New Haven, 1998), 170–1, 303–4, 393.

[64] Sir Walter Ralegh, *The Discoverie of the Large, Rich, and Bewtifull Empyre of Guiana* (London, 1596), 99; Lawrence Keymis, *A Relation of the Second Voyage to Guiana* (London, 1596), sig. [A4]ᵛ; [Robert Gray,] *A Good Speed for Virginia* (London, 1609), sig. B[1]ᵛ; Daniel Price, *Sauls Prohibition Staide* (London, 1609), sig. F2ʳ; Sir William Alexander, *An Encouragement to Colonies* (London, 1624), 8.

for *Castile*.[65] The subsequent success of the Catholic monarchies in effecting conversion in South and Central America 'may justly be coumpted rather a perversion'; nevertheless, the Protestant princes could offer no evidence that they had converted even one unbeliever to refute the claim that 'they are the true Catholicke Churche because they have bene the onely converters of many millions of Infidells to Christianitie'.[66] Hakluyt's writings show no evidence of any interest in the primitive Church or the antecedents of Protestantism before the European Reformations. He offered no answer to that vexing question apocryphally asked by every Catholic to any Protestant: 'Where was your church before Luther?' However, he was clearly troubled by the fact that God had allowed Catholics to convert native Americans unchecked, and had thereby endowed the Roman Church with the mark of truth: a successful saving mission.

Hakluyt's works remained thoroughly English and not British (let alone, British and Irish) in scope. His aim was to chronicle the voyages, traffics and navigations of the English nation alone. This in itself did not necessarily make him an English nationalist, and there is no evidence in his writings that he believed England to be the elect nation. However, his work revealed the limits that contemporary nationhood placed on his historiographical and geographical horizons. He set 'Britain' firmly in the distant past, as when he stated that the scattering of colonies in Roman Britain meant that the Romans did not 'in effecte ha[ve] the Brittishe nation at commaundement'. The last truly British king, for Hakluyt as for other commentators like John Dee and later John Selden, had been Edgar, 'soveraigne lord of all the British seas, and of the whole Isle of Britaine it selfe'.[67] Beyond these references, there is no evidence in Hakluyt's works that he espoused the British history that had been so prominent in Anglo-British propaganda in the 1540s and that Spenser deployed in the 1590s to underpin his vision of a unified British monarchy within the Three Kingdoms. He presumably shared the scepticism of sixteenth-century humanists regarding the Galfridian British history. The use of that history in the Anglo-British propaganda of the 1540s had been something of a rearguard action, and Scottish opponents of its historiographical agenda countered it by appeals to humanist scholarship, especially Polydore Vergil's *Anglica Historia*. A British

---

[65] Hakluyt (ed.), *Principal Navigations* (1598–1600), III, 3.
[66] Hakluyt, *Particuler Discourse*, ed. Quinn and Quinn, 11.
[67] Hakluyt, *Particuler Discourse*, ed. Quinn and Quinn, 43; Hakluyt (ed.), *Principal Navigations* (1598–1600), sig. **ᵛ, 6–9.

empire – let alone *the* British Empire – was inconceivable for Hakluyt. Such a community lay neither in the past nor in the future; his conception of the English nation was at root Thomist and neo-Aristotelian, a *societas perfecta*, or even a self-sufficient *polis*, not a composite monarchy or the metropolis of an expansive territorial *imperium* on the late Roman model. It was hardly surprising that William Robertson credited Hakluyt with the inspiration for planting *English* colonies, nor that Froude identified him as the author of the *English* nation's 'prose epic'. It is therefore entirely fitting that the term 'British Empire' did not appear in any of his works.

With hindsight, and from the perspective of mid-Victorian Anglicanism, Samuel Purchas could be praised alongside Hakluyt as the Protestant co-founder of a commercial empire:

Purchas . . . carried on most effectively . . . the work which Hakluyt had so well begun; and to those two clergymen of the Church of England every one who would desire to see the earliest steps by which the commercial greatness of this nation has been attained must ever turn with gratitude.[68]

However, attention to Hakluyt and Purchas's differing conceptions of Britain, national election, anti-Catholicism, and eschatology prevents any facile assimilation of their respective projects. Purchas's geographical histories, unlike Hakluyt's, placed England firmly in the context of the history of the Three Kingdoms, of Europe, and of a wider world conceived within sacred time. Hakluyt took little interest in Ireland, and none in Scotland; he made only the most glancing references to the schemes of church history; and he presented no apocalyptic justification for English trade and settlement. In contrast, Purchas's attention to the Three Kingdoms of the Stuart multiple monarchy, his cosmopolitan historiography and his attempt to place British history within the wider schemes of theological time made his works strictly incomparable to Hakluyt's. For all their superficial similarities as memorialists of English overseas enterprise, and in spite of Purchas's acknowledged debt to his predecessor, their conceptions of Britain, of empire, of history and time distinguished Hakluyt and Purchas sharply from one another. They were linked most directly by their common effort to provide a natural jurisprudential account of the legitimacy of English trade, conquest and plantation, particularly in the Americas, as we shall see; however, even

---

[68] James S. M. Anderson, *The History of the Church of England in the Colonies and Foreign Dependencies of the British Empire*, 3 vols. (London, 1856), I, 493, n. 47.

in this set of arguments, Purchas's intellectual debts were wider, and his sources more broad ranging than Hakluyt's.

Hakluyt and Purchas have usually been contrasted in their editorial methods, rather than their intellectual frameworks, most often to Purchas's disadvantage. Hakluyt, the scrupulous, logical editor whose well-constructed narratives offered persuasive encouragement to English overseas enterprise, has always been preferred to Purchas, the supposedly indiscriminate accumulator of theological compendia, whose gargantuan collections, most especially *Hakluytus Posthumus, or Purchas His Pilgrimes* (1625) were far too unwieldy, indigestible and archaic in their religious imperatives to provide any inspiration for expansion.[69] Even the most sympathetic comparison concludes that, 'if Richard Hakluyt was the historian of the early English colonial effort, Samuel Purchas was its philosopher', as if Hakluyt had no philosophy (and hence no place in intellectual history) and Purchas no interest in history (and, hence, no historical structure to his thought).[70] Unlike Hakluyt, it has been further argued, Purchas 'was steeped in religion. His symbols and allusions are biblical rather than classical for the most part'; accordingly, he could be of little interest to secular intellectual history, and his increasing marginality and irrelevance since the late seventeenth century have been well earned.[71]

The comparison between Purchas's religiosity and Hakluyt's classicism – if that is understood to mean his humanist editorial methods and his attention to civil philosophy – is not entirely misplaced. Purchas stated in the introduction to his first major work, *Purchas His Pilgrimage* (1613) that '*Religion* is my more proper aime',[72] and this could stand as the epigraph to any of his major works. His crowning achievement was the four-volume compilation, *Purchas His Pilgrimes*, which he entitled *Hakluytus Posthumus*, both to acknowledge the debt he owed to Hakluyt's manuscript legacy and to create a connection between their two enterprises. *Hakluytus Posthumus* was nonetheless the culmination of the theo-

[69] C. R. Steele, 'From Hakluyt to Purchas', in Quinn (ed.), *The Hakluyt Handbook*, 1, 74–84; James P. Helfers, 'The Explorer or the Pilgrim? Modern Critical Opinion and the Editorial Methods of Richard Hakluyt and Samuel Purchas', *Studies in Philology*, 94 (1997), 160–86.

[70] L. E. Pennington, '*Hakluytus Posthumus*: Samuel Purchas and the Promotion of English Overseas Expansion', *Emporia State Research Studies*, 14, 3 (1966), 5.

[71] John Parker, 'Samuel Purchas, Spokesman for Empire', in Ton Croiset van Uchelen, Koerst van der Horst and Günter Schilder (eds.), *Theatrum Orbis Librorum: Liber Amicorum Presented to Nico Israel on the Occasion of his Seventieth Birthday* (Utrecht, 1989), 48; L. E. Pennington, 'Samuel Purchas: His Reputation and the Uses of His Works', in Pennington (ed.), *Purchas Handbook*, 1, 10.

[72] Samuel Purchas, *Purchas His Pilgrimage. Or Relations of the World and the Religions Observed in All Ages and Places Discovered, from the Creation to the Present* (London, 1613), sig. [¶4]ʳ.

logically structured oeuvre he had elaborated over the preceding decade and a half, from *Purchas His Pilgrimage*, via *Purchas His Pilgrim* (1619) to the least well-known of all his works, *The Kings Towre* (1623), a sermon preached at St Paul's Cross. In each of these works, Purchas situated the Stuart composite monarchy of James VI and I and his heir, Prince Charles, within the universal history of the struggle between the true and the false churches, and in particular the history of the Protestant cause in northern Europe. The salient dates in that history were 1588, 1600 and 1605, the moments when the Protestant wind had scattered the Spanish Armada, when James VI had escaped assassination at the hands of the Earl of Gowrie and his brother at Perth, and when the King, his family and his counsellors had been delivered from the Catholic menace of the Gunpowder Plot. Two of his early works can be tied directly to this chronology of the Protestant triumphs over 'the *Paganisme* of Antichristian Poperie'. Purchas dedicated his *Pilgrimage* to his patron, the Calvinist archbishop, George Abbot, on 5 November 1612, the anniversary of the Gunpowder Plot, 'in thankfulnesse to GOD for our later Deliverance'; meanwhile, he preached *The Kings Towre* on 5 August 1622, the anniversary of the foiling of the Gowrie Plot.[73] Most important in establishing Purchas's anti-popish intent in his major work, Purchas noted that *Hakluytus Posthumus* (like *The Kings Towre*) had been compiled over four summers of 'His Majesties College at Chelsea', which was 'a place of argument to move me to enter these Lists'. This was the college of controversial divinity led by the militant former dean of Exeter, Matthew Sutcliffe, and the very arsenal of anti-Catholic polemic during James's reign.[74]

The bulk of Purchas's work between 1621 and 1625 can therefore be linked directly to the purposes of polemical anti-Catholicism. This was the period of James's policy of religious irenicism in Europe, and comprehension in England was under greatest strain. During this time, English, and especially metropolitan, anti-Catholicism and opposition to Spain peaked in the agitations surrounding the proposed 'Spanish Match' between Prince Charles and the Spanish Infanta. Purchas

[73] Purchas, *Purchas His Pilgrimage*, sigs. [¶3]ʳ⁻ᵛ, 752; Samuel Purchas, *The Kings Towre, And Triumphant Arch of London* (London, 1623); Millar Maclure, *The Paul's Cross Sermons 1534–1642* (Toronto, 1958), 244; Peter E. McCullough, *Sermons at Court: Politics and Religion in Elizabethan and Jacobean Preaching* (Cambridge, 1998), 116–19, 122.
[74] Purchas, *Hakluytus Posthumus*, I, ii, 25; D. E. Kennedy, 'King James I's College of Controversial Divinity at Chelsea', in Kennedy, Diana Robertson and Alexandra Walsham, *Grounds of Controversy: Three Studies in Late 16th and Early 17th Century English Polemics* (Melbourne, 1989), 97–126.

preached *The Kings Towre* at the height of these agitations, and two of his fellow St Paul's Cross preachers were imprisoned and reprimanded in the following ten days for criticising the match.[75] The four major editorial discourses with which Purchas interlarded *Hakluytus Posthumus* – 'The Animadversions on the Said Bull of Pope Alexander' (*c.* 1621); 'Virginia's Verger' (1624), written in the aftermath of the 1622 'massacre' of English settlers in Virginia;[76] 'A Large Treatise of King SALOMONS Navie sent from Eziongeber to Ophir' (*c.* 1625); and 'The Churches Peregrination by this Holy Land way … or a Mysterie of Papall iniquitie revealed' (*c.* 1625)[77] – all served the purposes of Purchas's anti-papal polemic. The last two, especially, provided the scheme of sacred time within which English, British and more broadly Protestant enterprise had to be placed.

Purchas's sacred chronology placed the apocalyptic battle between the True Church and the Antichrist firmly in the present rather than the future. He followed post-millennial theologians like John Jewel, James Usher and George Downame to locate the beginnings of the reign of Antichrist in the eleventh century CE, with the succession of the Hildebrandine popes. At this point, Satan had been unbound from his thousand-year captivity, and the temporal pretensions of the Papacy had grown in Italy, in Christendom more generally (where the Papacy asserted the powers of interdiction, excommunication and deposition of princes), and beyond Europe (where it assumed jurisdiction over new-found lands). Those pretensions were nothing less than the signs that the '*mysticall Babylon*' of the Papacy wished to set itself up above those princes whom God had enthroned, and hence that 'the *Man of sinne* might *exalt himselfe above all that is called God*'. This could only be the ambition of the Antichrist who, like Christ himself, embodied a church, the one, true, the other, false.[78] This apocalyptic scheme not only distinguished his project qualitatively from Hakluyt's; it may, in due course, have accounted for its obsolescence, so closely tied was it to the religious polemics of the later Jacobean period.

Purchas's conception of England's place within sacred history ren-

[75] Anthony Milton, *Catholic and Reformed: The Roman and Protestant Churches in English Protestant Thought, 1600–1640* (Cambridge, 1995), 59–60.
[76] For an account of the manuscript of 'Virginia's Verger' see D. R. Ransome (ed.), *Sir Thomas Smith's Misgovernment of the Virginia Company by Nicholas Ferrar* (Cambridge, 1990), xi–xii.
[77] Purchas, *Hakluytus Posthumus*, I, i, 18–25; IV, 1809–26; I, 1–48; II, 1245–71.
[78] Purchas, *Hakluytus Posthumus*, II, 1270, 1271; compare Richard Crakanthorpe, *A Sermon at the Solemnizing of the Happie Inauguration of our Most Gracious and Religious Soveraigne King James* (London, 1609), sig. [G1]ʳ ᵛ.

dered his works at once more elect-nationalist and more cosmopolitan than Hakluyt's. Unlike Hakluyt, who had no conception of the supposed place of England in the scheme of divine election, Purchas identified it as a chosen nation, though not a uniquely chosen one, for it was only one component of *'this Israel* of Great Britaine', the Stuart multiple monarchy. Purchas's conception of that monarchy changed over the course of the 1610s and 1620s, in light of British and Irish colonisation in the Americas and in regard to the prospect of Prince Charles's accession to the thrones of the Three Kingdoms in 1625. For example, in 1613, Purchas hailed the Virginia settlement as a 'New Britaine' and 'the foundation of a *New Britanian* Common-wealth'.[79] Ten years later, in *The Kings Towre*, he marvelled 'how great a part of wide and wilde *America*, is now encompassed with *this*, and [James's] Crowne'. This was an extension of the British monarchy that had been secured by the union of the crowns in 1603, and expanded in turn by the British plantations in Ulster: 'that Trinitie of *England, Scotland, Ireland*, [was] made an unitie' and thereby lost 'the Barbarisme of Borderisme'.[80] Two years later, in *Hakluytus Posthumus*, Purchas tempered this cultural unionism with a federal vision of the British kingdoms' extension across the Atlantic: '(not to mention the *New Wales* there discovered) *England* hath her *Virginia, Bermuda, New England*; *Scotland*, a New Daughter of her owne name; yea, *Ireland* by the care of the present Deputie is now multiplying also in *America*, and his Majestie hath sowne the seedes of New Kingdomes in that New World'.[81] As in the dedication of the *Pilgrimes* to Prince Charles, so here Purchas recognised the impossibility of creating a conjunctively *British* empire that would encompass the Three Kingdoms and their American plantations. The very fact that England, Scotland, Ireland and even Wales were engaged in colonial ventures would ensure their constitutional separation from one another, as their differences were broadcast and transplanted. Nonetheless, they all remained part of a common anti-Catholic bloc within northern Europe – at least, if only the Protestant Irish were considered as loyal Stuart subjects – and could therefore be joined as limbs in the common cause of anti-popery, Christianity and European Christendom. If the British Empire were to have any role in salvation history, it would achieve it through the efforts of its individual members, united within international Calvinism as adversaries of the Roman Church and the great territorial monarchies of contemporary Europe, but not as an apocalyp-

---

[79] Purchas, *Purchas His Pilgrimage*, sig. [¶5]ʳ, 625, 631, 632.
[80] Purchas, *The Kings Towre*, 57, 86 9.   [81] Purchas, *Hakluytus Posthumus*, I, 13.

tic unit claiming a universal mission to be the last empire before the end
of sacred time.

Purchas in turn subsumed the Stuart kingdoms within a more cosmopolitan vision of Europe, defined culturally and religiously. He attributed Europe's primacy over the rest of the world in 'Men, Arts,
[and] Armes' to its peoples' possession and exploitation of the *nova
reperta*: stirrups, guns, the compass and long-distance navigation. These
were the features of a common European enterprise, shared by the
Spanish, the Portuguese, the French and the British in their commercial
and colonial activities: 'Nature hath yeelded herself to *Europaean*
Industry', just as the Americas were 'almost every where admitting
Europaean colonies'.[82] Yet Christianity – even, and perhaps particularly
the divided Christendom bequeathed by the Reformation – was the
fundamental marker of European distinction, and the guarantee of
Europe's special place within sacred history: 'Here are [God's] Scriptures, Oratories, Sacraments, Ministers, Mysteries. Here that Mysticall
Babylon, and that Papacie (if that bee any glory) which challengeth both
the Bishopricke and Empire of the World; and here the victory over that
Beast (this indeed is glory) by *Christian* Reformation according to the
Scriptures.'[83] This conception of European Christendom was neither
triumphalist nor optimistic. Instead, Purchas's researches into the religions of the world, contained in *Purchas His Pilgrimage* and *Purchas His
Pilgrim*, convinced him that Christianity was in retreat compared to
Islam: 'it is (in comparison) but a small part of the world, that soundeth
the sacred name of JESUS'. The prospects for Christian renewal were bleak
so long as Christendom remained divided, and the Papacy powerful: 'so
little a part of the World in name *Christian*! and so little not covered over
... with Antichristian Heresie!'[84]

Protestants in general might be the saving remnant within a contracting Christendom, but British Protestants had no special election among
them, and were as embattled as any. In the face of a Catholic league,
and in the knowledge that Christendom as a whole was contracting, it
was essential to maintain a common front among Protestants, and even
to recognise the commonalities among all members of the Catholic
Christian Church, whether Roman or otherwise. In pursuit of the first

[82] Purchas, *Hakluytus Posthumus*, I, 90–4; Denys Hay, *Europe: The Emergence of an Idea*, 2nd edn
(Edinburgh, 1968), 120–1.
[83] Purchas, *Hakluytus Posthumus*, I, 93.
[84] Purchas, *Purchas His Pilgrimage*, I, sigs. [¶4]ᵛ–[¶5]ʳ; Purchas, *Purchas His Pilgrim: Microcosmos, or The
Historie of Man* (London, 1619), 680, 701.

aim, Purchas had to exculpate the Protestant Dutch for their attacks on English merchants in the East Indies. The Amboyna massacre of 1623, in which Dutch officials in Indonesia executed ten English merchants, provoked a major crisis in Anglo-Dutch relations and hence within international Calvinism itself at the outset of the Thirty Years War. Purchas added a preface to *Hakluytus Posthumus* to explain that the English East India Company had made it necessary to mention the regrettable incident; in the spirit of Jacobean Protestant irenicism, he argued that the particular faults of individual Dutchmen could not be taken as general failings of the Dutch as a whole: 'these are personall faults of that East *Indie* Company, or some Commanders there, not of the whole Nation'.[85]

In his treatments of Spain, the Dutch and the strategic competition between the embattled forces of Protestantism and the threat of an anti-Christian Catholic league, Purchas carefully traversed the treacherous and often contradictory arguments of Jacobean foreign policy. During the last six years of James's reign (1619–25) – that is, in the period when Purchas wrote, compiled and published almost all of his major works – English foreign policy was markedly hispanophile, to the horror of militant Protestants, such as Purchas's patron, archbishop Abbot.[86] Support for the Protestant cause in Europe took on an ideological cast that identified the supporter with the opposition to James. Purchas trod the fine line of opposition to the Catholic cause and support for royal policy by directing his polemical fire against the Papacy as the Antichrist, rather than against the Spanish Monarchy itself. In the same way, his measured response to the Amboyna massacre upheld the integrity of the fragile Protestant cause without any denial of guilt on the part of the Dutch East India Company. The political subtlety of Purchas's negotiation of these disputes contrasts with the uninflected antihispanism of Hakluyt. The intensely local complexity of late Jacobean foreign policy, with its impact upon public opinion and thence upon Purchas's major works, may provide another reason for Purchas's inassimilability to later, starker narratives of the origins of the British Empire in unadulterated Elizabethan opposition to Spain.

Purchas's use of Spanish sources in fact strengthened his anti-popery.

[85] Purchas, *Hakluytus Posthumus*, I, sig. [¶6]ᵛ.
[86] On the foreign policy of this period see especially Simon Adams, 'Spain or the Netherlands? The Dilemmas of Early Stuart Foreign Policy', in Howard Tomlinson (ed.), *Before the English Civil War: Essays on Early Stuart Politics and Government* (London, 1983), 79–101, and for public reaction to it, Thomas Cogswell, *The Blessed Revolution: English Politics and the Coming of War, 1621–1624* (Cambridge, 1989).

This was not because he, like Hakluyt and others, could draw upon the
Black Legend of Spanish atrocities in the New World that was founded
in the writings of conscientious Spanish authors like Las Casas;[87] rather,
it was because he found an ally against papal universalism – and, hence,
the juridical claims of the Spanish Monarchy – in the *relectiones* of the
Spanish Thomist theologian, Francisco de Vitoria. In fact, Purchas was
the early-modern British writer who showed the greatest familiarity with
Vitoria's writings, and who made the most frequent use of them in his
assaults on the legitimacy of the papal authority by which Spanish rights
of *dominium* in the Americas had been asserted. In the *Pilgrimage*, he used
Vitoria's *relectio De Indis* (1539), 2.5, to argue for the injustice of the
Spanish presence in the Americas on the grounds that the 'Christian
Religion had [not] beene propounded in a meet sort to the Indians', and
hence the Spanish claim to *dominium* based on the mission to evangelise
was, for this and other reasons, illegitimate.[88] Elsewhere, he cited
Vitoria's *relectio De Potestate Civili* (1528), 1.5, to prove that all power comes
from God, not from the community, and hence that resistance to the
powers that be was disobedience to divine command.[89] Most decisively,
he twice cited Vitoria's first *relectio De Potestate Ecclesiæ* (1532), 5.1, to show
that the Pope has no *dominium* over the lands of the infidel, since he only
has power within the Church. This was the key to Vitoria's case '[t]hat
the Pope is not Lord of the World, [and] That the Temporall Power
depends not of him'.[90] This, in turn, provided a refutation of the
argument that dominion depends upon grace, and hence that infidelity
can justify dispossession, 'as if all the world were holden of the Pope in
Catholike fee', to which Purchas added the marginal note: 'Read also a
Spanish divine *Fr. à Victoria* in his *Relect. de Pot. Ecc. & de Indis*, He with
many arguments confuteth this pretended power of the Pope'.[91] Purchas's anti-popery was not therefore solely a reflex of his politics or a
conventional and unexamined puritan binary, nor was it simply a
function of his ecclesiology. It may have served political purposes in the
international turmoil of the early 1620s, and confirmed his position as a

---

[87] *Pace* the dismissive comments in William S. Maltby, *The Black Legend in England: The Development of Anti-Spanish Sentiment, 1558–1660* (Durham, NC, 1971), 26–7, 71–2.
[88] Purchas, *Purchas His Pilgrimage*, 750 (compare Purchas, *Hakluytus Posthumus*, I, ii, 23); Francisco de Vitoria, *De Indis* (1539), 2–5, in *Vitoria: Political Writings*, ed. Anthony Pagden and Jeremy Lawrance (Cambridge, 1991), 271.
[89] Purchas, *Hakluytus Posthumus*, I, 15; Vitoria, *De Potestate Civili* (1528), 1.5, in *Vitoria: Political Writings*, ed. Pagden and Lawrance, 16 (quoting also Romans 13).
[90] Purchas, *Hakluytus Posthumus*, I, 16; I, ii, 23; Vitoria, I *De Potestate Ecclesiæ* (1532), 5.1, in *Vitoria: Political Writings*, ed. Pagden and Lawrance, 84 (quoting I Corinthians 5: 12).
[91] Purchas, *Hakluytus Posthumus*, I, 16.

defender of the Protestant cause in Europe. However, it was far from unreflective and depended instead upon originally Thomist anti-papal (and anti-Lutheran) arguments that could be turned as easily against Protestants as Roman Catholics, in pursuit of conformity at home and legitimate rights of possession abroad.

Purchas's publications were therefore consistently anti-papal and only incidentally anti-Spanish. To deny the legitimacy of papal donation was not to deny the legitimacy of Spanish possessions in the New World. Purchas confessed, 'I question not the Right of the Spanish Crowne in those parts: *Quis me constituit judicem?* ... I quarrell the Pope onely', thereby echoing Hakluyt, who nearly forty years earlier had repeated Jesus's question.[92] This judicious reluctance to adjudicate was of a piece with Purchas's delicate compromises elsewhere in his works. Though he shared the apprehension of his patron, archbishop Abbot, that the Roman Catholic Church was not a true church, and was indeed the embodiment of the Antichrist, he also tried to sustain a common Christian front against infidelity, in Europe and in the wider world. The expansion of commerce would be the conduit of Christianity, and would aid the realisation of Purchas's cosmopolitan vision, in which 'so many Nations as so many persons hold commerce and intercourse of amitie withall ... the West with the East, and the remotest parts of the world are joyned in one band of humanitie, and why not also to Christianitie?'[93] Similarly, though Purchas successfully avoided giving offence to the authorities during the *bouleversements* of late Jacobean foreign policy towards the Dutch and the Spanish, he did attempt to open up juridical space within which the subjects of the Three Kingdoms could make their own claims both against competing European colonial powers and against the native Americans. Moreover, he reconciled the potentially colliding claims of those kingdoms by proposing a federal vision of a British union that had been secured by the accession of the Stuarts to the thrones of England and Ireland after 1603. In all of these fraught reconciliations, Purchas turned to a wide array of intellectual resources to provide a theologically informed, politically nuanced and constantly revised vision of Britain, its overseas possessions, and the wider context of sacred and secular time within which they operated.

[92] Purchas, 'Animadversions on the Bull', in *Hakluytus Posthumus*, I, i, 20; compare Hakluyt, *Particuler Discourse*, ed. Quinn and Quinn, 96: 'our saviour Christe beinge requested and intreated to make a laufull devision of inheritaunce betwene one and his brother, refused to do yt, sayenge Quis me constituit Judicem inter vos?' (quoting Luke 12: 13–14).
[93] Purchas, *Hakluytus Posthumus*, I, 20–1.

The contextual complexity of Purchas's political and theological commitments proved inassimilable in later periods, just as his enormous compilations became increasingly indigestible. His later position as a progenitor of the British Empire owed more to his reputation as a compiler of narratives than to his editorial arguments; however, those arguments deserve to be taken more seriously, not only to recover Purchas from the condescension of posterity, but also to reveal just how little part an apocalyptic conception of the British Empire would play in the future, as the theologically reticent Hakluyt would be consistently preferred to the more intellectually eclectic Purchas. Each would be assimilated to the other as editors rather than as colonial theorists, and valued more as compilers than as philosophers. Only belatedly, in the Victorian era, would they be recovered as progenitors of the British Empire; for the intervening two centuries, John Locke's lukewarm commendation may stand: 'To geography, books of travel may be added. In that kind the collections made by our countrymen, Hakluyt and Purchas, are very good.'[94]

Despite their differing conceptions of history and of religion, of England and of Britain, Hakluyt and Purchas did agree that the first task of any argument in favour of English or British colonisation should be the refutation of the papal donation of the Americas to Spain, and hence the Papacy's powers of disposing dominion more generally. The rebuttal of such arguments for the scope of papal authority in secular matters both of sovereignty and property was not, of course, an exclusively Protestant enterprise, as Purchas's use of Vitoria's *relectiones* showed. However, once Spanish claims to *dominium* on the basis of the papal bulls had been refuted, it was still necessary for English (and Scottish) proponents of colonisation to provide alternative justifications for their rights of property and sovereignty in the Americas, especially. The effort to provide such justifications demanded the elaboration of arguments for *dominium* consistent with Protestant doctrine, but not solely reliant upon it; however, across the course of the seventeenth century, from Purchas to Locke, such arguments consistently avoided any appeal to what Purchas had seen as the 'Anabaptist' as much as Roman Catholic argument that '*Dominion is founded in grace*' (as Locke put it), and hence that rights of

[94] John Locke, 'Some Thoughts Concerning Study and Reading for a Gentleman' (1703), in *Locke: Political Essays*, ed. Mark Goldie (Cambridge, 1997), 353. (My thanks to Daniel Carey for this reference.) For Locke's ownership of works by Hakluyt and Purchas see John Harrison and Peter Laslett, *The Library of John Locke*, 2nd edn (Oxford, 1971), items 1374, 2409.

property derived from the state of the possessor's soul, just as the soteriological state of the dispossessed could provide justification for their dispossession. As the concluding section of this chapter will show, the ideological origins of the British Empire were identifiably Protestant only in so far as they related to rights of possession, and not as they informed the empire with a saving mission, a particular place within eschatological time or a distinctive location within what Locke called 'the Sacred Geography'.[95]

Hakluyt, in the 'Particuler Discourse', differed from his successors in his espousal of a version of the argument that dominion depended upon grace. In his refutation of the papal disposing power, Hakluyt charged that Alexander VI had mistaken the order of his priorities in donating the newly-discovered lands to the Spanish Monarchy: rather than charge the Spanish king with a mission to evangelise the pagans, he should first have preached to them himself; if they refused obstinately to repent,

> he mighte have pronounced the severe and heavie judgemente of God againste them shewinge out of the worde of God that one kingdomme is translated from another for the sinnes of the Inhabitantes of the same, and that God in his justice woulde surely bring somme nation or other upon them to take vengeaunce of their synnes and wickednes.[96]

In this form, Hakluyt's argument was in part a version of the classic Calvinist theory that God may send bad rulers as scourges to punish a wicked people; however, he went on to support the papal claim to depose kings and dispose kingdoms – just the power that Purchas, and all later Protestant theorists, denied that the Papacy possessed, whether in the New World or elsewehere.[97] For Purchas, the papal assertion of deposing made Protestants 'more happy than baptized Kings: for we may enjoy our Possessions, our Professions as more free, at least not impaired by Baptisme'. With the threat of such power hanging over Catholic princes, it might in fact be better not to be baptised at all. Hypocrites and heathens might have only a 'Naturall right' to their property, while Christians had 'publike and private civill rights and tenures', argued Purchas, but that distinction did not empower

[95] Purchas, *Hakluytus Posthumus*, I, 16; IV, 1810; John Locke, *A Letter Concerning Toleration* (1685), ed. James H. Tully (Indianapolis, 1983), 50, 35; Pagden, *Lords of All the World*, 47–8.
[96] Hakluyt, *Particuler Discourse*, ed. Quinn and Quinn, 99–100.
[97] Hakluyt, *Particuler Discourse*, ed. Quinn and Quinn, 100: 'the Popes can shewe goodd Recordes that they have deposed Emperors, y^t they have translated Empires from one people to another ... and that they have taken kingdommes from one nation and gaven them to another'.

dispossession, 'for they are villains not to us: but to our and their Lorde'.[98]

Hakluyt, Purchas and their contemporaries faced the dilemma of justifying European possessions in the absence of any claims to papal donation, or the derivation of *dominium* from grace. For both Hakluyt and Purchas, the argument began with the authority of English land-holders and the English Crown in Ireland, rather than comparable claims in America. Roman Catholic critics of Protestant arguments for *dominium* attempted to show that Spain's claims in the New World were as well grounded as English claims in Ireland because both relied upon papal donation: the Spanish, upon the Alexandrine bulls of 1493; the English, upon the bull *Laudabiliter* of 1156. In reply, both Hakluyt and Purchas denied that English rights of property or authority in Ireland descended from such donation. As Hakluyt noted, the bull was promulgated after Henry II's invasion, and had anyway been ignored by the Irish kings. Those kings had voluntarily submitted in 1171, added Purchas, and the English conquest had been completed in 1186: 'by his Sword', added Purchas, 'not the Popes Keyes ... together with the submission of the Irish, [the English] obtayned that Soveraigntie'. English claims in Ireland had thereafter been based upon submission, conquest and prescription, just as Spanish claims in the Americas depended upon 'Discoverie ... the Sword, Prescription, subjection of the Inhabitants, long and quiet Possession'.[99] Purchas's theoretical interest in such claims extended only so far as they could be applied to European – not least British – assertions of *dominium* in the New World, particularly against the claims of the native population. Whether they could be sufficient to ensure enduring title was another matter, for the case of Ireland was hardly reassuring: as Sir John Davies had noted in 1612, 'the conquest was but slight and superficial, so the pope's donation and the Irish submissions were but weak and fickle assurances'.[100]

In comparison with five hundred years of English involvement in Ireland, the halting attempts by the English to plant in Virginia since the 1580s demanded far more strenuous justification. The records of a conciliar debate *in utramque partem* from the Council of the Virginia Company in 1607–8 reveal the constraints within which early seven-

[98] Purchas, *Hakluytus Posthumus*, I, ii, 25; IV, 1810 (marginal note: 'Christians may not spoile Heathens').

[99] Hakluyt, *Particuler Discourse*, ed. Quinn and Quinn, 100; Purchas, *Hakluytus Posthumus*, I, ii, 21, 20.

[100] Sir John Davies, *A Discovery of the True Causes Why Ireland Was Never Entirely Subdued [And] Brought Under Obedience of the Crown of England Until the Beginning of His Majesty's Happy Reign* (1612), ed. James P. Myers, Jr (Washington, DC, 1988), 74.

teenth-century argument operated, especially in so far as such argument
had to be consonant with Protestant Christianity. Those who supported
the production of a document to reassure investors 'of ye Justice of y^e
action' took their rhetorical task to be a twofold one, to show that English
justifications were 'not only comparatively to be as good as ye Spaniards
... but absolutely to be good agaynst ye Naturall people'. This entailed
the refutation of the 'Donation of Alexander, which is so grounded upon
the principles of theyr religion that some of their best authors have
pronounced yt Heresy to doubt yt'; it also demanded ideological justifications that, in turn, would provide a more secure foundation for English
rights of both *imperium* and *dominium* than those the Spanish had relied
upon. One participant recapitulated the history of Spanish arguments
for dispossession since the early sixteenth century to show that even the
battery of intellectual resources marshalled by the Spanish Church, the
religious orders, and civil and canon lawyers had been incapable of
providing secure justifications for both *imperium* and *dominium*. Originally,
the Spanish Crown had employed neo-Aristotelian arguments 'to pros-
ecute ye Indians as Barbar's, and therby Naturally slaves':

> When after 50 years his fryars declyn'd him from that severe and unJust course,
> and he labourd by men of all learninge to provide himselfe of a more acceptable
> title, all ye reasons, which were prepared to him, by men of discourse, from y^e
> Indians transgressing ye Law of Nature; from his Civilians for their denying
> commerce: from his Canonists by ye Donation: and from his Devines, by
> propogation of religion, ... can be gathered for him no title, of Dominion or
> Property, but only a Magistracy, and Empiry, by which he is allowed to remove
> such impediments, as they had agaynst ye knowledge of Religion.[101]

This astute summary of the Spanish debate over dispossessing the
barbarian concluded with the dilemma that would also bedevil the
English and Scottish Crowns, and their chartered agents, in their efforts
to justify colonies in North America. Arguments derived from the civil
or religious incapacity of the Indians might be sufficient, under the
terms of a donation or charter which charged the necessity of conversion, to support claims of 'a Magistracy, and Empire', but did so in the
face of almost universal agreement that grace does not confer 'title, of
Dominion or Property'.[102] In light of the Spanish example, the company

---

[101] 'Reasons against the publishinge of the Kinges title to Virginia' (*c.* 1607–08), Bod. MS Tanner
93, f. 200, printed in D. B. Quinn (ed.), *New American World: A Documentary History of North America
to 1612*, 5 vols. (New York, 1979), III, 418–19.
[102] Anthony Pagden, 'Dispossessing the Barbarian: The Language of Spanish Thomism and the
Debate over the Property Rights of the American Indians', in Pagden (ed.), *Languages of Political
Theory in Early-Modern Europe*, 82–8.

decided not to offer a full-scale official defence of its *dominium* or its *imperium* in Virginia. That task, at least in the case of the Virginia settlement, would be left to an eclectic cast of promoters, preachers and propagandists who would, in due course, like the Spanish, have to retreat from their original arguments and search for an ideological justification for settlement that could overcome the crisis generated by that initial eclecticism.[103] The problem of uniting *dominium* and *imperium* would persist, however, as the fundamental and ultimately combustible dilemma at the core of British imperial ideology.

Biblical precedents provided ambivalent charters for the Scots and the English to oppose the papal donation. God's commands in the book of Genesis to subdue the earth and to go forth and multiply provided justifications for emigration and settlement in the New World on the grounds that they were issued to all mankind, not simply to Adam or to Abraham and his seed (Genesis 1:28, 9:1).[104] Combined with the other two most frequently cited texts from the New Testament, Matthew 24:14 (that the Gospel might be preached throughout the whole world to prepare for the last days) and Mark 13:10 (that it should be published among all nations), scriptural precedent could sanction the English to 'plant as well as preach, and . . . subdue as well as teach', in the words of Richard Eburne.[105] Protestant theorists, in particular, were keen to prove from scripture the legitimacy of any emigration and plantation. The first recorded 'deduction and plantacion of a Colonie' was that of the Jews under Moses, though even that was only a divinely-aided example of a process of multiplication and migration that had populated the whole world since the Flood.[106] The problem with such arguments, reassuring though they may have been to those who doubted the scriptural basis for colonisation, whether in Ireland or North America, was that they were not solely applicable to Protestants. If there were indeed a divine command to subdue the earth, to multiply and to

---

[103] Fitzmaurice, 'The Civic Solution to the Crisis of English Colonization', 34–43.

[104] John Cotton, *God's Promise to His Plantation* (London, 1630), 5–6; [John White,] *The Planters Plea* (London, 1630), 1.

[105] Richard Eburne, *A Plaine Pathway to Plantations* (London, 1624) 7; compare George Benson, *A Sermon Preached at Paules Crosse the Seaventh of May, M.DC.IX* (London, 1609), 92.

[106] 'Certeyn Notes & Observations Touching the Deducing & Planting of Colonies' (*c.* 1607–09), BL MS Cotton Titus B. x, f. 402ᵛ; Alexander, *Encouragement to Colonies*, 1–2; Eburne, *Plaine Pathway to Plantations*, ed. Wright, 41–2, 57–8, 102, 111, 126; [White,] *The Planters Plea*, 1–2; Sir Robert Gordon of Lochinvar, *Encouragements. For Such as Shall Have Intention to Bee Undertakers in the New Plantation of CAPE BRITON, Now New Galloway, in America* (Edinburgh, 1625), sig. B[1]ʳ⁻ᵛ; [William Vaughan,] *The Golden Fleece . . . Transported from Cambrioll Colchos, Out of the Southermost Part of the Iland, Commonly Called Newfoundland* (London, 1626), pt III, 34.

exercise dominion over all creatures, that command had been addressed to all of humanity, not any particular portion of it. This did not,
of course, render such proofs untenable by British Protestant proponents of colonisation; however, they were clearly insufficient as arguments against the claims of other European monarchies, even if they
could be turned to account against the native populations.

Apprehensions of the eschatological significance of British settlement
remained largely distinct from justifications for possession or sovereignty. The most important early seventeenth-century English millenarian, Joseph Mede, speculated in his *Clavis Apocalyptica* (1627) that the
armies of Gog and Magog of Revelation 20:8–9 would rise up from 'the
Hemisphere against us', that is, from the Americas. When an anxious
clerical correspondent, William Twisse, asked Mede whether the New
World, lately revealed by providence, would be the New Jerusalem or
Gog and Magog, Mede replied to the query by distinguishing between
the legitimacy of the plantations and their place in sacred time: 'Concerning our Plantation in the *American* world, I wish them as well as any
body; though I differ from them far, both in other things, and in the
grounds they go upon.' Mede expressed little hope that the native
peoples could be converted to Christianity, not least because he thought
them a colony of Satan's choosing, brought from the north into America. It would be appropriate to 'affront' Satan in North America by
planting Protestants, but this in itself could not provide adequate
'grounds' for the English colonies to 'go upon'.[107] Even those, like the
Dorchester patriarch, John White, who did identify the New World as a
place to 'raise a bulworke against ye kingdom of antichrist wch ye Jesuits
labour to rere in all parts of ye world', did not suggest that the English
Church alone had an exclusive mission: 'the church since christs tyme is
to be considered universall without respect of countrey'. To remove to
New England would not therefore be a desertion of the English Church,
but rather the edification of one 'particular church' as a branch of the
church universal.[108] However justifiable such an action might be in

---

[107] Joseph Mede, *The Works of the Pious and Profoundly-Learned Joseph Mede, B.D.* (London, 1664), 713
('A Conjecture Concerning Gog and Magog in the Revelation'), 979 (Twisse to Mede, 2 March
1635), 980 (Mede to Twisse, 23 March 1635). On the Mede–Twisse correspondence see
especially John Bowman, 'Is America the New Jerusalem or Gog and Magog? A Seventeenth
Century Theological Discussion', *Proceedings of the Leeds Philosophical and Literary Society*, 6 (1950),
445–52, and J. A. de Jong, *As the Waters Cover the Sea: Millennial Expectations in the Rise of
Anglo-American Missions 1640–1810* (Kampen, 1970), 25–6.

[108] [John White,] 'General Observations for ye Plantation of New England' (1632?), PRO co 1/6,
ff. 172^r–73^r, printed in Frances Rose-Troup, *John White, The Patriarch of Dorchester and the Founder of
Massachusetts 1575–1648* (London, 1930), 424, 425; [White,] *The Planters Plea*, 6–9, 17.

order to spread the Gospel, it, too, did not provide any grounds for English colonies to go upon.

Even John Winthrop, during his dispute with Roger Williams over English land-claims in Massachusetts, admitted this in defence of English *dominium* and the Crown's *imperium* in New England. Williams had charged that all of the English settlers 'lye under a synne of unjust usurpation upon others possessions', to which Winthrop replied: 'our title to what we possesse: it is not Religious (as he supposethe) neither dothe our Kinge challenge any right heer by his Christianyty'. But, on this point at least, Williams agreed with Winthrop: the 'great sin' in the New England patents was the point 'wherein Christian Kinds (so calld) are invested with Right by Virtue of their Christianitie, to take and give away the Lands and Countries of other men'.[109]

The divine commands in Genesis, and the injunctions of the Gospels, together encouraged and legitimated migration and even evangelisation. However, neither argument could provide a foundation for exclusive *dominium*, or the grounds for secular *imperium*, not least because they applied in the first instance to all human beings, and in the second, to all Christians. Christianity alone, as Winthrop and Williams agreed, could not be a sufficient basis for title to land or sovereignty. The claim that God's grant of the earth to Adam (Genesis 1:28) authorised all succeeding humans to spread across the face of the earth paralleled Sir Robert Filmer's argument that this divine commission had made Adam monarch of the whole world, and his successors absolute monarchs.[110] Locke, in the first *Treatise of Government* (*c.* 1681), accused Filmer of thereby confounding *imperium* with *dominium*, and further denied that 'by this Grant God gave him not *Private Dominion* over the Inferior Creatures, but right in common with all Mankind; so neither was he *Monarch*, upon the account of the Property here given him'.[111] Mere succession from Adam would not be argument enough for either absolute monarchy or rights of dominion.

[109] John Winthrop to John Endecott, 3 January 1634, in *Winthrop Papers: III 1631–1637* (Boston, 1943), 147, 148; John Cotton, *Master John Cottons Reply to Master Roger Williams* (1647), in *The Complete Writings of Roger Williams*, 7 vols. (New York, 1963), II, 44–7; Williams, *The Bloody Tenent Yet More Bloody* (1652), in Williams, *Complete Writings*, IV, 461. On the context of the Williams–Winthrop dispute see Jennings, *Invasion of America*, 138–44, and Moynihan, 'The Patent and the Indians', 9–11.

[110] Sir Robert Filmer, *Patriarcha* (*c.* 1632) and *Observations Upon Aristotles Politiques* (1652), in *Filmer: Patriarcha and Other Writings*, ed. Johann P. Sommerville (Cambridge, 1991), 7, 281–2 (citing John Selden, *Mare Clausum seu De Dominio Maris* (London, 1635), Bk I, ch. 4).

[111] John Locke, *First Treatise of Government* (*c.* 1681), §24, in *Locke: Two Treatises of Government*, ed. Peter Laslett, rev. edn (Cambridge, 1988), 157; James Tully, *A Discourse on Property: John Locke and His Adversaries* (Cambridge, 1980), 60.

The 'naturall right to replenish the whole earth' as derived from the divine injunctions of Genesis could still provide a charter for settlement, but only if such settlement took place in 'vacant places' (as Purchas put it).[112] This argument added a scriptural command to the agriculturalist justification for colonisation first propounded by Sir Thomas More in 1516, and repeated by Rowland White and the Smiths in Elizabethan Ulster. From the 1620s to the 1680s in Britain, and then in North America, Australia and Africa well into the nineteenth century, the argument from vacancy (*vacuum domicilium*) or absence of ownership (*terra nullius*) became a standard foundation for English and, later, British dispossession of indigenous peoples.[113] On these grounds, God's commands to replenish the earth and assert dominion over it provided a superior right to possession for those who cultivated the land more productively than others, and hence who adopted a sedentary, agricultural existence on the land.

The most extensive presentation of this argument was, of course, John Locke's, in the fifth chapter of the *Second Treatise of Government*. As James Tully and others have shown, Locke was heir to the tradition of agriculturalist theorising derived from his seventeenth-century Protestant predecessors, as he elaborated a justification for rights of *dominium* that would hold equally well in England and America. What other commentators seem not to have noticed, however, is that one reason Locke needed to provide such an argument was that he had also offered a compelling refutation of the argument that dominion conferred grace in the *Letter Concerning Toleration* (1685), when he argued that such a claim depended upon the wider argument that the civil power has authority in matters of conscience: admit that, and there could be no limit to the powers of the civil magistrate. 'No man whatsoever ought therefore to be deprived of his Terrestrial Enjoyments, upon account of his Religion', Locke argued,

Not even *Americans*, subjected unto a Christian Prince, are to be punished either in Body or in Goods for not imbracing our Faith and Worship. If they are perswaded that they please God in observing the Rites of their own Country,

---

[112] Purchas, *Hakluytus Posthumus*, IV, 1811.

[113] On the progress of this argument, and especially its relevance to Locke, see James Tully, 'Rediscovering America: The *Two Treatises* and Aboriginal Rights', in Tully, *An Approach to Political Philosophy: Locke in Contexts* (Cambridge, 1993), 149–55, 166–71; Barbara Arneil, *John Locke and America: The Defence of English Colonialism* (Oxford, 1996), 109–17, 141–3; Alan Frost, 'New South Wales as *Terra Nullius*: The British Denial of Aboriginal Land Rights', *Historical Studies*, 19 (1981), 513–23; and, more generally, Kent McNeil, *Common Law Aboriginal Title* (Oxford, 1989).

and that they shall obtain Happiness by that means, they are to be left unto God and themselves.

The application of such an argument was universal: 'For the reason of the thing is equal, both in *America* and *Europe*'.[114] Just as there could be no disposing power attributed to the Papacy, so no European prince could be allowed any right of possession on grounds of religious belief alone, not even the English. As Locke (and others) reaffirmed in 'The Constitutions of Carolina' of 1669, 'since ye Natives of yt place who will be concernd in o^r Plantation are utterly strangers to Christianity whose Idollatry Ignorance or mistake gives us noe right to expell or use y^m ill'.[115] Other foundations, and better justification, would have to be found to justify rights of *dominium* in the New World, and the agriculturalist argument, with its scriptural foundations, and its apparent applicability to the perceived social structure of the Amerindians, offered just such an argument, with enduring effects for later theories of property. Locke's may therefore have been the first, and perhaps only, theory of property in seventeenth-century England that was explicitly Protestant in its orientation (without falling into the error of equating grace with fitness for dominion) and applicable to colonial as well as municipal contexts.

In the long run, '[t]he real issue ... was not private ownership but public sovereignty', however, and hence *imperium*, not *dominium*.[116] This was not a question susceptible to a specifically Protestant answer, though its solution was attempted by many Protestants, often ordained ones, from the 1580s to the 1680s and beyond. Hakluyt's exposition of Aristotle and his Thomistic commentators, Purchas's reliance on Vitoria, and the Virginia Company's intimate interests in the history of Spanish colonial ideology together attested the impossibility of deriving any specifically and exclusively Protestant origins for British imperial ideology. Similarly, Hakluyt's lack of interest in the dimensions of sacred time, doctrines of election or eschatology more generally, and Purchas's cosmopolitan refusal to identify England, or Britain, as a peculiarly 'elect' nation, prevented any easy assimilation of their foundational

---

[114] Locke, *Letter Concerning Toleration*, ed. Tully, 43.

[115] [John Locke, *et al.*,] 'The Constitutions of Carolina' (21 July 1669), PRO 30/24/47/3, ff. 58–9, printed in *Locke: Political Essays*, ed. Goldie, 178; *The Fundamental Constitutions of Carolina* (n.p., n.d. [London, 1672]), 18. On the authorship of the 'Constitutions', and the dating of the printed version, see John Milton, 'John Locke and the Fundamental Constitutions of Carolina', *Locke Newsletter*, 21 (1990), 111–33.

[116] Thomas Flanagan, 'The Agricultural Argument and Original Appropriation: Indian Lands and Political Philosophy', *Canadian Journal of Political Science*, 22 (1989), 602; compare Jennings, *Invasion of America*, 138–40.

works to a conception of the British Empire as a millennial vehicle or
even as a community defined by any precise definition of Protestantism.
Finally, the eclectic use of the Bible, as much as the impossibility of
finding any specifically Protestant justifications for migration and settlement, provided only common Christian justifications for British colonisation. In sum, there were no identifiably and exclusively Protestant
origins of British imperial ideology, and a religious genealogy for the
British Empire would not emerge until the early eighteenth century, in
the bishop-bibliographer White Kennett's *Bibliothecæ Americanæ Primordiæ*
(1713).[117] Britons, as much as Europeans, had to face the disarming fact
that their sacred resources, as much as their secular ones, provided no
convincing means of squaring the circle by justifying *imperium* and
dominium at the same time, and interdependently. For this reason, the
ideological origins of the British Empire remained fissured and unstable
as much because of, as in spite of, the contribution of Protestantism.

[117] [Kennett], *Bibliothecæ Americanæ Primordiæ*, ix, and *passim*; on Kennett's enterprise see G. V.
Bennett, *White Kennett, 1660–1728* (London, 1957), 192.

CHAPTER 4

The empire of the seas, 1576–1689

... who ever is Dominus Maris, may eo Titulo clayme dominion in & over all ye Navigable waters of ye whole world, wch have communication & Interfluence with each other.[1]

Even more persistent and reassuring than the Protestant myth of the origins of the British Empire was the belief that it was an empire of the seas. The conventional chronology of the Empire's origins, which located them in the reign of Elizabeth I, nourished that belief and anchored it in a particular maritime history. The originating agents of empire were the Elizabethan sea-dogs, Gloriana's sailor-heroes who had circumnavigated the globe, singed the King of Spain's beard, swept the oceans of pirates and Catholics, and thereby opened up the sea-routes across which English migrants would travel, and English trade would flow, until Britannia majestically ruled the waves. The myth was persistent not least because it enshrined an inescapable truth: the British Empire *was* an empire of the seas, and without the Royal Navy's mastery of the oceans, it could never have become the global empire upon which the sun never set. Yet that maritime mastery was not complete until the end of the Napoleonic Wars, and the force of the myth derives in large part from the nineteenth-century celebration of an oceanic hegemony whose origins were traced back to the exploits of Drake, Hawkins and Ralegh. The myth was reassuring, not least in the two centuries before the Victorian zenith of the British Empire, because it served to distinguish the Empire from the territorial empires of antiquity (especially Rome's) and from contemporary land-empires such as the Holy Roman Empire or the Spanish Monarchy's possessions in the Americas. An empire of the seas would not be prey to the overextension and military dictatorship which had hastened the col-

[1] Sir William Petty, ['Dominion of the Sea'] (1687), BL Add. MS 72865, f. 120^r (also in BL MS Lansdowne 1228, f. 59^r).

lapse of the Roman Empire, nor would it bring the tyranny, depopulation and impoverishment which had hastened the decline of Spain. The British empire of the seas was both historically novel and comparatively benign; it could therefore escape the compulsions that destroyed all previous land-based, and hence obviously military, empires. In short, it could be an empire for liberty.

This enduring and encouraging myth was largely responsible for the *cordon sanitaire* erected between the history of the metropolitan state and the history of an empire defined by its ultramarine existence. It was enduring precisely because it provided both metropolitans and provincials with a bridge between the constituent parts of the Empire; it was encouraging because it also divided the provinces and the metropole, allowing the former a degree of autonomy and the latter a prophylactic against the debilitating infections of extensive empire. These characteristics may also explain why British maritime ideology has been so little studied, and why its genesis has not been investigated historically.[2] The geographical fact of Britain's insularity implied that it would naturally become a maritime power, at once distinct from the 'Continent' of Europe and linked oceanically to its extra-European empire. Because Britain's maritime destiny seemed compelled by nature, it was by definition beyond historical analysis; similarly, because Britain's natural situation divided it physically from the rest of Europe, its history could be seen as unavoidably exceptional. A fact so stubborn could hardly be historical; a history so exceptional was inassimilable to other European norms. British naval mastery came to seem as inevitable as the expansion of the British Empire, and each would be subject to the same complacent amnesia. If the myth indeed had a history, it would become more contingent and hence less inspiring.

The conventional narrative of British maritime history has tended to follow the history of the rise and fall of British naval mastery. It has therefore been most often told as a story of the influence of sea-power upon history, in the manner of Alfred Thayer Mahan, or, conversely, as a study of the influence of history – meaning economics, politics and strategy – upon sea-power.[3] Only recently has the history of Britain itself been considered as a naval history, tied to the chronology of the history of

<hr>

[2] The only book-length study of this mythology is Cynthia Fansler Behrman, *Victorian Myths of the Sea* (Athens, Ohio, 1977); an important analysis of, and contribution to, the myth is Carl Schmitt, *Land and Sea* (1942), trans. Simona Draghici (Washington, DC, 1997).

[3] A. T. Mahan, *The Influence of Sea Power upon History 1660–1783* (Boston, 1890); Paul Kennedy, *The Rise and Fall of British Naval Mastery* (London, 1976).

the Three Kingdoms and, not least, that of their territorial waters.[4] To rewrite British history in this way is idiomatic for the late sixteenth and seventeenth centuries, for it was then that debates about the extent and form of the British kingdoms, and the limits of monarchical *imperium* and *dominium*, often turned on disputes regarding maritime jurisdiction. Both the realm of England and the kingdom of the Scots were defined oceanically as well as territorially, and on occasion they collided with one another in the definitions of their respective boundaries. Claims to jurisdiction over the foreshore, home waters, fishing and navigation around Britain were specifically British instances of wider European debates which were conducted on a global scale, and most often in the language of the laws of nature and of nations. Because such arguments linked local disputes with cosmopolitan concerns, and because the history of British maritime ideology extends from the most parochial issues of coastal jurisdiction to the broadest questions of property, commerce and the freedom of the seas, the ideological history of the British Empire can, to a large extent, be reconstructed from the history of these maritime disputes. Such a reconstruction depends upon the reintegration of British arguments with pan-European debates, and therefore parallels the process by which defining rule over the seas around Britain came, in due course, to be the origins of British assertions of naval mastery.

The history of British maritime ideology in the sixteenth and seventeenth centuries follows the history of the conception of Britain itself. There could obviously not be any pan-British arguments in favour of maritime supremacy until the state itself had been defined as a collectively British kingdom; competing English and Scottish maritime ideologies were either subsumed within, or survived alongside, comprehensively British conceptions throughout the course of these centuries. A major achievement in the ideological history of the British Empire would be the creation of just such a pan-British conception of the Empire as an oceanic entity, equipped with its own historical foundations and destiny, though this would not come to full fruition until the late 1730s, in Bolingbroke's *Idea of a Patriot King* (1738) and James Thomson's 'Rule, Britannia' (1740), for instance. This demanded not only the integration of conflicting English and Scottish conceptions of the empire of the seas, but also the elaboration of a series of distinct yet interlocking arguments regarding *dominium* over the foreshore and over territorial waters, and the extent and limits of fishing and navigation on the high seas.

---

[4] N. A. M. Rodger, *The Safeguard of the Sea: A Naval History of Britain, I: 660–1649* (London, 1997).

Such arguments provide an essential connection between the histories conventionally deemed 'domestic' (and territorial) and 'imperial' (that is, trans-oceanic) because they depended upon the same fundamental incommensurability between *imperium* and *dominium* encountered by the theorists of real property examined in the last chapter. They also provide a necessary link between the histories of the Three Kingdoms and of Europe, because the arguments over maritime *imperium* and *dominium* were pan-European in scope, involving theorists from England, Scotland, Spain, Portugal and the United Provinces, and just as often derived from disputes over herring-fishery in the home waters of European states as from competition between those states and their trading-companies in the East or West Indies. The relationship between British arguments in these disputes therefore follows the contours of the ideological history of Britain as closely as it tracks the relationship of that history to the narrative of extra-European rivalry. It also reveals the indissoluble ideological connection between the two.

Arguments for or against particular conceptions of *dominium* or *imperium* over the seas were far from exclusively English, and had Ciceronian and Stoic roots. As Cicero put it early in *De Officiis*, in a passage cited at some point by almost every later theorist of property, 'there is no private property by nature' (*sunt autem privata nulla natura*) (*De Officiis*, I. 7. 21). Property becomes private 'either by ancient usurpation, men finding them void and vacant, or by victory in warre, or by legall condition or composition in peace' (*aut vetere occupatione, ut qui quondam in vacua venerunt, aut victoria ... aut lege, pactione, condicione*).[5] However, he continued, everything produced by the earth is for the benefit of humanity as a whole, and humans are born to help one another (*De Officiis*, I. 7. 22). On such Stoic principles, private property would be sanctioned, and should be protected, but the maxim of mutual assistance also provided the basis for rights of traffic and commerce, to facilitate reciprocity and to strengthen the cosmopolitan bonds between peoples. The air and the sea, 'so farre as they have not by possession of other men before, or otherwise by their own Nature cannot be appropriated, are Natures Commons', Samuel Purchas argued; by the law of nature and of nations, 'Nature within and without us, by everlasting Canons hath decreed Communitie of trade the World thorow whereas by Nature all the Earth was common Mother, and in equall community to be enjoyed

---

[5] Cicero, *De Officiis*, I. 7. 21; Richard Eburne, *A Plaine Pathway to Plantations* (London, 1624), 17.

of all hers'.[6] On such grounds, commerce should be free and the seas open to all. This natural jurisprudential claim would become the basis of all later British assertions of the freedom of the seas.

Purchas's claims echoed those of Francisco de Vitoria in *De Indis* that the *ius gentium* guaranteed rights of travel, hospitality and commerce throughout the world. Vitoria had argued that the apparent contradiction between the division of property (*divisio rerum*) and these rights of universal visitation and communication was only apparent, since 'it was never the intention of nations to prevent men's free mutual intercourse with one another by this division'. The denial of such intercourse could be grounds for just war. To uphold that right against those who denied it would be the Spaniards' first just title in the New World. Likewise, according to the *Institutes*, II. I. I–4, the high seas, rivers and ports were the common property of all, from which no one could be barred. By the determination of the natural, divine and human law, freedom of commerce, and travel were as certain as the common right of all humanity to the seas, whose products as *res nullius* become the property of the first appropriator, as the *Institutes*, II. I. 12, recorded in the law *Feræ Bestiæ*.[7] Vitoria's argument was intended to challenge both the universalism of the papacy and the supposedly Protestant claim that only grace conferred *dominium*. As such, it proved useful to Purchas, for example, in his counterclaims to the papal donations and as the positive basis for freedom of trade and navigation.

Vitoria's attempted resolution of the tension between the necessity of private property and the natural bond created by commerce was not sufficient to prevent debate regarding the relative merits of closed seas (*mare clausum*) and free seas (*mare liberum*), and hence over the extent of both *imperium* and *dominium* in the foreshore, territorial waters and the high seas. Disagreements between the Stuart monarchy and its North Sea neighbours over the extent and limits on fishing rights converged on the same problems, as did the juridical collisions between the English and the Dutch trading companies over rights of navigation in the East Indies. The extent of royal *dominium* generated some of the fiercest political arguments in the years preceding the English Civil Wars, not least when that *dominium* was claimed over the foreshore, and *imperium*

---

[6] Samuel Purchas, *Hakluytus Posthumus, or Purchas His Pilgrimes*, 4 vols. (London, 1625), I, 5 (marginal note, '*Sunt autem privata nulla natura*. Cic.'), 6.

[7] Francisco de Vitoria, *De Indis* (1539), 3. 1, in *Vitoria: Political Writings*, ed. Anthony Pagden and Jeremy Lawrance (Cambridge, 1991), 278–80, quoted in marginal note to Purchas, *Hakluytus Posthumus*, I, 16: '*Barbari sunt veri domini & publicè & privatim. Jus autem gentium ut quod in nullius bonis est, occupanti cedat. d §. fere best.*'

was likewise asserted over the inland counties for the support of the navy in the Ship-Money cases. These various arguments precipitated competing conceptions of England, Scotland, Britain and the British Empire as maritime communities. In due course, such conceptions also underlay the ideological definition of Britain as a maritime power, with a commercial destiny based on its natural insularity. Britons would support freedom of trade even as they ring-fenced the British Atlantic Empire with the Navigation Acts; they would also assert the freedom of the seas while they claimed to rule the waves. This squaring of the circle to assimilate the conception of *mare liberum* with that of *mare clausum* was one of the greatest ideological underpinnings of the later British Empire. The origins of that achievement lay in the sixteenth and seventeenth centuries, in debates of local significance within Britain that also participated in wider arguments of European and even global scope, from the reign of Elizabeth I to the eve of the Glorious Revolution.

The link between maritime ideology and the history of Britain first appeared in the writings of John Dee. As we have seen, Dee's conception of the 'Brytish Empire' revived the Galfridian genealogy deployed in the propaganda for the 'Rough Wooing' and appealed to that propaganda in support of England's claim to suzerainty over Scotland. Dee's expansion of the Edwardian 'empire of Great Britain' to include 'the Royalty and Soveraity of the seas adjacent, or environing this Monarchy of England, Ireland, and (by right) Scotland, and the Orknayes allso' marked a novel advance beyond the strictly territorial conception of the British Empire found in the earlier period.[8] This addition of maritime *imperium* in itself helps to explain the prominence Dee later assumed in accounts of the origins of the British Empire, and also the oblivion into which the mid-sixteenth-century proponents of an exclusively territorial, Anglo-British empire fell. So long as the British Empire was defined oceanically more than territorially, the search for its ideological origins would have to begin with those who explicitly conceived it as an empire of the seas. Though Dee was certainly not the first to use the concept of the British Empire – and acknowledged his debt to those among his predecessors who were the originators of the vernacular term – he was the first to theorise the maritime conception of the British Empire.[9]

[8] John Dee, *General and Rare Memorials Pertayning to the Perfect Arte of Navigation* (London, 1577), 6.
[9] On which see especially William H. Sherman, *John Dee: The Politics of Reading and Writing in the English Renaissance* (Amherst, Mass., 1995), 148–200.

Dee expanded and elaborated his conception of the maritime dimensions of the British Empire over two decades, until it became the defining feature of the empire itself. In his earliest extensive discussion of the boundaries of the British Empire ('Brytanici Imperii Limites' (1576), Dee was most concerned to establish the legality of Elizabeth's claims to the islands of the northern Atlantic (including Britain, Ireland, Iceland, Greenland and Friesland) on the basis of her descent from King Arthur, the last emperor of these isles, to reaffirm her claim to the sovereignty of Scotland and to prove her rights of *imperium* over the eastern seaboard of North America, 'partlie *Jure Gentium*, partlie *Jure Civilis*; and partlie *Jure Divino*'. This entailed the refutation of Spanish and Portuguese claims made on the basis of first discovery and papal donation, but did not include the assertion of the *dominium maris* over the intervening oceans.[10] The following year, Dee supplemented these territorial claims with maritime ones in the *General and Rare Memorials Pertayning to the Perfect Arte of Navigation* (1577), which advised Elizabeth to institute a 'Petty Navy Royal' for the protection of the British seas, cited Pericles and Pompey the Great on, respectively, Athenian naval supremacy and the Roman recovery of the *imperium maris*, and concluded with what would become, for later writers, a standard aetiological appeal to the sea-sovereignty of King Edgar, 'one of the perfect Imperiall Monarchs of this Brytish Impire', over all of the oceans adjoining Britain, Ireland and the British isles.[11] Yet even this was modest in comparison with the all-encompassing conception of maritime dominion Dee presented in his culminating work on the subject, the 'ΘΑΛΛΑΤΟΚΡΑΤΙΑ ΒΡΕΤΤΑΝΙΚΗ' (1597). On the basis of Edgar's 'Title Imperiall', the English claim to the French throne, the fealty-oath of the Scottish kings and 'the Law of Nature; The Law of Nations; The Law of true and constant Amitie: Yea the Law of God', Dee asserted Elizabeth's '*Sea Jurisdiction and soveraigntie absolute*' over the seas for one hundred miles around England's coasts, the English Channel, the western shore of Scotland and 'a mighty portion of the Sea Sovereigntie in that Ocean' between Scotland and North America, as well as over the 'OCEANUS BRITANNICUS: or MARE BRITANNICUM' between England and Denmark, Friesland and Holland.[12] No one until Sir William Petty (a century later) would claim such an expansive domain

[10] John Dee, 'Brytanici Imperii Limites' (22 July 1576), BL Add. MS 59681, ff. 9ʳ, 11ʳ, 33ʳ.
[11] Dee, *General and Rare Memorials*, 6–8, 38 (quoting Thucydides, *History of the Peloponnesian War*, II. 62), 39, 56, 57–60.
[12] John Dee, 'ΘΑΛΛΑΤΟΚΡΑΤΙΑ ΒΡΕΤΤΑΝΙΚΗ' (8 September 1597), BL MS Harl. 249, ff. 95ᵛ–96ʳ, 97ʳ, 98ʳ, 99ᵛ–100ʳ, 102ʳ; Sherman, *John Dee*, 192–200.

for an English or British *mare clausum* in European waters, and not until the 1650s would even non-legal assertions of the oceanic ambit of the British Empire extend so far.

Dee's conception of the British Empire as a compact territorial core at the heart of a far-reaching Atlantic and northern European *mare clausum* was anomalous in Elizabeth's reign, and entirely at odds with the otherwise consistently maintained Tudor commitment to the freedom of the seas. Before the regal union of 1603, the English and Scottish Crowns defined the maritime dimensions of their realms differently, and promoted competing and incompatible conceptions of their *imperium* and *dominium*. Thus, the English Crown argued for *mare liberum* on the natural jurisprudential grounds that 'all are at liberty to navigate the vast ocean, since the use of the sea and the air are common to all. No nation or private person can have a right to the ocean, for neither the course of nature nor public usage permits any occupation of it'. This conception of negative community in which all could claim a common right of navigation, because none could exercise exclusive dominion, was used in 1580 to refute Spanish claims of maritime *imperium* in the West Indies. The Spanish ambassador had appealed for restitution of property seized by Sir Francis Drake from Spanish settlements and ships in the Americas, to which the English replied that it was against the law of nations (*contra ius gentium*) for the Spanish to have excluded foreigners from commerce in the Indies; the papal donation was invalid since 'prescription without possession is not valid' (*præscriptio sine possessione haud valeat*); because the sea, like the air, could not be possessed, the Spanish could not therefore exclude the English from any part of it.[13] Like the more general arguments for British maritime supremacy, these particular assertions of the insufficiency of prescription to guarantee possession and the freedom of the seas for navigation would become staples of later British imperial ideology.

In the late 1590s, Richard Hakluyt used the same natural jurisprudential grounds to refute Spanish claims in the Indies based on the Alexandrine bulls. The English could by right travel and trade in the Indies,

---

[13] William Camden, *Annales* (1580), Eng. trans. (London, 1605), 309, quoted in Edward P. Cheyney, 'International Law under Queen Elizabeth', *English Historical Review*, 20 (1905), 660; Thomas Wemyss Fulton, *The Sovereignty of the Sea* (Edinburgh, 1911), 107–12. Compare Patricia Seed, *Ceremonies of Possession in Europe's Conquest of the New World 1492–1640* (Cambridge, 1995), 10, who truncates her citation of the same passage in order to show that the English mode of legal argument was different from the Spanish, and indeed any other European power's, though the argument in favour of *mare liberum* (which Seed does not quote) was of course far from being exclusively English.

and not even the Pope could deprive rulers and their subjects of this 'righte of navigation in the sea, & the right of traffique' which was available to everyone by the law of nations; '[s]eing therfore, that the sea & trade are common by the lawe of nature and of nations, it was not lawfull for the Pope, nor is it lawfull for the Spaniard, to prohibite other nations from the communication & participation of this lawe'. Hakluyt specifically cited Drake's case as an example of the lawful pursuit of trade and navigation, and concluded, in line with the English Crown's case, that he and other English sailors had a right to 'defend themselves, & lawfully continue traffique wth the Indians'.[14] In this, Hakluyt's assumption of *mare liberum* was more representative of Elizabethan policy than Dee's vision of an English Atlantic *mare clausum*. The same English argument in favour of *mare liberum* appeared in 1602 in the context of fishing rights in the northern seas, over which the Danish Crown asserted *mare clausum* in an attempt to exclude the English. Once again, the English Crown claimed that the seas were open to all persons and hence all nations, and that the king of Denmark, like any other ruler or realm, might exercise jurisdiction over the sea adjacent to his territory, in the interests of securing navigation against piracy and enemy action; however, he could not claim *dominium* over it: the sea was as free as the air, and all might therefore resort to it.[15]

While the English Crown before the regal union of 1603 supported *mare liberum* on the high seas, the Scottish monarchy asserted the opposite principle of *mare clausum* in home waters. Compared to the English, the Scots were more dependent on their fisheries than on their agriculture for subsistence, and hence were more protective of their coastal and oceanic fishing grounds. They also made comparatively little investment in inter-oceanic trade beyond northern Europe, and therefore had less cause than the English to dispute the freedom of the oceans. While the English made common fishing agreements with their neighbours, the Scots instead asserted their right to 'reserved waters', an exclusion zone around the realm of 14 or 28 miles from the shore. Soon after his accession to the English throne in 1603, James began to enforce Scottish policies of *mare clausum* in all of the 'British' seas around the coasts of England and Scotland, and thus reversed the more liberal Elizabethan policies that had allowed foreign access to English waters for both

---

[14] [Richard Hakluyt,] 'Whither an Englishman may trade into the West Indies with certain answers to the Popes Bull' (*c.* 1595–98), PRO co 1/1, f. 108^r, printed in *The Original Writings and Correspondence of the Two Richard Hakluyts*, ed. E. G. R. Taylor, 2 vols. (London, 1935), II, 424, 425.

[15] Cheyney, 'International Law under Queen Elizabeth', 670.

fishing and navigation.[16] This change of policy marked a shift both towards a pan-British conception of the adjacent seas, and hence one closer to the earlier vision of John Dee in the 1570s, and towards a conception of the British empire based on the royal prerogative, and including the territory of the Three Kingdoms as well as the seas around and between them.

The first major legal dispute involving James's Kingdom of Great Britain over this new policy immediately put this specifically Scoto-British assertion of *mare clausum* at the heart of the global argument over rights of dominion precipitated by the publication of Hugo Grotius's *Mare Liberum* in 1609. In that year, James issued a proclamation banning unlicensed foreigners (meaning, particularly, the Dutch) from the coastal fisheries around Britain and Ireland. This reversal of the English policy of *mare liberum* in favour of the Scottish practice of *mare clausum* has been authoritatively described as 'the beginning of the English pretension to the sovereignty of the sea'.[17] It seemed hardly coincidental to James's subjects that an anonymous tract upholding *mare liberum* in favour of the Dutch appeared in Leiden in the same year. Though the East Indian context was uppermost in Grotius's argument, this did not prevent Britons from imagining that his claims to freedom of the seas were made at the expense of their own demands for new restrictions on Dutch fishing-rights: 'K[ing] James coming in the Dutch put out *Mare Liberum*, made as if aimed at mortifying the Spaniards' usurpation in the W. and E. Indyes, but aimed indeed at England', noted one commentator in 1673.[18] Grotius's work, a fragment of the larger treatise *De Jure Prædæ* (*On the Law of Plunder*), had been written as an apology for the capture in 1603 of the Portuguese carrack *St Catharine* by the Dutch East India Company. Chapter XII was published as *Mare Liberum* at the insistence of the Dutch East India Company in the context of the negotiations towards what would become the Twelve Years' Truce between Spain and the United Provinces. Grotius justified Dutch rights of trade and navigation in the East Indies against the claims of the Portuguese by arguing from natural law principles that anything *publicum* – such as the air, the sea and the shore of that sea – was the common property of all, and hence could be the private property of none. The polemical purpose of this was clear: to deny that any state could make the sea an accessory to its realm, and to enforce freedom of

---

[16] Fulton, *Sovereignty of the Sea*, 76–85, 105–7, 124–5. [17] Fulton, *Sovereignty of the Sea*, 10.
[18] Material prepared for the English ambassadors to the Congress of Cologne, 1673, quoted in Fulton, *Sovereignty of the Sea*, 347, n. 1.

navigation throughout the ocean, as a Dutch counterblast to Portuguese claims of *dominium* over the seas on grounds of first discovery, papal donation, rights of conquest or title of occupation.[19]

The international debate on the sovereignty of the sea inspired by Grotius's *Mare Liberum* provoked the most important ideological counter-definitions of the European overseas empires of the early seventeenth century. It drew predictably hostile responses from Justo Seraphim de Freitas in Portugal and Juan Solórzano y Pereira in Spain. However, the first response to the work came from neither Spain nor Portugal but from Scotland. William Welwod, the Professor of Civil Law at the University of St Andrews, had produced the first independent treatise on sea law in Britain in 1590;[20] his chapter 'Of the Communitie and Proprietie of the Seas', in *An Abridgement of All Sea-Lawes* (1613), answered Grotius by supporting British fishing rights and *mare clausum*, and indeed was the only response to *Mare Liberum* to which Grotius himself replied. If God had meant the sea to be free, Welwod argued, he would not have charged humanity to subdue the earth and rule over the fish (Genesis 1:28), 'which could not be, but by subduing of the waters also'. As God had divided the earth after the Flood, so he had divided the sea, which therefore could be distinguished by boundaries, despite its fluidity. On these grounds, Welwod argued, princes might claim *dominium* over the sea around their coasts, to reserve their fishing stocks to their own kingdoms, even while the wider ocean remained '*mare vastum liberrimum*'.[21] At the instigation of Anne of Denmark, Welwod pressed his argument further in *De Dominio Maris* (1615), albeit in ignorance of Grotius's unpublished reply to his earlier

[19] Hugo Grotius, *Mare Liberum: Sive De Jure quod Batavis Competit ad Indicana Commercia* (Leiden, 1609). On the work and its context see C. G. Roelofsen, 'Grotius and the International Politics of the Seventeenth Century', in Hedley Bull, Benedict Kingsbury and Adam Roberts (eds.), *Hugo Grotius and International Relations* (Oxford, 1990), 104–12; Roelofsen, 'The Sources of *Mare Liberum*: The Contested Origins of the Doctrine of the Freedom of the Seas', in Wybo P. Heere (ed.), *International Law and its Sources: Liber Amicorum Maarten Bos* (The Hague, 1989), 93–124; Richard Tuck, *Philosophy and Government, 1572–1651* (Cambridge, 1993), 169–79.
[20] On Welwod see Fulton, *Sovereignty of the Sea*, 352–5; T. Callander Wade, 'Introduction', in *The Sea Law of Scotland* (1590), ed. Wade, in Scottish Texts Society, *Miscellany Volume* (Edinburgh, 1933), 23–36; David M. Walker, *The Scottish Jurists* (Edinburgh, 1985), 84–6.
[21] William Welwod, *An Abridgement of All Sea-Lawes* (London, 1613), 61–72; Hugo Grotius, 'Defensio Capitis Quinti Maris Liberi Oppugnati a Guilielmo Welwodo … Capite XXVII ejus Libri … cui Titulum Fecit Compendium Legum Maritimarum' (1615), printed in Samuel Muller, *Mare Clausum: Bijdrage tot de Geschiedenis der Rivaliteit van Engeland en Nederland in de Zeventiende Eeuw* (Amsterdam, 1872), 331–61, and translated as 'Defence of Chapter V of the *Mare Liberum*', in Herbert F. Wright, 'Some Less Known Works of Hugo Grotius', *Bibliotheca Visseriana*, 7 (1928), 154–205.

work.[22] Welwod's arguments foreshadowed the Portuguese response to Grotius by Seraphim de Freitas,[23] as well as those of Selden's *Mare Clausum*. Selden in fact owned both of Welwod's works, and drew on *De Dominio Maris* when writing *Mare Clausum* to affirm 'the *Dominion* or *Ownership* of the *Sea*, incompassing the Isle of *Great Britain*, as belonging to the Empire of the same'.[24] That claim to the freedom of the seas was therefore originally a *Scoto*-British maritime ideology, in which Scottish theories were expanded to justify Anglo-British practices.

The British reception of Grotius's *Mare Liberum*, not all of it as adversarial as Welwod's, abounded with ironies. Grotius's contentions were obviously applicable to British arguments in their disputes with the Dutch about fishing in northern waters. In 1618, apparently in preparation for renewed negotiations with the Dutch over coastal fishing rights, a member of the English delegation took 'Notes out of a book called Mare liberum' and appended citations from Welwod's *De Dominio Maris* to show that the Scotsman had 'materially' refuted Grotius. Thus forearmed, it might be possible to rebut Dutch claims, based on Grotian arguments, for freedom of fishing in the British seas.[25] Grotius's arguments could also easily be turned against the Dutch in pursuit of freedom of navigation in the East Indies. In this context it is notable that the first English translation of the *Mare Liberum*, 'The Free Sea', was also the last surviving work by Richard Hakluyt, and it was presumably undertaken at the instigation of the East India Company.[26] Relations between the English and Dutch in the East Indies reached an impasse in 1612–13, which could only be broken by negotiations between representatives of the two companies. This offered the English an opportunity to

[22] [William Welwod,] *De Dominio Maris, Juribusque ad Dominium Præcipue Spectantibus Assertio Brevis et Methodica* (London, 1615); J. D. Alsop, 'William Welwood, Anne of Denmark and the Sovereignty of the Sea', *Scottish Historical Review*, 49 (1980), 171–4.

[23] Justo Seraphim de Freitas, *De Justo Imperio Lusitanorum Asiatico Adversus Grotii Mare Liberum* (Valladolid, 1625); C. H. Alexandrowicz, 'Freitas *Versus* Grotius', *British Yearbook of International Law*, 35 (1959), 162–82.

[24] [John Selden,] *Of the Dominion, Or, Ownership of the Sea*, trans. Marchamont Nedham (London, 1652), 1. Selden's annotated working copies of Welwod's *Abridgement* and *De Dominio Maris* are Bodleian Library shelfmarks 4° G. 26. Jur. Seld., 6 and 8; the latter is quoted in Selden, *Mare Clausum seu De Dominio Maris* (London, 1635), 293–4.

[25] [Sir Julius Caesar,] 'Notes Out of a Book Called Mare Liberum, sive De Jure Quod Batavis Competit ad Indicana Commercia Dissertatio' (*c.* 1618), BL MS Lansdowne 142, ff. 384ʳ–86ʳ; Fulton, *Sovereignty of the Sea*, 185–6, n. 4.

[26] Hugo Grotius, trans. Richard Hakluyt, 'The Free Sea or A Disputation Concerning the Right wᶜʰ yᵉ Hollanders Ought to Have to the Indian Marchandize for Trading' (*post* 1609), Inner Temple Library, MS 529. Hakluyt translated other Dutch material (in Latin) relating to the East Indies for the Company in 1614: D. B. Quinn, 'A Hakluyt Chronology', in Quinn (ed.), *The Hakluyt Handbook*, 2 vols. (London, 1974), 324, 328.

turn the principle of the freedom of the seas, which the Dutch had recently asserted against the Spanish and the Portuguese, against the Dutch themselves; most ironically of all, that principle was thrown in the face of Hugo Grotius himself, who was one of the four Dutch commissioners sent to negotiate with the English East India Company.

The English had no compunction in demanding *mare liberum* in the East Indies though they had earlier asserted *mare clausum* in the British seas, as the Dutch, 'contrary to the generall law of nations which admitteth a communion and liberty of commerce, would seek as much as lyes in them to hinder [the English] from tradeing in those parts'. Their argument was, in effect, Grotian, though the English commissioners may have been unaware that they were addressing *Mare Liberum*'s author, because the work had remained anonymous since its publication four years earlier. The English rebuttal concluded with a quotation from the '*assertor Maris liberi*' to the effect that, under the *ius gentium*, freedom of trade (*commercandi libertas*) cannot be restricted without the consent of all peoples: the source of the principle was, of course, Grotius, in the eighth chapter of his *Mare Liberum*. To this, Grotius himself replied that Dutch commercial restrictions relied upon treaties with the Indian rulers, and (citing the fifth chapter of *Mare Liberum*) 'the proponent of *mare liberum* does not disagree with this, and establishes liberty everywhere before agreement has been given' (*ubique libertatem statuit ante consensum praestitum*).[27] Grotius's self-defence (though he did not acknowledge it as such) was shrewd, not least because it left the larger natural jurisprudential claim to freedom of navigation and commerce unchallenged. It also marks a stage in the transition towards Grotius's mature theory of property in *De Jure Belli ac Pacis* (1625), in which he established the role of consent as fundamental to the transition from universal community to private property.[28] As this Anglo-Dutch dispute revealed, particular claims to *imperium* and *dominium* over seas and ports established by law or treaty remained in tension with the more general assertion of *mare liberum*, in accordance with the law of nature and of nations. Such claims also gained a more general significance as part of

[27] G. N. Clark, 'Grotius's East India Mission to England', *Transactions of the Grotius Society*, 20 (1934), 54, 78–80; English Commissioners to Dutch Commissioners, 9 May 1613 (O.S.), and Dutch Commissioners' reply, 13 May 1613 (O.S.), in G. N. Clark and W. J. M. van Eysinga, *The Colonial Conferences between England and the Netherlands in 1613 and 1615*, Bibliotheca Visseriana, 15 (1940), 116, 126. Curiously, Hugh Trevor-Roper, 'Hugo Grotius and England', in Trevor-Roper, *From Counter-Reformation to Glorious Revolution* (London, 1992), 52–3, overlooks Grotius's role in these discussions.
[28] Richard Tuck, *Natural Rights Theories: Their Origin and Development* (Cambridge, 1979), 77.

the wider European revival of natural law, especially as it was used to establish rights of property, both for individuals and for states.

Anglo-Dutch rivalry later inspired the most famous Grotian response to Grotius's theory of *mare liberum* in John Selden's *Mare Clausum*. Selden originally drafted his work in 1618, in response to the crisis in Anglo-Dutch fishing relations that year, but it did not appear in print until 1635. By the time it was published, Selden had been able to digest Grotius's *De Jure Belli ac Pacis*, and was therefore able to produce 'a deeply Grotian work'.[29] Selden, like so many of his predecessors, began from the premise that God's commission in Genesis 9:1–2 had left the earth in common to all humanity, and also cited Cicero *De Officiis*, I. 7. 22, to the effect that in nature there was no private property. Only when men tired of this negative community did they wish to establish rights of individual possession; they did so by agreement, as Grotius had shown in *De Jure Belli ac Pacis*, II. 2. 2. Selden's task was to prove, *contra* the *Mare Liberum*, that the dominion over the sea could be demonstrated in law and had been established in fact. Selden showed at length that 'by the Customs of almost all and the more noble Nations that are known to us, such a Dominion of the Sea is every where admitted', and hence that the sea was as capable of possession as the land or moveable goods, *pace* Grotius and the only other defender of the freedom of the seas Selden acknowledged, the Spanish humanist jurist, Fernando Vásquez de Menchaca.[30] Once this had been established, he could go on to the argument from fact, which proved that 'the *Britains* were Lords of the *Northern Sea*, before they were subdued by the *Romans*. And that the Sea and the Land were *made one entire Bodie* of the *British Empire*' ('... *Et Mare & Tellurem* unicum Imperii Britannici corpus *constituisse*'); that '[t]he Empire of the waters ever followed the Dominion of the Island' ('*Undarum imperium insulae dominium semper secutum est*'); and that the *dominium maris* had been continuously exercised by the English kings since Edgar, as even Grotius had admitted, in his panegyric verses celebrating the accession of James VI and I to the English throne.[31]

Selden's argument from law, and the theory underlying his conception of the British Empire of the seas, was more novel, and hence

---

[29] Tuck, *Philosophy and Government*, 213.

[30] Selden, *Mare Clausum*, 12, 14, 29; Selden, *Of the Dominion, Or, Ownership of the Sea*, trans. Nedham, 18, 23, 42. On Vásquez see especially Annabel Brett, *Liberty, Right and Nature: Individual Rights in Later Scholastic Thought* (Cambridge, 1997), 165–204, and Anthony Pagden, *Lords of All the World: Ideologies of Empire in Spain, Britain and France c. 1500 – c. 1800* (New Haven, 1995), 56–61.

[31] Selden, *Mare Clausum*, 133, 137, 177–8, 303–4; Selden, *Of the Dominion, Or, Ownership of the Sea*, trans. Nedham, 201, 207, 273, 457–9.

controversial (though Grotius himself never replied to it at length). The main precedent for the conception of the Crown's prerogative implied by Selden's conception of *mare clausum* derived from the English Crown's property in the foreshore. From time immemorial until 1569, the English common law presumed that every man's manor extended down to the low-water mark, and hence that the Crown could claim no property (*dominium*) in the foreshore though it could rightfully assert its jurisdiction (*imperium*) there, as over anything else public. In 1569, however, Thomas Digges argued that the original negative community did not prevent any assumption of *dominium* over nature's commons, such as the sea or the foreshore:

True it is that Jure naturali the seaes are common so likewise is the earth and everye other thinge whatsoever, for as *Cicero* saithe *privatum natura nihil est* [*De Officiis*, I. 7. 22]. But the Civile Lawes and all such as comment on them confesse that even as of olde time private men, eyther by first discoverie or antique possession, might purchase propertie in such particular tenements as theye possessed and by lawe of nature were common, even so maie kings *absolute princes* and *comon*-weales does in the Seas adjacent to their *Territories*.

Digges maintained that, like ship-wrecks, treasure-trove, and waifs and strays, the foreshore could not become the property of any particular subject, and therefore fell under the *dominium* of the Crown. By this argument for the extensive power of the royal prerogative, any waste lands became the property of the Crown. However, as Digges hastened to point out, such a claim over the foreshore did not entail an extension of royal *imperium*, 'forasmutche as the princes *Jurisdiction* is as well on the sea as on the lande, but it were an ill exchandge to lose *Proprietye*, for *Jurisdiction*, where bothe of duetye to the Prince therein are due'.[32] Such 'taking away of men's right, under the colour of the King's title to land, between high and low water marks', would become in due course one of the grievances complained of in the Grand Remonstrance of 1641, along with the 'new unheard-of tax of ship-money', which was also justified with reference to prerogative claims in Selden's *Mare Clausum*.[33]

[32] Thomas Digges, 'Arguments Prooving the Queenes Majes^ties Propertye in the Sea Landes, and Salt Shores Thereof, and that No Subject Can Lawfully Hould Eny Parte Thereof but by the Kinges Especiall Graunte' (c. 1568–69), BL MS Lansdowne 105, printed in Stuart A. Moore, *The History of the Foreshore and the Law Relating Thereto* (London, 1888), 202–3, 185, 187, 194.
[33] 'The Grand Remonstrance' (1 December 1641), in Samuel Rawson Gardiner (ed.), *The Constitutional Documents of the Puritan Revolution 1625–1660*, 3rd edn (Oxford, 1906), 212, 211; Moore, *History of the Foreshore*, xxxi; W. P. Drever, 'Udal Law and the Foreshore', *Juridical Review*, 16 (1904), 200–1.

Ship-Money was one of two major political test cases that compelled the English and the Scots to define their relative and mutual claims to *mare clausum* in the 1630s, as Charles I demanded 'British' fishing rights against the Dutch and as he simultaneously pressed his claim to marine taxation over the inland counties of England. In the first case, the status of the island of Britain as a maritime unit was denied; in the second, and relatedly, the inescapably maritime nature of the English realm was defiantly asserted. Charles's attempt to exclude the Dutch from British fishing grounds revealed the limitations of Anglo-Scottish maritime co-operation. The Scottish royal burghs had originally petitioned Charles to prevent Dutch incursions into their coastal waters, to which Charles responded with a plan for a British fishery allowing English, Scots, Irish and naturalised subjects equal access to all of the waters adjacent to the British Isles on the prerogative grounds that fishing rights in all of the Three Kingdoms 'properlie belong to our imperiall crowne'.[34] The confederation of fishing associations – set up to monopolize all the catching, processing and marketing of fish around the coasts of Britain and Ireland – collapsed under the impact of local Scottish resistance, especially in the western Isles, as the Scots objected to being 'confound[ed]' with the English 'under the name of great Britane altho ther be no unioun as yitt with England nor the style of Great Britane received there'.[35] The prerogative claim in this case to *mare liberum* clearly benefited the English more than the Scots, who therefore turned the traditional Scottish claim to *mare clausum* against English encroachments, in opposition to the presumption of a common British fishery.

Simultaneously, the English Crown invoked the same principle against the Dutch with the revision and publication of John Selden's *Mare Clausum* in 1635. According to the Kentish antiquarian Sir Roger Twysden, the coincidence of the publication of *Mare Clausum* with the increased exaction of Ship-Money led people to 'imagin that booke was not set out so much to justyfy the clayme abroad, as the actyon of raysing the money at home'. Twysden claimed that '[t]he booke itself is in every man's hands'; it was clearly in the hands of the judges who tried the Ship-Money case against the Buckinghamshire resister, John Hampden, in 1637, for they cited it six times to show that the king was

---

[34] Allan I. Macinnes, *Charles I and the Making of the Covenanting Movement, 1625–1641* (Edinburgh, 1991), 108 (quoted); Fulton, *Sovereignty of the Sea*, 209–45; John R. Elder, *The Royal Fishery Companies of the Seventeenth Century* (Glasgow, 1912), 35–53.

[35] *The Register of the Privy Council of Scotland*, 2nd ser., IV (1630–2), ed. P. Hume Brown (Edinburgh, 1902), 57.

lord of the sea as well as of the land, that he had *dominium* as well as *imperium* over it, and that it had been customary in England for the inland counties to be taxed for the defence of the sea in cases of necessity, according to the king's determination.[36] However, Selden's arguments from law were more notorious, because of their association with the Ship-Money trial, and would be rendered obsolete by the Crown's insistence on *mare liberum* after the Restoration.

The Crown justified the levying of Ship-Money, and its extension to the inland counties, on grounds of national defence against the imminent threats presented by 'certain thieves, pirates, and sea-robbers, as well as Turks, enemies of Christianity, and others confederated together'.[37] The security of the realm was therefore at stake, and the judgment that this was a case of sufficient danger to allow extraordinary taxation was left to the king to make. The argument between Hampden's lawyers and the judges of the Court of Exchequer turned on the scope and limits of the king's discretionary power when deciding what provisions should be made for the national defence. Historians of political thought have accordingly treated it as an episode in the history of reason-of-state argument, or as a moment in the definition of the respective powers of king and parliament on the eve of the Civil Wars.[38] It was, of course, both, but it was also a central episode in the ideological definition of England (though not 'Britain' in this case) as a maritime realm.

The judges who ruled in favour of the crown in Hampden's case insisted that the king had both dominion and jurisdiction over the seas around England. The dominion of the sea had to be upheld, argued Lord Coventry, 'for safety sake . . . The Wooden Walls are the best walls of the kingdom; and if the riches and wealth of the kingdom be respected for that cause, the Dominion of the Sea ought to be respected'. He thereby conflated two separate arguments, which defined both the

---

[36] Sir Roger Twysden, quoted in Kenneth Fincham, 'The Judges' Decision on Ship Money in February 1637: The Reaction of Kent', *Bulletin of the Institute of Historical Research*, 57 (1984), 235; 'Proceedings in the Case of Ship-Money, between the King and John Hampden, Esq., in the Exchequer, 13 Charles I. A.D. 1637', in *A Complete Collection of State Trials . . . From the Earliest Period to the Year 1783*, ed. T. B. Howell, 21 vols. (London, 1816), III, cols. 928, 934, 1023, 1210, 1226, 1247. On the context of the Ship-Money dispute, and Selden's place within it, see especially Martin Dzelzainis, 'The Case of Ship-Money and its Aftermath', in Dzelzainis, *The Ideological Origins of the English Revolution* (Cambridge, forthcoming). My thanks to Dr Dzelzainis for the opportunity to read this chapter in typescript.

[37] Writ of 22 May 1637, in *Complete Collection of State Trials*, ed. Howell, III, col. 848.

[38] Peter N. Miller, *Defining the Common Good: Empire, Religion and Philosophy in Eighteenth-Century Britain* (Cambridge, 1994), 43–7; Michael Mendle, 'The Ship Money Case, *The Case of Shipmony*, and the Development of Henry Parker's Parliamentary Absolutism', *The Historical Journal*, 32 (1989), 513–36.

rights of the English Crown and the nature of the English nation. Since the prosperity and the safety of the nation depended upon the security of its defences, those defences ought to be maintained by all necessary means. The greatest of those defences was the sea, and the sea was an appurtenance of the Crown of England, according to the Stuart principle of *mare clausum*. Decisions regarding the welfare of the realm were judgments to be made according to the royal prerogative, and so the judgment that England's maritime safety was in danger, and hence that extraordinary fiscal measures should be taken to protect it, was entirely in the hands of the king. On the canonistic principle that what affects all should be borne by all (*quod omnes tangit, per omnes debet supportari*), Coventry and his fellow-judges argued that the burden of maritime defence should be carried by all the counties of England, whether coastal or inland, so that even taxpayers in Buckinghamshire, like John Hampden, would be liable for the cost of equipping and maintaining a ship for the defence of the realm.[39]

The justices who ruled against Hampden adjudged that all subjects of the Crown were liable for maritime defence because all benefited from the security and prosperity of the seas around England. Yet in doing so they, like John Selden and earlier Thomas Digges, defined England as a maritime polity on the basis of the royal prerogative. By this argument, the English were necessarily a maritime nation in so far as they were subject to a king whose dominions included the seas around his realm. Such a prerogative definition of *dominium* was questioned early in the Civil War, when those among Hampden's judges who had decided in favour of the Crown were impeached in the Long Parliament. As Edmund Waller argued in his speech against Sir Edward Crawley, the invasion of the property-rights of Englishmen in the name of national defence, when decided by the king alone without consulting Parliament, was a threat to liberty rather than the means to protect it: 'God and nature have given us the sea', he argued, 'as our best guard against our enemies; and our ships, as our greatest glory above other nations . . . how barbarously would these men [the judges who had ruled against Hampden] have let in the sea upon us at once, to wash away our liberties; . . . making the supply of our navy a pretence for the ruin of our nation!'[40]

[39] *Complete Collection of State Trials*, ed. Howell, III, cols. 838, 858, 1224 (compare cols. 848, 1308, writ of 22 May 1637).

[40] *Complete Collection of State Trials*, ed. Howell, III, col. 1303 (compare Henry Parker, *The Case of Ship-Mony Briefly Discoursed* (London, 1640)). Waller's copy of the 1652 translation of Selden's *Mare Clausum* is Folger Shakespeare Library shelfmark S2432.

There was therefore no necessary connection between the empire of the seas and the liberty of Englishmen, especially when that liberty was defined as security of property, the nation's naval defence provided the expedient for extraordinary fiscal exactions, and the maritime definition of the realm depended on the extent of prerogative power.

These arguments in favour of the English Crown's dominion over the seas nonetheless proved essential for the Rump Parliament just before the outbreak of the Anglo-Dutch War of 1652.[41] The Commonwealth printed or reprinted tracts written to support the Stuart monarchy's sovereignty of the seas in support of their own arguments against the Dutch. For example, Sir John Boroughs's *The Soveraignty of the British Seas* (c. 1633) appeared in print for the first time in 1651, to show that both by fact (*factum*) and right (*ius*), princes possessed *dominium* in, and *imperium* over, the seas around their realms. Boroughs cited a series of precedents, from the Romans and Saxons through to Bracton (via Edgar, the 'Imperator & dominus' of the British seas), to show 'that the Kings of *England* by immemoriall prescription, continuall usage, and possession . . . have ever held the Soveraigne Lordship of the Seas of *England*', while King Charles had now 'enlarged his Dominions over a great part of the Westerne *Indies*; by meanes of which extent of Empire . . . the trade, and persons of all Nations . . . must of necessitie, first, or last, come within compasse of his power, and jurisdiction'.[42] A year later, in 1652, the Council of State paid Marchamont Nedham £200 to translate the fullest version of these arguments, in the form of Selden's *Mare Clausum*.[43] By adopting Boroughs's and Selden's arguments, in the sovereignty of the seas, as in so many other matters, the Commonwealth and the Protectorate republicanised the appurtenances of the Stuart monarchy. Though Nedham admitted that Selden had revised his work 'at the command of the *late Tyrant*', he nevertheless left his arguments from both law and fact untouched, and hence derived the Rump's claim to dominion over the Narrow Seas from his claim that 'the King of *Great Britain* is Lord of the Sea flowing about, as an inseparable and perpetual Appendant of the British Empire' ('*Serenissimum Magnae Britanniae Regem maris circumflui, ut individuæ ac perpetuæ Imperii Britannici appendicis, Dominum esse*').[44]

[41] Steven C. A. Pincus, *Protestantism and Patriotism: Ideologies and the Making of English Foreign Policy, 1650–1668* (Cambridge, 1996), 70, 72.
[42] Sir John Boroughs, *The Soveraignty of the British Seas* (London, 1651), 1–3, 21, 160–1, 163–5; compare [Donald Lupton,] *Englands Command on the Seas, Or, The English Seas Guarded* (London, 1653), 41–51.
[43] *Calendar of State Papers, Domestic: 1652–53*, ed. Mary Everett Green (London, 1878), 486.
[44] Selden, *Mare Clausum*, sig. b2ʳ; Selden, *Of the Dominion, Or, Ownership of the Sea*, trans. Nedham, sig. (e2)ᵛ.

The prefatory poem prefixed to Nedham's translation of *Mare Clausum* revealed ambivalence about the project of defending a republican regime on the basis of a 'British Empire' defined by the extent of royal prerogative. 'Neptune to the Common-Wealth of England' elucidated the work's accompanying engraving – the first representation of Britannia as the ruler of the waves – as if it were part of an emblem-book. A submissive and imploring Neptune begs assistance from the victorious Britannia, who is helmed and breast-plated as Minerva, treading the standards of Scotland and Ireland beneath her feet in the wake of Cromwell's military conquest of the British Isles in 1651–52, and carrying a tiny Nike, like the Athena of the Parthenon, tutelary deity of the Athenian empire of the seas.[45] Neptune implores Britannia not simply to preserve but to extend her sea-dominion, in order to claim the sovereignty of seas by right of conquest rather than simply by inheritance from England's kings: 'For Sea-Dominion may as well bee gain'd/ By new acquests, as by descent maintained'. This acknowledged the prerogative claim to Britain's coastal waters which the Rump maintained, but also imagined the extension of sea-dominion in the name of the 'Angliae Respub.' beyond the Narrow Seas and at the expense of the Dutch.[46] This poem contributed to the burgeoning maritime mythology of the eighteenth century in various musical settings, including a truncated one by Haydn from 1794, but without acknowledgement of its republican roots.[47]

Selden's work provided the foundation for later claims to dominion over the seas in the name of a 'British Empire'. In May 1654, rumour in Paris had it that Oliver Cromwell wanted to become 'emperor of the seas *occidentalis* ... an old pretension of the kings that were heretofore of England' on the basis of Selden's arguments in *Mare Clausum*.[48] This echoed claims that circulated in 1654–55 that Cromwell would become emperor of Great Britain, or even in one especially extravagant

[45] On the Stuart transformation of Britannia into Pallas Athene/Minerva see Madge Dresser, 'Britannia', in Raphael Samuel (ed.), *Patriotism*, 3 vols. (London, 1989), III: *National Fictions*, 30–2.

[46] 'Neptune to the Common-Wealth of England', in Selden, *Of the Dominion, Or, Ownership of the Sea*, trans. Nedham, sig. [b1]ʳ⁻ᵛ. David Norbrook has ingeniously suggested Thomas Chaloner as the possible author of the poem, on the basis of the anagrammatic signature, 'Κλαρεαμοντοσ': Norbrook, *Writing the English Republic: Poetry, Rhetoric and Politics, 1627–1660* (Cambridge, 1999), 294, n. 146.

[47] [Marchamont Nedham,] 'Invocation of Neptune, and His Attendant Nereids, to Britannia, on the Dominion of the Sea' (n.p., n.d. [London, 1784?]), BL shelfmark 1870. d. 1 (110) (libretto for setting by Friedrich Hartman Graf, 1784); Joseph Haydn, *Mare Clausum* (1794), ed. H. C. Robbins Landon (Vienna, 1990), Hoboken XXIV a: 9.

[48] Letter of intelligence, 27 May 1654, in *A Collection of the State Papers of John Thurloe*, ed. Thomas Birch, 7 vols. (London, 1742), II, 287.

account, emperor of the West Indies,[49] and recalled King Edgar's style
as emperor of the British seas (revived by Selden and Boroughs, among
others).[50] This flurry of rumour came in the aftermath of the military
pacification of Ireland, the conquest of Scotland in 1650–51 and the
elevation of Cromwell to the position of Protector in December 1653.
The Cromwellian union achieved what the Stuart kings had failed to
provide: the consolidation of England, Ireland, Scotland and all the
territories belonging thereto into a political unit with a single head.
However, it did so not least by relying on the prerogative powers of
dominium over the seas inherited from the Stuarts. An earlier Protector,
the Duke of Somerset, had attempted to create an empire of Great
Britain by conquering Scotland, but it took Cromwell, another hammer
of the Scots turned Protector, to fulfil his aim. Though the title of
'Emperor', or ruler over multiple dominions, was never formally
awarded to Cromwell, the rumour that it might be hinted at a desire for
equality with the other rulers of Europe, and a recognition of the
Commonwealth's unique achievement in creating an archipelagic state
within the British Isles and over the seas adjacent to them. When the
Protectoral warship, the *Naseby* (also known as the *Great Oliver*) was
launched, the effigy on its prow depicted Cromwell trampling Scottish,
Irish, Dutch, French, Spanish and English victims under his horse's feet,
in an image derived from the portrait of King Edgar on the sovereign.
However, the commingling of regal and republican claims on which
these images relied was inevitably inflammatory after the Restoration.
Cromwell's image was torn from the *Naseby*, and the ship was renamed
the *Royal Charles*.[51] Selden's *Mare Clausum* itself had to be 'restored' to its
monarchical purity by James Howell in 1663, who warned readers that
Nedham had foisted the translation upon them 'in the name of a
Commonwealth, instead of the kings of *England*'.[52] This was a relief to at
least one early reader, Samuel Pepys, who took his copy of Nedham's

[49] Arnold Oskar Meyer, 'Der Britische Kaisertitel zur Zeit des Stuarts', *Quellen und Forschungen aus italienischen Archiven und Bibliotheken*, 10 (1907), 231–7; David Armitage, 'The Cromwellian Protectorate and the Languages of Empire', *The Historical Journal*, 35 (1992), 531–4.
[50] Dee, *General and Rare Memorials*, 56; Boroughs, *Soveraignty of the British Seas*, 21; Selden, *Mare Clausum*, 178; William Ryley, Sr, 'The Soveraigntie of the English Seas Vindicated and Proved, by Some Few Records ... Remayning in the Tower of London' (c. 1652), BL MS Harl. 4314, f. 10ʳ; John Evelyn, *Navigation and Commerce, Their Original and Progress* (London, 1674), 94.
[51] Bernard Capp, *Cromwell's Navy: The Fleet and the English Revolution* (Oxford, 1989), 5–6, 362, 369; *The Diary of Samuel Pepys*, ed. Robert Latham and William Matthews, 11 vols. (London, 1970–83), I, 136, 154.
[52] John Selden, *Mare Clausum; The Right and Dominion of the Sea in Two Books*, ed. James Howell (London, 1663), sig. a[1]ʳ; for Howell's earlier concern about using monarchical prerogative to support republican sovereignty of the seas, and proposing a replacement for Selden's *Mare Clausum*, see Howell to Council of State, [May 1652], BL Add. MS 32093, f. 370ʳ.

translation to his bookseller in 1662 'to cause the title of my English *Mare Clausum* to be changed and the new title, dedicated to the King, to be put to it, because I am ashamed to have the other seen dedicate[d] to the Commonwealth'.[53]

Anyone who discoursed on the sovereignty of the sea after Selden, 'will certainly incurr the whole censure of writing an Iliad after Homer', wrote Sir Philip Meadows, a diplomat and former Latin Secretary to the Commonwealth.[54] In his highly Seldenian 'Observations Concerning the Dominion and Sovereignty of the Seas' (1673), which Meadows originally presented to Charles II during the Third Anglo-Dutch War, he remarked that various peoples had historically claimed dominion over several seas, including the Athenians, the Carthaginians, the Rhodians and the Romans, but 'this was Force and Empire, without Property, an Usurpation, not a Right'; only the 'Feudists' in later times had held that kings could claim *dominium directum* because they possessed the *imperium* over them. In his dedication of his manuscript to Samuel Pepys, Meadows situated his work in the context of the Anglo-Dutch Wars, and stated his aim as the prevention of any excessive assumptions by others regarding the powers of the Crown, not least by enemies like the Dutch, who would construe expanded claims to the empire of the seas as advances towards universal monarchy.[55] When he came to publish it in 1689, he offered it as a means to prevent any misunderstanding between the Dutch and the English, in order to defend the British seas against the encroachments of 'the Continent' (meaning, presumably, France). Like Selden, he assumed the original community of the earth on Ciceronian grounds; also like Selden, he attributed the origins of private property to consent, as Grotius had argued; like Sir William Petty (as we shall see), he identified complete sea-sovereignty as the amalgamation of *dominium* and *imperium*, property and supreme rule and jurisdiction, based on law, rather than fact or force alone: ''tis one thing to be Master of it in an Historical and Military sense, by a Superiority of Power and Command, as the General of a Victorious Fleet is, another thing to be Master of it in a legal sense, by a Possessory Right, as the true Owner and Proprietor is'.[56]

[53] Pepys, *Diary*, ed. Latham and Matthews, IV, 205.
[54] Sir Philip Meadows, 'Observations Concerning the Dominion and Sovereignty of the Seas' (1673), BL Add MS 30221, ff. 13^{r-v} (copy dedicated to Samuel Pepys, 2 January 1686/87).
[55] Meadows, 'Observations Concerning the Dominion and Sovereignty of the Seas', BL Add MS 30221, ff. 16^v, 20^v, 42^v–43^r; Meadows, *Observations Concerning the Dominion and Sovereignty of the Seas: Being an Abstract of the Marine Affairs of England* (London, 1689), sig. [B4]^r; Fulton, *Sovereignty of the Seas*, 524–6, greatly downplays Meadows's Seldenian arguments.
[56] Meadows, *Observations Concerning the Dominion and Sovereignty of the Seas*, 'To the Reader'; sig. B1^v, 1 (quoting Cicero, *De Officiis*, I. 7. 21), 2, 4, 9–10.

Meadows's assimilation of *dominium* and *imperium* over the British seas was perhaps the last such assertion of a whole-heartedly Seldenian conception of the empire of the seas. Both at the time of its composition, and at the moment of its publication in 1689, his treatise captured the shifting associations of the empire of the seas in the post-Restoration era. The geopolitical competition between England and its continental neighbours was cast in the idiom of universal monarchy, the attempt by either Holland or France to achieve the hegemony of Europe by maritime supremacy and commercial monopoly. In 1673, Meadows had attempted to allay any possibility that English pretensions to the sovereignty of the seas could be interpreted as such an ambition for universal monarchy in the era of Anglo-Dutch rivalry.[57] When the treatise appeared in print, it also fit the temper of the times for, in the aftermath of the Glorious Revolution, such rivalry had ceased, as the decade and a half between 1662 and 1678 had seen the focus of English fears of universal monarchy shift from the Dutch to the French.[58] Any English assumptions of *mare clausum* were also abandoned in pursuit of a policy of *mare liberum* across the oceans of the world. As a matter of law, Selden's arguments in *Mare Clausum* were effectively irrelevant by 1689.[59] However, his historical arguments from fact for English *dominium* and *imperium* over the British seas became a *locus classicus* for later students of the subject; as late as 1732, James Oglethorpe, the promoter of the Georgia colony, recommended that 'Whoever would be fully informed concerning the Figure which *England* has made in all Ages, in Maritime Affairs, may find abundance of curious matter in Selden's *Mare Clausum*'.[60]

Meadows was not alone in attempting to resolve the theoretical conundrum of combining *imperium* and *dominium*, over the sea as over land. Among the last seventeenth-century theorists to attempt a reconciliation in relation to the sea rather than for landed property was the political economist Sir William Petty, who turned not to John Selden but rather to Thomas Hobbes (an early admirer of *Mare Clausum*) for assistance.[61] The key to Petty's theory was his Hobbesian understanding

---

57 Compare Sir Philip Meadows, 'Reflections upon a Passage in Sr William Temple's Memoirs Relating to our Right of Dominion in the British Seas' (1692), BL Add. MS 30221, ff. 55ʳ–61ᵛ.
58 Steven C. A. Pincus, 'The English Debate over Universal Monarchy', in John Robertson (ed.), *A Union for Empire: Political Thought and the British Union of 1707* (Cambridge, 1995), 37–62.
59 Fulton, *Sovereignty of the Seas*, 523, 533.
60 [James Edward Oglethorpe,] *A New and Accurate Account of the Provinces of South-Carolina and Georgia* (1732), in *The Publications of James Edward Oglethorpe*, ed. Rodney M. Baine (Athens, GA, 1994), 234.
61 On Hobbes's reading of Selden's *Mare Clausum* see Hobbes to Mr Glen, 6/16 April 1636, and Hobbes to William Cavendish, Earl of Newcastle, 13/23 June 1636, in *The Correspondence of Thomas Hobbes*, ed. Noel Malcolm, 2 vols. (Oxford, 1994), I, 30, 32.

of the commensurability of *dominium* and *imperium*. As he put it in the opening to his major tract on the dominion of the sea (1687):

The Words Soveraignity & Empire doe signify even as Large a Power as Mr Hobs attributes to his Leviathan That is to say, a Power & Right of doing all things that are naturally possible. So as Empire in & over any certain scope or circuit of Ground whether dry or covered with water signifies a Right & power over ye lives Liberties & fortunes of all that Live within ye same & a right to all Things being or produced therein. Dominion over ye same Land or ground, signifies onely such a Right as Landlords have to their Estates of Inheritance . . . So as ye Dominus Maris hath ye same right to all ye fish & other productions of ye seas as any Landlord hath to ye Corne & Cattle accrewing from his Lands . . . [62]

Petty's plan offered the monarchy of James II the chance to become the arbiter of European affairs by asserting its dominance over the European seas; the British monarch would thereby emerge as a Hobbesian sovereign, guaranteeing protection in return for obedience, at least upon the seas. Petty argued that this was necessary because the various maritime states of northern Europe 'are as to sea-affaires in ye state of Nature and there is bellum omnium contra Omnes betweene them . . . Whereas if all and every of them did transferre their Rights unto some One of their Number, Peace & profitt would ensue'.[63] Petty consistently maintained the necessity of a *mare clausum* as an essential defence for the Three Kingdoms in many of his reformative projects for the restoration of Britain and Ireland, particularly in the 1680s. This would be an essential alternative to territorial conquest, and hence the means to prevent military overstretch for the Stuart monarchy; it would also not face the costs of continental commitments, and avoid the nuisance of internal disputes about sovereignty.[64] Petty presented the alternatives in 1687: 'Whether it bee to ye King of Englands Interest to acquire More Territory then hee now hath or rather to bee Effectuall Soveraine of a reall *Mare Clausum* attaineable only to himself'.[65] Though theoretically potent, Petty's plan was practically impossible: it might be plausible to combine *imperium* and *dominium* in the figure of a Leviathan-like *dominus maris*, but providing the rows of signal-ships – manned by convicts who also busily knitted stockings and manufactured fishing-

---

[62] Petty, 'Dominion of the Sea', BL Add. MS 72865, f. 119^r; BL MS Lansdowne 1228, f. 58^r.

[63] Petty, 'Dominion of the Sea', BL Add. MS 72865, ff. 127^v–128^r; BL MS Lansdowne 1228, f. 65^v.

[64] Sir William Petty, 'Ten Tooles for Making ye Crowne & State of England More Powerfull Then Any Other in Europe' (1687), BL Add. MS 72866, ff. 109^{r-v}; Petty, 'Of ye Mare Clausum,' BL Add. MS 72893, f. 34^r; Petty, 'Of a Mare Clausum' (1687), BL Add. MS 72893, f. 36^r.

[65] Sir William Petty, 'A Probleme' (1687), BL Add. MS 72885, f. 126^v.

nets, and moored between the north of Ireland and Scotland, from Kinsale to the Scilly Islands, the Scillies to the French coast, between northern Scotland and Norway, the Isle of Wight and Cap le Hague, and between Dover and France – was not.[66]

Petty presented his conception of 'a reall *Mare Clausum*' not as an alternative to the plantation of colonies in North America,[67] but rather as a warning against English territorial ambitions in Europe. Yet his suggestion was both backward looking and belated, because William III's successful invasion of England and Ireland in 1688–91 would ultimately eliminate the Anglo-Dutch rivalry which had done so much to encourage English attachment to a European *mare clausum*, and open an era in which the freedom of the seas again came to distinguish English ideology and policy. However, Petty's opposition between land and sea, and the armies and navies necessary to exercise *dominium* and *imperium* over them, also looked forward, as did his political-economic conception of Britain and Ireland as a unit within Northern Europe and the wider Atlantic world. Both the navalist ideology implicit in Petty's work and the coincident commitment to commerce would become crucial components of British imperial ideology in the decades following the Restoration. Not least, their confluence could provide a possible solution to one of the greatest of the historical conundrums that bedevilled British conceptions of empire since the late sixteenth century: how to reconcile empire with liberty. The answer was clear, according to Petty. He quoted a Dutch student of naval architecture, who in turn had appealed to a more eminent ancient authority: 'Such as Desire Empire & Liberty says Aristotle let Them Encourage the Art of Ship-building'.[68] Petty had turned to Hobbes in search of a means to reconcile *imperium* and *dominium*; the rapprochement between *imperium* and *libertas*, two classically opposed but equally admired values, would be no less challenging. The empire of the seas and freedom of commerce would be the major solutions to this dilemma, as the next two chapters will show.

---

[66] Sir William Petty, 'Of a Mare Clausum', BL Add. MS 72866, ff. 122ʳ–123ᵛ.

[67] Compare Petty, 'Ten Tooles', BL Add. MS 72866, f. 109: '9 That American Colonyes, The East India & African Trades as also a Mare clausum may bee considered.'

[68] 'Die heerschen wil, zegt *Aristoteles*, en vry zijn, rechte t'zijnent een vaerdige Scheeps-bouw op': Nicolaes Witsen, *Aeloude en Hedendaegsche Scheeps-bouwen Bestier: Waer in Wijtloopigh wert Verhandelt, de Wijze van Scheeps-timmeren, by Grieken en Romeynen* (Amsterdam, 1671), sig. *3ʳ, quoted in Sir William Petty, 'A Treatise of Navall Philosophy in Three Parts', BL Add. MS 72854, f. 106ᵛ.

CHAPTER 5

Liberty and empire

Empire is of two kinds, *Domestick* and *National*, or *Forrain* and *Provinciall*.[1]

The dilemma of providing simultaneous and equally persuasive justifications of both *dominium* and *imperium* bedevilled theorists of real property and of maritime law. The dilemma was not necessarily insoluble, because there was no paradox involved in making such parallel claims to property and jurisdiction: the one did not necessarily threaten the other, though, as the Spanish Monarchy had discovered decades before the English and Scottish Crowns would, the two claims were not dependent upon one another, and each needed a separate and distinct argument. A more intractable dilemma arose from the tension between the competing demands of two overwhelmingly desirable but ultimately irreconcilable goals, liberty and empire. A variety of solutions to this dilemma had emerged by the later seventeenth century and, as William Petty noted in the 1680s, it may have been more apparent than real. However, for the classical – above all, Roman – historical and moral traditions within which the majority of early-modern British theorists had been educated, *libertas* and *imperium* remained seemingly incompatible values. This was hardly confined to those who asserted the primacy of Roman moral and political thought as a means of contemporary self-understanding. So widespread was knowledge of classical history, among the generally educated as well as the more technically learned, that the problem of how to achieve empire while sustaining liberty became a defining concern of British imperial ideology from the late sixteenth century onwards. This resulted in part from the reception of Machiavelli's *Discorsi*, but even the attention to the moral lessons delivered by that Florentine would not have aroused such interest had

---

[1] James Harrington, *The Common-Wealth of Oceana* (London, 1656), 4; *The Political Works of James Harrington*, ed. J. G. A. Pocock (Cambridge, 1977), 163.

there been no prior concern with the historical and theoretical dilemmas that underlay them. Machiavelli did present the most compelling modern dissection of the problem of sustaining empire while maintaining liberty, and it was to him that British thinkers most frequently
turned. Nonetheless, they relied, as did Machiavelli himself, on Roman
historians such as Sallust for their understanding of this persistent
dilemma.

Both classical and contemporary history showed that liberty gave
birth to republics and that republics strove to safeguard that liberty both
internally, for the flourishing of their citizens, and externally, for the
security and grandeur of the republic itself. Theory reinforced the
historical connection between republican government and liberty. The
commitment to liberty under the law, a liberty with responsibility for the
collective well-being of the community, has distinguished the republican
tradition from its classical origins through to its contemporary revival.[2]
Though the Machiavellian branch of the early-modern republican
tradition affirmed this central commitment to liberty, it insisted equally
strongly on the primacy of greatness (*grandezza*) in defining the character
of the commonwealth. Machiavelli began his analysis of *grandezza* historically with the expulsion of the Tarquins from Rome and theoretically from the origins of that greatness in republican liberty. 'It is truly
remarkable to observe the *grandezza* which Athens attained in the space
of a hundred years after it had been liberated from the tyranny of
Pisistratus,' he remarked in *Discorsi*, II. 2: 'But most marvellous of all is it
to observe the *grandezza* Rome attained after freeing itself from its kings.'
The reason for this rapid acquisition of greatness was not far to seek.
Only when the good of the commonwealth was paramount would cities
become great, for 'it is beyond question that it is only in republics that
the common good (*il bene comune*) is looked to properly in that all that
promotes it is carried out'.[3]

Machiavelli inherited this equation between greatness and republican
liberty from Sallust, the most popular of all classical historians in
early-modern Europe.[4] In the opening chapters of the *Bellum Catilinæ*,

[2] Philip Pettit, 'Liberalism and Republicanism', *Australian Journal of Political Science*, 28 (1993),
Special Issue, 164–9; Pettit, *Republicanism: A Theory of Freedom and Government* (Oxford, 1997), 35–41.
[3] Niccolò Machiavelli, *Discorsi sopra la prima deca di Tito Livio*, ed. Giorgio Inglese (Milan, 1984), 287
(*Discorsi*, II. 2): 'Ma sopra tutto maravigliosissima è a considerare a quanta grandezza venne Roma
poi che la si liberò da' suoi Re. La ragione è facile a intendere, perché non il bene comune è
quello che fa grandi le città'; compare *Discorsi*, I. 58. On the Romans' own dating of their civic
liberty from the abolition of the monarchy see Chaim Wirszubski, *Libertas as a Political Idea at Rome
during the Late Republic and Early Principate* (Cambridge, 1950), 5.
[4] Peter Burke, 'A Survey of the Popularity of Ancient Historians, 1450–1700', *History and Theory*, 5

VII, Sallust argued that the establishment of the Republic in Rome had released the talents of the Roman people which had formerly been repressed under the rule of the kings. So great was the popular thirst for glory that it was indeed remarkable (*incredibile*) how the *civitas* grew once it had recovered its liberty.[5] This passage from Sallust became the *locus classicus* for the equation between republican liberty and the greatness of a free state. Augustine cited it in his discussion in the *City of God*, V. 12, of the divine favour which had allowed Rome to be the vehicle for the expansion of Christianity; following Augustine, the author of the *De Regimine Principum*, I. 5. 2–3, also quoted it and remarked further, in Sallustian vein, that under republican government 'when [persons] see that the common good is not in the power of one, each attends to it as if it were their own, not as if it were something pertaining to someone else'. Closer to Machiavelli's own time and to his immediate political concerns, both Coluccio Salutati and Leonardo Bruni deployed the same passage in praise of the greatness of republican Florence.[6]

This Sallustian and Machiavellian tradition encouraged the belief that the greatness of the republic derived originally from its liberty. However, Sallust's continuation of his narrative showed that the consequences of pursuing such *grandezza* would lead inevitably to the loss of that liberty both for the republic and for its citizens. The martial virtue and concern for the public good that the citizens exhibited when they had been freed from the repressions of monarchy may have propelled the remarkable growth of the Roman Republic, but (as Sallust regretfully reported) fortune then turned against Rome. The virtuous and the courageous became greedy, ambitious and impious; the character of the republic was changed, and the government itself became cruel and intolerable (*Bellum Catilinæ*, x. 1–6).[7] Sallust located this declension quite precisely in Roman history during the dictatorship of Lucius Sulla. From that point onward, the pursuit of individual advantage replaced the effort to protect the good of the community, the army which had been sent to conquer distant lands became debilitated by luxury, and all of the former virtues that had sustained Rome in its acquisition of

---

(1966), 136–7; Patricia Osmond, 'Sallust and Machiavelli: From Civic Humanism to Political Prudence', *Journal of Medieval and Renaissance Studies*, 23 (1993), 407–38.

5 Sallust, *Bellum Catilinæ*, VII. 3, in *Sallust*, ed. and trans. J. C. Rolfe (London, 1931), 12–14; Quentin Skinner, *Liberty Before Liberalism* (Cambridge, 1998), 61–4.

6 Augustine, *De Civitate Dei, Libri XII*, eds. B. Dombart and A. Kalb, 2 vols. (Leipzig, 1928–9), I, 212; Ptolemy of Lucca, *On the Government of Princes: De Regimine Principum*, trans. James M. Blythe (Philadelphia, 1997), 70–1; Osmond, 'Sallust and Machiavelli', 410–20.

7 Sallust, *Bellum Catilinæ*, x. 1–6, in *Sallust*, ed. and trans. Rolfe, 16–18; Skinner, *Liberty Before Liberalism*, 64–5.

territory and greatness were scorned and abandoned (*Bellum Catilinæ*, XI. 4–7, XII. 1–2).[8]

Machiavelli followed Sallust not only in his account of the origins of Roman *grandezza* but also in his analysis of Roman declension. Rome had used two methods to facilitate its territorial expansion. It had armed the plebs and admitted foreigners to citizenship, but these methods had led to tumults and hence to internal instability (*Discorsi*, I. 6).[9] Though Machiavelli's defence of such tumults marked his greatest departure from pre-humanist republicans' attachment to internal peace, his argument that such tumults contributed to the decline of the Roman Republic was merely one part of his analysis of the contribution of expansion towards the destruction of Roman liberty. Rome's *grandezza* could not have been achieved without the necessary extension of military commands, he argued, but this had led directly to servitude (*servitù*) for the Roman people; the liberty which had been won with the expulsion of the monarchy ended during the dictatorships of Sulla and Marius, which in turn provided the precedent for the tyranny of Julius Caesar and the loss of popular liberty under the emperors (*Discorsi*, III. 24).[10]

Machiavelli's major advance beyond the limits of Sallust's argument was to show that it would be impossible for any state to avoid the compulsions of expansion, and hence to escape the loss of its liberty. Rome could never have achieved *grandezza* without instituting the practical measures that had led to internal dissension and hence to the destruction of its republican liberty; likewise, those states that did not follow the expansionist policies of the Romans rendered themselves vulnerable to conquest by others and would still lose their liberty as their competitors overran them in due course. Machiavelli's counterexamples were Venice and Sparta, the states that had, respectively, refused in the interests of internal harmony to arm the plebs and declined to increase population by admitting foreigners to citizenship. Each had hoped thereby to resist the temptation to expand in order to safeguard the liberty of the commonwealth. Sparta remained stable for eight hundred years until the Theban revolt checked its ambitions to occupy all the cities of Greece; Venice similarly lost its liberty along with all of its territories on the *terraferma* in one day at the battle of Agnadello in 1509.[11]

---

[8] Sallust, *Bellum Catilinæ*, XI. 4–7, XII. 1–2, in *Sallust*, ed. and trans. Rolfe, 18–20.

[9] Machiavelli, *Discorsi*, I. 6, ed. Inglese, 77–8.

[10] Machiavelli, *Discorsi*, III. 24, ed. Inglese, 529–30.

[11] Niccolò Machiavelli, *Legazione e commissarie*, ed. Sergio Bertelli, 3 vols. (Milan, 1964), III, 1188–1205; Felix Gilbert, 'Machiavelli e Venezia', *Lettere Italiane*, 21 (1969), 389–98; Innocenzo Cervelli, *Machiavelli e la Crisi dello Stato Veneziana* (Naples, 1974).

'What will happen to the others if this [republic] burned and froze in a few days only?' Machiavelli asked. 'And if justice and force and union for so great an *impero* did not avail?' (*Decennale*, II, 178–80).[12] The alternatives were stark: a republic could pursue *grandezza*, or it could safeguard its liberty and maintain tranquil but temporary security. Such security could not be guaranteed, because the republic would be forced to expand and all would be lost. Machiavelli's recommendation was unequivocal: *grandezza* was a greater good than stability. 'Wherefore' (in the words of James Harrington), 'you are to take the course of Rome'.[13]

Once Machiavelli had shown that attack was the best form of defence, and that Roman *ordini* would be the essential base for a successful martial republic, he defined more precisely the means by which an *impero* should be enlarged, and the conditions that would make expansion possible. A territory could be augmented by leagues of confederacy, as the Tuscans had done; by unequal confederations, with the expansive power keeping the headship of any league to itself, as Rome had done; or, least effectively of all, by simply annexing conquered territory without confederation, thus bringing instability and collapse upon republics like Athens and Sparta which could not support the weight of new conquest (*Discorsi*, II. 4). To hold such acquisitions, many soldiers and settlers would be needed, so every effort should be made to increase the population. A small root could not support a great trunk, so 'whoever would make any City great, and apt for Dominion (*faccia grande imperio*), must endeavour with all industry to throng it with inhabitants, otherwise it will be impossible to bring it to any great perfection'.[14] The 'true ways of enlarging an empire' (*acquistare imperio*) were therefore to increase the population; to ally with, and not to subject, other states; to dispatch colonies into conquered territory; to put war-booty into the public coffers; to campaign by means of battles not sieges; to keep individuals poor in order to increase public wealth; and to maintain military discipline. The only viable alternative to taking the course of

[12] Niccolò Machiavelli, *Decennale*, in Machiavelli, *Il teatro e gli scritti letterari*, ed. Franco Gaeta (Milan, 1965), 264: 'Che fia degli altri se questo arse ed alse/ in pochi giorni? e se a cotanto impero/ iustizia e forza e unione non valse?'; *Machiavelli: The Chief Works and Others*, trans. Allan H. Gilbert, 3 vols. (Durham, NC, 1965), III, 1461. Compare Machiavelli, *Dell'asino d'oro*, v, 49–60, in Machiavelli, *Il teatro e gli scritti letterari*, ed. Gaeta, 287–8.

[13] Harrington, *Oceana*, in *Political Works*, ed. Pocock, 330.

[14] Machiavelli, *Discorsi*, II. 3, ed. Inglese, 301: 'Quegli che disegnono che una città faccia grande imperio, si debbono con ogni industria ingegnare di farla piena di abitori'; trans. Henry Neville, in *The Works of the Famous Nicholas Machiavel* (London, 1680), 337. Henry Neville's English translation of Machiavelli was the one most frequently quoted by British authors of the eighteenth century, and is therefore the one used here.

Rome would be to rein in ambition, prohibit expansion, adopt a
defensive posture, and make good internal laws, like the
commonwealths of Germany: 'whoever takes any other course, rather
ruines than advantages himself, for new Conquests are prejudicial a
thousand ways, and especially when your force does not encrease with
your Territory, and you are not able to keep what you conquer' (*Discorsi*,
II. 19).[15]

Machiavelli's analysis of expansion therefore offered three possibilities. A state could follow the course of Rome and order itself internally to
be capable of mastering its external environment. It would be shaken by
popular dissent, its life span would be limited, but it would nonetheless
be glorious and would ride the flux of time. The German republics
presented the second possibility, that of defensive stability and curbed
ambition, which seemed to have been successful, at least temporarily.
Finally, the model of Sparta, Athens or Venice, which guaranteed
internal tranquillity and stability, could be followed, but only if neither
necessity nor greed forced the state to expand (*Discorsi*, II. 3–4). Machiavelli's recommendation to follow the *ordine romano* instead was not
unequivocal. The main reason to prefer the course of Rome was not
glory but security in a world of change and ambition. The Roman
model would incur the cost of dissent between the nobility and the
people; most damagingly, the further the marches of the empire extended away from the centre, the greater was the need to prolong
military commands. This would lead to partisanship in the army, giving
such men as Marius, Sulla and Caesar the means to effect constitutional
overthrow. The empire might not have expanded so rapidly without
that prolongation of commands, but it would not thereby have fallen so
quickly into servitude (*servitù*) (*Discorsi*, III. 24).[16] *Imperio* and *libertà* would,
at last, be incompatible.

As Maurizio Viroli has suggested, 'in recommending the Roman
model, Machiavelli was actually sacrificing the substance of the *vivere
politico* in the pursuit of greatness'.[17] One of Machiavelli's most hostile
critics, the Venetian Paolo Paruta, made just such a charge. Paruta's

---

[15] Machiavelli, *Discorsi*, II. 19, ed. Inglese, 347: 'E chi si governa altrimenti, cerca non la sua vita ma
la sua morte e rovina; perché in mille modi e per molte cagioni gli acquisti sono dannosi. Perché
gli sta molto bene insieme acquista imperio e non forze; e qui acuista imperio e non forze
insieme, conviene che rovini'; trans. Neville, in *Works of … Machiavel*, 358. Compare Maurizio
Viroli, *Machiavelli* (Oxford, 1998), 139–42.

[16] Machiavelli, *Discorsi*, II. 3–4, III. 24, ed. Inglese, 301–7, 530.

[17] Maurizio Viroli, 'Machiavelli and the Republican Idea of Politics', in Gisela Bock, Quentin
Skinner and Maurizio Viroli (eds.), *Machiavelli and Republicanism* (Cambridge, 1990), 158–9;
compare Viroli, *Machiavelli*, 127.

Discorsi Politici (1599) dismissed the Florentine's *Discorsi* as 'already buried in oblivion', and asked, contrary to Machiavelli:

who can doubt but that the true end of a City is to have her Citizens live vertuously, not the inlarging of her Empire? . . . the perfection of Government lies in making a City vertuous, not in making her Mistress of many Countries. Nay the increasing of Territories, as it is commonly coupled with some injustice, so it is remote from the true end of good Laws, which never part from what is honest. Governments which aim at Empire are usually short lived; which denotes their imperfection.[18]

Machiavelli would have answered Paruta's charge by invoking the inescapable compulsions of *necessità, ambizione* and the flux of human affairs (*Discorsi*, I. 6). His crucial insight was to link the strength of internal institutions to the pressures of external policy, thereby to show that '[t]he Conquests of *Common-wealths* that are ill Governed, and contrary to the Mould of the *Romans*, do conduce more to the Ruine, than Advancement of their Affairs' (*Discorsi*, II. 19).[19] This was the lesson taught by Venice, Sparta and the Athenian commonwealth; the commonwealths of contemporary Germany had not yet been tested in this way, but Machiavelli believed that all rulers demand ever larger dominions, however aware they might be of the costs, and that they too would be tried before too long.[20]

Machiavelli's distinction between the stable, defensive yet ultimately vulnerable commonwealth for preservation, and the tumultuous, aggressive, and finally servile commonwealth for expansion drew upon Polybius's discussion of the peculiar fate of the Roman Republic. Polybius had also contrasted Rome with Sparta, wherein Lycurgus's legislation had ensured harmony among the citizens, kept the territory intact and preserved his country's liberty by equally dividing landed property and banning money, as well as by instituting military training. However, Lycurgus had not left any safeguards against territorial aggrandisement on the part of the Spartans, so that 'when the Lacedaemonians attempted to win supremacy in Greece it was not long before they were in danger of losing their liberty'. Polybius's conclusion was therefore the one that Machiavelli followed: 'the Spartan constitution is deficient, and

[18] Paolo Paruta, *Politick Discourses*, trans. Henry, Earl of Monmouth (London, 1657), III, 10.
[19] Machiavelli, *Discorsi*, II. 19, ed. Inglese, 344: 'Che gli acquisti nelle republiche non bene ordinate, e che secondo la romana virtù non procedano, sono a ruina, non a esaltazione di esse'; trans. Neville, in *Works of . . . Machiavel*, 357.
[20] Machiavelli, *Decennali*, II, 181–92, and *Dell'Asino d'Oro*, V, 37–87, in *Il teatro e gli scritti letterari*, ed. Gaeta, 264–5, 287–8.

... the Roman is superior and certainly better devised for the attainment of power' (*Historiæ*, VI. 48–50).[21] Rome was best fitted for empire, Sparta for liberty, but in the end neither could endure. Sparta would be tempted to expand, and Rome would be debilitated by the seductions of petty competition for public office and the pleasures of indolent luxury. Machiavelli faced this pessimism squarely, but saw no alternative to the servitude compelled by overambitious expansion: that way destruction lay, but at least the bitter pill of servitude would be sweetened by the brief taste of glory that came with *grandezza*.

The Machiavellian compound of Sallust's moral account of Roman decline and Polybius's constitutional analysis provided an enduring model for later republicans to understand the competing pressures of liberty at home and expansion abroad. British republicans, in particular, attempted to reconcile the convergent, but antagonistic, claims of empire and liberty in the century between the Elizabethan *fin-de-siècle* and the Glorious Revolution, and beyond. The Machiavellian typology of republics for expansion and those for stability first appeared as a tool to analyse English policy in 1594 when Richard Beacon, the disaffected former Queen's Attorney for the Irish county of Munster, published his Machiavellian 'Politique Discourse' on the state of Ireland, *Solon His Follie* (1594). In a paraphrase of *Discorsi*, I. 6, one of the interlocutors in Beacon's dialogue argued that a 'peaceable & permanent' commonwealth should follow the example of the Spartans, in not admitting foreigners, and that of the Venetians, in fortifying a naturally defensible site; however, 'such as shall ayme at honour and glory', must take the course of Rome, and naturalise foreigners, arm the people, and make alliances. Yet neither form of commonwealth 'may be founde so happy and permanent, but at the last ... they fall with their owne weight and poyse to the ground', the difference being that the state aiming at honour (or, in Machiavelli's terms, the commonwealth for expansion) 'leaveth the image of true glory, as a lively picture, to invest a perpetuall memory of a worthy and excellent Institution'. In these terms, to be a commonwealth for preservation was fit only for 'servile commonweales', like Pisa, Cremona or Ireland under English subjection. It was, of course, possible that Machiavelli's dilemma was a false one, and hence that it might be possible for a commonwealth to combine the

---

[21] Polybius, *The Rise of the Roman Empire*, trans. Ian Scott-Kilvert (Harmondsworth, 1979), 344; on Machiavelli's debt to Polybius see especially Gennaro Sasso, 'Polibio e Machiavelli: costituzione, potenza, conquista', in Sasso, *Studi su Machiavelli* (Naples, 1967), 223–80.

liberty of a free state with territorial expansion. As one character in *Solon His Follie* asked, 'may not one selfesame common-weale, ayme at the one and the other?' 'No, verily', came the reply in the form of a paraphrase of *Discorsi*, II. 3: a commonwealth for preservation was like a tree with a slender root – it could not stay upright for long if it extended itself too far or too fast. There could be no escape from the compulsions of Machiavelli's categories. The dilemma remained: which form of state should be imitated, and hence in the end which form of destruction or decline to face?[22]

The challenge of maintaining liberty while pursuing empire returned prominently in republican thought after 1649. Sallust and Machiavelli in particular provided republicans with the means to understand the military successes of the Rump in Britain, Ireland and Europe, as well as with a series of warnings regarding the consequences of territorial expansion for hard-won republican liberty. The republican moment of 1649–53 – from the declaration of the Commonwealth to Cromwell's forcible dissolution of the Long Parliament – inspired a variety of Englishmen to apply the lessons learnt from the classical republics to their own political situation. John Lilburne, in exile, first read Machiavelli, Livy and Plutarch in these years.[23] In the same period Marchamont Nedham's *The Case of the Commonwealth of England Stated* (1650), and his editorials for the government organ *Mercurius Politicus* in 1651–52, applied ancient history to modern politics, and drew upon a wide range of classical and contemporary sources to celebrate the successes of the Rump and to point the way forward for republican regeneration. During these years, John Milton acted as licenser of *Mercurius Politicus* during the period when most of Nedham's republican editorials were published, and he seems to have begun reading Machiavelli's *Discorsi* seriously in November 1651, just as the first of them began to appear.[24] He was soon applying the Roman

[22] Richard Beacon, *Solon His Follie* (1594), ed. Clare Carroll and Vincent Carey (Binghamton, 1996), 86, 87. On Beacon's debt to Machiavelli see generally Sydney Anglo, 'A Machiavellian Solution to the Irish Problem: Richard Beacon's *Solon His Follie* (1594)', in Edward Chaney and Peter Mack (eds.), *England and the Continental Renaissance: Essays in Honour of J. B. Trapp* (Woodbridge, 1990), 153–64; Markku Peltonen, 'Classical Republicanism in Tudor England: The Case of Richard Beacon's *Solon His Follie*', *History of Political Thought*, 15 (1994), 469–503; and specifically on his debt to *Discorsi*, I. 6, Peltonen, *Classical Humanism and Republicanism in English Political Thought, 1570–1640* (Cambridge, 1995), 99–102.
[23] Perez Zagorin, *A History of Political Thought in the English Revolution* (London, 1954), 18.
[24] William Riley Parker, *Milton: A Biographical Commentary*, 2nd edn, ed. Gordon Campbell, 2 vols. (Oxford, 1996), I, 394, II, 993–4; James Holly Hanford, 'The Chronology of Milton's Private Studies', *Publications of the Modern Languages Association of America*, 36 (1921), 281–3; Maurice Kelley, 'Milton and Machiavelli's *Discorsi*', *Studies in Bibliography*, 4 (1951–2), 123–7.

example to the analysis of the English constitution, as Herman Mylius reported in January 1652.[25]

The relevance of Sallust's analysis was not lost on either Milton or Nedham. In the immediate aftermath of the regicide, they had high hopes of the potential for liberty to foster greatness, and both cited Sallust to affirm this belief. In 1649, on the title-page of *Eikonoklastes*, Milton displayed Sallust's opinion that the monarchy had declined into tyranny, and hence that good men became suspect and their virtue a danger (*Bellum Catilinæ*, VI. 7, VII. 1–2), a passage to which he had also alluded at the opening of *The Tenure of Kings and Magistrates* a few months earlier.[26] The following year, Nedham continued Sallust's narrative on the title-page of *The Case of the Commonwealth of England Stated* (1650) with the epigraph, 'Incredibile est memoratu, quantum adeptâ libertate, in brevi *Romana* civitas creverit' (*Bellum Catilinæ*, VII. 3), a verdict he repeated elsewhere in *The Case*.[27] Sallust's words clearly informed Nedham's most ringing endorsement of the Rump's foreign policy in January 1652: just as the loss of liberty debilitates a people morally, he told the readers of *Mercurius Politicus*, 'so on the other side, the People ever grow magnanimous & gallant upon a recovery; witness at present the valiant Swisses, the Hollanders, and also our own Nation; whose high atchievments may match any of the Ancients, since the extirpation of Tyranny, and a re-establishment of our Freedom in the hands of the People'.[28]

The republican confidence of the years under the Rump evaporated during the course of the Cromwellian Protectorate. Both Nedham and Milton came to believe that the story of moral decline, from freedom with greatness to servitude wrought by ambition, narrated by Sallust and warned against by Machiavelli, had – perhaps inevitably – run its course in Britain between 1649 and 1656. The evidence for Nedham's disillusionment comes from the version of his republican editorials published as *The Excellencie of a Free State* in 1656. When first published in *Mercurius Politicus* in 1651–52, these articles presented a set of warnings to the infant republic along with his celebrations of its fortitude. Liberty for the people, its most effective guardians, could only be secured once

---

[25] Leo Miller, *John Milton and the Oldenburg Safeguard* (New York, 1985), 128.
[26] John Milton, *Complete Prose Works*, gen. ed. Don M. Wolfe, 8 vols. (New Haven, 1953–82), III, 190. On Milton's reading of Sallust, his favourite historian, see especially Nicholas von Maltzahn, *Milton's History of Britain: Republican Historiography in the English Revolution* (Oxford, 1991), 75–7; Martin Dzelzainis, 'Milton's Classical Republicanism', in David Armitage, Armand Himy and Quentin Skinner (eds.), *Milton and Republicanism* (Cambridge, 1995), 22–4.
[27] Marchamont Nedham, *The Case of the Commonwealth of England Stated* (London, 1650), 85.
[28] *Mercurius Politicus*, 85 (22 January 1652), 1352.

kingship had been thoroughly uprooted; it could only be maintained if the exercise of power could be limited by rotation of civil and military office-holders.[29] The reward for liberty and free assemblies would be power abroad and the extension of the empire. Yet, like Machiavelli and Sallust, Nedham warned that Rome's expansion had brought in luxury, a standing army, and the extension of military commands. A succession of tyrants ensued. Liberty was lost, and with liberty, the Empire itself.[30] When reprinted in 1656, these warnings looked like predictions, and they became a stick with which to beat the Protector.[31]

Sallust's awed account of the achievements of Rome's new-won liberty had been celebratory when cited in *The Case of the Commonwealth* in 1650, but it became bitterly nostalgic when repeated in 1656; similarly, Nedham's praise of the Rump's foreign policy in 1652, when amended in *The Excellencie of a Free State*, became a lament for the republican opportunity which had been squandered by the Protector: 'the People ever grow magnanimous & gallant upon a recovery [of freedom]; witness at present the valiant Swisses, the Hollanders and *not long since* our own Nation when declared a Free-State, and a Re-establishment of our Freedom in the hands of the people procured, (*though not secured*) what noble Designs were undertaken and prosecuted with Success?'[32] Likewise, in 1660 Milton echoed Nedham's frustration with the failure to secure the free-state in *The Readie and Easie Way*, as he put the achievement of republican *grandezza* firmly in the English past: 'Nor were our actions less both at home and abroad then might become the hopes of a glorious rising Commonwealth; nor were the expressions both of the Army and of the People ... other than such as testifi'd a spirit in this nation no less noble and well fitted to the liberty of a Comonwealth, then in the ancient Greeks or Romans'. Like Nedham, he thought that the Dutch had not squandered their chance to be 'a potent and flourishing Republick', though England had conspicuously failed to become 'another *Rome* in the west'.[33]

[29] *Mercurius Politicus*, 77 (27 November 1651), 1222; 72 (23 October 1651), 1141; 78 (4 December 1651), 1238 (compare *Mercurius Politicus*, 79 (11 December 1651), 1256; 81 (25 December 1651), 1289; 92 (11 March 1652), 1461; 100 (6 May 1652), 1572; 101 (13 May 1652), 1588).

[30] *Mercurius Politicus*, 82 (1 January 1652), 1304, 1305–6; 85 (22 January 1652), 1349, 1351; 88 (12 February 1652), 1394–5; 90 (26 February 1652), '1435' (*sc.* 1427); 103 (27 May 1652), '1511' (*sc.* 1611).

[31] Harrington, *Political Works*, ed. Pocock, 13; Blair Worden, 'Milton and Marchamont Nedham', in Armitage, Himy and Skinnner (eds.), *Milton and Republicanism*, 175.

[32] Marchamont Nedham, *The Excellencie of a Free State* (London, 1656), 19 (which reprints the passage from Nedham, *The Case of the Commonwealth*, 85), 58 (my emphases).

[33] Milton, *Complete Prose Works*, VII, 357; in the second edition of *The Readie and Easie Way*, 'our actions' became 'their actions': Milton, *Complete Prose Works*, VII, 420.

Milton and Nedham's jaundiced realisation that the British republic had failed in its promise to secure liberty sprang from their common disillusionment with the Cromwellian Protectorate. As Nedham's allusions to Sallust and the pointed revisions of his editorials from *Mercurius Politicus* indicated, that declension had taken place between 1649 and 1656; its agent was Cromwell himself, who played the role of the dictator, Sulla, within the revival of the Sallustian and Machiavellian narrative. Other opponents of the Protector thought him as bad as, or even worse than, Sulla, a military dictator whose office had been made permanent, and had thereby paved the way for the return of monarchy.[34] Milton seems to have shared this assessment. On the title-page of the second edition of *The Readie and Easie Way*, in April 1660, he quoted Juvenal: 'et nos/consilium dedimus *Syllae*, demus populo nunc' ('we, too, gave advice to Sulla; now we give it to the people').[35] Milton had offered counsel to the Protector in the quite practical sense that he had been one of his Latin Secretaries, but also in that he had warned against the temptations of expansion, for instance, in the *Defensio Secunda* (1654).[36] That advice had gone unheeded; Cromwell had revealed himself as a Sulla; the great tower of the Commonwealth had fallen and, by 1660, the Sallustian decline had clearly been repeated.

The failure of Cromwell's so-called Western Design against the Spanish Caribbean in 1654–55 was a crucial moment in the decline of republican faith in the Protectorate, just as it seems to have accelerated the Protector's own loss of self-confidence.[37] To many former adherents of the 'Good Old Cause', it illustrated the declension predicted by Sallust and Machiavelli whenever any commonwealth for preservation tried to become a commonwealth for expansion. Henry Vane saw the Spanish victory as a punishment for national sin brought in by the corrupted agent, Cromwell.[38] Milton conspicuously failed to herald the foreign policy achievements of either Rump or Protectorate in verse, unlike

---

[34] *Cromwell's Conspiracy. A Tragy-Comedy, Relating to our latter Times ... Written by a Person of Quality* (London, 1660), sig. [A2]ᵛ; P. W. Thomas, *Sir John Berkenhead 1617–1679* (Oxford, 1969), 188.

[35] Juvenal, *Satires*, 1. 15–16, adapted in Milton, *Complete Prose Works*, VII, 405.

[36] Milton, *Complete Prose Works*, IV, 673, 681.

[37] See generally Blair Worden, 'Oliver Cromwell and the Sin of Achan', in Derek Beales and Geoffrey Best (eds.), *History, Society and the Churches* (Cambridge, 1985), 125–45; Karen Ordahl Kupperman, 'Errand to the Indies: Puritan Colonization from Providence Island through the Western Design', *William and Mary Quarterly*, 3rd ser., 45 (1988), 70–99; David Armitage, 'The Cromwellian Protectorate and the Languages of Empire', *The Historical Journal*, 35 (1992), 531–55.

[38] Sir Henry Vane, *A Healing Question* (London, 1656), 1, 3–4, 14–15, 23–4.

Andrew Marvell or Edmund Waller, for example.[39] Nedham republished the editorials from *Mercurius Politicus*, in which he lamented the waste of the Rump's achievements, to coincide with the Second Protectoral Parliament in 1656, where Cromwell attempted to justify his proceedings against Spain. That Parliament also provided the opportunity for James Harrington to publish *The Commonwealth of Oceana*, another major republican work critical of the Protectorate. The challenge of combining liberty and empire was central to the argument of the *Oceana*. Harrington's solution to the dilemma implicitly criticised the Protector for his failure to provide the constitutional settlement which would have guaranteed that the British republic secured under the Rump successfully pursued its military designs beyond Britain and Ireland.

The Machiavellian distinction between Rome and Sparta (or Venice) was fundamental to Harrington's presentation of the options that the British republic faced under the Protectorate. Harrington paraphrased the whole of Machiavelli's discussion from *Discorsi*, I. 6, on the grounds that 'he that will erect a commonwealth against the judgment of Machiavel, is obliged to give such reasons for his enterprise as must not go on begging'.[40] The *Oceana* constituted an attempt to break free from compulsions of the Machiavellian categories that afflicted both static and expansive republics by proposing measures that could maintain the internal stability of an externally expanding commonwealth. Harrington proposed measures to prevent the kind of strife between the plebs and the nobility that had destroyed Roman liberty, thereby making Oceana 'a commonwealth for increase, and upon the mightiest foundation that any hath been laid from the beginning of the world'. Harrington's solution was, like Machiavelli's, based upon the Roman model of unequal leagues, in which the metropolitan state retained the leadership, rather than the subordination of conquered territory (like the Athenians or the Spartans) or confederation on the Tuscan model. To 'take the course of Rome' would ensure the maintenance of liberty and the achievement of *grandezza*; Oceana might then became what Harrington (*contra* Machiavelli) thought Rome to have been, 'a commonwealth ... both for increase and preservation', as he put it in *The Prerogative of Popular Government* (1658).[41]

[39] On which see especially Margarita Stocker and Timothy Raylor, 'A New Marvell Manuscript: Cromwellian Patronage and Politics', *ELR*, 20 (1990), 106–62, and the important correction in Elsie Duncan-Jones, 'Marvell, R. F. and the Authorship of "Blake's Victory"', in Peter Beal and Jeremy Griffiths (eds.), *English Manuscript Studies*, 5 (London, 1995), 107–26.
[40] Harrington, *Oceana*, in *Political Works*, ed. Pocock, 273–4.
[41] Harrington, *Oceana*, in *Political Works*, ed. Pocock, 160, 446.

Harrington's Oceana could be a commonwealth both for increase and preservation because it was theoretically and practically distinct from the territorial empires of the past. By adopting a policy of unequal leagues, Oceana could avert the dangers of military conquest. Those dangers would be even easier to avoid because Oceana would primarily be a maritime republic, as its name suggested. Yet, as Machiavelli had recalled, even the greatest of maritime commonwealths, like Venice, had been tempted to expand, and had thereafter suffered swift collapse. Oceana would escape this destructive compulsion by virtue of its mastery of the sea, rather than by allowing the sea to master it: 'The sea giveth law unto the growth of Venice, but the growth of Oceana giveth law unto the sea'. Moreover, Oceana would pursue a tutelary mission whose purpose had been carefully defined by Cicero in *De Officiis* to distinguish it from a conquering and martial empire:

> This is a commonwealth of the fabric that hath an open ear, and a public concernment. She is not made for herself only, but given as a magistrate of God unto mankind, for the vindication of common right and the law of nature. Wherefore saith Cicero of the ... Romans, *Nos magis patronatum orbis terrarrum suscepimus quam imperium*, we have rather undertaken the patronage than the empire of the world.

Following Cicero further, Harrington noted that the Romans planted colonies, but also preserved the liberties of the territories they colonised; thus Rome, 'in confirming of liberty, ... propagated her empire'. This Ciceronian reconciliation of *libertas* and *imperium* could be the model for any well-ordered republic to expand without endangering the liberty of its own citizens, and would therefore be inspiration enough 'to take the course of Rome'.[42]

Harrington's argument that power followed property – and hence that *imperium* sprang from *dominium* – was more immediately successful than his attempted solution to the dilemma of protecting *libertas* while also extending *imperium*.[43] His critics in the last years of the Protectorate ironically compared Harrington's republican utopia to Jamaica – the sole prize left from Cromwell's Western Design – as the greatest white elephants of the British republic. One squib against the Harringtonian Rota Club ordered 'That *Harrington*'s Aphorisms and other political slips be recommended to the English Plantation in *Jamaica*, to try how they

---

[42] Harrington, *Oceana*, in *Political Works*, ed. Pocock, 160, 323 (quoting Cicero, *De Officiis*, II. 27, with *patronatum* substituted for Cicero's *patrocinium*), 329–30.
[43] '... there is no maxim more infallible and holding in any science, than this in politics: that empire is founded in property': Henry Neville, *Plato Redivivus* (c. 1681), in *Two English Republican Tracts*, ed. Caroline Robbins (Cambridge, 1969), 87.

will agree with that Apocryphal Purchase'; Samuel Butler thought that Harrington himself should be sent to Jamaica, to see whether Oceana could be planted there.[44] Such contemporary criticism makes it all the more remarkable that Harrington would later be identified as a thoroughgoing imperialist, who had successfully reconciled liberty and empire, and thereby provided a prophecy of the British Empire as it gave laws to the sea and exported liberty across the globe. For example, J. A. Froude entitled his federalist travel-narrative *Oceana; or England and Her Colonies* (1886) in homage to Harrington's supposed vision of the British Empire as maritime and free.[45] Historians have since rarely questioned Froude's assessment of *Oceana*'s contribution to British imperial ideology, nor doubted that Harrington was 'an important determinant in the intellectual pedigree of that system of colonies, dominions, and "leagues" by which Britain came in time in truth to give "law unto the Sea"', 'a rip-roaring England-firster', and 'a prophet of the rule of the propertied and of the British Empire' after 1688.[46] Yet only in retrospect did Harrington's work become so fundamental to the Empire's ideological origins. His work began as part of the republican critique of the Protectorate's failure to safeguard liberty while expanding its *imperium*, and was consigned to oblivion by Harrington's critics. Only when read out of context could *Oceana*'s counterfactual counsel to Cromwell appear to be the solution to the dilemma of empire and liberty.

Harrington's solution to that dilemma was not so conclusive that his successors abandoned the typology of expanding and non-expanding commonwealths, ignored Machiavelli's own account of the methods and results of expansion, or ceased their own search for the means to reconcile liberty and empire.[47] After the Restoration, Algernon Sidney shared the republican analysis of the declension of the Commonwealth. He rehabilitated Machiavelli's typology during the mid-1660s in his *Court Maxims* (c. 1663–64). Sidney's spokesman for republicanism in the dialogue judged the condition of England to be 'without discipline, poor, discontented, ... [and] easily subdued', and hence peculiarly

44 *Decrees and Orders of the Committee of Safety of the Commonwealth of Oceana* (London, 1659), 3; [Samuel Butler,] *The Acts and Monuments of Our Late Parliament* (London, 1659), 10; see also *Democritus Turned Statesman* (London, 1659), 4; *Eight and Thirty Queries Proposed* (London, 1659); H. F. Russell Smith, *Harrington and His Oceana* (Cambridge, 1914), 100–1.

45 J. A. Froude, *Oceana; or England and Her Colonies* (London, 1886), 1–4.

46 Zera S. Fink, *The Classical Republicans*, 2nd edn (Evanston, 1962), 188–9; Judith Shklar, 'Ideology-Hunting: The Case of James Harrington', *American Political Science Review*, 53 (1959), 677–8; Christopher Hill, *The Experience of Defeat: Milton and Some Contemporaries* (London, 1984), 206.

47 Blair Worden, 'English Republicanism', in J. H. Burns and Mark Goldie (eds.), *The Cambridge History of Political Thought 1450–1700* (Cambridge, 1991), 466–8.

vulnerable to Europe's aspiring universal monarch, Louis XIV. In such a condition, any nation that could not aspire to hegemony must resist it at all costs, for '[f]reedom is the greatest advantage next to dominion'. The spokesman for the court argues that it is not dominion alone that should be sought but rather that 'enlargement of dominion and increase of riches and power by conquest' benefit a nation, to which the commonwealthman makes the Machiavellian reply that only a nation constituted for enlargement can profit, even temporarily, from expansion; moreover, 'if government be constituted for other ends, that in a society we may live free, happy and safe', conquest would only be an advantage if it promoted those quite precise goals. Conquests destroyed Sparta and put an end to its 'liberty and glory'; Venice and the Swiss Confederation would be vulnerable if they expanded; even the Spanish Monarchy had been 'weakened, dispeopled, and ruined by its own conquests'. Only conquests that did not tend to corrupt the manners of a nation could be justified. Once again, Rome was the great historical example. In the 'fullness of liberty', the law safeguarded the freedom of individuals, since '[t]he Roman virtue was the effect of their good laws and discipline', and Rome's enemies proved no match for it. Nevertheless, '[l]ess glory might have been more permanent', and 'success followed with a prodigious affluence of riches, introduced ambition and avarice, raising some citizens above the power of the law. Then did that victorious people turn its conquering hand into its own bowels, and fell by its own sword.'[48]

Sidney's resuscitation of Machiavelli's warnings about the moral dangers of expansion without adequate constitutional precautions was intended less to school the readers of his manuscript in the best methods to acquire a territorial empire, let alone a universal monarchy, than to affirm the necessity of upholding fragile liberty in a world dominated by reason of state politics. When Sidney returned to the problems of liberty and empire in the *Discourses Concerning Government* (1681–83), he refused to adjudicate between states like Sparta that found 'felicity rather in the fullness and stability of liberty, integrity, virtue and the enjoyment of their own than in riches, power, and dominion over others' like Rome. This could be illustrated by the history of the commonwealths of Italy that fought so valiantly against Rome before they were absorbed into the Republic: '[t]he power and virtue of the Italians grew up, decayed and perished with their liberty', but once 'they were all brought under

---

[48] Algernon Sidney, *Court Maxims*, ed. Hans W. Blom, Eco Haitsma Mulier and Ronald Janse (Cambridge, 1996), 78, 155, 15–16, 136–7.

the Romans, either as associates or subjects, they made the greatest strength that ever was in the world'. Sidney also repeated the Sallustian maxim that the institution of republican liberty in England would lead to the same outburst of courage and industry that the ancient republics had experienced on the recovery of their liberty: 'Men would have the same love to the publick as the Spartans and the Romans had, if there was the same reason for it' – witness the English Commonwealth in the early 1650s, the Swiss Confederation, and the Dutch Republic.[49]

Despite his admiration for classical republics, Sidney accepted one of the major tenets of modern reason of state, that trade provided the sinews of war: 'the best judges of these matters have always given the preference to those constitutions that principally intend war, and make use of trade as assisting to that end', since 'those only can be safe who are strong'.[50] As late seventeenth-century commentators noted, earlier republican theorists' admiration for Sparta – which had banned negotiable currency under the laws of Lycurgus, in order to prevent commerce – was now unsustainable in a world where commerce was a major reason of state. The political economists of the 1690s agreed that European states, whether republics or monarchies, could no longer afford to choose whether they would be self-sufficient or expansive, nor whether they should be trading or war-making commonwealths. They were all now interdependent, so that the Spartan option of economic autarchy was no longer viable: even Harrington had recognised that, though 'the Spartan could have no trade, the Oceaner may have all'.[51]

War and trade were now inextricably linked in ways that challenged some of the most cherished tenets of the republican tradition, but which might yet allow the reconciliation of liberty and empire. Charles Davenant, for one, expressed the moralistic concern that commerce would bring in luxury, and luxury, debility, but recognised that the commercial conditions of contemporary Europe rendered trade a 'necessary evil' for every state. Commerce would now be the only guarantee of either stability or greatness, and since a nation could no longer be a Sparta, it should take the course of Venice (and other commercial republics) in order to reach the eminence of Rome – but with one major proviso, that it should not lead to the military expansion that had caused the collapse of Roman liberty: 'if trade cannot be made subservient to

[49] Algernon Sidney, *Discourses Concerning Government*, ed. Thomas G. West (Indianapolis, 1990), 204, 213, 216.
[50] Sidney, *Discourses Concerning Government*, ed. West, 204–5.
[51] Harrington, *Oceana*, in *Political Works*, ed. Pocock, 238.

the nation's safety, it ought to be no more encouraged here than it was
in Sparta: And it can never tend to make us safe, unless it be so managed
as to make us encrease in shipping and in the breed of seamen'. An
empire of the seas could provide *grandezza* without the need for large
armies, extended military commands, or the takeover of civilian government by overmighty generals. Instead, maritime empire could enrich
the nation, render it stable in the arena of international power politics,
and offer greatness without endangering liberty.[52]

The empirical observation that republics like Florence, Venice and
the Dutch Republic had been so economically vibrant in the early-
modern period strengthened the theoretical connection between liberty
and commerce. For instance, Henry Parker in his *Of a Free Trade* (1648)
had attributed that connection to the influence merchants had over the
administration in 'popular states', while Davenant later argued, with a
crucial revision of Sallust's analysis of the origins of greatness in liberty,
that 'industry has its first foundation in liberty', and that the absolute
monarchies of contemporary Europe would fail in achieving commercial greatness just as their predecessors in ancient times had failed to
gain the glory of *grandezza*: 'They who are either slaves, or who believe
their freedoms precarious, can neither succeed in trade nor meliorate a
country'; the territorial monarchies of Europe, for all their designs on
universal monarchy, would inevitably fail because their hegemonic
power would lead to institutional absolutism and hence economic
decay: 'all these great monarchies degenerate into tyranny, with which
trade is incompatible'.[53] Empire could only be compatible with liberty if
it were redefined as maritime and commercial, rather than territorial
and military. As George Savile, Marquis of Halifax, had argued in the
late 1660s, 'Our Scituation hath made Greatnesse abroad by land
Conquests unnaturall things to us', as the collapse of the cross-channel
Angevin monarchy in the fifteenth century had shown. '[T]he reasonable enjoyments of a free people', such as the English, had to be
distinguished from 'one by which Empire is to bee extended at such an
unnaturall price'. The only natural course for a state like England to

[52] Charles Davenant, *An Essay upon the Ways and Means of Supplying the War* (1695) and *An Essay upon the
       Probable Methods of Making the People Gainers in the Balance of Trade* (1699), in *The Political and
       Commercial Works of Charles Davenant LL.D.*, ed. Charles Whitworth, 5 vols. (London, 1771), I, 30, II,
       275. On Davenant see especially Istvan Hont, 'Free Trade and the Economic Limits to National
       Politics: Neo-Machiavellian Political Economy Reconsidered', in John Dunn (ed.), *The Economic
       Limits to Modern Politics* (Cambridge, 1990), 41–120.
[53] Henry Parker, *Of a Free Trade* (London, 1648), 3, 4; Davenant, *Discourses on the Public Revenues* (1698)
       and Davenant, *An Essay upon Universal Monarchy* (1701), in Davenant, *Political and Commercial Works*,
       ed. Whitworth, II, 35, IV, 34.

take would be one which sprang from its geographical situation and historical experience: 'wee are a very little spot in the Map of the World, and made a great figure onely by trade, which is the Creature of Liberty'.[54] On this analysis, not only would empire be at last reconciled with liberty, but liberty would be its essential foundation.

If liberty were the precondition for successful commerce, and commerce was the cause of greatness, then liberty would be the guarantee of commercial *grandezza*. This syllogism demanded the redefinition of empire. As Nicholas Barbon put it in 1690, '*Trade* may be Assistant to the Inlarging of Empire; and if an Universal Empire, or Dominion of very Large Extent, can again be raised in the World, It seems more probable to be done by the help of *Trade*; By the Increase of Ships at Sea, than by Arms at Land'. Any state aspiring to universal empire, whether benign or malign, should therefore look to the sea for its dominion, 'For those Things that Obstruct the Growth of Empire at Land, do rather Promote its Growth at Sea': the sea has enough room for a great population, fortifications cannot hinder shipping, the diffusion of knowledge has 'added an Unlimited Compass to the Naval Power' and Gothic liberty 'best argues with such an Empire'. Though Barbon gave the Dutch their due for their seaborne challenge to Spanish and French attempts 'to Raise an Universal Empire upon the Land', he affirmed that England was the true seat of the empire of the sea. As an island, it needed no military force for its defence; it was well supplied with harbours; and the people were naturally courageous. 'The Monarchy is both fitted for Trade and Empire.' England could thus 'extend its Dominion over all the Great Ocean: An Empire not less glorious, and of a much larger Extent, than either *Alexander*'s or *Caesar*'s'.[55]

The argument that trade depended upon liberty, and that liberty could therefore be the foundation of empire, became especially prominent in the so-called Standing Army debate that arose after the Treaty of Ryswick in 1697. Though a large standing army had proved its worth as a check to the expansionist ambitions of that aspiring universal monarch, Louis XIV, the nub of the debate was what should be done with the victorious army in peacetime. Those who favoured its disbandment, now that its contingent purpose had been served, juxtaposed the liberty of the citizen militia to the potential tyranny and slavery of a standing army such as that King William possessed. According to John

---

[54] George Savile, Marquis of Halifax, 'A Rough Draft of a New Modell at Sea' (*c.* 1666–67), in *The Works of George Savile Marquis of Halifax*, ed. Mark N. Brown, 3 vols. (Oxford, 1989), I, 297, 300.

[55] N[icholas] B[arbon], *A Discourse of Trade* (London, 1690), 40–1, 57, 60, 61.

Trenchard and Walter Moyle, in the germinal pamphlet of the debate, the example of Rome presented a dire warning to Britain. Instead of a standing army, England should 'give Laws to the Universe' with her hardy sailors and sturdy ships because '[t]he Sea is our element'.[56] Trenchard later encapsulated this argument in one of the *Cato's Letters* (1720–23), on which he collaborated with Thomas Gordon: 'Trade and Naval Power the Offspring of Civil Liberty only, and cannot subsist without it'. Trenchard agreed with Davenant that the whole commercial infrastructure of an absolute monarchy was precarious because it was not protected from the depredations of the monarch by laws that secured property, and he also argued that the luxurious demands of the court necessarily distorted the productive capacity of the nation. However, in a commonwealth where law did safeguard liberty, property would be secure, republican moderation would drive consumption, and the demands of trade would ensure that the nation's military needs were upheld not by soldiers (who might be the tools of tyranny) but by sailors, who presented no threat to the liberty that their duty defending commerce could only promote. For these reasons, liberty would guarantee success in the competition for commercial *grandezza*, because 'despotick monarchs, though infinitely powerful at land, yet could never rival Neptune, and extend their empire over the liquid world'.[57]

The vision of a maritime trading empire, and the diagnosis of England's fitness to capture it, identified the success of a trading nation with the liberty of its government, distinguished territorial conquest from the unlimited potential of empire upon the sea, and thus laid the foundations for a blue-water policy designed to enrich England while defeating universal monarchy in Europe. A typology thereby emerged which would hold sway for at least half a century. The Bourbon monarchies were ambitious for universal monarchy, their designs lay on the continent of Europe, their monarchies were absolute, and hence they could not flourish as commercial powers. England (and, after 1707, Great Britain) was a free government, which encouraged rather than depressed trade, and its destiny lay in the empire of the sea rather than in territorial conquest, which was a danger to liberty itself, as well as a diversion from the nation's true commercial interests. Such arguments

---

[56] [John Trenchard with Walter Moyle,] *An Argument, Shewing that a Standing Army is Inconsistent with a Free Government, and Absolutely Destructive to the Constitution of the English Monarchy* (London, 1697), 8, 18.

[57] John Trenchard and Thomas Gordon, *Cato's Letters: Or, Essays on Liberty, Civil and Religious, and Other Important Subjects*, ed. Ronald Hamowy, 2 vols. (Indianapolis, 1995), I, 442, 445–6, 447.

could, however, cut in two directions when applied to the competitive relations among the Three Kingdoms themselves. They were adopted by the Scottish republican, Andrew Fletcher, in his contribution to the debate on the relative merits of militias and a standing army in 1698, when he counselled his countrymen: 'The Sea is the only empire which can naturally belong to us. Conquest is not our interest'.[58] This in turn provided inspiration for the Scots to pursue their own commercial reason of state by attempting to create a maritime, commercial empire centred on the isthmus of Darien. Yet the pursuit of independent commerce by Scotland inevitably collided with the imperatives of English trade. Three years later, at the beginning of the War of the Spanish Succession, Fletcher warned the Scots of the dangers of English (and Dutch) appeals to these same arguments: 'Might they not for ever establish in themselves the empire of the sea, with an entire monopoly of Trade?'[59] The empire of the seas could therefore provide a threat to liberty for a dependent or unequal province within a composite monarchy; it could also guarantee the liberty of the monarchy as a whole.

The Sallustian and Machiavellian dilemma of how to combine liberty and empire remained incompletely resolved, even in an era of commercial reason of state and maritime expansion. The possibility that empire now consisted of trade, and the wealth it generated, seemed to offer the chance for liberty to remain intact, as ships, rather than armies, and sailors, not soldiers, safeguarded the empire of the seas. Such a maritime regime seemed naturally fitted to the situation of England – perhaps even of Britain – and would ensure that the corruptions and debilities which had beset classical and modern republics (as they threatened their stability by attempting expansion) need no longer destroy the liberty of its citizens. Yet, because commercial compulsions were competitive rather than integrative, the ideological contribution of this argument necessarily remained limited until well after the British union of 1707. It could only be applied to the British monarchy as a whole once that monarchy was conceived of as possessing a single set of commercial interests, and could only be extended to the wider anglophone Atlantic world when it, too, was perceived as possessing a similar community of interests.

[58] Andrew Fletcher, *A Discourse of Government With Relation to Militia's* (Edinburgh, 1698), in *Andrew Fletcher: Political Works*, ed. John Robertson (Cambridge, 1997), 30.
[59] [Andrew Fletcher,] *A Speech Upon the State of the Nation; In April 1701* (1701), in *Political Works*, ed. Robertson, 128.

CHAPTER 6

The political economy of empire

> ... the *Theory* of TRADE is a Princely Science, and the true Regula-
> tion of it the *Key of Empire*.[1]

In the decades following the Stuart Restoration, it became increasingly
clear that the dilemma classically formulated by Sallust and pointedly
revived by Machiavelli was coming under challenge as a prescription for
modern Europe and its overseas possessions. The growth of commerce
marked a novel epoch in human affairs, in which the Roman and
neo-Roman apprehension that liberty might be threatened by empire
was less relevant, and less revealing, because the very definition of
'empire' itself was changing. The warnings of classical and modern
republicans, in this regard at least, might be of only limited guidance to
understanding contemporary politics. As Nicholas Barbon argued in
1690,

> *Livy*, and those Antient Writers ... have been very exact in describing the
> several forms of Military Discipline, but take no Notice of *Trade*; and *Machiavel* a
> Modern Writer, and the best, though he lived in a Government, where the
> Family of *Medicis* had advanced themselves to the Sovereignty by their Riches,
> acquired by Merchandizing, doth not mention *Trade*, as any way interested in
> the Affairs of State.[2]

Writing fifty years later, David Hume agreed: 'Trade was never esteemed an affair of state till the last century; and there is scarcely any
ancient writer on politics, who has made mention of it. Even the
ITALIANS have kept a profound silence with regard to it, though it has
now engaged the chief attention, as well of ministers of state, as of
speculative reasoners.'[3] The most prominent of those Italians had been

[1] [William Wood,] *A Survey of Trade* (London, 1718), vi.
[2] N[icholas] B[arbon], *A Discourse of Trade* (London, 1690), sig. A3ʳ ᵛ.
[3] David Hume, 'Of Liberty and Despotism' (1741), in Hume, *Essays, Moral, Political and Literary*, ed.
Eugene F. Miller (Indianapolis, 1985), 88 9.

146

Machiavelli, whose supposed silence on the matter of commerce Hume remarked upon in the late 1730s: 'There is not a word of Trade in all Matchiavell, which is strange considering that Florence rose only by Trade'.[4] This note is found among Hume's early memoranda, sandwiched between quotations from Cicero's *De Officiis* and Sir Josiah Child's *A New Discourse of Trade* (1665), as if Hume were passing intellectually from an ancient world of republican mores to the more modern compulsions of commercial society.[5] Such a transition had been under way in the British republican tradition at least since the work of Algernon Sidney. That transition marked an important stage in the ideological history of the British Empire, as it became more persuasive, because now more intellectually plausible, to argue that liberty and empire might be reconciled, both theoretically and historically, within the discourse of political economy.

Political economy as a distinct discipline, with a canon of classic texts and a set of definite problems, was the child of the nineteenth century; however, it had a longer heritage as a theoretical language that defined the polity itself in terms of its fiscal, financial and commercial capacities rather than exclusively in relation to its constitution, the civic personality of its citizens or its teleology. Karl Marx agreed with Hume that its origins could be found in the seventeenth century, and attributed its paternity to Sir William Petty,[6] and hence, by extension, to the emergent disciplines of statistics and 'political arithmetic'. However, Hume's description of late seventeenth-century economic discourse was more idiomatic to the period than Marx's. The fundamental principle of late seventeenth-century political economy was the recognition that commerce was now, in Hume's words, 'an affair of state' for every European polity.[7] As the Irishman, Richard Lawrence, noted in 1682, for all states

---

[4] National Library of Scotland, MS 23159, item 14, f. 16, printed in 'Hume's Early Memoranda, 1729–1740: The Complete Text', ed. Ernest Campbell Mossner, *Journal of the History of Ideas*, 9 (1948), 508.

[5] Though for Machiavelli's passing remarks on the subject of trade see Niccolò Machiavelli, *The Prince*, ed. Russell Price and Quentin Skinner (Cambridge, 1989), 79 (*Principe*, XXI); Machiavelli, *Discorsi sopra la prima deca di Tito Livio*, ed. Giorgio Inglese (Milan, 1984), 300 (*Discorsi*, II. 2); Machiavelli, *Florentine Histories*, trans. Laura F. Banfield and Harvey C. Mansfield, Jr. (Princeton, 1988), 361 (*Istorie Fiorentine*, VIII. 36).

[6] Tony Aspromourgos, 'The Life of William Petty in Relation to his Economics: A Tercentenary Interpretation', *History of Political Economy*, 20 (1988), 337. Terence Hutchison, *Before Adam Smith: The Emergence of Political Economy, 1662–1776* (Oxford, 1988), 3, is sceptical of Marx's attribution of paternity to Petty; Neal Wood, *Foundations of Political Economy: Some Early Tudor Views on State and Society* (Berkeley, 1994), proposes instead mid-sixteenth-century English parentage.

[7] Istvan Hont, 'Free Trade and the Economic Limits to National Politics: Neo-Machiavellian Political Economy Reconsidered', in John Dunn (ed.), *The Economic Limits to Modern Politics* (Cambridge, 1990), 41–120.

it had become 'a principal Piece of State-policy to know how to encrease
their own and lessen their neighbours Trade . . . espousing the Interest of
Trade as the Darling of State'.[8] 'Is there anything in the World, that
should be thought a Matter of State more than Trade, especially in an
Island...?', asked Charles Davenant in 1696.[9] 'It's now beyond all
Controversie', affirmed a Scottish commentator in the same year, 'that
it is the Interest of all Nations to increase their Trade; the Increase of
which begetteth Wealth, and Riches, which now in the time of Warr
doth more contribute to the Preservation of a Nation, then the multitude and the valour of it's Men'.[10] With this central maxim, political
economy provided the arguments with which the competing interests of
England, Scotland and Ireland could be promoted, as well as a broader
framework within which economic competition and integration could
be understood.

Political economy was therefore not merely a technical discipline, but
provided the means to describe and explain the relationships among the
Three Kingdoms, in the context of the wider Atlantic economy. It
was both intellectually integrative and ideologically disintegrative: as
economics linked the interests of the Three Kingdoms and the Atlantic
world, so politics sharpened the competition between those interests,
especially in the aftermath of the Glorious Revolution. This language
of interest and policy presented a new means to understand the
relations among the Three Kingdoms, and to define their connections
with the wider Atlantic world. Economic interests defined states and
nations as well as empires, but they defined them competitively. As
J. H. Elliott has noted, empire – in the modern sense of commerce,
supported by independent fleets and plantations – could provide the
alternative to subordination within a composite monarchy for a
kingdom like Scotland, as it had earlier for Portugal or the United
Provinces.[11] In such circumstances, differing definitions of empire collided, and conceptual, as well as political, solutions had to be found for
novel dilemmas.

The triangular relations between England, Ireland and Scotland
provided the shifting contexts for the economic redefinition of empire in
the decades following the Restoration. Ireland's ambiguous status in
English policy, as constitutionally a kingdom with its own legislature,

---

[8] Richard Lawrence, *The Interest of Ireland in Its Trade and Wealth Stated* (Dublin, 1682), pt 1, 9.

[9] [Charles Davenant,] *An Essay on the East-India Trade* (London, 1696), 7.

[10] *A Letter from a Gentleman in the Country to His Friend at Edinburgh* (Edinburgh, 1696), 3.

[11] J. H. Elliott, 'A Europe of Composite Monarchies', *Past and Present*, 137 (Nov. 1992), 59.

but economically a colonial dependency, generated a series of debates on the status of the Irish commerce, the powers of the Irish Parliament and Ireland's place in the Atlantic economy in which discussions of statehood and nationality were cast in the language of colony and empire. These discussions paralleled and at times intersected with those around Anglo-Scottish relations, especially in the aftermath of the Glorious Revolution. In this context, there was no doubt on either side that Scotland was an ancient kingdom and that its Parliament was sovereign; the precise nature of its relation to England was more debatable, as feudal conceptions of dependency (reminiscent of those appealed to in the 1540s) in the name of the English imperial crown were deployed against economic arguments for independence, based on the *imperium* of the Scottish Parliament and the advantages of a separate commercial empire for the Scots.[12] These interlocking arguments reached a climax early in the reign of Queen Anne during the debate on Anglo-Scottish Union. By the resulting Treaty of Union, England joined Scotland in the United Kingdom of Great Britain with a common legislature, a single crown and access to the commerce of an empire now British rather than just English. However, neither Ireland nor the American colonies were offered admission to the Union, and they remained dependencies of a British state that stood at the heart of a transatlantic composite monarchy of unequal communities defined by the Navigation Acts and, increasingly, by mercantilist legislation from the British Parliament. The Union of 1707 sharply distinguished a range of different available conceptions of empire, from the incorporating union of Great Britain, through the semi-colonial dependency of Ireland to the colonial semi-autonomy enjoyed by the American and Caribbean colonies. It thus incorporated a yet sharper form of disunity within the British Empire than had existed before, even as it also enshrined diversity between the Churches and legal systems of England and Scotland.

Before the British Union of 1707, the Navigation Acts had regulated political-economic relations between the Three Kingdoms as they had also formally defined the limits of the English commercial empire. Under the terms of the Acts, Scotland and Ireland had been treated differently, according to English assessments of their respective threats to English commerce. Scotland had been strictly excluded from the

---

[12] William Ferguson, 'Imperial Crowns: A Neglected Facet of the Background to the Treaty of Union of 1707', *Scottish Historical Review*, 53 (1974), 22–44.

mercantile system defined by the Acts because it was held to be a potential rival to English commerce; Ireland, meanwhile, had been included within the ambit of the Acts, as a docile dependency of England, rather than a commercial competitor.[13] This double standard was evident to contemporaries. '[A]re we not all the Subjects of one King, and Members of the same Commonwealth?' Richard Lawrence asked rhetorically. 'We may be the first', he answered, 'and not the second, though the Scots are Subjects to the same King'.[14] All might be subjects within the Stuart composite monarchy, but that would not render them equal citizens of the same commonwealth, let alone partners within a comprehensively British empire: commercial reasons of state dictated otherwise. In terms of political economy, the various communities of Britain and Ireland were considered as economically and constitutionally distinct. The main question for English protectionists was whether Ireland or Scotland could command an independent commerce; for their Irish and Scottish counterparts, the question was instead whether such economic independence demanded the sovereignty of an independent legislature as its guarantee and foundation. The decades after the Glorious Revolution brought these two arguments together into the single question of whether it was possible to have economic union without institutional – meaning, above all, parliamentary – union. This would, in due course, become a central question in relations between the American colonies and Great Britain in the mid-eighteenth century.

The dictates of economic reason of state ensured that the English Parliament judged Ireland's commercial expansion to be a threat to England's prosperity. The English Parliament's Cattle Acts of 1663 and 1667 had restricted one of the most vibrant areas of Ireland's commerce and thereby depleted the supplies of bullion that might have fuelled the economy. Ireland lacked banks and a mint, and hence both cash and credit; the consequently high rates of interest stifled commercial enterprise. Though the Irish economy was expanding in the later seventeenth century, these factors nonetheless limited the rate of its growth and the nature of change.[15] Recent scholarship has tended to downplay the impact of English legislation on Irish economic perform-

---

[13] See [Sir Walter Harris,] *Remarks on the Affairs and Trade of England and Ireland* (London, 1691), 33–9, for a report of contemporary Irish complaints.
[14] Lawrence, *The Interest of Ireland*, 115.
[15] Raymond Gillespie, *The Transformation of the Irish Economy 1550–1700*, Studies in Irish Economic and Social History, 6 (Dublin, 1991), 53–7.

ance, at least in so far as that legislation is seen as the expression of a determined state policy of mercantilist regulation in favour of England.[16] Ireland was subject to discriminatory English legislation throughout the latter half of the seventeenth century, however imperfectly applied. It had been specifically included within the ambit of the Navigation Acts, but the inadequate enforcement of the 1663 Staple Act (which required that all enumerated articles be landed in England before re-export to Ireland) led in turn to the 1671 Staple Act, which effectively ended the direct legal flow of sugar and tobacco to Ireland. That Act lapsed in 1680 and was not restored until 1685, when English trading interests demanded that Ireland be treated not simply as a colonial dependency of the English economy but rather as a potential competitor with England, especially in the Atlantic staple trade to the sugar islands of the Caribbean.[17]

It was in this context that Sir William Petty conceived his Hobbesian solution to the problem of competing sovereignties as a northern European *mare clausum* centred on England. This maritime amalgamation of *imperium* and *dominium* was not his only attempt to reconceive the relations between England and Ireland in these years. His most drastic answer to the dilemma of the unequal relationship between the two kingdoms came in his last major work, the 'Treatise of Ireland' (1687), in which he proposed the transplantation of the majority of the Irish population into England.[18] This would have left some 300,000 people in Ireland to administer the country as a cattle-ranching dependency of England. It would also deny Ireland the institutional autonomy it had fitfully claimed through its own Parliament: 'Whereas there are Disputes concerning the Superiority of Parliament; now there will need no Parliament in Ireland to make Laws among the Cow-Herds and Dairy-Women'. Petty's proposal cut across the religious and ethnic divisions of contemporary Ireland by treating its inhabitants solely according to their economic relations with the Crown, their tenants and landlords, whether as employers or employees.[19] His briefer version of the plan, 'A Probleme' (1687), omitted some of the features which made the 'Treatise'

---

[16] Compare Hugh Kearney, 'The Political Background to English Mercantilism, 1695–1700', *Economic History Review*, 11 (1959), 484–96, with Patrick Kelly, 'The Irish Woollen Export Prohibition Act of 1699: Kearney Revisited', *Irish Economic and Social History*, 7 (1980), 22–44.

[17] Thomas M. Truxes, *Irish-American Trade, 1660–1783* (Cambridge, 1988), 1–16.

[18] On Petty's unionism see James Kelly, 'The Origins of the Act of Union: An Examination of Unionist Opinion in Britain and Ireland, 1650–1800', *Irish Historical Studies*, 25 (1987), 238–40.

[19] Sir William Petty, 'A Treatise of Ireland' (1687), BL Add. MS 21128, in *The Economic Writings of Sir William Petty*, ed. Charles Henry Hull, 2 vols. (Cambridge, 1899), 11, 559, 568.

a comprehensively British vision of population, power and profit, such as
the parallel proposal to depopulate the Scottish Highlands and leave
them to the care of 100,000 herdsmen, to the benefit of lowland Scotland
and England.[20] Nevertheless, both redactions concluded with similar
warnings for the English empire as a whole – that it would not be in
England's interests to contemplate any further territorial expansion, and
that the substitute for a territorial empire (with all of the military, and
hence fiscal, commitments that it raised) should be 'a reall *Mare Clausum*'
between and around the islands of Britain and Ireland.[21]

Petty's conception of the English empire firmly included the American colonies, though his perception of their place within that empire
variously emphasised political and economic factors. For example, he
speculatively proposed a 'grand House of Peers' for a federal Parliament
including members from England, Ireland, Scotland and '10 more out
of ye rest of his Ma^{tys} Dominions in Asia, Affrica & America, all men out
of the best Estates within y^r respective Provinces'. This was not intended
as a substitute for the various legislatures within the Three Kingdoms,
or, indeed, for the colonial assemblies, 'but doth equally superintend
them all'. He also envisaged a colonial council, with representation from
Ireland, Scotland, the American colonies, Asia and Africa, to advise the
English Parliament. This would not have had the powers of his 'House
of Peers', but, like that grander constitutional conception, it would have
assumed the equal dependence of the two British kingdoms and the
various English overseas possessions upon the English Parliament. Petty
designed colonial settlements which could readily be planted in either
Ireland or America, and debated with himself 'Whether It bee better to
transplant out of England into Ireland or America'? In the context of the
1680s, his plans were visionary, but his speculations remained private.
However, they did indicate, albeit precociously, the possibilities for
reconsidering the relations between the Three Kingdoms and the
American colonies. In a stray note, Petty located the four parts of 'The
King of Englands Empire' in 'His European Islands', the American
islands and mainland colonies, and the Asian and East Indian trades.
Such a comprehensive vision of empire – as territorial, colonial and
commercial – was novel in its extent, though conservative in that it

---

[20] Sir William Petty, 'A Probleme' (1687), BL Add. MS 72885, ff. 124^r–26^r, in *The Petty Papers*, ed.
Marquis of Lansdowne, 2 vols. (London, 1927), I, 64–7; Petty, 'A Treatise of Ireland', in *Economic
Writings*, ed. Hull, 572.

[21] Petty, 'A Probleme', in *Petty Papers*, ed. Lansdowne, II, 67; Petty, 'A Treatise of Ireland', in
Economic Writings, ed. Hull, 573.

encompassed all of these elements within the regal *imperium* of the English (not even yet a *British*) Crown.[22]

Petty did not live to see the effects of the Glorious Revolutions on the Three Kingdoms. If he had, the experience might have dampened his enthusiasm for non-sectarian, rationally-calculated solutions to the problem of Anglo-Irish political and economic relations. However, he would not have been surprised to see that the Three Kingdoms did not benefit equally from the settlements of 1688–89. Only in England (and, possibly, some colonies on the American mainland) did the Glorious Revolution represent the victory of law, liberty and localism against absolutism, subordination and centralisation,[23] and 'Ireland did not experience the Glorious Revolution in the sense in which the term is understood in the history of England and Scotland'.[24] The English Parliament reaffirmed its claims to supremacy over the Irish Parliament, as it also reimposed and extended the post-Restoration restrictions on Irish trade. As the Anglo-Irish Williamite Richard Cox put it aphoristically in a pamphlet addressed to the Convention Parliament in 1689, 'Ireland is part of the Dominions of *England*, and a Kingdom subordinate to it … Without the Subjection of *Ireland*, *England* cannot flourish, and perhaps subsist'.[25] This may have been partly intended to reassure the Convention that the 'English' in Ireland knew to whom they owed their dutiful obedience at this contested moment, but admissions like this opened the way more broadly for the assertion of English parliamentary supremacy not solely over the settler population in Ireland, but over their own Parliament and over their economy too.

The Revolution Settlement in Ireland had restored the Irish Parliament as a semi-permanent part of government there. This in turn encouraged the potential for collision between the newly self-confident legislatures in England and Ireland.[26] That English Whiggism would

---

[22] Sir William Petty, 'Of a grand House of Peers', BL Add. MS 72866, ff. 8ʳ, 10ʳ; Petty, 'Of a generall Council for Plantation, Manufactures, Trade, Religion & appointments,' BL Add. MS 72866, f. 174ʳ; Petty, 'Questions concerning American Plantations' (1685), BL Add. MS 72866, f. 68ʳ; Petty, untitled fragment, BL Add. MS 72866, f. 148ʳ.

[23] Jack P. Greene, 'The Glorious Revolution and the British Empire, 1688–1783', in Lois G. Schwoerer (ed.), *The Revolution of 1688–89: Changing Perspectives* (Cambridge, 1992), 260–71. Greene's use of 'Britain' where he in fact means 'England' in this essay obscures the differences between the Revolutions in England, Scotland and Ireland, and makes his Whiggish account of the 'Glorious Revolution' as a single 'British' event untenable, at least for the period 1688–1707.

[24] Patrick Kelly, 'Ireland and the Glorious Revolution', in Robert Beddard (ed.), *The Revolutions of 1688: The Andrew Browning Lectures 1988* (Oxford, 1991), 163.

[25] [Sir Richard Cox,] *Aphorisms Relating to the Kingdom of Ireland* (London, 1689), 1–2.

[26] Patrick Kelly, 'Ireland and the Glorious Revolution', in Beddard (ed.), *The Revolutions of 1688*, 182–3.

also bring no immediate advantage to Ireland was evident from the brief
burst of unionist sentiment aroused by the uncertainties of the Jacobite
War after 1689.[27] The 'Remarks shewing that it is not to the interest of
England that Ireland should remain a separate kingdom' (1690) argued
in the language of English whiggery that Ireland was the home of
arbitrary government and passive obedience, and that these Jacobite
corruptions could easily be reintroduced into England. The author was
less concerned with the potential benefits of union for Ireland than with
the political and moral dangers of maintaining the then current dispen-
sation of domination and dependency between England and Ireland.
Even Poynings' Law provided no defence against the influx of arbitrary
government from Ireland into the 'English empire', since it placed the
ultimate decision-making power in the hands of king and council rather
than parliament. The only solution could be complete and incorporating union between England and Ireland on the model of the Anglo-
Welsh union of the early sixteenth century which had incorporated the
English and the Welsh into one polity, with a single defining 'interest'.
Such a union would also allow for the more direct economic exploitation of Ireland than had previously been possible, so that the newly
absorbed kingdom 'might be made more profitable to England than all
the foreign plantations'. The author presented the Irish economy less as
a threat to the English, by virtue of its cheaper costs for labour,
production and raw materials, than as the backdoor through which
hostile European powers might enter to oppose English economic
interests.[28] This analysis was accordingly cast in a comparative geopolitical and historical framework, from the Anglo-Welsh union to the
contemporary Williamite wars in Europe; by specifically comparing the
profits from Ireland with those to be made from the 'foreign plantations', it intimated that the political-economic context for considering
Ireland now encompassed the Atlantic as well as the Three Kingdoms.

   The analogy between the economic benefits to be derived from the
American and Caribbean colonies and those from Ireland only encouraged the belief among the English that Ireland should be treated less as a
kingdom than as a colony. In the aftermath of the Jacobite War, and in
the face of the fact that Ireland had been pacified by force of arms, it also

---

[27] James Kelly, 'The Origins of the Act of Union', 240–41; Jim Smyth, ' "No Remedy More
   Proper": Anglo-Irish Unionism before 1707', in Brendan Bradshaw and Peter Roberts (eds.),
   British Consciousness and Identity: The Making of Britain, 1533–1707 (Cambridge, 1998), 311–14.
[28] 'Remarks shewing that it is not to the interest of England that Ireland should remain a separate
   kingdom' (1690), in *Calendar of State Papers, Domestic: 1690–91*, ed. W. J. Hardy (London, 1898),
   201–6.

became easier for the English and the Anglo-Irish to claim that Ireland had been conquered, and hence that it should be held in subjection to England. The distinction elaborated by Francis Annesley in 1698, between a 'Colony for Trade' and a 'Colony for Empire', was a telling one in the case of Ireland. The plantations of the West Indies and the forts and factories of Africa and the East Indies were 'Colonies for Trade' in Annesley's terms, and comprised small groups of metropolitans, either 'sent forth to plant Commodities which your native Country does not produce' or 'to negotiate a Trade with the Natives'. Their trade would therefore be reserved to the metropolis, in return for which the colonists would be defended by the home country and enriched by their risk-taking; such colonists would continue to identify themselves as metropolitans and would thereby present no danger by claiming independence. 'Colonies for Empire', however, were closer to the neo-classical model, and were designed 'to keep great Countries in subjection, and prevent the charge and hazard of constant Standing Armies'. Their commerce would be unrestrained by the metropolis as a necessary reward for the emigrants' commitment to maintaining the dependency of the conquered territory and its inhabitants.[29]

Annesley's two models were each inflected by post-Machiavellian commercial concerns, though only the model of a 'Colonies for Trade' could be usefully applied to Ireland or, more specifically, to the 'English' community in Ireland. 'They are Englishmen sent over to conquer *Ireland*, your Countrymen, your Brothers, your Sons, your Relations, your Acquaintance', he informed the English House of Lords: should they then be subject to economic restrictions that had never even been applied to the 'Irish and Popish' population in Ireland?[30] There were only two ways to keep a conquered country in subjection, by arms or by colonies. The former was always too dangerous and too costly; the latter had the sanction of history, and had not only been the method adopted by Rome, but also what 'our Ancestors did to secure *Ireland*, and is the easiest, least chargeable, and least dangerous Method'. Annesley clearly drew upon neo-classical and Machiavellian analyses of territorial expansion, and warned with a Machiavellian metaphor that Rome's conquests extended so far 'that their Government grew top-heavy, the

[29] [Francis Annesley,] *Some Thoughts on the Bill Depending Before the Right Honourable the House of Lords, For Prohibiting the Exportation of the Woollen Manufactures of Ireland to Foreign Parts* (Dublin, 1698), 8–9. Though the pamphlet is usually attributed to Sir Richard Cox, I follow Kelly, 'The Irish Woollen Export Prohibition Act of 1699', 35, n. 47, in attributing it instead to Annesley.

[30] [Annesley,] *Some Thoughts on the Bill*, 16, 15.

Trunk was not large enough to support its branches';[31] however, his deviations from Machiavelli's prescriptions in the *Discorsi* were as signifi-cant as his additions. Though Machiavelli had indeed recommended in both the *Discorsi* and the *Principe* that conquered territories should be held by force of arms or, preferably, by colonies, he had also counselled that the best way for a state to expand and maintain its *impero* would be by leagues, whether equal or unequal (*Discorsi*, I. 6; II. 4; II. 19; *Principe*, V). In the context of Anglo-Irish relations, this would have implied the necessity of viceregal government or, at best, progress towards ever-closer incorporating union.[32] This latter option entailed a recognition that Ireland was a separate but equal kingdom with sovereign institu-tions capable of making alliances; at least, it demanded the admission that Ireland and England should be partners in a British composite monarchy, joined under the same head, albeit unequal in their relations. As the progress of the union debates in Ireland and Scotland would show, this became increasingly implausible as a solution to the problems of Anglo-Irish relations, even as it became the most realistic option for England and Scotland to pursue.

The continuing relevance of Machiavelli's analysis of provincial gov-ernment, even in the age of political economy, reinforced the tendency to think of Ireland as a colony, and hence to distinguish it from Scotland. Henry Maxwell's *Essay upon an Union of Ireland with England* (1703) argued that there were three ways of 'maintaining Conquests, or annexed Governments': colonies; unequal leagues; or military occupa-tion. The latter option was the policy most suitable for absolute govern-ments, and was most fraught with danger, as Roman history taught. If the metropolitan state failed to change its military commanders, then overmighty generals, like Sulla, Marius, Julius Caesar and Augustus, would destroy 'the Liberty of the Commonwealth'. In light of these neo-Roman, and neo-Machiavellian, warnings, the case of Ireland was clear: either '*England* must suffer *Ireland* to live in liberty, or else they must maintain it in subjection to a constant force', though this would contradict and threaten England's constitutional principles as a limited monarchy. There remained only three options: direct rule by England; strict regulation of Irish commerce to render it entirely dependent on England; and incorporating union, on the Welsh model. Maxwell recommended the last course of action, as the one likely to be most

---

[31] [Annesley,] *Some Thoughts on the Bill*, 6; compare Machiavelli, *Discorsi*, II. 3.
[32] For a Machiavellian analysis of the necessity for viceregal goverment (derived explicitly from *Discorsi*, II. 19), see *The Present State of Ireland*, 165–6.

economically and politically beneficial to England: 'as the wealth of *England* Centres in *London*, so must the Wealth of *Ireland* Centre in England'.[33]

William Molyneux, in *The Case of Ireland ... Stated* (1698), had assimilated Ireland to Scotland as equal dominions under the English crown, and therefore denied that Ireland should be conceived of in the same terms as the plantations of the Americas: 'Do not the Kings of *England* bear the *Stile of Ireland* amongst the rest of their Kingdoms? Is this Agreeable to the nature of a *Colony*? Do they use the Title of Kings of *Virginia, New-England,* or *Mary-Land*?'[34] On such constitutional grounds, Ireland was not of course a colony in the strict meaning of the term, unlike the plantations on the North American continent. But that did not mean that it was impossible to imagine that the status of Ireland and of the plantations could be considered as constitutionally, politically or economically equal. Even after the Anglo-Scottish Union of 1707, the continuing Anglo-Irish disputes over judicial appeals and Wood's Halfpence exacerbated the tensions generated by the failure to extend to Ireland the union that incorporated Scotland with the Anglo-Welsh state. The Anglo-Scottish Union in fact made it even harder to imagine Ireland as a kingdom, and (in the words of Patrick Kelly) 'the tendency to think of Ireland as merely the first of England's colonies was greatly reinforced'.[35]

Against the English proponents of mercantilist restraint, Francis Annesley had argued that the Anglo-Irish had no desire to compete directly with the English in the European race for commercial pre-eminence: 'They are not contending for Power or great Riches; they neither Trade to the *East Indies, Turkey,* or *Africa*; they have neither *Hamborough, Hudsons-Bay, Green-land,* or *Russia* Companies; they have no Fleets or Plantations; they ask only the common Benefits of Earth and Air.'[36] In the context of the late 1690s, this was intended not simply as a reassurance to the English Parliament, and to the economic interests represented therein, that Ireland presented no threat to English colonial trade; it was also intended to drive a wedge between the perceived interests of Ireland and those of Scotland. In the years following the Revolution, the

---

[33] [Henry Maxwell,] *An Essay upon an Union of Ireland with England* (Dublin, 1703), 3–4, 5, 7, 11–14, 33.
[34] William Molyneux, *The Case of Ireland ... Stated* (1698), ed. J. G. Simms (Dublin, 1977), 75–6, 115.
[35] Patrick Kelly, 'Ireland and the Glorious Revolution', in Beddard (ed.), *The Revolutions of 1688*, 188.
[36] [Annesley,] *Some Thoughts on the Bill*, 8.

Scots had begun to pursue their own independent colonial ventures, in direct competition with the English and in contravention of the Navigation Acts. 'Fleets and plantations' would be the alternative to dependency within a composite monarchy ruled from London, and hence an economic solution to the inequalities enshrined in the Union of the Crowns. The failure to create a Scottish colonial empire changed the terms of the problem and narrowed the political possibilities until incorporating union seemed the only viable option.

Compared to England's experience, the Glorious Revolution in Scotland was much more radical in the contractarian obligations it imposed on the monarchy, and in the overhaul of the institutions of church and state which accompanied it. In due course, the assertion of Scottish sovereignty set the English and the Scottish Parliaments against each other, as each promoted the commercial reasons of state of their respective kingdoms. The Revolution Settlement in Scotland put the Scottish Parliament on the defensive in support of its national interests in the mid-1690s, especially when those interests were construed in the prevailing discourse of national wealth and independence. Scottish political economists had come to realise in the wake of the Revolution that 'Colonies for Trade' offered an escape from the unequal relations of composite monarchy as much as the means by which a province could be bound into it. They had learned their lessons from the English and the Dutch, and argued that the best way to avoid provincial subjection within the Williamite composite monarchy would be for Scotland to pursue an independent colonial trade of its own by instituting its own mercantile fleet and colonies.[37] The Scottish Privy Council had begun investigating mercantilist means to promote national prosperity after the appointment of James, Duke of York, as lord high admiral of Scotland, and to this end they proposed a carrying trade, supported by the protection of domestic shipbuilding and the expansion of the Scottish fleet. This inevitably implied a challenge to the Navigation Acts, though that challenge only threatened Anglo-Scottish relations with the resurgence of English Parliamentary mercantilism after 1688.[38] The revival in 1693 of plans for an independent Scottish trade to challenge the English Acts initially made common cause with English merchants who wished to evade the East India Company's monopoly, so that an

[37] On the state of the Scottish economy in the 1690s see Richard Saville, *Bank of Scotland: A History 1695–1995* (Edinburgh, 1996), chs. 1–3.
[38] Eric J. Graham, 'In Defence of the Scottish Maritime Interest, 1681–1713', *Scottish Historical Review*, 71 (1992), 89–90.

Anglo-Scottish trading group proposed setting up a joint-stock company. The East India Company compelled its allies in the English Parliament to oppose the move; thus, Scottish investment alone financed the newly founded Company of Scotland trading to Africa and the Indies.[39]

The economic hardships of the 1690s, including famine and the restrictive effects of the Navigation Acts, led the Scots into their first encounter with the literature of economic improvement, and the Company of Scotland's proposed commercial empire centred on the isthmus of Panama was the most striking fruit of this encounter. The company's Darien colony was intended to be the alternative to provincial dependency within the Williamite composite monarchy, as well as an economic defence against the aspiring universal monarchs of contemporary Europe.[40] It was justified as a necessity in a world where the longest purse and the largest population guaranteed military success, and in which the greatest empire to be captured was the empire of the seas. 'It is the interest and policy of all Governments to improve the naturall product of a Country and to encourage foreign trade ... the experience of all Nations makes appear that nothing contributes so effectually to these ends as foreign plantations'.[41] In an era of standing armies financed by public debt, money was now the sinews of war, and trade was the most reliable means of creating national wealth: 'For as *Trade* is a richer and more dureable *Mine* than any in *Mexico* or *Peru* ... so in proportion to its plenty of *Money*, will ... [a nation] flourish at Home, and be terrible Abroad'.[42] The main promoter of the colony, William Paterson, justified the settlement as a free port, sustained by general naturalisation, its commercial wealth providing the key to the empire of the seas. With the large population such policies would create, Paterson argued, Scotland need have no fear of depopulation, 'Trade will increass Trade, ... money will begett money' and, he concluded (echoing both James Harrington and Nicholas Barbon): '[t]hus this Door of the

[39] G. P. Insh, 'The Founding of the Company of Scotland Trading to Africa and the Indies', *Scottish Historical Review*, 21 (1924), 288–95; Insh, 'The Founders of the Company of Scotland', *Scottish Historical Review*, 25 (1928), 241–54.
[40] David Armitage, 'The Scottish Vision of Empire: Intellectual Origins of the Darien Venture', in John Robertson (ed.), *A Union for Empire: Political Thought and the British Union of 1707* (Cambridge, 1995), 102–9.
[41] 'Memoriall in behalf of the Scots Company Trading to Africa and the Indies', National Archives of Scotland, Dalhousie Muniments, GD 45/1/161, ff. 2ʳ ᵛ; also in NAS, Leven and Melville Muniments, GD 26/13/105.
[42] C. K., *Some Seasonable and Modest Thoughts Partly Occasioned By, and Partly Concerning the Scots East-India Company* (Edinburgh, 1696), 4.

Seas, and the key of the universe with any thing of a Reasonable management will of Course enable its proprietors to give Laws to both Oceans and to become Arbitrators of the Commerciall world, without being lyable to the fatigues, expences and dangers, or contracting the Guilt and blood of Alexander and Cesar'.[43]

The attempt to settle a commercial emporium at Darien, and with it to bring Scottish commercial independence from England, ended in defeat, disaster and despair. However, the debate surrounding the Company of Scotland was the most sophisticated and wide ranging controversy before the debate on the Union, and marked the beginnings of what would become the Scottish Enlightenment's peculiarly creative engagement with political economy.[44] The shifting national and international contexts created by the disputed successions to the Spanish, English and Scottish thrones in the opening years of the eighteenth century raised the strategic necessity of incorporating union between England and Scotland and lent the isthmus of Panama a new geopolitical significance. Scottish pamphleteers executed an expedient volte-face in order to show the English that it was now in their interests to support and participate with the Scots in their isthmian venture. Under the shadow of a potential Bourbon universal monarchy encompassing both the French and Spanish dominions, argued one memorialist, the Scottish settlement provided strategic and financial defences and the way to 'be ready at hand to seize on Antichrists pouch', the Spanish bullion-mines in the Americas. All of the historic differences between England and Scotland – from the Wars of Independence to the divergence in church government – could be smoothed over by the profits of trade, for 'an union of Interest is the likeliest way to procure ane union of affections'. Thus bound together by economic interest, and with traditional dissensions tamed, the advantages of union would be clear: 'we are united under the same crown, and together make the greatest Bulwark of the Protestant Religion'.[45]

On similar grounds, Paterson proposed that a free port at Darien could help to unite the British kingdoms profitably and indissolubly. Under Paterson's new plan for a pan-British enterprise, the Scottish

---

[43] William Paterson to the Company of Scotland, 17 January 1700, National Library of Scotland, MS Adv. 83. 7. 5, f. 56ʳ.

[44] John Robertson, 'The Scottish Enlightenment', *Rivista Storica Italiana*, 108 (1996), 808–14.

[45] National Library of Scotland, Dunlop Papers, MS 9255 (*c.* 1699), ff. 217ᵛ, 218ʳ, 220ʳ (endorsed 'That its the Interest of England to joyn with the Scots in their Colony of Caledonia'); compare [William Seton of Pitmedden,] *The Interest of Scotland in Three Essays* (n.p., 1700), 60; [George Ridpath,] *The Great Reasons and Interests Consider'd Anent the Spanish Monarchy* (n.p., 1702), 36–7.

emporium would benefit the Anglo-British *imperium*: united 'into one empire, whereof England [is] to be the centre country, and London to be the centre city' and 'by means of these storehouses of the Indies, this island, as it seems by nature designed, will of course become the emporium of Europe'.[46] A monarchy with a single crown, a state with a single representative assembly, and a market with a single metropolitan emporium might safeguard the interests of both England and of Scotland.[47] Yet since the crown was to pass in a line of succession originally chosen by the English, the Parliament of Great Britain was to be held in Westminster, and the emporium based in London, it became clear that this was to be a British Empire founded on English terms, if not exclusively to England's advantage.

Such an argument for the benefits of union to the metropolis rather than the province was anathema to the Scottish republican Andrew Fletcher of Saltoun, an investor in the Company of Scotland and a dyspeptic student of modern political economy, particularly in his last works in which he argued against the incorporating union of England and Scotland. As Fletcher lamented in 1704, 'trade is now become the golden ball, for which all the nations of the world are contending, and the occasion of so great partialities, that not only every nation is endeavouring to possess the trade of the whole world, but every city to draw all to itself'.[48] The logic of political economy compelled every nation to strive for the profits of a colonial empire; equally, that ruthless logic determined that some nations would remain, or at worst become, colonies, in so far as they and their populations were subordinated to the overmastering and unchallengeable economic interests of other nations. Fletcher feared that too ready a capitulation to this political-economic logic by the Scots would lead them to cede their historic status as a separate kingdom, only to be bullied and impoverished into dependency as Ireland had been by England for centuries past. Fletcher drew many of his arguments in the *Account of a Conversation* from the work of Sir William Petty, William Molyneux and Henry Maxwell. From Petty, Fletcher appropriated the ironic argument that the population of

---

[46] William Paterson, 'Proposal for settling on the Isthmus of Darien, releasing the nations from the Tyranny of Spain by throwing open the Trade of S[ou]th America to all Nations' (1 Jan. 1702), BL Add. MS 12437, in *The Writings of William Paterson*, ed. Saxe Bannister, 3 vols. (London, 1859), I, 156, 158.

[47] John Robertson, 'Union, State and Empire: The Britain of 1707 in its European Setting', in Lawrence Stone (ed.), *An Imperial State at War: Britain from 1688 to 1815* (London, 1994), 247–8.

[48] Andrew Fletcher, *An Account of a Conversation Concerning a Right Regulation of Governments for the Common Good of Mankind* (1704), in *Andrew Fletcher: Political Works*, ed. John Robertson (Cambridge, 1997), 193.

Ireland should be transplanted to England to prevent any further
economic competition; from Molyneux, he drew the arguments that
Ireland was founded on union, not conquest, and that the native Irish
were conquered, but the English colony was not, so that Ireland was still
a kingdom, and not a colony; and from Maxwell, Fletcher apparently
took the Machiavellian arguments that the English 'have never shown
the least disposition to unite with any other nation, though such as either
stood upon equal terms with them, or such as they conquered, or even
planted'.[49]

This would be an enduring lesson from the era of the Glorious
Revolution, the rise of political economy and the Anglo-Scottish and
Anglo-Irish union debates, as the arguments from that era would set the
terms of the debate for relations between Great Britain and its overseas
possessions for much of the succeeding century. Though there had been
various plans for a union among the English colonies in North America
during the seventeenth century,[50] there were none for specifically *imperial* union until the turn of the eighteenth century. For example, the
English man-midwife and economic projector, Hugh Chamberlen, proposed in 1702 incorporating not only England and Scotland but 'also
Ireland, and the *American* Plantations, into one and the same Body, under
the same Liberties, and *Legislative*, as well as Executive Power'.[51] Because
Chamberlen wrote five years before the Treaty of Union went into
effect, he did not identify this legislative and defensive union as a
specifically 'British' empire. The anonymous author of *The Queen an
Empress, and Her Three Kingdoms One Empire* (1706) did, however, and
proposed an incorporating union of all Three Kingdoms under one
monarch, with a single legislature, a British Protestant church with a
patriarchal seat in London, and a pan-British nobility headed by the
eldest sons of the monarch, who would be the subordinate kings of
England, Scotland and Ireland and hold the titles of '*Princes of the British*

[49] Fletcher, *Account of a Conversation*, in *Political Works*, ed. Robertson, 194, 199, 196–7: compare Petty,
'A Treatise of Ireland'; Molyneux, *The Case of Ireland*, 30–9; [Maxwell,] *An Essay upon an Union of
Ireland with England*, 3–4 (cf. Machiavelli, *Discorsi*, ii. 4). The parallels with Petty and Molyneux are
noted in Fletcher, *Political Works*, ed. Robertson, 194, n. 16; 199, n. 26. The copy of Maxwell's
Essay in the Folger Shakespeare Library (shelf-mark DA496 1703 M3 Cage), its cover inscribed
'For Mr Fletcher', is presumably Andrew Fletcher's.

[50] Frederick D. Stone, (comp.) 'Plans for the Union of the British Colonies of North America,
1643–1776', in Hampton L. Carson (ed.), *History of the Celebration of the One Hundredth Anniversary of
the Promulgation of the Constitution of the United States*, 2 vols. (Philadelphia, 1889), ii, 439–503; *An Essay
upon the Government of the English Plantations on the Continent of America* (London, 1701).

[51] [Hugh Chamberlen,] *The Great Advantages to Both Kingdoms of Scotland and England By an Union* (n.p.,
1702), 7; Chamberlen also suggested that the United Provinces should join this defensive union
against the French: *Great Advantages to Both Kingdoms*, 32.

Empire. This 'Empire of *Great Britain*' could then be the Protestant counterweight to French universal monarchy in Europe, an argument whose force was not lost on those who negotiated the Treaty of Union between England and Scotland, but who left Ireland out of the newly-united kingdom and retained diversity-in-unity in Anglo-Scottish ecclesiology and law.[52] However, only the 'Three Kingdoms' would become one empire; the transatlantic colonies would be no part of this new 'British Empire'. Only after the Union of 1707 was it possible to imagine that the English would communicate their rights of parliamentary representation and free trade to anyone other than themselves. Even then, the anomalous position of Ireland – dependent but not united – presented a great stumbling-block to any integrative concept of a British Empire.

English political economists in the 1690s had seen both Ireland and Scotland as threats to the supremacy of their own economy, but for very different reasons. The possibility that Scotland's potential success in the plantation trade might lead that kingdom to open up Ireland as its primary market made it imperative that Ireland be more closely subjected to English economic regulation and thus treated as a 'Colony for Trade' as much as a 'Colony for Empire'. If the Scots proposed to use the sovereignty of their Parliament and the relative maturity of their financial institutions to promote a colonial empire that might allow them to declare their independence of the English Parliament and even the English Protestant succession, then Ireland must more firmly be regulated as a colony and not allowed to pursue its own independent economic destiny as yet another competitive kingdom. This line of argument was pursued by the Bristol merchant John Cary, who perhaps did more than any other English writer of the 1690s to present the political economy of England and its dependencies as a single, interdependent system.[53] As Cary put it in his *Essay on the State of England* (1695), 'I take *England* and all its Plantations to be one great Body, those being so many Limbs or Counties belonging to it',[54] though he saw this English colonial empire as being in competition with the Scots to the North and held that Ireland was simply one of those plantations, and should be

[52] *The Queen an Empress, and Her Three Kingdoms One Empire* (London, 1706), 22, 31.
[53] For a succinct overview of Cary's political economy in its Bristolian context see David Harris Sacks, *The Widening Gate: Bristol and the Atlantic Economy, 1450–1700* (Berkeley, 1991), 339–43.
[54] John Cary, *An Essay on the State of England in Relation to its Trade, its Poor, and its Taxes, For Carrying on the Present War Against France* (Bristol, 1695), 66–7.

treated as such. The two major recommendations of the *Essay* struck at Ireland particularly, as Cary insisted that the plantation-trade should be made more dependent upon England than hitherto, and that England should become 'a Market for all the Wool of *Christendom*' in order that England should have the economic capacity to continue the Williamite war against France. Ireland should be treated on the same terms as the American plantations by repealing the Cattle Acts, since they had only encouraged the Irish to seek foreign outlets for their products, and hence to become dangerously industrious. It should also have its woollen trade confined to the export of raw material to England so that, like the other colonies, its interests could be entirely subordinated to England's.[55]

Cary became in due course one of the major proponents of the English Parliament's bill to restrict the exportation of Irish wool and was one of five English authors to offer replies to William Molyneux's *The Case of Ireland ... Stated*.[56] However, his prominence in these debates has distracted attention from his wider political-economic vision, particularly the connections he made between Ireland, Scotland and the American plantations. These connections were made clearer for his metropolitan English readership by the separate publication in 1696 of those sections of his *Essay* that concerned not only Irish but also Scottish trade.[57] This publication suggests that Cary's target was not solely the Irish woollen manufactory, but also the Scottish Parliament with its plans for a joint-stock company. Cary notoriously used the reprint of the *Essay* to reaffirm his argument that the kingdom of Ireland should be reduced to the status of a colony and its products harnessed for the benefit of England. He also drew his English readers' attention to the stirrings of economic innovation in Scotland, where woollen manufactures, a fishery company and plantations were being proposed. Though he discouraged the idea that any nation like Scotland which lacked a vibrant manufacturing base could raise the capital to finance a plantation trade, he nonetheless realised the dangers of a second British kingdom's possession of colonies for trade:

[55] Cary, *An Essay on the State of England*, sigs. A4ᵛ–[A5]ʳ; 10–11, 97–8; compare [Cary,] *To the Freeholders and Burgesses of the City of Bristol* (n.p., n.d. [Bristol, 1698?]), 3. A similar point about the Cattle Acts was made by the Board of Trade, 29 April 1697: PRO CO 381/10, f. 44ᵛ.
[56] John Cary, *A Vindication of the Parliament of England, In Answer to a Book Written by William Molyneux of Dublin, Esq.* (London, 1698); Patrick Kelly, 'The Irish Woollen Export Prohibition Act', 26–8. Molyneux, *The Case of Ireland ... Stated*, ed. Simms, 143–4, lists the English replies, to which should be added Charles Davenant, *An Essay upon the Probable Means of Making a People Gainers in the Balance of Trade* (1698), in *The Political and Commercial Works of Charles Davenant LL.D.*, ed. Charles Whitworth, 5 vols. (London, 1771), II, 239–59.
[57] John Cary, *A Discourse Concerning the Trade of Ireland and Scotland* (London, 1696), comprises Cary, *An Essay on the State of England*, 89–113.

I cannot see what advantage the *Scotch* can make at this time of day, by setling Plantations; which if they do attempt we must be sure to take care of *Ireland*, and by reducing it to the terms of a Colony, prevent their selling their Product there, which I am apt to think is the main thing they aim at.[58]

Cary was not alone in perceiving the interconnections between English, Scottish, Irish and colonial commerce. His antagonist Francis Brewster saw that the success of Scotland's East India trade would only deprive England of such advantages as it had in the Irish market.[59] Cary's ally and interlocutor, John Locke, from his vantage point on the English Board of Trade, had at least as expansive a vision of the British Atlantic world's commerce, even if he did not present a single, comprehensive survey of its interrelations in the way that Cary did. Though Locke's writings on interest and coinage form the most important part of his economic legacy,[60] he also deserves respect for his attention to the workings of the post-Revolutionary Atlantic economy.[61] Locke was the official on the Board of Trade who paid closest heed to the progress of the Company of Scotland's activities in the late 1690s,[62] and it was Locke who co-ordinated the board's efforts to promote linen manufacture in Ireland as an alternative to the Irish woollen industry.[63] Locke's interest in the prospects for the English woollen industry had been a central concern of his brief position-paper, 'For a Generall Naturalization' (1693), in which he had also shown himself aware of the dangers that depopulation had posed to the Spanish monarchy's possessions in the Indies. In line with the prescriptions of other contemporary political economists, Locke argued that wealth no longer lay in land, but rather in trade and hence also in the population necessary for extensive manufactures.[64] In the words of the manuscript addition he made to the *Second Treatise* in the late 1690s, '[t]his shews, how much numbers of men are to be preferd to largenesse of dominions, and that the increase of

[58] Cary, *Discourse*, 12–13; Cary, *Essay*, 111–13.

[59] [Sir Francis Brewster,] *A Discourse Concerning Ireland and the Different Interests Thereof, In Answer to the Exon and Barnstaple Petitions* (London, 1698), 52–4.

[60] *Locke on Money*, ed. Patrick Hyde Kelly, 2 vols. (Oxford, 1991).

[61] On which see especially Louise Fargo Brown, *The First Earl of Shaftesbury* (New York, 1933), chs. IX–X.

[62] Maurice Cranston, *John Locke: A Biography* (London, 1957), 444–6; Armitage, 'The Scottish Vision of Empire', in Robertson (ed.), *A Union for Empire*, 110. For Board of Trade documents relating to the Darien venture see Bod. MS Locke c. 30, ff. 33^r, 49^r–52^v, 53^r, 112^r–15^v, 116^r–18^v, 126^r, 127^r–28^v.

[63] See especially [John Locke,] report of the Board of Trade, 31 August 1697, in H. R. Fox Bourne, *The Life of John Locke*, 2 vols. (London, 1876), II, 363–72, which was the scheme 'pitched upon' by the Board of Trade: PRO CO 381/10, f. 107^v. For Board of Trade documents relating to the Irish woollen dispute see Bod. MS Locke c. 30, ff. 65^r–66^v, 67^r–68^{v}v, 69^r, 70^r–77^v, 78^r–81^v, 82^r–83^v, 84ff.

[64] John Locke, 'For a Generall Naturalization' (1693), in *Locke on Money*, ed. Kelly, II, 487–92.

lands [*sc.*, hands] and the right employing of them is the great art of government'.[65] This would be a problem for an extended and composite commonwealth, such as that formed by England and Ireland, as much as for a unitary polity.

Locke's arguments in the 1690s showed his awareness of the larger archipelagic and Atlantic context within which political-economic argument was now necessarily being played out. Yet, as the disputes over the Woollen Bills and the Company of Scotland showed, economic argument in the British Atlantic world after the Glorious Revolution readily became political and constitutional argument. The existence of three legislatures within the Three Kingdoms, each of which could be used as the instrument for the promotion of competing economic interests, inevitably led to collisions and confrontations, especially when the most powerful of them, the English Parliament, had such a freshly renewed sense of its own supremacy. An all-encompassing vision of political economy such as Cary's or Locke's at once allowed all of the British dominions to be seen as part of a single economic system, while the compulsions of contemporary political-economic theory revealed that the parts of that system would necessarily remain in tension with each other so long as they pursued separate economic interests.

Metropolitan analyses of the place of the colonies within an empire now increasingly defined by the terms of political economy converged on a series of common theoretical assumptions and historical lessons, many of which seemed to have been reaffirmed by recent Anglo-Irish and Anglo-Scottish relations. The three most influential analysts of the political economy of the plantations were Josiah Child, Charles Davenant and William Wood.[66] All three agreed with Locke that population, rather than territory – and hence 'hands', not 'lands' – was the most important commodity for a flourishing polity, whether a state or an empire.[67] The historical experience of the Dutch and the Spanish supported this contention: the Dutch, a landless people, had increased their wealth enormously by commerce, and had encouraged population by means of religious toleration; over the course of a century, the

[65] John Locke, *Second Treatise*, § 42, ll. 21–3, in *Two Treatises of Government*, ed. Peter Laslett, rev. edn (Cambridge, 1988), 297–8.
[66] Sir Josiah Child, *A New Discourse of Trade* (London, 1698), 178–216, ch. x, 'Concerning Plantations'; Charles Davenant, *Discourses on the Public Revenues and on the Trade of England* (1698), 'Discourse III: On the Plantation Trade', in Davenant, *Political and Commercial Works*, ed. Whitworth, ii, 1–76; [William Wood,] *Survey of Trade*, 131–94, pt iii, 'The Great Advantages of our Colonies and Plantations to Great Britain, and our Interest in Preserving and Encouraging them, and how they may be further Improved'.
[67] Child, *New Discourse of Trade*, 179, 180; Davenant, 'On the Plantation Trade', in Davenant, *Political and Commercial Works*, ed. Whitworth, ii, 26, 29; [Wood,] *Survey of Trade*, 162.

Spanish, their former governors, had become impoverished and de-populated in Europe, so that their colonies had been a cause of decline rather than a source of greatness.[68] All three authors therefore found it necessary to refute the charge that England's colonies would destroy the metropolis by drawing migrants across the Atlantic. On the contrary, they argued, the flourishing colonies encouraged manufactures, shipping and employment at home, to the advantage of England. However, this could only be sustained by firm regulation of the colonies, under the terms of the Navigation Acts: mercantilist protection, for the benefit of the metropolis, was the key to a flourishing empire, and any signs of colonial independence would have to be quashed, as they had been in Ireland, in order to continue the favourable relationship between England (after 1707, Britain) and its colonies.[69] In 1775, all three writers' discourses on colonies would be collected to provide an argument for conciliation between the colonies and the metropolis, 'with a View of showing the *Americans* the Stake they risque in the present Contest',[70] thereby confirming the apparent utility of this mercantilist analysis to the metropolitan conception of the British Empire.

Politics and economics converged to provide the analytical framework within which the relations between England, Ireland, Scotland and the American colonies would be understood for at least half a century after the Glorious Revolution, an event that had not only 'deliver'd the People of *Great Britain* from Popery and Slavery', as Wood noted, but also 'gave them that which is inseparable from their being Freemen, a *Liberty of Trading to any Part of the known World*'.[71] Despite the unequal effects of the Glorious Revolution for the Three Kingdoms and for the colonies, and despite the constitutional differences that were made all the more obvious by the Union of 1707, that association of religious and civil liberty with freedom of trade became an enduring ideological foundation of the British Empire.[72]

This argument found graphic expression in Sir James Thornhill's decoration of the Upper Hall at Greenwich Hospital between 1718 and 1725. Though less elaborate than the spectacular allegory of William

---

[68] Child, *New Discourse of Trade*, 181–2, 189–90; Davenant, 'On the Plantation Trade', in Davenant, *Political and Commercial Works*, ed. Whitworth, II, 30; [Wood,] *Survey of Trade*, 134.

[69] Child, *New Discourse of Trade*, 194, 216; Davenant, 'On the Plantation Trade', in Davenant, *Political and Commercial Works*, ed. Whitworth, II, 10, 24–5; [Wood,] *Survey of Trade*, 137.

[70] *Select Dissertations on Colonies and Plantations*, ed. Charles Whitworth (London, 1775), v, 1–23 (Child), 27–84 (Davenant), 87–113 (Wood).

[71] [Wood,] *Survey of Trade*, 181.

[72] Jack P. Greene, 'Empire and Identity from the Glorious Revolution to the American Revolution', in P. J. Marshall (ed.), *The Oxford History of the British Empire*, II: *The Eighteenth Century* (Oxford, 1998), 208–13, 221–3.

and Mary spreading peace and liberty throughout Europe that covers the ceiling of the Lower Hall of the Hospital, the Upper Hall's paintings aptly depicted the post-Revolutionary, and post-Union, Anglo-British imperial ideology. Neptune and Britannia, 'attended by *Reason* of *State* and *Love* of her *Country*', greet William III at Torbay; the four continents and all the gods of the sea acclaim Queen Anne; justice and peace accompany George I's landing at Greenwich, alongside St George crushing the dragon of 'Popery' and the cringing figure of Jacobite 'Rebellion'. The argument of this suite of paintings concludes in two paintings to show 'that our *Trade, Commerce,* and *Publick Wealth* are chiefly owing to our NAVY', in the form of allegories of '*Salus Publica*' and '*Securitas Publica*', each linking naval power, commerce and the good of the *res publica*.[73] Thornhill's neo-classical celebration of commercial reason of state showed that the discourse of political economy was not incompatible with neo-Roman conceptions of the *res publica*, nor was it necessary to counterpose them. Reason of state could be cast as *salus publica*, and public safety readily redefined in economic terms to suit the demands of a modern state.

Confirmation that Barbon and Hume had been premature in their announcement of the irrelevance of Machiavelli to the modern, commercial world came from James Edward Oglethorpe. Oglethorpe contributed to the creation of an informal eighteenth-century canon of colonial writings by combining Machiavellianism with political economy in his *Select Tracts Relating to Colonies* (1732). The work was part of his campaign to promote the new settlement of Georgia, and justified the colony with testimony from Francis Bacon's essay 'On Plantations', the Dutch political economist Pieter de la Court, William Penn, Josiah Child and Machiavelli. Oglethorpe skilfully excerpted 'the *Florentine Historian*' to show that he recommended a plan remarkably similar to Oglethorpe's own for Georgia, a colony founded on a plan of 'Religion, Liberty, good Laws, the Exercise of Arms, and Encouragement of Arts', particularly after the Roman model recommended in *Discorsi*, II. 6.[74]

---

[73] [Sir James Thornhill,] *An Explanation of the Painting in the Royal Hospital at Greenwich* (London, n.d.), 14, 20; Edward Croft-Murray, *Decorative Painting in England 1537–1837*, 2 vols. (London, 1962), I, 76, 268–9.

[74] [James Edward Oglethorpe,] *Select Tracts Relating to Colonies* (London, n.d. [1732]), sig. A[3]ʳ, 1–4 (Bacon); 5–17 (Machiavelli, *Istorie Fiorentine*, II; *Principe*, III; *Discorsi*, I.1; I.10; I.11; I.21; II.6; II.7; II.19); 18–25 (de la Court); 26–30 (Penn); 31–40 (Child); for Oglethorpe's sources see [Leigh and Sotheby,] *A Catalogue of the Entire and Valuable Library of General Oglethorpe, Lately Deceased* (London, 1788), items 292, 562, 1111, 1864; on the authorship and dating of the work see Rodney M. Baine, 'James Oglethorpe and the Early Promotional Literature for Georgia', *William and Mary Quarterly*, 3rd ser., 45 (1988), 104–5. Compare James Edward Oglethorpe, *Some Account of the Design of the Trustees for Establishing Colonys in America* (1732), ed. Rodney M. Baine and Phinizy Spalding (Athens, Ga., 1990), 5–10.

Machiavelli may have been mostly silent regarding commerce as a reason of state, but he could certainly still supply pointed advice for the promotion of a modern colony; such counsel could also be aptly combined with the most modern analyses of commercial compulsions, to offer a rounded, and persuasive, account of the means and reasons for settling new plantations at such a late date. Oglethorpe's subtle rapprochement between Machiavellianism and political economy offered one resolution of the ancient dilemma of *imperium* and *libertas*, in line with the recommendations of modern reason of state. It seemed from this, as also from Thornhill's prominent representations of the post-Revolutionary British *salus publica*, that Barbon's and Hume's announcements of the death of Machiavellianism in the modern commercial world were, perhaps, somewhat exaggerated.

CHAPTER 7

Empire and ideology in the Walpolean era

When Britain first, at heaven's command,
Arose from out the azure main,
This was the charter of the land,
And guardian angels sung this strain –
'Rule, Britannia, rule the waves;
Britons never will be slaves'.[1]

It is now an historiographical commonplace that the 1730s and early 1740s marked a watershed in the history of the British state and empire. Both British and American historians take the decade on either side of 1740 as a pivotal moment in the histories of nationalism, patriotism and national identity. They do so because this seems to be the moment at which British identity began to coalesce within Britain itself, a generation after the Anglo-Scottish Union of 1707, to mark 'the birth of a powerfully self-confident British nationalism'.[2] 'It was precisely during these early conflicts in the formation of British markets that the symbols of the British nation came into being': the Union flag, 'God Save the King', 'Rule, Britannia', the rules of cricket and Edmund Hoyle's codification of whist, quadrille, backgammon and chess.[3] At the same time, it has been argued, 1740 marked the end of the period – roughly corresponding to the length of a single lifetime – in which communications around the British Atlantic world had changed substantially and irreversibly. From this point onward, a British Atlantic community became conceivable in practice as 'colonial leaders initiated changes in the meaning of the word "empire" to include themselves and their localities in an organic union with the British Isles in what, by 1740, was

---

[1] James Thomson, *Alfred: A Masque* (London, 1740), 42–3.
[2] T. H. Breen, 'Ideology and Nationalism on the Eve of the American Revolution: Revisions *Once More* in Need of Revising', *Journal of American History*, 84 (1997), 19.
[3] Peter Linebaugh, *The London Hanged: Crime and Civil Society in the Eighteenth Century* (Cambridge, 1992), 116–17.

coming to be called the "British Empire"'.[4] All the British Empire needed to overcome its institutional heterogeneity was a common ideology. This could readily be supplied in the form of the burgeoning British nationalism generated in the metropolis. However, the exchange from the metropolis to the provinces ultimately fostered dissolution rather than integration. In due course, the aggressiveness of that nationalism, the unredeemable promises made to the colonists in the form of the rights of Englishmen, and the fissile consequences of the export of British political theory together ensured that the British Atlantic Empire would sunder and then be refashioned in the decades after the Seven Years War. It was in that period that, although 'new concepts of empire were slow to emerge, language and terminology began to change, as those associated with the dominion of the seas based on liberty no longer seemed appropriate'.[5]

During the second quarter of the eighteenth century, the anglophone inhabitants of the Atlantic world began for the first time habitually to describe their community as the 'British Empire'. This British Empire included the United Kingdom of Great Britain and its dependencies within Europe; Britain's insular possessions in the West Indies; and the continental colonies of British North America. Sometimes, though not always, it also encompassed the slave-stations, factories and forts of Africa and the East Indies, and it was increasingly acknowledged that 'the general NAVIGATION of *Great Britain* owes all its *Encrease* and *Splendor* to the Commerce of its *American* and *African Colonies*', and hence to the slave-trade, 'the next valuable Branch of Trade belonging to the *British Empire*'.[6] Such a conception of a united British Empire demanded the union of a substantive idea of Britishness with a redefinition of inherited ideas of empire. That idea of a 'British Empire' also had to be sufficiently broad to encompass the pluralism of a multinational and multi-denominational polity, while necessarily narrow enough to exclude those deemed unworthy of its political benefits. As we have seen, the *concept* of the British Empire – as a particular kind of political community that incorporated various peoples and territories and which could be described as British, rather than English or Scottish alone, for example – had a long history, stretching back to the mid-sixteenth century.

[4] Ian K. Steele, *The English Atlantic: 1675–1740: An Exploration of Communication and Community* (New York, 1986), 278; compare Richard Koebner, *Empire* (Cambridge, 1961), ch. 3.
[5] P. J. Marshall, 'Britain and the World in the Eighteenth Century: I, Reshaping the Empire', *Transactions of the Royal Historical Society*, 6th ser., 8 (1998), 10.
[6] [Malachy Postlethwayt,] *The African Trade, The Great Pillar and Support of the British Plantation Trade in America* (London, 1745), 6, 20.

However, various *conceptions* of the British Empire continued to offer competing ideological descriptions of that community. 'The concepts we have settle for us the form of the experience we have of the world', the philosopher Peter Winch has noted. 'That is not to say that our concepts may not change; but when they do, that means that our concept of the world has changed too'.[7] This is perhaps especially true when such concepts define the nature and limits of the polity itself. Accordingly, if it is possible to pinpoint the emergence of a new language to describe the British Empire, then the examination of that language should reveal the existence of a new conception of the Empire itself.[8]

That the British Empire was conceived as a political community incorporating Britain, Ireland and the plantations during the 1730s can be seen from the works of moral philosophers, historians, pamphleteers and poets across the whole range of private and public discourse. By being conceived at this time – during the years of Sir Robert Walpole's tenure as chief minister – the British Empire acquired a distinctive history, genealogy and ideology. This conception was criticised and challenged even at the moment it emerged. It was therefore originally an ideology, not an identity; that is, it was a contribution to political argument, and not a normative self-conception. It may have become an identity later, but that development should not obscure its beginnings in political ideology, or the causes that ideology promoted. Both the ground-breaking work of Kathleen Wilson and the recent magisterial survey of British imperial 'identity' in the long eighteenth century by Jack P. Greene have each assumed the category of identity as an idiomatic and unproblematic one in this period.[9] However, this begs the question of how it became possible for Britons to conceive of the Anglo-British monarchy and its overseas dependencies as members of a single community at all, let alone how they adopted that conception as a distinctive 'identity'. Clearly, such a conception demanded something more geographically expansive than the perception of a contiguous territorial unit: it depended on a conception of the state and its authority, whether embodied in the monarchy or legislated by Parliament,

[7] Peter Winch, *The Idea of a Social Science and its Relation to Philosophy*, 2nd edn (London, 1990), 15.
[8] Quentin Skinner, 'Language and Social Change', in James Tully (ed.), *Meaning and Context: Quentin Skinner and His Critics* (Princeton, 1988), 119–33; Terence Ball, James Farr and Russell L. Hanson (eds.), *Political Innovation and Conceptual Change* (Cambridge, 1989).
[9] Kathleen Wilson, 'Empire, Trade and Popular Politics in Mid-Hanoverian Britain: The Case of Admiral Vernon', *Past and Present*, 121 (Nov. 1988), 74–109; Wilson, *The Sense of the People: Politics, Culture and Imperialism in England, 1715–1785* (Cambridge, 1995); Jack P. Greene, 'Empire and Identity from the Glorious Revolution to the American Revolution', in P. J. Marshall (ed.), *The Oxford History of the British Empire*, II: *The Eighteenth Century* (Oxford, 1998), 208–30.

though not contained within a British imperial church; it also had to be extended to encompass a more expansive conception of the nation.

The conception that emerged in the 1730s defined Britain and the British Empire (at least for the generation after the War of Jenkins's Ear) as Protestant, commercial, maritime and free. 'This vision, predicated on a mixture of adulterated mercantilism, nationalistic anxiety and libertarian fervor, was clearly both rose-colored and self-serving' and (no doubt for this reason) proved 'immensely attractive to domestic publics' – and, it might be added, to many provincial publics, too.[10] It found its greatest purchase in the oppositional polemics of the 1730s and early 1740s, where it provided a counter-argument to the supposed pusillanimity of Walpole's government, which had patiently refused to be drawn into a commercial war with Spain until 1739.[11] James Thomson's ode 'Rule, Britannia' was the most lasting expression of this conception.[12] As might be expected from the aggressively Anglicising son of a Scottish Whig mother and a Lowland Presbyterian minister father, Thomson defined the polity as 'Britain', the divinely-ordained island lifted from the sea 'at heaven's command', destined to rule the waves, whose people were promised both positive and negative liberty ('Britons never will be slaves'; 'thou shalt flourish great and free'). This commercial thalassocracy would be home to the 'Muses', the liberty-loving women who would be protected, like the feminised isle herself, by 'manly hearts to guard the fair'. Thomson's Britannia therefore ruled an empire of difference, defined by its oppositions, where men would defend women, freemen would not be slaves, liberty would defeat tyranny, and the empire of the seas would outlive, outfight and outprosper military monarchies with territorial dominions.

The popularity of 'Rule, Britannia' kept alive this conception of the British Empire. Nonetheless, according to the best recent student of early eighteenth-century oppositional patriotism, Thomson's 'apparently straightforward expression of patriotism ... proves resistant to analysis'.[13] The same might be said of the larger conception transmitted by

[10] Wilson, *The Sense of the People*, 157; compare Nicholas Rogers, *Whigs and Cities: Popular Politics in the Age of Walpole and Pitt* (Oxford, 1989), 58–9.
[11] For a defence of Walpole's actions see R. W. Harding, *Amphibious Warfare in the Eighteenth Century: The British Expedition to the West Indies 1740–42* (Woodbridge, 1991), ch. 1.
[12] On the genesis and reception of 'Rule, Britannia', see William Hayman Cummings, *Dr. Arne and Rule, Britannia* (London, 1912), 111–36.
[13] Christine Gerrard, *The Patriot Opposition to Walpole: History, Politics, and National Myth, 1720–1742* (Oxford, 1994), 3; though compare Clement Ramsland, 'Britons Never Will Be Slaves: A Study in Whig Political Propaganda in the British Theatre, 1700–1742', *Quarterly Journal of Speech*, 28 (1942), 393–9; Linda Colley, *Britons: Forging the Nation, 1707–1837* (New Haven, 1992), 11.

the ode. The prevalence during the anti-Walpolean agitations and long thereafter of the conception of the character of Britain and its empire as Protestant, commercial, maritime and free has rendered it seemingly natural and inarguable, as no doubt its proponents intended it should be.[14] Though this conception persisted throughout the eighteenth century and has endured since, it did not stand alone or unchallenged as a conception of empire, either then or now. For these reasons, 'God Save the King' – a product of the years of the War of the Austrian Succession, but more martial, more monarchical and more obviously hierarchical than 'Rule, Britannia', as befit its anti-Jacobite rather than precisely anti-Walpolean or anti-Spanish origins[15] – would be the preferred anthem during the British Empire's late eighteenth-century period of aristocratic authoritarianism. In light of these alternatives, and in the knowledge that the competition between conceptions of empire would burgeon in the years following the Peace of Paris of 1763, it is more important to historicise this conception, rather than accept that it became normative (as many historians have effectively done). Thereby it might be possible to understand where it came from, how it came to be attached to a particular concept of the British Empire as an Atlantic community, and indeed what were the effects of its endurance.

The limits to the emergence of an integrative conception of the British Empire beyond the Three Kingdoms can be seen in the early topographical histories of the English – later, British – empire. Such histories assumed the economic importance of overseas possessions to England, but largely failed to see them as integral parts of a single polity. For example, Nathaniel Crouch's *The English Empire in America* (1685) traversed the mainland colonies from Newfoundland to Carolina, then travelled the islands from Bermuda to Jamaica, an arrangement that remained unchanged in six later editions up to 1739. His aim was to 'discover the Acquisitions and Dominions of the *English* Monarchy in *America*',[16] thereby to delineate the 'empire' in the western hemisphere as a set of political communities distinct from, though subordinate to, the English monarchy. In 1708, Crouch's successor as an imperial topographer, John Oldmixon, described 'the British Empire in Amer-

---

[14] Gerald Berkeley Hertz, *British Imperialism in the Eighteenth Century* (London, 1908), 7–59.

[15] William H. Cummings, *God Save the King: The Origin and History of the Music and Words of the National Anthem* (London, 1902), 29–30, 32; on the supposed origins of 'God Save the King' as also a celebration of Vernon's victory at Portobello, see Cummings, *God Save the King*, 50–7.

[16] 'R. B.' [Nathaniel Crouch,] *The English Empire in America: Or a Prospect of His Majesties Dominions in the West-Indies* (London, 1685), 1.

ica', to show the economic advantages of a commercial (rather than a territorial) empire to Britain. Oldmixon acknowledged that it was difficult 'for an exact History of all the *British Empire* in the *West-Indies* to be fram'd by one Man in *America* or *Europe*'. He adopted the mercantilist analysis of Child and Davenant to confirm that migrants were not lost to Britain, that the plantations saved rather than expended money by virtue of import-substitution, and that neo-classical anxieties about colonisation were now analytically irrelevant: 'the Arguments brought from Antiquity will be of no use to the Enemies of Colonies'. Rome may have secured its conquests by colonies, but the British colonies were even more advantageous for the simple reason that 'the Safety of a Nation is of greater Consequence than its Extent of Empire'.[17] These arguments remained largely unchanged when Oldmixon published a new edition of his work during the 'present Juncture' of the Anglo-Spanish War, even as the extent of the '*British Empire* on the *Continent*' had expanded to include Oglethorpe's recently settled and strategically vulnerable Georgia colony.[18]

The concepts of the British Empire propagated by Crouch and Oldmixon were firmly transatlantic, at least from the perspective of the metropolis. Their object of inquiry was the 'British Empire *in* America' or the 'British Empire *of* America', not a collective or even collaborative British Empire that incorporated the British plantations and colonies into a single community alongside the Three Kingdoms of Britain and Ireland. Metropolitan attempts to rationalise the structure of the Hanoverian dominions remained transatlantic. The first major survey of the 'State of the British Plantations in America' since the Dominion of New England, produced for the Board of Trade in 1721, had delineated George I's 'Plantations on the Continent of America' colony by colony (though omitting Newfoundland and Hudson's Bay, because not under 'civil government') rather than attempt to describe an integrated and pan-Atlantic British Empire. The report assumed no unity between the plantations and the metropolis, except in so far as all were joined under the sovereignty of the crown. Yet if *imperium* was unitary, *dominium* was divided, as various proprietors, patentees and royal governments claimed separate rights of property, based on the right of first discovery, occupation or cession. The report recommended

---

[17] [John Oldmixon,] *The British Empire in America, Containing the History of the Discovery, Settlement, Progress and Present State of All the British Colonies, on the Continent and Islands of America*, 2 vols. (London, 1708), I, xiv, xix–xx, xxxv–xxxvi, xxxvii.

[18] [John Oldmixon,] *The British Empire in America*, 2nd edn, 2 vols. (London, 1741), I, v, xii, 525–41.

that the Crown reassume all the proprietary governments to ensure that 'all the British Colonies in America hold immediately of one Lord, & have but one joint purpose to pursue'.[19] This recommendation that *imperium* and *dominium* should be conjoined was not, of course, taken up. Its failure perpetuated a necessarily unstable conception of the British Empire whose internal contradictions could be adroitly exploited by those like Thomas Jefferson and John Adams, who could easily show that, since first discovery had been undertaken by individuals and not by the British state, Parliament could make no claims over the colonists who were encompassed only by royal *imperium*.[20]

The emergence of a pan-Atlantic conception of the British Empire coincided with the next wave of reform of the colonial administration in the 1730s, and sprang initially from a cadre of imperial officials and provincials, some of whom had been involved in the drafting of the 1721 report. 'In the decade preceding the renewal of war with Spain and France, the home government took the first steps in conceiving and implementing a theory of empire suitable for a mature colonial system'.[21] Such a theory had to reconcile the paradox of a mercantilist colonial system informed by post-Revolutionary political ideology, which promised the Anglo-British 'rights of Englishmen' to all free inhabitants of the colonies while subordinating their economic activities to the needs of the metropolis. That it failed to do so had as much to do with the abrupt termination of the experiment in the face of Anglo-Spanish conflict at the end of the 1730s as it did with the unwillingness of Walpole's government to relax the demands of metropolitan mercantilism in favour of greater autonomy for the colonists. The failure of Walpole and his ministers to square the circle and fashion a suitable theory of empire nonetheless had two important consequences. The very attempt encouraged various Britons throughout the Atlantic world to conceive of themselves as partners in a single polity; meanwhile, the failure of it left the responsibility for fashioning a mutually acceptable ideology of empire to the opposition; anything as systematic as a theory would have demanded the resolution of contradictions, as well as the

[19] 'State of the British Plantations in America' (8 September 1721), in *Documents Relative to the Colonial History of the State of New-York*, ed. E. B. O'Callaghan, 11 vols. (Albany, 1853–61), v, 591–630.
[20] Thomas Jefferson, 'Refutation of the Argument that the Colonies Were Established at the Expense of the British Nation' (1776), in *The Papers of Thomas Jefferson, I: 1760–1776*, ed. Julian P. Boyd (Princeton, 1950), 277–84; [John Adams and Daniel Leonard,] *Novanglus and Massachusettensis: or Political Essays* (Boston, 1819), 79; Michael Kammen, 'The Meaning of Colonization in American Revolutionary Thought', *Journal of the History of Ideas*, 31 (1976), 337–58.
[21] James A. Henretta, *'Salutary Neglect': Colonial Administration under the Duke of Newcastle* (Princeton, 1972), 94.

necessary reforms – whether to strengthen metropolitan control, or to allow greater colonial autonomy – to overcome the paradoxes.[22]

A Scottish baronet and former deputy governor of Pennsylvania, Sir William Keith presents a good example of the shift that took place between the 1720s and the late 1730s. In 1721, he had been one of the informants behind the Board of Trade's report, and in 1728, in another survey of the British American colonies, he firmly subordinated the interests of the colonies to those of Britain, on the grounds that 'a lesser publick Good must give place to a greater'.[23] Yet by 1738, the impoverished Keith had thrown in his lot with the opposition to Sir Robert Walpole. He dedicated his *History of the British Plantations in America* – the first volume of a projected series anatomising all of the British possessions in the western hemisphere – to Frederick, Prince of Wales, and later endorsed the 'universal Satisfaction' at the declaration of war with Spain in 1739.[24] In the introduction to his *History*, Keith offered a broadly civic-humanist account of the origins and development of civil government in the British colonies. In line with the often-quoted prescriptions of the 106th of *Cato's Letters*, Keith argued that only gentle treatment of the colonies by the metropolis could ensure that the benefits of mercantilism would be sustained. He identified liberty as the promotion of the common good, and by assuming that it was 'altogether impracticable to separate and divide the Interest of the Subject in the *British* Plantations from that of the whole State', he defined that good as common both to the metropolis and to the plantations.[25] As he affirmed elsewhere in 1739, 'the common Interest of the *British* State or Commonwealth, most certainly includes the Subjects of *America*'.[26] This conjunctive concept of the '*British* State or Commonwealth' as including the subjects in the plantations sprang from Keith's experience in the colonies; it also reflected the priorities of the Opposition, for whom those colonies were integral parts of the British possessions threatened

---

[22] On the general problem illustrated by this particular instance see Jack P. Greene, *Peripheries and Center: Constitutional Development in the Extended Polities of the British Empire and the United States 1607–1788* (Athens, Ga., 1986).

[23] [Sir William Keith,] 'A Short Discourse on the Present State of the Colonies in America' (November 1728), PRO co 5/4, f. 170'; printed in Keith, *A Collection of Papers and Other Tracts, Written Occasionally*, 2nd edn (London, 1749), 174.

[24] [Sir William Keith,] *Some Useful Observations on the Consequences of the Present War with Spain* (London, n.d. [1740]), 1–6.

[25] Sir William Keith, *The History of the British Plantations in America* (London, 1738), 4–5, 12, 15; Roy N. Lokken, 'Sir William Keith's Theory of the British Empire', *The Historian*, 25 (1963), 403–18.

[26] [Sir William Keith,] 'Proposal for the Establishing by Act of Parliament the Duties upon Stampt Paper and Parchment in All the *British American* Colonies' (1739), in [Keith,] *Two Papers on the Subject of Taxing the British Colonies in America* (London, 1767), 18.

by Spain which should therefore be defended against Spanish depreda-
tion, even at the cost of transatlantic war.

The creation of a pan-Atlantic concept of the British Empire emerged
at the same time in the Caribbean, as can be seen from the pamphlets of
the Barbadian planter John Ashley. Ashley's words from 1743 have often
been cited as evidence of the emergence of a concept of 'the *British*
Empire, taking all together as one body, viz. *Great Britain, Ireland,* and the
Plantations and *Fishery* in *America,* besides its possessions in the *East-Indies*
and *Africa*'.[27] Though this may have been a precocious example of a
concept that would become widespread in the aftermath of the Seven
Years War, it was in fact somewhat belated among Ashley's own
changing concepts of the British Empire. For example, in 1732 he had
argued for increased metropolitan attention 'to protect and cherish its
West-India colonies, confound their Enemies, and assert and gloriously
maintain The *British* Empire in *America*'.[28] If his concept in 1743 was
pan-Atlantic, in 1732 it had been firmly transatlantic, locating the British
Empire in the western hemisphere, as perhaps one among many concentric British empires, though certainly as a British empire detached
from, albeit superintended by, the metropolis. By 1740, in the third of his
interventions into debate on West Indian tariffs and revenues, Ashley
defined the sugar colonies as 'a Branch of the *British* Dominions on
which the Wealth and Naval Power of *Great Britain* does in great
measure depend', linked by British shipping, supplied with British
goods, and enriching Britain by its products, and hence inextricably
bound together by a set of common interests to form one '*British*
Nation'.[29] His remark of 1743 was therefore a restatement of this vision
of pan-imperial interests in the British Atlantic world; only at that point
did he define that congeries of interests as the *British* Empire.

The major dependency of the 'British Empire in Europe' was, of
course, Ireland.[30] However, the emergent British Empire of the Walpolean era was relatively little celebrated by patriot opinion in Ireland.
Instead, the Irish concept of the British Empire had always sprung from
various strands of unionism. For example, the anonymous author of *The*

---

[27] John Ashley, *The Second Part of Memoirs and Considerations Concerning the Trade and Revenues of the British Colonies in America* (London, 1743), 94 (compare *ibid.*, sigs. A1ᵛ–A2ʳ, 96), cited in, for example, Koebner, *Empire*, 88, and P. J. Marshall, 'Introduction', in Marshall (ed.), *The Oxford History of the British Empire II: The Eighteenth Century*, 7.

[28] [John Ashley,] *The British Empire in America, Consider'd* (London, 1732), 29.

[29] [John Ashley,] *Memoirs and Considerations Concerning the Trade and Revenues of the British Colonies in America* (London, 1740), 11, 26.

[30] Jean Louis de Lolme, *The British Empire in Europe: Part the First, Containing an Account of the Connection Between the Kingdoms of England and Ireland, Previous to the Year 1780* (Dublin, 1787).

Present State of Ireland (1673) described Ireland as 'one of the chiefest members of the *British* Empire' and 'like to prove profitable to the Prince, and at all times a good additional strength to the *Brittish Empire*', by which was meant the Anglo-British monarchy based in London.[31] From the other side of the confessional divide, Father Peter Walsh argued in 1674 for the transnational community of British and Irish Catholics, 'those in this famous Empire of *Great Britain*, that continue in Ecclesiastical Communion with the *Catholick* Bishop of old *Rome*'.[32] Walsh denied that there was any necessary collision between allegiance to the Stuart monarchy and communion with Rome, but such an imperial perspective sat more comfortably with the Protestant Anglo-Irish argument in the 1690s 'that we are of one Religion, that we are a Province of their Empire, and have neither Laws nor Governors but of their sending us'.[33]

Though '[t]he 1730s and 1740s . . . represent the nadir for pro-union sentiment on both sides of the Irish Sea', Irish unionists did appeal to a conception of the British Empire cast in the idiom of political economy.[34] For example, Samuel Madden lamented the fact that Ireland had failed to benefit from British prosperity, liberty and civility, and hence to profit from 'the Inheritance of our Ancestors, who were sent hither to enlarge the *British* Empire and Commerce'. He proposed, among other solutions, internal colonisation of the country to increase population and production to 'put our selves a Degree or two above the *Savage Indians*', the strenuous avoidance of luxury goods, and, ultimately, incorporating union with England, rather than immiserating dependency, to make Ireland 'a vast Support and encrease to the *English* Empire, wealth and strength in the World'.[35] Madden drew upon the work of the Ulsterman, Arthur Dobbs, who, as a colonial governor and promoter of the North-West Passage, elaborated one of the most comprehensive concepts of the British Empire in the mid-eighteenth century, ranging from Ireland to Hudson's Bay.[36] In 1729, Dobbs promoted

[31] *The Present State of Ireland: Together with Some Remarques Upon the Antient State Thereof* (London, 1673), sigs. A2ᵛ–3ʳ, 79.
[32] Peter Walsh, *A Letter to the Catholicks of England, Ireland, Scotland, and All Other Dominions under His Gracious Majesty Charles II* (London, 1674), 1.
[33] [John Hovell,] *A Discourse upon the Woollen Manufactury of Ireland and the Consequences of Prohibiting its Exportation* (London, 1698), 8.
[34] James Kelly, 'The Origins of the Act of Union: An Examination of Unionist Opinion in Britain and Ireland, 1650–1800', *Irish Historical Studies*, 25 (1987), 245.
[35] [Samuel Madden,] *Reflections and Resolutions Proper for the Gentlement of Ireland* (Dublin, 1738), 26, 50–51, 57, 124.
[36] For Madden's use of Dobbs see [Madden,] *Reflections and Resolutions*, 96, 115, 190, 224.

the comparative ability of Ireland to 'add considerably to the Power of the *British Empire*' by its trade and manufactures, not as a competitor to 'the Seat of Empire' in Britain, but as 'the choicest Jewel and Acquisition of the *Crown* and People of England'.[37] In the same year, he presented Sir Robert Walpole with a comprehensive scheme for the economic development of the British American colonies, and he proposed British settlements in California and Easter Island as the key to British trade in the South Seas.[38] Anglo-Irish union was the commercial and constitutional cornerstone of Dobbs's concept of the British Empire, though that in itself revealed the range of concentric empires within the British Empire, each of which maintained different relations with the metropolis.

The emergence of a pan-Atlantic concept of the British Empire was the product of an epistemological as much as a conceptual shift. Before it became necessary to conceive the nature of the connection between the metropolis and the plantations, that connection had to be perceived. Progress towards such an apprehension of the nature of the British Empire as a unity had undoubtedly been made during the course of the seventeenth century, whether in the creation of various British Atlantic communities by migration and communication, by the rise of mercantilist thought, or by the statutory prescriptions of Parliament which had bound the colonies to the metropolis within a single trading system since promulgation of the first Navigation Acts. However, the precise nature of that epistemology of empire was not described until David Hume's *Treatise of Human Nature* (1739–40), which he researched and wrote during the latter years of Robert Walpole's regime and published at the opening of the War of Jenkins's Ear.

In his discussion 'Of Contiguity, and Distance in Space and Time' (*Treatise*, II. 3. 7–8), Hume noted that though distance both in space and in time affects the strength of our imagination, and hence the force of our passions, 'the consequences of a removal in *space* are much inferior to those of a removal in *time*'. Thus, twenty years in the lifetime of one person would greatly diminish the acuity of memory; with that dimin-

---

[37] Arthur Dobbs, *An Essay on the Trade and Improvement of Ireland* (Dublin, 1729), sig. a[1]^v, [a2]^r, 66; on Dobbs see Desmond Clarke, *Arthur Dobbs, Esq., 1689–1765* (London, 1958); Raymond Gillespie, 'The Ulster of Arthur Dobbs', in D. Helen Rankin and E. Charles Nelson (eds.), *Curious in Everything: The Career of Arthur Dobbs of Carrickfergus 1689–1765* (Carrickfergus, 1990), 1–5.

[38] Dobbs, 'Memorial on the Northwest Passage' (1731), in William Barr and Glyndwr Williams (eds.), *Voyages in Search of a Northwest Passage*, 2 vols. (London, 1994), I, 9–36; Dobbs, *An Account of the Countries Adjoining to Hudson's Bay, in the North-West Part of America* (London, 1744), 167–8; Trevor Parkhill, 'Arthur Dobbs: Colonial Undertaker and Governor of North Carolina', in Rankin and Nelson (eds.), *Curious in Everything*, 15–22.

ution would come a parallel abatement of our sentiments regarding actions distant in time. However, a distance of a thousand leagues will not have an effect proportional to a similar distance in time. Hume's example, though passing, was significant in the context of the emergence of a pan-Atlantic concept of the British Empire: 'A *West-India* merchant will tell you', he reported, 'that he is not without concern about what passes in *Jamaica*; tho' few extend their views so far into futurity, as to dread very remote accidents'.[39] As we will see, Hume was both the acutest analyst of the concept of identity in British philosophy of the 1730s and the sharpest critic of the emergent ideology with which the British Empire was being equipped at the same time. By this example, though, he showed, even fleetingly, that action at a distance – specifically, action at an *imperial* distance – could excite the passions and create intellectual connections. As Thomas Haskell, among others, has argued, just such a conception of 'action at a distance' helps to provide an epistemological explanation for the emergence of the abolitionist movement in the 1790s: without such an expansive conception of causation, it was literally inconceivable that humanitarian sentiment could have acted effectively on a global, or at least hemispheric, scale.[40] Hume revealed the connection between distance and sentiment that the economic connections within an imperial community could create. He did not share the sentiment of passionate connection he diagnosed in the West India merchant, but he was aware that a concept of imperial contiguity, even across Atlantic spaces, had emerged, and that it was associated in particular with those who had specific financial and commercial interests in the colonies, like the merchants of Glasgow and, no doubt, planters like John Ashley.

The concept of the British Empire as a congeries of territories linked by their commerce, united with common interests and centred politically upon London, was therefore originally provincial, and arose among unionists in Ireland, planters in the Caribbean and officials in the mainland colonies over the course of the first quarter of the eighteenth century. It was the product above all of a group of colonial administrators, merchants and politicians, for whom an appeal to a common

---

[39] David Hume, *A Treatise of Human Nature* (1739–40), ed. L. A. Selby-Bigge and P. H. Nidditch, 2nd edn (Oxford, 1978), 429 (II. 3. 7, 'Of Contiguity, and Distance in Space and Time'); Carlo Ginzburg, 'Killing a Chinese Mandarin: The Moral Implications of Distance', in Olwen Hufton (ed.), *Historical Change and Human Rights: The Oxford Amnesty Lectures 1994* (New York, 1995), 67.

[40] Thomas Bender (ed.), *The Antislavery Debate: Capitalism and Abolitionism as a Problem in Historical Interpretation* (Berkeley, 1992).

interest with Britain was a necessary strategy to encourage equal treatment for their compatriots, whether under the terms of the Navigation Acts or within the constitutional framework of the United Kingdom. Their concept of the British Empire, projected from the provinces back to a metropolitan audience, was both the expression of their own interests and the means to develop a coincident appreciation of a common interest among their British audiences. This strategic use of the British Empire as the conceptual realisation of these interests explains the widespread use among these provincials of the language of the common good, frequently cast (as in the work of Sir William Keith, for example) in the idiom of neo-Roman republicanism. When metropolitans adopted their concept of the British Empire, as they began to do with increasing frequency in the late 1730s, theirs would be the derivative discourse, not that of the provincials. The metropolitan contribution was to add to this provincial concept of the British Empire the classic conception of that empire as Protestant, commercial, maritime and free.

The crucible of that conception was the agitations preceding the Anglo-Spanish War of Jenkins's Ear, and the oppositional circles which encouraged them. As Horatio Walpole later noted:

> the depredations of the Spaniards upon the british Commerce in the West Indies ... had given a handle to the disaffected and discontented party encreased by the accession of those in Parliament who belonged to the Court of the late weak, imprudent and undutiful prince of Wales, to raise a great ferment in the Nation to occasion warm debates in Parliament and strong resolutions and addresses to the Crown ...[41]

As Adam Smith also pointed out, the succeeding conflict was in essence a 'colony war',[42] fought to defend British possessions overseas and to protect rights of free navigation on the high seas. The War of Jenkins's Ear became notorious in the later eighteenth century as an example of popular pressure overcoming governmental resolve and hence, one might say, as a triumph of ideology over policy.[43] In 1796, Edmund Burke used the example of the war for his own special pleading, and

[41] [Horatio Walpole,] 'Mr Walpole's Apology', BL Add. MS 9132, f. 99ʳ.
[42] Adam Smith, *An Inquiry into the Causes and Nature of the Wealth of Nations* (1776), ed. R. H. Campbell, A. S. Skinner and W. B. Todd, 2 vols. (Oxford, 1976), II, 616; Smith, 'Thoughts on the State of the Contest with America, February 1778', in *The Correspondence of Adam Smith*, ed. E. C. Mossner and J. S. Ross, rev. edn (Oxford, 1987), 382.
[43] Compare Isaac De Pinto, *Letters on the American Troubles* (London, 1776), 47; Alexander Hamilton, *Federalist*, VI, in James Madison, Hamilton and John Jay, *The Federalist Papers* (1788), ed. Isaac Kramnick (Harmondsworth, 1987), 107–8.

moralised the force of public opinion in the opening stages of the war and in the push towards Walpole's fall as a cynical process which had backfired on its perpetrators: 'There has not been in this century any foreign peace or war, in its origin, the fruit of popular desire, except this war that was made with Spain in 1739'. The execration of Walpole for caving in to the opposition's demands for war, and the opposition's later admission that their conduct was insincere, showed that '[t]hey who stir up the people to improper desires, whether of peace or war, will be condemned by themselves. They who weakly yield to them will be condemned by history.'[44]

History fostered ideology. In the pamphlets preceding the war, the origins of the British Empire were traced back to the Welsh Prince Madoc and the discoveries of John and Sebastian Cabot to refute Spanish claims of first discovery in the Americas, and Bartolomé de Las Casas was liberally quoted as evidence of Spain's destructive policies there.[45] Anti-Spanish propaganda opposing the Spanish Match in 1623, which itself had made use of Elizabethan precedent, was reprinted as evidence of England's long-standing defence of the Protestant religion and position as arbiter of Europe, keeping the balance of power in check.[46] The dangers of peace between France and Spain and the claims of England's West India trade were recalled in speeches given by Sir Thomas Roe and Sir Benjamin Rudyerd in 1641.[47] Sir John Boroughs's treatise defending Britain's right to the seas from the time of the first Anglo-Dutch War was reprinted: 'There needs no Apology for Republishing, at this Time, the following excellent little Treatise', wrote its editor.[48] Anglo-Spanish tensions in 1711 and 1726–27 were also brought to mind with the first publication of manuscript memoranda recommending an attack on Buenos Aires and a West Indian offensive.[49] Elizabeth I was consistently hailed as the founder of the British

---

[44] Edmund Burke, *First Letter on a Regicide Peace* (20 October 1796), in *The Writings and Speeches of Edmund Burke IX*, ed. R. B. McDowell (Oxford, 1991), 226, 228.

[45] *The British Sailor's Discovery* (London, 1739), 11, 12–14, 17, reprinted in *Old England For Ever, Or, Spanish Cruelty Display'd* (London, 1740); [Micaiah Towgood,] *Spanish Cruelty and Injustice a Justifiable Plea for a Vigorous War with Spain* (London, 1741), 17–26.

[46] [John Reynolds,] *Vox Coeli* (London, 1623), sig. A3^r–*^{r}, 42–56, 86–9, reprinted in *The Merchant's Complaint Against Spain* (London, 1738), 5–16, 44–58, 59–63. On *Vox Coeli* see Thomas Cogswell, *The Blessed Revolution: English Politics and the Coming of War, 1621–1624* (Cambridge, 1989), 290.

[47] [Sir Thomas Roe,] *A Speech Delivered in Parliament by a Person of Honour* (London, 1739), originally published as *Sir Thomas Roe His Speech in Parliament* (London, 1641); *ibid.*, 17–20, [Sir Benjamin Rudyerd,] *A Speech Concerning a West-India Association* (London, 1641).

[48] Sir John Boroughs, *The Soveraignty of the British Seas* (London, 1739), sig. A2r.

[49] *A Proposal for Humbling Spain* (London, 1739), 1–42; [John Campbell (ed.),] *Memoirs of the Duke of Ripperda*, 2nd edn (London, 1740), 377–90.

Empire, for 'it was owing, in a great Measure, to that Great and Glorious Princess Queen *Elizabeth* . . . that *Great-Britain*, at present, is not only so Rich a Kingdom, but so powerful at Sea, and Master of so considerable a Number of Islands and such vast Tracts of Land in *America*';[50] her supposed speech at Tilbury was revived, and the Armada of 1588 held before the public as a sign of lost valour.[51]

The war had begun with patriot demands for a blue-water war in the West Indies: 'The Empire of the Seas is ours; we have been many Ages in Possession of it; we have had many Sea-Fights, at a vast Effusion of Blood, and Expences of Treasure, to preserve it; and preserve it we still must, at all Risks and Events, if we have a Mind to preserve ourselves'.[52] The first victory of the conflict seemed to confirm this policy, as Admiral Edward Vernon destroyed the fortifications of Porto Bello in November 1739, the news of which was greeted with a flood of poems, pageants and medals that extolled the achievements of an admiral who had long been an oppositional figure himself, and boosted the wider opposition to Walpole by inflaming public opinion against his half-hearted policies and indifference to Britain's true interests.[53] 'Rule, Britannia' was first sung just as Vernon was preparing a second fleet in August 1740. Such blue-water triumphalism was effective mainly as a response to the threats of territorial universal monarchy in Europe, and the passage of the war was widely conceived in such terms,[54] especially as the theatre of conflict moved decisively from the Caribbean to central Europe. One cynical commentator even suggested that the Anglo-Spanish War and the war in Europe were both fomented by France, 'the first with a view to exhaust and impoverish the power and wealth of Britain; and the

[50] *Reasons for Giving Encouragement to the Sea-Faring People of Great-Britain, in Times of Peace or War* (London, 1739), 14.

[51] *Reasons for a War Against Spain* (London, 1737; rptd 1738), 37, 38–40; *The British Sailor's Discovery*, 49–51. [Philip Morant,] *The Tapestry Hangings of the House of Lords: Representing the Several Engagements between the English and Spanish Fleets in the . . . Year MDLXXXVIII* (London, 1739) presented engravings of the Armada tapestries in the House of Lords at an expedient moment.

[52] C. Ferguson, *A Letter Address'd to Every Honest Man in Britain* (London, 1738), 17.

[53] On the significance of the Vernon agitation, see Wilson, 'Empire, Trade and Popular Politics', and Gerald Jordan and Nicholas Rogers, 'Admirals as Heroes: Patriotism and Liberty in Hanoverian England', *Journal of British Studies*, 28 (1989), 201–24.

[54] For graphic representations see, for example, *Catalogue of Prints and Drawings in the British Museum . . . Political and Personal Satires*, ed. Dorothy George, 11 vols. (London, 1870–1954), III, item 2421 (in which the Spanish Queen is seen proclaiming 'France is my aid, the Universe my right', and is opposed by Admiral Vernon with the motto 'Thus we chastise our Insolent oppressors' on a representation of the siege of Portobello), item 2431, 'The European Race, Heat IIId', (in which Fleury is dressed as 'Universal Monarchy') and item 2449, 'The European State Jockies Running a Heat for the Ballance of Power' (in which Fleury tries to catch smoke, inscribed 'Universal Monarchy', in a sack).

latter, to subjugate the Austrian opponent, who had long blocked up the passage between France and universal empire'.[55]

The public agitations which preceded the war formed the context for Henry St John, Viscount Bolingbroke's *Idea of a Patriot King* (1738) which, like Thomson's 'Rule, Britannia', was originally written for the private circle of Frederick, Prince of Wales.[56] Bolingbroke skilfully deployed the shibboleths of mercantilist libertarianism to argue that Britain was naturally a maritime and hence a commercial nation whose interests would be best protected by the blue-water patriarchalism of a Patriot King. Bolingbroke had elsewhere followed the Sallustian and Machiavellian narrative that located the origins of Roman greatness in the acquisition of liberty after the expulsion of the Tarquins, but warned that '[a] wise and brave people will neither be cozened, nor bullied out of their liberty, but a wise and brave people may cease to be such; they may degenerate'.[57] In light of such a possibility, it would be necessary to erect a constitution that could prevent such corruption by protecting popular liberty, while bearing in mind the compulsions of mercantilist political economy. This was the task that Bolingbroke set himself while writing *The Idea of a Patriot King*. The Patriot King would hold the balance between Britain's political parties in order to prevent the corruption of Parliament; Bolingbroke had argued throughout the early 1730s that such corruption would threaten liberty by denying popular political participation, undermine property rights in pursuit of invasive taxation and raise the spectre of permanent standing armies that might be turned against the British people rather than their enemies.

The Patriot King's external policies would be consonant with these internal procedures by acknowledging the interests of Britain as an island nation, and hence as a commercial republic, thereby providing the foundations for prosperity and the survival of liberty. The sea was Britain's natural element and a navy its natural defence force. Continental commitments in Europe would only encourage the growth of a standing army, while concentrating resources upon the navy would render Britain 'the guardian of liberty' throughout Europe. The sources

---

[55] Richard Rolt, *An Impartial Representation of the Conduct of the Several Powers of Europe, Engaged in the Late General War*, 4 vols. (London, 1749–50), I, xiii; compare *Impartial Representation*, I, 171–2: '... while the house of Austria flourished in a condition to oppose the designs of France, the ballance of power was preserved, and the liberty of Europe remote from the destruction of an arbitrary and universal monarchy'. The volume was dedicated to Admiral Vernon.

[56] Gerrard, *The Patriot Opposition to Walpole*, 3, 190–91.

[57] Henry St John, Viscount Bolingbroke, *A Dissertation Upon Parties* (1733–34), in *Bolingbroke: Political Writings*, ed. David Armitage (Cambridge, 1997), 111.

of greatness would be commercial, not territorial: 'To give ease and encouragement to a manufactory at home, to assist and protect trade abroad, to improve and keep in heart the national colonies, like so many farms of the mother country, will be the principal and constant parts of the attention of such a prince'. Bolingbroke concluded that if such a prince could be found – or trained – nothing could be more inspiring than '[a] king, in the temper of whose government, like that of Nerva, things so seldom allied as empire and liberty are intimately mixed, co-exist together inseparably, and constitute one real essence'.[58] The Patriot King's reign would therefore reconcile the traditionally opposed ideals of *imperium* and *libertas*, as the ruler of a free and prosperous people whose colonies were farms of the mother-country and whose fleets ruled the waves.

The allusion to 'Rule, Britannia' is not accidental, of course, because Thomson may have had access to Bolingbroke's manuscript through the medium of Alexander Pope.[59] All that separated the two works was the news of naval victory in the Caribbean, which allowed Thomson to buttress Bolingbroke's confident counsel with the fact of amphibious triumph. What they shared, of course, was the conception of the British Empire as commercial, maritime and free – perhaps not explicitly Protestant in the deistical Bolingbroke's work, but certainly anti-Catholic, and hence Protestant enough for mid-eighteenth-century pur-poses. *The Idea of a Patriot King* went unscathed by the later attacks on Bolingbroke's heterodoxy, but it lost favour during the British Empire's late eighteenth-century, counter-revolutionary, authoritarian phase, as did 'Rule, Britannia' – further evidence of the contingency of the conception of the British Empire contained therein, and of the competi-tion it faced later in the century.[60] Bolingbroke's solution to the dilemma of empire and liberty was historically speculative and theoretically unstable. It was speculative because it depended so heavily on the unreliable reversionary interest of the heir to the throne, Frederick, Prince of Wales; moreover, it was unstable because it required the emergence of a monarch committed above all to the public good, who

---

[58] Bolingbroke, *The Idea of a Patriot King* (1738, rev. 1749), in *Bolingbroke: Political Writings*, ed. Armitage, 278, 277, 293: compare Tacitus, *Agricola*, III. 2: 'Nerva Caesar res olim dissociabiles miscuit, *principatum* et libertatem', crucially revised by Francis Bacon in the *Advancement of Learning* as 'divus Nerva res olim insociabiles miscuisset, *imperium* et libertatem,' in Bacon, *Francisci Baconis ... Opera Omnia*, ed. John Blackbourne, 4 vols. (London, 1730), II, 439 (my emphases).

[59] James Sambrook, *James Thomson 1700–1748: A Life* (Oxford, 1991), 202–3.

[60] Linda Colley, 'The Apotheosis of George III: Loyalty, Royalty and the British Nation, 1760–1820', *Past and Present*, 102 (Feb. 1984), 104; David Armitage, 'A Patriot for Whom? The Afterlives of Bolingbroke's Patriot King', *Journal of British Studies*, 36 (1997), 413.

would hence be that republican oxymoron, a patriot king. Though the authority of monarchs was never deemed decisively incompatible with a neo-Roman conception of liberty, later British thinkers within the republican and neo-Roman traditions found it increasingly difficult to identify a patriot king or to endorse any particular monarch for their Nerva-like combination of empire and liberty.[61]

The crisis of Walpole's ministry provided the occasion for other philosophers to consider the relationship between a metropolitan state and its colonies as a legitimate topic for moral and civil philosophy. For example, the anonymous author of the *Essay on Civil Government* (1743) apologised retrospectively for the prominence of colonial questions in his treatise, but admitted that the work had been completed in 1738–39, during the anti-Spanish and anti-Walpolean agitations. The *Essay* argued that the end of civil government was the protection of property, and took a whiggish turn in allying property with liberty. More novel, but characteristic of the period, was the expansive conception of property, both national and personal, that the author expounded.[62] The right to real property, for instance, derived from first occupation, and '[a] long continuance of possession without interruption from the former proprietor, gives a just right to the present occupier', as in the case of the formerly 'uninhabited and unpossessed places of America'. This right to property also authorised national defence of colonial possessions against any 'prince [who] aims at universal monarchy' (as the Spanish Monarchy was repeatedly accused of planning to do before the War of Jenkins's Ear). Commerce as much as land required such defence, the author continued, even if a true care for this crucial component of national wealth was lacking under the premiership of Walpole: 'In some countries, the navy is a chief strength' for such defence; such was the case in Britain. The author thus provided blue-water Lockeanism as a foundation for the British Empire, as a justification for war against Spain, and as a stick with which to beat the Walpolean government.[63] In just such works lay the origins of the 'Whig imperialism' of the later

---

[61] Quentin Skinner, *Liberty Before Liberalism* (Cambridge, 1998), 53–5.

[62] For an immediately contemporary discussion of 'the Right of the Dominion of Lands in America', derived from the *ius gentium*, see Harman Verelst, 'Some Observations on the Right of the Crown of Great Britain to the North West Continent of America' (16 April 1739), PRO co 5/283, ff. 1–53.

[63] *An Essay on Civil Government: In Two Parts: Part I. An Enquiry into the Ends of Government, and the Means of Attaining Them. Part II. Of the Government and Commerce of England; with Reflections on Liberty and the Method of Preserving the Present Constitution* (c. 1738–39) (London, 1743), viii–ix, 9, 36, 150–51, 294; compare [Alexander Campbell,] *APETE-ΛΟΓΙΑ or An Enquiry into the Original of Moral Virtue* (London, 1728), 99–172, 'Moral Virtue Promotes Trade and Aggrandizes a Nation'.

eighteenth century – a vision of the British Empire as Protestant, commercial, maritime and free founded on the sanctity of property as much at home as abroad, in the metropolis and in the colonies.[64]

Alongside the mercantilist and metrocentric strain in civil philosophy in the 1730s, there was also an anti-imperial and philocolonial strand.[65] This was represented most notably by the Hiberno-Scot Francis Hutcheson's *A System of Moral Philosophy*, which he composed between 1734 and 1737, in the period before the anti-Spanish agitations but in the aftermath of the Excise Crisis and the darkest days of Walpole's premiership.[66] Hutcheson questioned the very foundations in rights of *dominium* upon which the British Empire rested, and argued that '[n]o person or society . . . can by mere occupation acquire such a right in a vast tract of land quite beyond their power to cultivate'. This denial of the juridical basis on which the British Empire in America was claimed was in its own way as Lockean as that of the author of the *Essay on Civil Government*, but took seriously Locke's sufficiency condition for legitimate possession.[67] Hutcheson went even further, and proposed colonial independence should the mother-country impose 'severe and absolute' power over its provinces. 'The insisting on old claims and tacit conventions', he concluded, 'to extend civil power over distant nations, and form grand unwieldy empires, without regard to the obvious maxims of humanity, has been one great source of human misery'.[68]

Hutcheson's critique of 'grand unwieldy empires' and of property rights derived from first occupation formed the basis of David Hume's sceptical response to the conception of the British Empire that was becoming normative during the Anglo-Spanish War. Hume's *Treatise on Human Nature* and the first two volumes of his *Essays, Moral and Political* (1741–42) appeared during the last years of the Walpolean regime and the first of the Anglo-Spanish War as it bled into the War of the Austrian

[64] P. J. Marshall, 'Parliament and Property Rights in the Eighteenth-Century British Empire,' in John Brewer and Susan Staves (eds.), *Early Modern Conceptions of Property* (London, 1996), 530–44.
[65] Compare Guido Abbattista, *Commercio, colonie e impero alla vigilia della Rivoluzione Americana: John Campbell pubblicista e storico nell'Inghilterra del. sec. XVIII* (Florence, 1990).
[66] W. R. Scott, *Francis Hutcheson: His Life, Teaching and Position in the History of Philosophy* (Cambridge, 1900), 113–14, 210–11.
[67] Gopal Sreenivasan, *The Limits of Lockean Rights in Property* (Oxford, 1995), 48–50; compare [William Wood,] *A Survey of Trade* (London, 1718), 160–62.
[68] Francis Hutcheson, *A System of Moral Philosophy* (c. 1734–37), 2 vols. (Glasgow, 1755), I, 326–7, II, 308–9; Caroline Robbins, '"When It Is That Colonies May Turn Independent": An Analysis of the Environment and Politics of Francis Hutcheson (1694–1746)', in *Absolute Liberty: A Selection from the Articles and Papers of Caroline Robbins*, ed. Barbara Taft (Hamden, Conn., 1982), 135–6, 159–64; David Fate Norton, 'Francis Hutcheson in America', *Studies on Voltaire and the Eighteenth Century*, 154 (1976), 1560–63.

Succession. Hume judged foreign policy to be one of the major dividing issues between ministry and opposition. 'Unnecessary wars, scandalous treaties, profusion of public treasure, oppressive taxes, every kind of mal-administration is ascribed to [Walpole]' by the opposition, while the panegyrics on the minister show that '[t]he honour and interest of the nation supported abroad, public credit maintained at home, persecution restrained, faction subdued; the merit of all these blessings is ascribed solely to the minister'.[69] Yet in relation to foreign affairs in the years immediately preceding the publication of the *Essays*, Hume's typology may be seen as deliberately muddying the waters, because it was the opposition which had called for '[t]he honour and interest of the nation [to be] supported abroad', and the government which had stood firm against '[u]nnecessary wars', especially against the Spanish. Hume referred even more pointedly to the battle over public opinion of the period as an illustration of the matter likely to cause most surprise to a foreigner on visiting Britain, the freedom of its press: 'If the administration resolve upon war, it is affirmed, that, either wilfully or ignorantly, they mistake the interests of the nation, and that peace, in the present situation of affairs, is infinitely preferable. If the passion of the ministry lie towards peace, our political writers breathe nothing but war and devastation, and represent the pacific conduct of the government as mean and pusillanimous'[70] – as had been done by the opposition during the anti-Spanish agitations. The only hint of Hume's partiality over the question of the war came in 'A Character of Sir Robert Walpole', in which he affirmed that '[d]uring his time trade has flourished, liberty declined, and learning gone to ruin'.[71] When asked to defend this judgement, Hume wrote that trade had flourished 'so far as the administration has been pacific, and private property has been preserved inviolate', thereby implicitly aligning himself with those who had urged conciliation with Spain.[72]

In his early memoranda from the late 1730s, in his *Essays* and in the *Treatise on Human Nature*, Hume challenged the ideological foundations of the anti-Walpolean, pro-imperial campaign. He questioned the basis

[69] David Hume, 'That Politics May Be Reduced to a Science' (1741), in Hume, *Essays, Moral, Political and Literary*, ed. Eugene F. Miller (Indianapolis, 1985), 28.

[70] David Hume, 'Of the Liberty of the Press' (1741), in Hume, *Essays*, ed. Miller, 9. On ministerial meanness and pusillanimity, compare [Joseph Trapp,] *The Ministerial Virtue: Or, Long-Suffering Extolled in a Great Man* (London, 1739), an ironic sermon on Walpole's ability to 'turn the other cheek'.

[71] David Hume, 'A Character of Sir Robert Walpole' (1742), in Hume, *Essays*, ed. Miller, 576.

[72] Robert C. Elliott, 'Hume's "Character of Sir Robert Walpole": Some Unnoticed Additions', *Journal of English and Germanic Philology*, 48 (1949), 369.

of the whiggish view that 'commerce can never flourish but in a free government', an argument which others had extended to the flourishing of the arts and sciences. Hume's answer was to adduce the example of France, even as a counter to the evidence that trade has always established itself in free governments from Tyre and Athens through to modern Holland and England, the maritime powers whose rise had largely invalidated Machiavellian maxims. Politeness arises in monarchies and courts, not in republics, and in particular the new 'civilised monarchies' of Europe (so different from the 'little disorderly principalities of ITALY' that were Machiavelli's concern) were great nurseries of the civilised arts, France among them, because favour comes from the sovereign, who must be impressed by the pleasant cultivation of any supplicant.[73] If commerce were less vibrant in an absolute monarchy, Hume argued, it was for much the same reason: under such a monarchy, the pursuit of commerce would be not less secure (for all of the reasons presented by Trenchard and Gordon in *Cato's Letters*, for example), but rather less *honourable*, because '[b]irth, titles, and place, must be honoured above industry and riches'.[74] Hume thus steered a course away from a whiggish determinism that placed trade solely as the child of liberty. 'Multitudes of people, necessity, and liberty, have begotten commerce in HOLLAND', but if those conditions were not essential for its growth, nor would they be sufficient to foster polite arts.[75]

Hume shared none of the misgivings of those who saw in commerce a conduit of corruption; the target of his concern was extensive territorial empire, not trade. Though he admitted that 'no probable reason can be assigned for the great power of the more ancient states above the modern, but their want of commerce and luxury', a return to the ancient maxims of policy in the interests of reason of state rather than the happiness of a state's subjects would be impossible. To abolish commerce would be both unnatural and demand violent restraints upon the inclination of subjects: 'Now, according to the most natural course of things, industry and arts and trade encrease the power of the sovereign as well as the happiness of the subjects'. Under these changed conditions, only the unequivocal testimony of history could persuade anyone that the government of Sparta was anything other than 'a mere philosophical whim or fiction'. So small a number of helots had been able to

---

[73] Hume, 'Of Liberty and Despotism' (1741), and 'Of the Rise and Progress of the Arts and Sciences' (1742), in Hume, *Essays*, ed. Miller, 92, 124, 126–7.
[74] Hume, 'Of Liberty and Despotism', in Hume, *Essays*, ed. Miller, 93.
[75] Hume, 'Of the Rise and Progress of the Arts and Sciences', in Hume, *Essays*, ed. Miller, 113.

support so many Spartans only because there was no desire for luxury items.[76] Thereby, one part of the population had been condemned to abject submission under the authoritarian rule of another. As Hume pointed out in 'Of Refinement in the Arts', this meant that a free government could never have been maintained, because the demand for luxury items was the first link in a chain which ultimately fastens liberty. The demand for luxury stimulated commerce and industry; the peasants who cultivate the land can become 'rich and independent' while the balance of property shifts also to the tradesmen and merchants. By the Harringtonian mechanism of authority following land-holding, the 'middling rank of men' are empowered and since such men are 'the best and firmest basis of public liberty', that liberty is strengthened.[77]

Hume commended the 'agreeable entertainment' to be derived from reading history, not least of which was '[t]o remark the rise, progress, declension, and final extinction of the most flourishing of empires'. In one of his early memoranda he signalled his own interest in the pathology of empires in the comprehensive account he gave of the mechanism by which empires naturally expand and die:

> There seems to be a natural Course of Things, which brings on the Destruction of great Empires. They push their Conquests till they come to barbarous Nations, which stop their Progress, by the Difficulty of subsisting great Armies. After that, the Nobility & considerable Men of the conquering Nation & best Provinces withdraw gradually from the frontier Army, by reason of its Distance from the Capital & barbarity of the Country, in which they quarter: They forget the Use of War. Their barbarous Soldiers become their Masters. These have no Law but their Sword, both from their bad Education, & from their distance from the Sovereign to whom they bear no Affection. Hence Disorder, Violence, Anarchy, & Tyranny, & Dissolution of Empire.[78]

Elsewhere in his essays, Hume warned against the consequences of imperial overstretch, both for the metropolis and the provinces. Free governments in particular are 'ruinous and oppressive' to their provinces, he argued, because such governments discriminate against their new subjects and turn a blind eye to the egregious abuses of provincial governors, as absolute monarchs do not: 'What cruel tyrants were the ROMANS over the world during the time of their commonwealth!'

[76] Hume, 'Of Commerce', in Hume, *Essays*, ed. Miller, 258, 260, 259, 257.
[77] Hume, 'Of Refinement in the Arts', in Hume, *Essays*, ed. Miller, 277.
[78] David Hume, 'Of the Study of History' (1741), in Hume, *Essays*, ed. Miller, 566; National Library of Scotland MS 23159, item 14, f. 27, printed in 'Hume's Early Memoranda, 1729–1740: The Complete Text', ed. Ernest Campbell Mossner, *Journal of the History of Ideas*, 9 (1948), 517.

Empire, like commerce, was a self-regulating system, however – once it had reached its point of furthest extension, it must inevitably contract and collapse.[79]

Hume also argued in the *Treatise* that first discovery could not provide a legitimate justification for dominion over a whole continent.[80] To take possession of the part did not create property in the whole. After all, what would this imply if an invader were to land on one of the British Isles, and claim it? 'The empire of *Great Britain* seems to draw along with it the dominion of the *Orkneys*, the *Hebrides*, the isle of *Man*, and the isle of *Wight*; but the authority over those lesser islands does not naturally imply any title to *Great Britain*'.[81] This effectively only deprived the British colonists of their claims to *dominium* in the Americas, by denying that their first discoveries could provide solid claims for current occupation. Hume's strictly archipelagic usage of the term 'empire of *Great Britain*' also implicitly questioned the emergent pan-Atlantic concept of the British Empire by harking back to sixteenth-century conceptions of the British monarchy as a strictly contiguous empire, and by avoiding the concept of the British Empire as a commercial, or maritime, entity.

Hume's affront to the more extensive concept of the British Empire was not unparalleled at the time. The security demands of the Anglo-Spanish War led Walpole's chief adviser on colonial policy (and, earlier, translator of Caesar's *Commentaries*), Martin Bladen, to propose a common defence structure for the colonies, along with a 'Plantation Parliament': 'That we might be better secured, of their Dependance, and they, better intitled, to our Protection', though all under the authority of the Crown, 'for the general protection and advantage of the British Empire in America' in 1739.[82] This was, again, a transatlantic, not a pan-Atlantic conception. Meanwhile, and delving even further back into the earliest conceptions of Britain's empire, the 'Brutan' history of the origins of Britain was still being played out poetically by

---

[79] Hume, 'That Politics May be Reduced to a Science' (1741), in Hume, *Essays*, ed. Miller, 18–19.

[80] Compare Verelst, 'Some Observations on the Right of the Crown of Great Britain . . .,' PRO co 5/283, f. 5ᵛ: 'this Right arising from the first discovery is the first and fundamental Right of all European Nations, as to their Claim of Lands in America'.

[81] Hume, *Treatise of Human Nature*, ed. Selby-Bigge and Nidditch, 507, 510, note; compare Hume to William Strahan, 25 March 1771, in *The Letters of David Hume*, ed. J. Y. T. Greig, 2 vols. (Oxford, 1932), II, 240–41.

[82] Martin Bladen, 'Reasons for Appointing a Captain General for the Continent of North America' (27 December 1739), in Jack P. Greene, 'Martin Bladen's Blueprint for Colonial Union', *William and Mary Quarterly*, 3rd ser., 17 (1960), 524, 525; Julius Caesar, *Commentaries*, trans. Martin Bladen (London, 1705).

the aesthetic theorist Hildebrand Jacob in *Brutus the Trojan; Founder of the British Empire* (1735). In this poem, the British Empire was the *Imperium Britannicum*, the monarchy of Great Britain bequeathed by Brutus to his sons. It was therefore strictly archipelagic in extent, and did not even encompass Ireland, let alone the transatlantic colonies.[83] In 1740, Alexander Pope was also planning an epic on the theme of Brutus's civilising mission to conquer Britain, which would have been not only an allegory of the British deliverance from tyrannous subjection – Brutus lands at Torbay, as had William III in 1688 – but also a recommendation of colonisation as improvement 'without the guilt of a conquest'.[84]

Hume's sceptical Whiggism led him to doubt that there was any historical link between the peculiar constitutional and legal character of the British state and the success of its overseas trade, and generated a subtle but sweeping critique of the whole enterprise of empire up to the mid-eighteenth century, and with it, of the emergent conception of the British Empire itself. He questioned the very juridical basis upon which the English, the Scots and hence the British after 1707 based their territorial claims, especially in the supposedly 'waste' lands of North America. He challenged the very denotation of the term 'British Empire', and returned it to a solely archipelagic construction which denied the incorporation or even the association of the other territories, provinces, colonies and factories that contemporaries increasingly encompassed within the term. He would even have denied the very possibility of such an entity's possessing any unitary character, ideology or identity, because even Britain itself lacked the necessary 'moral' foundations he thought essential to any definition of national character.[85] If this were true of post-Union Britain, then not only was the Anglo-British state still something less than a nation, but any wider conception of a British Empire beyond the island of Britain would have an even weaker claim to a settled or common identity. Yet if Hume feared for the ascendancy of the 'British Empire', he need not have worried. The classic conception of the British Atlantic Empire as Protestant, commercial, maritime and free flourished for little more than three decades, from the mid-1730s (when Hume began his philosophi-

[83] Hildebrand Jacob, *Brutus the Trojan; Founder of the British Empire* (London, 1735).
[84] Pope, 'Brutus' (*c.* 1740), BL MS Eg. 1950, ff. 4ʳ–6ᵛ; synopsis paraphrased in Owen Ruffhead, *The Life of Alexander Pope, Esq.* (London, 1769), 418, 414, 420 (footnote). On 'Brutus', see Friedrich Bric, 'Pope's Brutus', *Anglia*, 63 (1939), 144–85; Donald J. Torchiana, 'Brutus: Pope's Last Hero', in Maynard Mack (ed.), *Essential Articles for the Study of Alexander Pope* (Hamden, Conn., 1968), 705–23; Miriam Leranbaum, *Alexander Pope's 'Opus Magnum' 1729–1744* (Oxford, 1977), 155–74.
[85] Hume, 'Of National Characters' (1748), in Hume, *Essays*, 198.

cal career) to the mid-1760s, when the Atlantic Empire began to un-
ravel in the aftermath of the Seven Years War. Indeed, Hume rejoiced
at its dissolution even in his dying days.[86]

Notwithstanding Hume's scepticism, the ideological redefinition of
the British Empire which took place in the late Walpolean era provided
an enduring conception of that empire that was not confined to British
observers. Hume might have appreciated the fact that one of the most
resilient accounts of that concept came from Bordelais magistrate
Charles Secondat, baron de Montesquieu, in the twenty-seventh chapter of Book XVIII of *Esprit des Lois* (1748).[87] This work was also, in part,
the result of the War of Jenkins's Ear, because British embargoes on
French wine during the War of the Austrian Succession had forced the
vigneron to retreat to his study, and complete his treatise.[88] Montesquieu argued that the compulsions diagnosed by Machiavelli were no
longer applicable to modern politics: 'One has begun to be cured of
Machiavellianism (*machiavélisme*), and one will continue to be cured.'
Princes had gradually abandoned this *machiavélisme* as they realised that
only moderation brings prosperity, and that commerce was now the
sole source of such prosperity. Trade, for Montesquieu, not only rendered Machiavelli's maxims outdated; it made his principles harmless.
Britain was the only nation in Europe whose constitution was construc-
ted to promote liberty – just as Rome was built for expansion, Sparta
for war, Israel for religion, Marseilles for trade, China for natural
tranquillity, and Rhodes for navigation. In particular, the separation of
powers between the executive and the legislative branches of government prevented any toppling over into arbitrary power, whether monarchical or oligarchical, and the citizens rested secure in the knowledge
that they had nothing to fear from one another. Britain retained its
liberty at home by constitutional separation, while it maintained its
integrity abroad by eschewing overseas conquest, which would weaken
it, by planting colonies 'to extend its commerce more than its domination', and by being defended by a navy, not by a standing army. 'As
one likes to establish elsewhere what is established at home', Montes-

[86] Hume to Sir Gilbert Elliot of Minto, 22 July 1768; Hume to William Strahan, 25 October 1769; Hume to Strahan, 11 March 1771; Hume to Strahan, 26 October 1775; Hume to Strahan, 13 November 1775, in Greig (ed.), *Letters of David Hume*, II, 184, 210, 237, 300–1, 304–5; J. G. A. Pocock, 'Hume and the American Revolution: The Dying Thoughts of a North Briton', in *Virtue, Commerce and History: Essays on Political Thought and History, Chiefly in the Eighteenth Century* (Cambridge, 1985), 125–41.
[87] Charles Secondat, Baron de Montesquieu, *The Spirit of the Laws* (1748), trans. Anne Cohler, Basia Miller and Harold Stone (Cambridge, 1989), 325–33.
[88] Robert Shackleton, *Montesquieu: A Biography* (Oxford, 1956), 201, 206.

quieu continued, 'it would give the form of its government to the people of its colonies':

> The dominant nation, inhabiting a big island and being in possession of a great commerce, would have all sorts of facilities for forces upon the seas; and as the preservation of its liberty would require it to have neither strongholds, nor fortresses, nor land armies, it would need an army on the sea to protect itself from invasions; and its navy would be superior to that of all other powers, which, needing to employ their finances for a land war, would no longer have enough for a sea war.
>
> A naval empire has always given the peoples who have possessed it a natural pride, because, feeling themselves able to insult others everywhere, they believe that their power is as boundless as the ocean.

If its terrain were fertile, then the people would be self-sufficient, not ambitious for conquest, and hence secure in the liberty their constitution guaranteed for them. 'This is the people', he concluded, 'who have best known how to take advantage of these three great things at the same time: religion, commerce, and liberty'.[89] Liberty would foster commerce, and Britain could become everything that the aspirant universal monarchies of seventeenth-century Europe were not, and could not be – an empire for liberty.

The origins, the transferability and the contestability of the conception of the British Empire as Protestant, commercial, maritime and free are what mark it as an ideology – rather than as an identity. Only by studying it as an ideology is it possible to understand why it failed to provide an enduring and stable identity. This fact seems to have been realised, in two rather different ways, by John Adams, in the context of the American controversy of the 1770s, and by G. W. F. Hegel a generation after American Independence. As Adams famously pointed out in 1774, 'the terms "British Empire" are not the language of the common law, but the language of newspapers and political pamphlets'. The possessions of the British Crown could not be an empire, said Adams, because that term smacked both of Imperial Rome and of the civil law; nor could they be strictly called 'British', because most of the colonies in North America had been planted long before the Treaty of Union created the United Kingdom of Great Britain in 1707.

---

[89] Montesquieu, *The Spirit of the Laws*, 156 (XI. 5), 157–65 (XI. 6), 328–9 (XIX. 27); John Robertson, 'Universal Monarchy and the Liberties of Europe: David Hume's Critique of an English Whig Doctrine,' in Nicholas Phillipson and Quentin Skinner (eds.), *Political Discourse in Early Modern Britain* (Cambridge, 1993), 364–8.

He thereby threw down a challenge to the ideological origins of the British Empire as they had appeared in the 1730s and 1740s, a challenge almost as devastating as Hume's, but more direct.[90] The concept of the British Empire was a fiction, and not even a legal fiction at that. The pamphlets in which the language of the 'British Empire' had first appeared were more often provincial than metropolitan originally, but during the Seven Years War the concept had been more widely disseminated, even if the prevailing conceptions of that empire changed and proliferated.

Hegel likewise understood the ideology of the British Empire not as a concept but as a conception. In a crucial passage of his introductory lectures on the philosophy of world history, Hegel argued that the true history of a nation consists in the process whereby the *Geist*'s conception of itself is realised in the various, interconnected activities of that nation, such as the state, religion, art, justice and foreign affairs. All of these spheres of life were not connected in all nations, he stated (citing China and India), but where they were, the informing activity of the *Geist* could be felt in every area. Where these spheres were completely integrated, the self-consciousness of the nation would be realised in the lives of the members of the state. The nation's history would nourish that self-consciousness, just as that self-consciousness would be the realisation of the *Geist* itself. To illustrate this central point, Hegel turned to 'England' for evidence. 'If he is asked', Hegel reported, 'any Englishman will say of himself and his fellow citizens that it is they who rule the East Indies and the oceans of the world, who dominate world trade, who have a parliament and trial by jury, etc. It is deeds such as these which give the nation its sense of self-esteem' (*Selbstgefühl*).[91]

Hegel's illustration is remarkable for so accurately capturing what had been a dominant, but not unchallenged, British conception of empire in the long eighteenth century: as derived from Britain's historic achievements as a maritime power, as a commercial economy, and as a parliamentary democracy with a common-law tradition. Hegel omitted only Protestantism from his account of British national self-consciousness, but this was perhaps less a 'deed' expressive of the British *Geist* than it was a direct expression of the informing *Geist*

90 [Adams and Leonard,] *Novanglus and Massachusettensis*, 30, 79.
91 'Frägt man einen Engländer, so wird jeder von sich und seinen Mitbürgen sagen, sie seien die, die Ostindien und das Weltmeer beherrschen, den Welthandel besitzen, Parlament und Geschworenengerichte haben usf. Diese Taten machen das Selbstgefühl des Volkes aus': G. W. F. Hegel, *Die Vernunft in der Geschichte*, ed. Johannes Hoffmeister (Hamburg, 1955), 122; Hegel, *Lectures on the Philosophy of World History: Introduction*, trans. H. B. Nisbet (Cambridge, 1975), 101–3.

itself.[92] This conception of 'English' identity could be traced back in its classic form to the anti-Walpolean ideology of the 1730s and early 1740s, when it became attached for the first time to a concept of the British Empire as a single pan-Atlantic community. It was therefore the dominant conception during the formative years of Samuel Johnson, William Pitt and Edmund Burke and hence of the generation of politicians and writers around the British Atlantic world who would debate, defend, decry and administer the British Empire during the Seven Years War, the aftermath of the Peace of Paris and through the American Revolution.

This conception found new leases of life in nineteenth-century arenas as varied as the cult of Nelson and the evangelical missionary movement.[93] The expansion of British trade seemed to confirm Britain's commercial destiny, especially since this was bolstered by the indispensable and universally acknowledged supremacy of the Royal Navy on the sea-routes of the world after 1815: 'the magnitude and splendour of the resources which have been thus developed cannot fail to fill the mind of every British subject with exultation and gratitude to the Supreme Being for the numerous blessings conferred on this highly favoured nation'.[94] The success of the coincident campaigns for Parliamentary reform and the abolition of slavery within the Empire merely confirmed what Britons had known about themselves at least since 1688: that they were the greatest defenders of liberty within Europe, and throughout the wider British imperial world.[95] Even rule over India came gradually to be cast as benign, progressive tutelage expressive of Britain's historically unique combination of empire and liberty – now increasingly cast as liberalism, especially in the imperial context.[96] Under these conditions, the conception of the British Empire fostered the imperial amnesia diagnosed by J. R. Seeley. The various British Empires of the nineteenth

[92] Hegel, *Die Vernunft in der Geschichte*, ed. Hoffmeister, 124–33.

[93] Jordan and Rogers, 'Admirals as Heroes', 201–24; Andrew Porter, '"Cultural Imperialism" and Protestant Missionary Enterprise, 1780–1914', *Journal of Imperial and Commonwealth History*, 25 (1997), 367–91.

[94] Patrick Colquhoun, *A Treatise on the Wealth, Power, and Resources of the British Empire, In Every Quarter of the World, Including the East Indies*, 2nd edn (London, 1815), 88.

[95] Seymour Drescher, 'Cart Whip and Billy Roller: Antislavery and Reform Symbolism in Industrializing Britain', *Journal of Social History*, 15 (1981), 3–24; Robin Blackburn, *The Overthrow of Colonial Slavery 1776–1848* (London, 1988), 436–59; Colley, *Britons*, 359–60.

[96] Thomas R. Metcalf, *Ideologies of the Raj*, The New Cambridge History of India, III: 4 (Cambridge, 1994), ch. 2; Bhikhu Parekh, 'Liberalism and Colonialism: A Critique of Locke and Mill', in J. P. Nederveen Pieterse and Bhikhu Parekh (eds.), *The Decolonization of Imagination: Culture, Knowledge, and Power* (London, 1995), 92–6; Uday Singh Mehta, *Liberalism and Empire: A Study in Nineteenth-Century British Liberal Thought* (Chicago, 1999).

century were multiethnic and multidenominational, polyglot and poly-morphous, and defied capture within any single definition. However, the conception of the British Empire as Protestant, commercial, mari-time and free lingered, vestigially but reassuringly. As Hegel perhaps recognised, more than many recent historians, this conception of the British Empire was a classic example of an identity that was originally an ideology.

Bibliography

PRIMARY SOURCES

MANUSCRIPTS

Bodleian Library, Oxford

MS Locke, c. 30.
  MS Tanner 93, 'Reasons against the publishinge of the Kinges title to Virginia' (*c.* 1607–8), f. 200.

British Library, London

Add. MS 6128: John Mason, 'Instrumentorum Quorundam Authenticorum Exemplaria Aliquot ... Ex quibus planum fit ... Reges Scociæ in fide fuisse Regum Anglie, regnumque Scocie, Reges Anglie tanquam superiores dicti regni Dominos, per sacramentorum fidelititatis [*sic*] agnovisse' (1549).

Add. MS 9132: [Horatio Walpole,] 'Mr Walpole's Apology', ff. 80–99.

Add. MS 30221: Sir Philip Meadows, 'Observations Concerning the Dominion and Sovereignty of the Seas' (1673), ff. 13–43.

Add. MS 30221: Sir Philip Meadows, 'Reflections upon a Passage in Sᵣ William Temple's Memoirs Relating to our Right of Dominion in the British Seas' (1692), ff. 55–61.

Add. MS 32093: Malet Collection, State Papers and Historical Documents, 1625–May 1660: James Howell to Council of State, f. 370.

Add. MS 59681: John Dee, 'Brytanici Imperii Limites' (22 July 1576).

Add. MS 72854: Sir William Petty, 'A Treatise of Navall Philosophy in Three Parts', ff. 99–104.

Add. MS 72865: Sir William Petty, ['Dominion of the Sea'] (*c.* 1674), ff. 118–38.

Add MS 72866: Sir William Petty, 'Ten Tooles for Making yᵉ Crowne & State of England More Powerfull Then Any Other in Europe' (1687), f. 109.

Add. MS 72866: Sir William Petty, 'Of a Mare Clausum', ff. 122–3.

Add. MS 72885: Sir William Petty, 'A Probleme' (1687), f. 126.

Add. MS 72893: Sir William Petty, 'Of ye Mare Clausum' (1687), f. 34.

Add. MS 72893: Sir William Petty, 'Of a Mare Clausum' (1687), f. 36.

Cotton MS Titus B. x: 'Certeyn Notes and Observations Touching the Deducing and Planting of Colonies' (*c.* 1607–9), ff. 402–9.

Eg. 1950: Alexander Pope, 'Brutus', ff. 4r–6v.

Harl. MS 36: [Sir Thomas Smith,] 'A Collection of Certain Reasons to Prove the Queen Majesty's Right to Have the Restitution of Calais' (3 April 1567), ff. 74–90.

Harl. MS 249: John Dee, 'ΘΑΛΛΑΤΟΚΡΑΤΙΑ ΒΡΕΤΤΑΝΙΚΗ' (1597), ff. 95–105.

Harl. MS 4314: William Ryley, Sr., 'The Soveraigntie of the English Seas Vindicated and Proved, by Some Few Records ... Remayning in the Tower of London' (*c.* 1652), ff. 1–26.

Lansdowne 142: [Sir Julius Caesar,] 'Notes Out of a Book Called Mare Liberum, sive De Jure Quod Batavis Competit ad Indicana Commercia Dissertatio' (*c.* 1618), ff. 384–6.

Lansdowne 1228: Sir William Petty, 'Dominion of the Sea', ff. 58–74.

Royal MS 12. G. XIII: Richard Hakluyt, 'Analysis, seu resolutio perpetua in octo libros Politicorum Aristotelis'.

Sloane MS 1982: Richard Hakluyt, 'Analysis, seu resolutio perpetua in octo libros Politicorum Aristotelis'.

Inner Temple Library, London

MS 529: Hugo Grotius, trans. Richard Hakluyt, 'The Free Sea or A Disputation Concerning the Right wch ye Hollanders Ought to Have to the Indian Marchandize for Trading' (*post* 1609).

National Archives of Scotland (formerly Scottish Record Office), Edinburgh

GD 26/13/105: Leven and Melville Muniments, 'Memoriall in behalf of the Scots Company trading to Africa and the Indies'.

GD 45/1/161: Dalhousie Muniments, 'Memoriall in behalf of the Scots Company trading to Africa and the Indies'.

National Library of Scotland, Edinburgh

MS 9255: Dunlop Papers.

MS 23159, item 14: David Hume, 'Early Memoranda, 1729–1740'.

MS Adv. 83. 7. 5: Company of Scotland Papers.

Public Record Office, Kew

30/24/47/3: [John Locke, et al.,] 'The Constitutions of Carolina' (21 July 1669).

CO 1/1: [Richard Hakluyt,] 'Whither an Englishman may trade into the West Indies with certain answers to the Popes Bull' (*c.* 1595–8), f. 108.

CO 1/6: [John White,] 'General Observations for ye Plantation of New England' (1632?), ff. 172–3.

CO 5/4: [Sir William Keith,] 'A Short Discourse on the Present State of the Colonies in America' (November 1728), ff. 164–78.

CO 5/283: Harman Verelst, 'Some Observations on the Right of the Crown of Great Britain to the North West Continent of America' (16 April 1739), ff. 1–53.

CO 381/10: Board of Trade Journals, 1697.

PRINTED WORKS

Acts of the Parliaments of Scotland, ed. T. Thomson and Cosmo Innes, 12 vols. (Edinburgh, 1814–75).

[Adams, John and Leonard, Daniel,] *Novanglus and Massachusettensis: or Political Essays* (Boston, 1819).

Alexander, Sir William, *An Encouragement to Colonies* (London, 1624).

[Annesley, Francis,] *Some Thoughts on the Bill Depending Before the Right Honourable the House of Lords, For Prohibiting the Exportation of the Woollen Manufactures of Ireland to Foreign Parts* (Dublin, 1698).

Arber, Edward (ed.), *A Transcript of the Registers of the Company of Stationers of London; 1554–1640 A.D.*, 3 vols. (London, 1875).

[Ashley, John,] *The British Empire in America, Consider'd* (London, 1732).

  Memoirs and Considerations Concerning the Trade and Revenues of the British Colonies in America (London, 1740).

Ashley, John, *The Second Part of Memoirs and Considerations Concerning the Trade and Revenues of the British Colonies in America* (London, 1743).

Augustine, *De Civitate Dei, Libri XII*, ed. B. Dombart and A. Kalb, 2 vols. (Leipzig, 1928–9).

Bacon, Francis, *Francisci Baconis . . . Opera Omnia*, ed. John Blackbourne, 4 vols. (London, 1730).

  The Letters and Life of Francis Bacon, ed. James Spedding, 7 vols. (London, 1862–74).

[B]arbon, [N]icholas, *A Discourse of Trade* (London, 1690).

Barr, William and Williams, Glyndwr (eds.), *Voyages in Search of a Northwest Passage*, 2 vols. (London, 1994).

Beacon, Richard, *Solon His Follie* (1594), ed. Clare Carroll and Vincent Carey (Binghamton, 1996).

Benson, George, *A Sermon Preached at Paules Crosse the Seaventh of May, M.DC.IX* (London, 1609).

Blackstone, William, *Commentaries on the Laws of England*, 4 vols. (London, 1765–69).

Bladen, Martin, 'Reasons for Appointing a Captain General for the Continent of North America' (27 December 1739), in Jack P. Greene, 'Martin Bladen's Blueprint for Colonial Union', *William and Mary Quarterly*, 3rd ser., 17 (1960), 516–30.

[Bodrugan, Nicholas,] *An Epitome of the Title That the Kynges Majestie of Englande, Hath to the Sovereigntie of Scotlande* (London, 1548).

Boroughs, Sir John, *The Soveraignty of the British Seas* (London, 1651).

The Soveraignty of the British Seas (London, 1739).

[Brewster, Sir Francis,] *A Discourse Concerning Ireland and the Different Interests Thereof, In Answer to the Exon and Barnstaple Petitions* (London, 1698).

The British Sailor's Discovery (London, 1739).

Burke, Edmund, *The Writings and Speeches of Edmund Burke IX*, ed. R. B. McDowell (Oxford, 1991).

[Butler, Samuel,] *The Acts and Monuments of Our Late Parliament* (London, 1659).

Caesar, Julius, *Commentaries*, trans. Martin Bladen (London, 1705).

Calendar of State Papers, Domestic: 1652–53, ed. Mary Everett Green (London, 1878).

Calendar of State Papers, Domestic: 1690–91, ed. W. J. Hardy (London, 1898).

Calendar of State Papers, Foreign Series, of the Reign of Elizabeth January–June 1583 and Addenda, ed. Arthur John Butler and Sophie Crawford Lomas (London, 1913).

Calendar of State Papers Relating to Scotland and Mary Queen of Scots 1547–1603, ed. Joseph Bain *et al.*, 13 vols. (Edinburgh, 1898–1969).

[Campbell, Alexander,] *ΑΡΕΤΕ-ΛΟΓΙΑ or An Enquiry into the Original of Moral Virtue* (London, 1728).

[Campbell, John (ed.),] *Memoirs of the Duke of Ripperda*, 2nd edn (London, 1740).

Carson, Hampton L. (ed.), *History of the Celebration of the One Hundredth Anniversary of the Promulgation of the Constitution of the United States*, 2 vols. (Philadelphia, 1889).

Cary, John, *An Essay on the State of England in Relation to its Trade, its Poor, and its Taxes, For Carrying on the Present War Against France* (Bristol, 1695).

A Discourse Concerning the Trade of Ireland and Scotland (London, 1696).

A Vindication of the Parliament of England, In Answer to a Book Written by William Molyneux of Dublin, Esq. (London, 1698).

[Cary, John,] *To the Freeholders and Burgesses of the City of Bristol* (n.p., n.d. [Bristol, 1698?]).

Catalogue of Prints and Drawings in the British Museum . . . Political and Personal Satires, ed. Dorothy George, 11 vols. (London, 1870–1954).

[Chamberlen, Hugh,] *The Great Advantages to Both Kingdoms of Scotland and England By an Union* (n.p., 1702).

Child, Sir Josiah, *A New Discourse of Trade* (London, 1698).

Clark, G. N., and W. J. M. van Eysinga, *The Colonial Conferences between England and the Netherlands in 1613 and 1615*, Bibliotheca Visseriana, 15 (1940).

Collectanea de Rebus Albanicis (Edinburgh, 1847).

Colquhoun, Patrick, *A Treatise on the Wealth, Power, and Resources of the British Empire, In Every Quarter of the World, Including the East Indies*, 2nd edn (London, 1815).

A Complete Collection of State Trials . . . From the Earliest Period to the Year 1783, ed. T. B. Howell, 21 vols. (London, 1816).

Conditions To Be Observed By the Brittish Undertakers, of the Escheated Lands in Ulster (London, 1610).

Corpus Iuris Civilis, ed. Paul Krueger, 4 vols. (Berlin, 1892).

Correspondance Politique de Odet de Selve, Ambassadeur de France en Angleterre (1546–1549), ed. Germain Lefèvre-Pontalis (Paris, 1888).

Cotton, John, *God's Promise to His Plantation* (London, 1630).

[Cox, Sir Richard,] *Aphorisms Relating to the Kingdom of Ireland* (London, 1689).

Craig, Sir Thomas, *De Unione Regnorum Britanniæ Tractatus* (1605), ed. C. Sanford Terry (Edinburgh, 1909).

Crakanthorpe, Richard, *A Sermon at the Solemnizing of the Happie Inauguration of our Most Gracious and Religious Soveraigne King James* (London, 1609).

Cromwell's Conspiracy. A Tragy-Comedy, Relating to our latter Times . . . Written by a Person of Quality (London, 1660).

[Crouch, Nathaniel,] *The English Empire in America: Or a Prospect of His Majesties Dominions in the West-Indies* (London, 1685).

Daniel, Samuel, *The First Part of the Historie of England* (London, 1612).

[Davenant, Charles,] *An Essay on the East-India Trade* (London, 1696).

Davenant, Charles, *The Political and Commercial Works of Charles Davenant LL.D.*, ed. Charles Whitworth, 5 vols. (London, 1771).

Davies, Sir John, *A Discovery of the True Causes Why Ireland Was Never Entirely Subdued [And] Brought Under Obedience of the Crown of England Until the Beginning of His Majesty's Happy Reign* (1612), ed. James P. Myers, Jr (Washington, DC, 1988).

A Declaration, Conteyning the Just Causes and Consyderations of this Present Warre with the Scottis (5 November 1542), in *The Complaynt of Scotlande wyth an Exortatione to the Thre Estaits to be Vigilante in Deffens of Their Public Veil*, ed. J. A. H. Murray (London, 1872), 191–206.

A Declaration of His Highness . . . Setting Forth, On the Behalf of this Commonwealth, the Justice of their Cause against Spain (London, 1655).

Decrees and Orders of the Committee of Safety of the Commonwealth of Oceana (London, 1659).

Dee, John, *General and Rare Memorials Pertayning to the Perfect Arte of Navigation* (London, 1577).

de Lolme, Jean Louis, *The British Empire in Europe: Part the First, Containing an Account of the Connection Between the Kingdoms of England and Ireland, Previous to the Year 1780* (Dublin, 1787).

Democritus Turned Statesman (London, 1659).

Dilke, C. W., *Greater Britain: A Record of Travel in the English-Speaking Countries during 1866 and '67*, 3 vols. (London, 1868).

Problems of Greater Britain (London, 1890).

A Discourse Concerning the Union (n.p., n.d.).

Dobbs, Arthur, *An Essay on the Trade and Improvement of Ireland* (Dublin, 1729).

An Account of the Countries Adjoining to Hudson's Bay, in the North-West Part of America (London, 1744).

Documents Relative to the Colonial History of the State of New-York, ed. E. B. O'Callaghan, 11 vols. (Albany, 1853–61).

Eburne, Richard, *A Plaine Pathway to Plantations* (London, 1624).

Eight and Thirty Queries Proposed (London, 1659).

Elder, John, 'A Proposal for Uniting Scotland with England, Addressed to King Henry VIII. By John Elder, Clerke, a Reddshanke' (*c.* 1542), BL MS King's 18. A. XXXVIII, in *The Bannatyne Miscellany*, 1, eds. Sir Walter Scott and David Laing (Edinburgh, 1827).

[Elder, John,] *The Copie of a Letter Sent in to Scotlande, of the Arivall and Landynge, and Moste Noble Marryage of the Moste Illustre Prynce Philippe, Prynce of Spaine, to the Moste Excellente Princes Marye Quene of England* (1555), in *The Chronicle of Queen Jane, and of Two Years of Queen Mary, and Especially of the Rebellion of Sir Thomas Wyat*, ed. John Gough Nichols (London, 1850), 136–66.

English and Irish Settlements on the River Amazon 1550–1646, ed. Joyce Lorimer (London, 1989).

An Essay on Civil Government: In Two Parts: Part I. An Enquiry into the Ends of Government, and the Means of Attaining Them. Part II. Of the Government and Commerce of England; with Reflections on Liberty and the Method of Preserving the Present Constitution (London, 1743).

An Essay upon the Government of the English Plantations on the Continent of America (London, 1701).

Evelyn, John, *Navigation and Commerce, Their Original and Progress* (London, 1674).

Ferguson, C., in *A Letter Address'd to Every Honest Man in Britain* (London, 1738).

[Ferrar, Nicholas,] *Sir Thomas Smith's Misgovernment of the Virginia Company by Nicholas Ferrar*, ed. D. R. Ransome (Cambridge, 1990).

Filmer, Sir Robert, *Filmer: Patriarcha and Other Writings*, ed. Johann P. Sommerville (Cambridge, 1991).

Fletcher of Saltoun, Andrew, *Andrew Fletcher: Political Works*, ed. John Robertson (Cambridge, 1997).

Freeman, E. A., *Lectures to American Audiences* (Philadelphia, 1882).

   Greater Greece and Greater Britain; and, George Washington, The Expander of England (London, 1886).

Freitas, Justo Seraphim de, *De Justo Imperio Lusitanorum Asiatico Adversus Grotii Mare Liberum* (Valladolid, 1625).

[Froude, J. A.,] 'England's Forgotten Worthies', *The Westminster Review*, n.s. 2, 1 (July 1852), 42–67.

Froude, J. A., *Oceana; or England and Her Colonies* (London, 1886).

Gardiner, Samuel Rawson (ed.), *The Constitutional Documents of the Puritan Revolution 1625–1660*, 3rd edn (Oxford, 1906).

Gordon of Lochinvar, Sir Robert, *Encouragements. For Such as Shall Have Intention to Bee Undertakers in the New Plantation of CAPE BRITON, Now New Galloway, in America* (Edinburgh, 1625).

[Gray, Robert,] *A Good Speed for Virginia* (London, 1609).

Grotius, Hugo, *Mare Liberum: Sive De Jure quod Batavis Competit ad Indicana Commercia* (Leiden, 1609).

'Defensio Capitis Quinti Maris Liberi Oppugnati a Guilielmo Welwodo ... Capite XXVII ejus Libri ... cui Titulum Fecit Compendium Legum Maritimarum' (1615), in Samuel Muller, *Mare Clausum: Bijdrage tot de Geschiedenis der Rivaliteit van Engeland en Nederland in de Zeventiende Eeuw* (Amsterdam, 1872), 331–61.

'Defence of Chapter V of the *Mare Liberum*', in Herbert F. Wright, 'Some Less Known Works of Hugo Grotius', *Bibliotheca Visseriana*, 7 (1928), 154–205.

Hakluyt, Richard, *A Particuler Discourse Concerninge the Greate Necessitie and Manifolde Commodyties that are Like to Growe to this Realme of Englande by the Westerne Discoveries Lately Attempted ... Known as Discourse of Western Planting* (1584), ed. David B. Quinn and Alison M. Quinn (London, 1993).

Hakluyt, Richard (ed.), *Divers Voyages Touching the Discoverie of America* (London, 1582).

De Orbe Novo Peter Martyris (Paris, 1587).

The Principall Navigations ... of the English People (London, 1589).

The Principal Navigations, Voyages, Traffiques and Discoveries of the English Nation, 3 vols. (London, 1598–1600).

Hakluyt, Richard the Elder and Richard Hakluyt, *The Original Writings and Correspondence of the Two Richard Hakluyts*, ed. E. G. R. Taylor, 2 vols. (London, 1935).

Harrington, James, *The Common-Wealth of Oceana* (London, 1656).

The Political Works of James Harrington, ed. J. G. A. Pocock (Cambridge, 1977).

[Harris, Sir Walter,] *Remarks on the Affairs and Trade of England and Ireland* (London, 1691).

Gabriel Harvey's Marginalia, ed. G. C. Moore Smith (Stratford-upon-Avon, 1913).

Haydn, Joseph, *Mare Clausum*, ed. H. C. Robbins Landon (Vienna, 1990).

Hayman, Robert, *Quodlibets; Lately Come Over from New Britaniola, Old Newfound-Land* (London, 1628).

Hegel, G. W. F., *Die Vernunft in der Geschichte*, ed. Johannes Hoffmeister (Hamburg, 1955).

Lectures on the Philosophy of World History: Introduction, trans. H. B. Nisbet (Cambridge, 1975).

Henrisoun, James, *An Exhortacion to the Scottes to Conforme Themselves to the Honourable, Expedient, and Godly Union Betweene the Two Realmes of Englande and Scotland* (1547), in *The Complaynt of Scotlande wyth ane Exortatione to the Thre Estaits to be Vigilante in Deffens of Their Public Veil*, ed. James A. H. Murray (London, 1872), 207–36.

'The Godly and Golden Booke for Concorde of England and Scotland', in *Calendar of State Papers Relating to Scotland and Mary Queen of Scots 1547–1603*, ed. Joseph Bain, *et al.*, 13 vols. (Edinburgh, 1898), I, 141–5.

Herbert, Sir William, *Croftus sive De Hibernia Liber* (*c.* 1591), ed. Arthur Keaveney and John A. Madden (Dublin, 1992).

Historical Manuscripts Commission, Report on the Manuscripts of the Duke of Buccleuch and Queensberry K.G., K.T., Preserved at Montagu House, Whitehall, ed. R. E. G. Kirk, 3 vols. (London, 1899–1926).

Historical Manuscripts Commission, Report on the Manuscripts of Lord de L'Isle and Dudley Preserved at Penshurst Place, ed. C. L. Kingsford, 5 vols. (London, 1925–1962).

Hobbes, Thomas, *The Correspondence of Thomas Hobbes*, ed. Noel Malcolm, 2 vols. (Oxford, 1994).

[Hovell, John,] *A Discourse upon the Woollen Manufactury of Ireland and the Consequences of Prohibiting its Exportation* (London, 1698).

Hume, David, *The Letters of David Hume*, ed. J. Y. T. Greig, 2 vols. (Oxford, 1932).
   A Treatise of Human Nature (1739–40), ed. L. A. Selby-Bigge and P. H. Nidditch, 2nd edn (Oxford, 1978).
   Essays, Moral, Political and Literary, ed. Eugene F. Miller (Indianapolis, 1985).

Hutcheson, Francis, *A System of Moral Philosophy*, 2 vols. (Glasgow, 1755).

Jacob, Hildebrand, *Brutus the Trojan; Founder of the British Empire* (London, 1735).

The Jacobean Union: Six Tracts of 1604, ed. Bruce R. Galloway and Brian P. Levack (Edinburgh, 1985).

James VI and I, *King James VI and I: Political Writings*, ed. Johann P. Sommerville (Cambridge, 1994).

Jefferson, Thomas, *The Papers of Thomas Jefferson*, I: 1760–1776, ed. Julian P. Boyd (Princeton, 1950).

Journals of the House of Commons From November the 8th 1547 . . . to March the 2d 1628 (London, n.d.).

K., C., *Some Seasonable and Modest Thoughts Partly Occasioned By, and Partly Concerning the Scots East-India Company* (Edinburgh, 1696).

Keith, Sir William, *The History of the British Plantations in America* (London, 1738).

[Keith, Sir William,] *Some Useful Observations on the Consequences of the Present War with Spain* (London, n.d. [1740]).

Keith, Sir William, *A Collection of Papers and Other Tracts, Written Occasionally*, 2nd edn (London, 1749).

[Keith, Sir William,] *Two Papers on the Subject of Taxing the British Colonies in America* (London, 1767).

[Kennett, White,] *Bibliothecæ Americanæ Primordiæ* (London, 1713).

Keymis, Lawrence, *A Relation of the Second Voyage to Guiana* (London, 1596).

Lamb, William, *Ane Resonyng of Ane Scottis and Inglis Merchand Betuix Rowand and Lionis* (1549), ed. Roderick J. Lyall (Aberdeen, 1985).

Lawrence, Richard, *The Interest of Ireland in Its Trade and Wealth Stated* (Dublin, 1682).

A Letter from a Gentleman in the Country to His Friend at Edinburgh (Edinburgh, 1696).

Llwyd, Humphrey, *Commentarioli Britannicæ Descriptionis Fragmentum* (Cologne, 1572).
   The Breviary of Britayne, trans. Thomas Twyne (London, 1573).

Locke, John, *Locke on Money*, ed. Patrick Hyde Kelly, 2 vols. (Oxford, 1991).
   Locke: Political Essays, ed. Mark Goldie (Cambridge, 1997).
   A Letter Concerning Toleration (1685), ed. James H. Tully (Indianapolis, 1983).
   Two Treatises of Government, ed. Peter Laslett, rev. edn (Cambridge, 1988).

[Lupton, Donald,] *Englands Command on the Seas, Or, The English Seas Guarded* (London, 1653).

Machiavelli, Niccolò, *The Works of the Famous Nicholas Machiavel*, trans. Henry Neville (London, 1680).

    Legazione e commissarie, ed. Sergio Bertelli, 3 vols. (Milan, 1964).

    Il teatro e gli scritti letterari, ed. Franco Gaeta (Milan, 1965).

    Machiavelli: The Chief Works and Others, trans. Allan H. Gilbert, 3 vols. (Durham, NC, 1965).

    Discorsi sopra la prima deca di Tito Livio, ed. Giorgio Inglese (Milan, 1984).

    The Prince, ed. Quentin Skinner and Russell Price (Cambridge, 1988).

[Madden, Samuel,] *Reflections and Resolutions Proper for the Gentlement of Ireland* (Dublin, 1738).

Madison, James, Alexander Hamilton and John Jay, *The Federalist Papers*, ed. Isaac Kramnick (Harmondsworth, 1987).

Martyr, Peter, *The Decades of the Newe Worlde or West India*, trans. Richard Eden (London, 1555).

[Maxwell, Henry,] *An Essay upon an Union of Ireland with England* (Dublin, 1703).

Meadows, Sir Philip, *Observations Concerning the Dominion and Sovereignty of the Seas: Being an Abstract of the Marine Affairs of England* (London, 1689).

Mede, Joseph, *The Works of the Pious and Profoundly-Learned Joseph Mede, B.D.* (London, 1664).

The Merchant's Complaint Against Spain (London, 1738).

Mercurius Politicus, 1651–2.

Milton, John, *Complete Prose Works*, gen. ed. Don M. Wolfe, 8 vols. (New Haven, 1953–82).

Molyneux, William, *The Case of Ireland . . . Stated* (1698), ed. J. G. Simms (Dublin, 1977).

Montesquieu, Charles-Louis de Secondat, Baron, *The Spirit of the Laws* (1748), trans. Anne Cohler, Basia Miller and Harold Stone (Cambridge, 1989).

[Morant, Philip,] *The Tapestry Hangings of the House of Lords: Representing the Several Engagements between the English and Spanish Fleets in the . . . Year MDLXXXVIII* (London, 1739).

More, Sir Thomas, *Utopia: Latin Text and English Translation*, ed. George M. Logan, Robert M. Adams and Clarence H. Miller (Cambridge, 1995).

Morley, John, *The Life of Richard Cobden*, 2 vols. (London, 1881).

Nedham, Marchamont, *The Case of the Commonwealth of England Stated* (London, 1650).

    The Excellencie of a Free State (London, 1656).

[Nedham, Marchamont,] 'Invocation of Neptune, and His Attendant Nereids, to Britannia, on the Dominion of the Sea' (n.p., n.d. [London, 1784?]).

Neville, Henry, *Plato Redivivus* (*c.* 1681), in *Two English Republican Tracts*, ed. Caroline Robbins (Cambridge, 1969), 61–200.

Nuttall, Zelia (ed.), *New Light on Drake* (London, 1914).

Nietzsche, Friedrich, *On the Genealogy of Morality* (1887), ed. Keith Ansell-Pearson, trans. Carol Diethe (Cambridge, 1994).

[Oglethorpe, James Edward,] *Select Tracts Relating to Colonies* (London, n.d. [1732]).

Oglethorpe, James Edward, *Some Account of the Design of the Trustees for Establishing Colonys in America* (1732), ed. Rodney M. Baine and Phinizy Spalding (Athens, Ga., 1990).

   The Publications of James Edward Oglethorpe, ed. Rodney M. Baine (Athens, Ga., 1994).

Old England For Ever, Or, Spanish Cruelty Display'd (London, 1740).

[Oldmixon, John,] *The British Empire in America, Containing the History of the Discovery, Settlement, Progress and Present State of All the British Colonies, on the Continent and Islands of America*, 2 vols. (London, 1708).

   The British Empire in America, 2nd edn, 2 vols. (London, 1741).

Original Letters Illustrative of English History, ed. Henry Ellis, 1st ser., 3 vols. (London, 1824).

Ortelius, Abraham, *Theatrum Orbis Terrarum* (Antwerp, 1570).

Paine, Thomas, *Common Sense; Addressed to the Inhabitants of America* (Philadelphia, 1776).

Parker, Henry, *The Case of Ship-Mony Briefly Discoursed* (London, 1640).

   Of a Free Trade (London, 1648).

Paruta, Paolo, *Politick Discourses*, trans. Henry, Earl of Monmouth (London 1657).

Paterson, William, *The Writings of William Paterson*, ed. Saxe Bannister, 3 vols. (London, 1859).

Patten, William, *The Expedition into Scotland of the Most Worthily Fortunate Prince Edward, Duke of Somerset* (1548), in *Tudor Tracts 1532–1588*, ed. A. F. Pollard (London, 1903), 53–158.

Pepys, Samuel, *The Diary of Samuel Pepys*, ed. Robert Latham and William Matthews, 11 vols. (London, 1970–83).

[Petty, Sir William,] *An Account of Several New Inventions &c.* (London, 1691).

Petty, Sir William, *The Economic Writings of Sir William Petty*, ed. Charles Henry Hull, 2 vols. (Cambridge, 1899).

Pinto, Isaac de, *Letters on the American Troubles* (London, 1776).

Polybius, *The Rise of the Roman Empire*, trans. Ian Scott-Kilvert (Harmondsworth, 1979).

[Postlethwayt, Malachy,] *The African Trade, The Great Pillar and Support of the British Plantation Trade in America* (London, 1745).

The Present State of Ireland: Together with Some Remarques Upon the Antient State Thereof (London, 1673).

Price, Daniel, *Sauls Prohibition Staide* (London, 1609).

A Proposal for Humbling Spain (London, 1739).

Ptolemy of Lucca, *On the Government of Princes: De Regimine Principum*, trans. James M. Blythe (Philadelphia, 1997).

Purchas, Samuel, *Purchas His Pilgrimage. Or Relations of the World and the Religions Oberved in All Ages and Places Discovered, from the Creation to the Present* (London, 1613).

   Purchas His Pilgrim: Microcosmos, or The Historie of Man (London, 1619).

The Kings Towre, And Triumphant Arch of London (London, 1623).

Hakluytus Posthumus, or Purchas His Pilgrimes, 4 vols. (London, 1625).

The Queen an Empress, and Her Three Kingdoms One Empire (London, 1706).

Quinn, D. B. (ed.), *New American World: A Documentary History of North America to 1612*, 5 vols. (New York, 1979).

Ralegh, Sir Walter, *The Discoverie of the Large, Rich, and Bewtifull Empyre of Guiana* (London, 1596).

Reasons for a War Against Spain (London, 1737; rptd 1738).

Reasons for Giving Encouragement to the Sea-Faring People of Great-Britain, in Times of Peace or War (London, 1739).

The Register of the Privy Council of Scotland: IX A.D. 1610–1613, ed. David Masson (Edinburgh, 1889).

The Register of the Privy Council of Scotland, 2nd ser., IV (1630–32), ed. P. Hume Brown (Edinburgh, 1902).

[Ridpath, George,] *The Great Reasons and Interests Consider'd Anent the Spanish Monarchy* (n.p., 1702).

Robertson, William, *The History of America*, 2 vols. (London, 1777).

[Roe, Sir Thomas,] *A Speech Delivered in Parliament by a Person of Honour* (London, 1739).

Rolt, Richard, *An Impartial Representation of the Conduct of the Several Powers of Europe, Engaged in the Late General War*, 4 vols. (London, 1749–50).

Ruffhead, Owen, *The Life of Alexander Pope, Esq.* (London, 1769).

St John, Henry, Viscount Bolingbroke, *Bolingbroke: Political Writings*, ed. David Armitage (Cambridge, 1997).

Sallust, *Sallust*, ed. and trans. J. C. Rolfe (London, 1931).

Seeley, J. R., *Lectures and Essays* (London, 1870).

The Expansion of England (London, 1883).

The Growth of British Policy, 2 vols. (Cambridge, 1895).

Introduction to Political Science: Two Series of Lectures (London, 1896).

'Introduction', in A. J. R. Trendell, *The Colonial Year Book for the Year 1890* (London, 1890), ix–xxvi.

Selden, John, *Mare Clausum seu De Dominio Maris* (London, 1635).

Mare Clausum; The Right and Dominion of the Sea in Two Books, ed. James Howell (London, 1663).

[Selden, John,] *Of the Dominion, Or, Ownership of the Sea*, trans. Marchamont Nedham (London, 1652).

Select Dissertations on Colonies and Plantations, ed. Charles Whitworth (London, 1775).

[Seton, William, of Pitmedden,] *The Interest of Scotland in Three Essays* (n.p., 1700).

[Seymour, Edward, Duke of Somerset,] *An Epistle or Exhortacion, to Unitie and Peace, Sent from the Lord Protector . . . To the Nobilitie, Gentlemen, and Commons, and Al Others the Inhabitauntes of the Realme of Scotlande* (5 February 1548), in *The Complaynt of Scotlande wyth an Exortatione to the Thre Estaits to be Vigilante in Deffens of Their Public Veil*, ed. James A. H. Murray (London, 1872), 237–46.

Sidney, Algernon, *Discourses Concerning Government*, ed. Thomas G. West (Indianapolis, 1990).

    Court Maxims, ed. Hans W. Blom, Eco Haitsma Mulier and Ronald Janse (Cambridge, 1996).

Smith, Adam, *An Inquiry into the Causes and Nature of the Wealth of Nations* (1776), ed. R. H. Campbell, A. S. Skinner and W. B. Todd, 2 vols. (Oxford, 1976).

    The Correspondence of Adam Smith, ed. E. C. Mossner and J. S. Ross, rev. edn (Oxford, 1987).

[Smith, Sir Thomas,] *A Discourse of the Commonweal of This Realm of England* (1549), ed. Mary Dewar (Charlottesville, Va. 1969).

[Smith, Sir Thomas, and Thomas Smith,] *A Letter Sent by I. B. Gentleman unto his Very Frende Mayster R. C. Esquire* (1572), in George Hill (ed.), *An Historical Account of the MacDonnells of Antrim* (Belfast, 1873), 405–15.

Speed, John, *The Theatre of the Empire of Great Britaine* (London, 1611).

Spenser, Edmund, *The Færie Queene* (1590–96), in *The Works of Edmund Spenser: A Variorum Edition*, eds. Edwin Greenlaw, Charles Grosvenor Osgood, Frederick Morgan Padelford and Ray Heffner, 11 vols. (Baltimore, 1932–57), I–VI.

[Spenser, Edmund,] *A View of the Present State of Ireland* (c. 1596), ed. Rudolf Gottfried, in *The Works of Edmund Spenser: A Variorum Edition*, eds. Edwin Greenlaw, Charles Grosvenor Osgood, Frederick Morgan Padelford and Ray Heffner, 11 vols. (Baltimore, 1932–57), IX, 39–231.

Thomson, James, *Alfred: A Masque* (London, 1740).

[Thornhill, Sir James,] *An Explanation of the Painting in the Royal Hospital at Greenwich* (London, n.d.).

Thurloe, John, *A Collection of the State Papers of John Thurloe*, ed. Thomas Birch, 7 vols. (London, 1742).

[Towgood, Micaiah,] *Spanish Cruelty and Injustice a Justifiable Plea for a Vigorous War with Spain* (London, 1741).

[Trapp, Joseph,] *The Ministerial Virtue: Or, Long-Suffering Extolled in a Great Man* (London, 1739).

Trusler, John, *The Difference, Between Words, Esteemed Synonymous, in the English Language*, 2 vols. (London, 1766).

Vane, Sir Henry, *A Healing Question* (London, 1656).

[Vaughan, William,] *The Golden Fleece . . . Transported from Cambrioll Colchos, Out of the Southermost Part of the Iland, Commonly Called the Newfoundland* (London, 1626).

de Vitoria, Francisco, *Vitoria: Political Writings*, ed. Anthony Pagden and Jeremy Lawrance (Cambridge, 1991).

Walsh, Peter, *A Letter to the Catholicks of England, Ireland, Scotland, and All Other Dominions under His Gracious Majesty Charles II* (London, 1674).

Weber, Max, *Weber: Political Writings*, ed. Peter Lassman and Ronald Speirs (Cambridge, 1994).

[Wedderburn, Robert,] *The Complaynt of Scotland* (c. 1550), ed. A. M. Stewart (Edinburgh, 1979).

Welwod, William, *An Abridgement of All Sea-Lawes* (London, 1613).

[Welwod, William,] *De Dominio Maris, Juribusque ad Dominium Præcipue Spectantibus Assertio Brevis et Methodica* (London, 1615).

[White, John,] *The Planters Plea* (London, 1630).

White, Rowland, 'Discors Touching Ireland', ed. Nicholas Canny, *Irish Historical Studies*, 20 (1977), 439–63.

Williams, Roger, *The Complete Writings of Roger Williams*, 7 vols. (New York, 1963).

Winthrop, John, *et al.*, *Winthrop Papers: III 1631–1637* (Boston, 1943).

Witsen, Nicolaes, *Aeloude en Hedendaegsche Scheeps-bouwen Bestier: Waer in Wijtloopigh wert Verhandelt, de Wijze van Scheeps-timmeren, by Grieken en Romeynen* (Amsterdam, 1671)

[Wood, William,] *A Survey of Trade* (London, 1718).

SECONDARY WORKS

Abbattista, Guido, *Commercio, colonie e impero alla vigilia della Rivoluzione Americana: John Campbell pubblicista e storico nell'Inghilterra del. sec. XVIII* (Florence, 1990).

Adams, James Truslow, 'On the Term "British Empire"', *American Historical Review*, 27 (1922), 485–9.

Adams, Simon, 'Spain or the Netherlands? The Dilemmas of Early Stuart Foreign Policy', in Howard Tomlinson (ed.), *Before the English Civil War: Essays on Early Stuart Politics and Government* (London, 1983), 79–101.

Alexandrowicz, C. H., 'Freitas *Versus* Grotius', *British Yearbook of International Law*, 35 (1959), 162–82.

Alford, Stephen, *The Early Elizabethan Polity: William Cecil and the British Succession Crisis 1558–1569* (Cambridge, 1998).

Alsop, J. D., 'William Welwood, Anne of Denmark and the Sovereignty of the Sea', *Scottish Historical Review*, 49 (1980), 171–4.

Anderson, James S. M., *The History of the Church of England in the Colonies and Foreign Dependencies of the British Empire*, 3 vols. (London, 1856).

Andrews, Kenneth R., *Trade, Plunder and Settlement: Maritime Enterprise and the Genesis of the British Empire, 1480–1630* (Cambridge, 1984).

Anglo, Sydney, 'A Machiavellian Solution to the Irish Problem: Richard Beacon's *Solon His Follie* (1594)', in Edward Chaney and Peter Mack (eds.), *England and the Continental Renaissance: Essays in Honour of J. B. Trapp* (Woodbridge, 1990), 153–64.

Armitage, David, 'The Cromwellian Protectorate and the Languages of Empire', *The Historical Journal*, 35 (1992), 531–55.

'The Scottish Vision of Empire: Intellectual Origins of the Darien Venture', in John Robertson (ed.), *A Union for Empire: Political Thought and the British Union of 1707* (Cambridge, 1995), 97–118.

'A Patriot for Whom? The Afterlives of Bolingbroke's Patriot King', *Journal of British Studies*, 36 (1997), 397–418.

'Literature and Empire', in Nicholas Canny (ed.), *Oxford History of the British Empire*, I: *The Origins of Empire* (Oxford, 1998), 99–123.

'Greater Britain: A Useful Category of Historical Analysis?' *American Historical Review*, 104 (1999), 427–45.

Armitage, David (ed.), *Theories of Empire, 1450–1800* (Aldershot, 1998).

Arneil, Barbara, *John Locke and America: The Defence of English Colonialism* (Oxford, 1996).

Asch, Ronald (ed.), *Three Nations – A Common History? England, Scotland, Ireland and British History c. 1600–1920* (Bochum, 1993).

Aspromourgos, Tony, 'The Life of William Petty in Relation to his Economics: A Tercentenary Interpretation', *History of Political Economy*, 20 (1988), 337–56.

Bailyn, Bernard, *The Ideological Origins of the American Revolution*, 2nd edn (Cambridge, Mass., 1992).

Baine, Rodney M., 'James Oglethorpe and the Early Promotional Literature for Georgia', *William and Mary Quarterly*, 3rd ser., 45 (1988), 100–6.

Baker, Keith Michael, 'On the Problem of the Ideological Origins of the French Revolution', in Baker, *Inventing the French Revolution: Essays on French Political Culture in the Eighteenth Century* (Cambridge, 1990), 12–27.

Ball, Terence, James Farr and Russell L. Hanson, (eds.), *Political Innovation and Conceptual Change* (Cambridge, 1989).

Barker, Sir Ernest, *The Ideas and Ideals of the British Empire* (Cambridge, 1941).

Bartlett, Robert, *The Making of Europe: Conquest, Colonization and Cultural Change 950–1350* (New Haven, 1993).

Bauckham, Richard, *Tudor Apocalypse* (Abingdon, 1978).

Beer, G. L., *The Origins of the British Colonial System 1578–1660* (London, 1908).

Behrman, Cynthia Fansler, *Victorian Myths of the Sea* (Athens, Ohio, 1977).

Bender, Thomas (ed.), *The Antislavery Debate: Capitalism and Abolitionism as a Problem in Historical Interpretation* (Berkeley, 1992).

Bennett, G. V., *White Kennett, 1660–1728* (London, 1957).

Bennett, George (ed.), *The Concept of Empire: Burke to Attlee, 1774–1947* (London, 1953).

Bennett, Josephine Waters, 'Britain Among the Fortunate Isles', *Studies in Philology*, 53 (1956), 114–40.

Bentley, Michael, 'The British State and its Historiography', in Wim Blockmans and Jean-Philippe Genet (eds.), *Visions sur le développement des états européens: théories et historiographies de l'état moderne* (Rome, 1993), 153–68.

Bindoff, S. T., 'The Stuarts and their Style', *English Historical Review*, 60 (1945), 192–216.

Blaas, P. B. M., *Continuity and Anachronism: Parliamentary and Constitutional Development in Whig Historiography and in the Anti-Whig Reaction between 1890 and 1930* (The Hague, 1978).

Blackburn, Robin, *The Overthrow of Colonial Slavery 1776–1848* (London, 1988).

Bloch, Marc, *The Historian's Craft*, trans. Peter Putnam (New York, 1953).

Bossuat, André, 'La Formule "Le Roi est empereur en son royaume": son emploi au XVe siècle devant le parlement de Paris', *Revue Historique de Droit Français et Etranger*, 4th ser., 39 (1961), 371–81.

Bourne, H. R. Fox, *The Life of John Locke*, 2 vols. (London, 1876).

Bowman, John, 'Is America the New Jerusalem or Gog and Magog? A Seventeenth Century Theological Discussion', *Proceedings of the Leeds Philosophical and Literary Society*, 6 (1950), 445–52.

Braddick, Michael J., 'The English Government, War, Trade, and Settlement, 1625–1688', in Nicholas Canny (ed.), *The Oxford History of the British Empire*, i: *The Origins of Empire* (Oxford, 1998), 286–308.

Brading, D. A., *The First America: The Spanish Monarchy, Creole Patriots, and the Liberal State 1492–1867* (Cambridge, 1991).

Bradshaw, Brendan, 'Robe and Sword in the Conquest of Ireland', in Claire Cross, David Loades and J. J. Scarisbrick (eds.), *Law and Government in Tudor England* (Cambridge, 1986), 139–62.

Bradshaw, Brendan, and John Morrill (eds.), *The British Problem: State-Formation in the Atlantic Archipelago c. 1534–1707* (Basingstoke, 1996).

Bradshaw, Brendan, and Peter Roberts (eds.), *British Consciousness and Identity: The Making of Britain, 1533–1707* (Cambridge, 1998).

Brady, Ciaran, 'The Road to the *View*: On the Decline of Reform Thought in Tudor Ireland', in Patricia Coughlan (ed.), *Spenser and Ireland: An Interdisciplinary Perspective* (Cork, 1989), 25–45.

Braudel, Fernand, *The Mediterranean and the Mediterranean World in the Age of Philip II*, trans. Siân Reynolds, 2 vols. (London, 1973).

Breen, T. H., 'Ideology and Nationalism on the Eve of the American Revolution: Revisions *Once More* in Need of Revising', *Journal of American History*, 84 (1997), 13–39.

Brett, Annabel, *Liberty, Right and Nature: Individual Rights in Later Scholastic Thought* (Cambridge, 1997).

Brie, Friedrich, 'Pope's *Brutus*', *Anglia*, 63 (1939), 144–85.

Brockliss, Laurence, and David Eastwood (eds.), *A Union of Multiple Identities: The British Isles c. 1750 – c. 1850* (Manchester, 1997).

Brown, Louise Fargo, *The First Earl of Shaftesbury* (New York, 1933).

Brunt, P. A., '*Laus Imperii*', in Brunt, *Roman Imperial Themes* (Oxford, 1990), 288–323.

Bryant, Arthur, *The History of Britain and the British Peoples*, 3 vols. (London, 1984–90).

Burgess, Glenn (ed.), *The New British History: Founding a Modern State, 1603–1715* (London, 1999).

Burke, Peter, 'A Survey of the Popularity of Ancient Historians, 1450–1700', *History and Theory*, 5 (1966), 135–52.

Burrow, John, *A Liberal Descent: Victorian Historians and the English Past* (Cambridge, 1981).

Bush, M. L., *The Government Policy of Protector Somerset* (London, 1975).

Butterfield, Herbert, *The Englishman and His History* (Cambridge, 1944).

Calder, Angus, *Revolutionary Empire: The Rise of the English-Speaking Peoples from the Fifteenth Century to the 1780s* (London, 1981).

Campbell, James, 'The United Kingdom of England: The Anglo-Saxon

Achievement', in Alexander Grant and Keith J. Stringer (eds.), *Uniting the Kingdom? The Making of British History* (London, 1995), 31–47.

Canning, J. P., 'Ideas of the State in 13th and 14th-Century Commentators on the Roman Law', *Transactions of the Royal Historical Society*, 5th ser., 33 (1983), 1–27.

Canny, Nicholas, *Kingdom and Colony: Ireland in the Atlantic World 1560–1800* (Baltimore, 1988).

    Making Ireland British, 1580–1650 (Oxford, forthcoming).

    'The Ideology of English Colonization: From Ireland to America', *William and Mary Quarterly*, 3rd ser., 30 (1973), 575–98.

    'Edmund Spenser and the Development of Anglo-Irish Identity', *Yearbook of English Studies*, 13 (1983), 1–19.

    'Fashioning "British" Worlds in the Seventeenth Century', in Nicholas Canny, Joseph Illick and Gary Nash (eds.), *Empire, Society and Labor: Essays in Honor of Richard S. Dunn, Pennsylvania History*, 54, supplemental vol. (College Park, Pa., 1997), 26–45.

Capp, Bernard, *Cromwell's Navy: The Fleet and the English Revolution* (Oxford, 1989).

Cave, Alfred A., 'Canaanites in a Promised Land: The American Indian and the Providential Theory of Empire', *American Indian Quarterly*, 12 (1988), 277–97.

Cervelli, Innocenzo, *Machiavelli e la crisi dello stato Veneziana* (Naples, 1974).

Cheyney, Edward P., 'International Law under Queen Elizabeth', *English Historical Review*, 20 (1905), 659–72.

Clark, G. N., 'Grotius's East India Mission to England', *Transactions of the Grotius Society*, 20 (1934), 45–84.

Clark, J. C. D., *The Language of Liberty 1660–1832: Political Discourse and Social Dynamics in the Anglo-American World* (Cambridge, 1995).

Clarke, Desmond, *Arthur Dobbs, Esq., 1689–1765* (London, 1958).

Claydon, Tony, and Ian McBride (eds.), *Protestantism and National Identity: Britain and Ireland, c. 1650 – c. 1850* (Cambridge, 1998).

Cogswell, Thomas, *The Blessed Revolution: English Politics and the Coming of War, 1621–1624* (Cambridge, 1989).

Colbourn, H. Trevor, *The Lamp of Experience: Whig History and the Intellectual Origins of the American Revolution* (Chapel Hill, 1965).

Colley, Linda, *Britons: Forging the Nation, 1707–1837* (New Haven, 1992).

    'The Apotheosis of George III: Loyalty, Royalty and the British Nation, 1760–1820', *Past and Present*, 102 (Feb. 1984), 94–129.

    'The Imperial Embrace', *Yale Review*, 81, 4 (1993), 92–9.

Collini, Stefan, Donald Winch and John Burrow, *That Noble Science of Politics: A Study in Nineteenth-Century Intellectual History* (Cambridge, 1983).

Collinson, Patrick, *The Birthpangs of Protestant England: Religious and Cultural Change in the Sixteenth and Seventeenth Centuries* (London, 1988).

    'A Chosen People? The English Church and the Reformation', *History Today*, 36, 3 (March 1986), 14–20.

Corrigan, Philip and Derek Sayer, *The Great Arch: English State Formation as Cultural Revolution* (Oxford, 1985).

Cranston, Maurice, *John Locke: A Biography* (London, 1957).

Croft-Murray, Edward, *Decorative Painting in England 1537–1837*, 2 vols. (London, 1962).

Cummings, William H., *God Save the King: The Origin and History of the Music and Words of the National Anthem* (London, 1902).

Dr. Arne and Rule, Britannia (London, 1912).

Davies, C. S. L., 'Slavery and Protector Somerset: The Vagrancy Act of 1547', *Economic History Review*, 2nd ser., 19 (1966), 533–49.

'International Politics and the Establishment of Presbyterianism in the Channel Islands: The Coutances Connection', *Journal of Ecclesiastical History*, 50 (1999), 498–522.

Davies, R. R., 'The English State and the "Celtic" Peoples 1100–1400', *Journal of Historical Sociology*, 6 (1993), 1–14.

'The Failure of the First British Empire? England's Relations with Ireland, Scotland and Wales 1066–1500', in Nigel Saul (ed.), *England in Europe 1066–1453* (London, 1994), 121–32.

Dawson, Jane, 'Two Kingdoms or Three? Ireland in Anglo-Scottish Relations in the Middle of the Sixteenth Century', in Roger A. Mason (ed.), *Scotland and England, 1286–1815* (Edinburgh, 1987), 113–38.

'William Cecil and the British Dimension of Early Elizabethan Foreign Policy', *History*, 74 (1989), 196–216.

'Calvinism and the *Gaidhealtachd* in Scotland', in Andrew Pettegree, Alastair Duke and Gillian Lewis (eds.), *Calvinism in Europe, 1540–1620* (Cambridge, 1994), 231–53.

'Anglo-Scottish Protestant Culture and Integration in Sixteenth-Century Britain', in Steven G. Ellis and Sarah Barber (eds.), *Conquest and Union: Fashioning a British State 1485–1725* (London, 1995), 87–114.

de Jong, J. A., *As the Waters Cover the Sea: Millennial Expectations in the Rise of Anglo-American Missions 1640–1810* (Kampen, 1970).

Dewar, Mary, *Sir Thomas Smith: A Tudor Intellectual in Office* (London, 1964).

Drayton, Richard, 'Knowledge and Empire', in P. J. Marshall (ed.), *The Oxford History of the British Empire*, II: *The Eighteenth Century* (Oxford, 1998), 231–52.

Drescher, Seymour, 'Cart Whip and Billy Roller: Antislavery and Reform Symbolism in Industrializing Britain', *Journal of Social History*, 15 (1981), 3–24.

Dresser, Madge, 'Britannia', in Raphael Samuel (ed.), *Patriotism: The Making and Unmaking of British National Identity*, 3 vols. (London, 1989), III: *National Fictions*, 26–49.

Drever, W. P., 'Udal Law and the Foreshore', *Juridical Review*, 16 (1904), 189–202.

Duncan-Jones, Elsie, 'Marvell, R. F. and the Authorship of "Blake's Victory"', in Peter Beal and Jeremy Griffiths (eds.), *English Manuscript Studies*, v (London, 1995), 107–26.

Durkan, John, 'Education: The Laying of Fresh Foundations', in John MacQueen (ed.), *Humanism in Renaissance Scotland* (Edinburgh, 1990), 123–60.

Dworkin, Ronald, *Taking Rights Seriously*, rev. edn (Cambridge, Mass., 1978).

Dzelzainis, Martin, *The Ideological Origins of the English Revolution* (Cambridge, forthcoming).

'Milton's Classical Republicanism', in David Armitage, Armand Himy and Quentin Skinner (eds.), *Milton and Republicanism* (Cambridge, 1995), 3–24.

Eisinger, Chester, 'The Puritans' Justification for Taking the Land', *Essex Institute Historical Collections*, 84 (1948), 131–43.

Elder, John R., *The Royal Fishery Companies of the Seventeenth Century* (Glasgow, 1912).

Elliott, J. H., 'A Europe of Composite Monarchies', *Past and Present*, 137 (Nov. 1992), 48–71.

'Empire and State in British and Spanish America', in Serge Gruzinski and Nathan Wachtel (eds.), *Le Nouveau Monde – mondes nouveaux: l'expérience américaine* (Paris, 1996), 365–82.

Ellis, Steven G., and Sarah Barber (eds.), *Conquest and Union: Fashioning a British State 1485–1725* (London, 1995).

Elton, G. R., 'The Tudor Revolution: A Reply', *Past and Present*, 29 (Dec. 1964), 26–49.

Facey, Jane, 'John Foxe and the Defence of the English Church', in Peter Lake and Maria Dowling (eds.), *Protestantism and the National Church in Sixteenth Century England* (London, 1987), 162–92.

Ferro, Marc, *Colonization: A Global History*, trans. K. D. Prithipaul (London, 1997).

Ferguson, William, 'Imperial Crowns: A Neglected Facet of the Background to the Treaty of Union of 1707', *Scottish Historical Review*, 53 (1974), 22–44.

Fieldhouse, David, 'Can Humpty-Dumpty be Put Together Again? Imperial History in the 1980s', *Journal of Imperial and Commonwealth History*, 12 (1984), 9–23.

Fincham, Kenneth, 'The Judges' Decision on Ship Money in February 1637: The Reaction of Kent', *Bulletin of the Institute of Historical Research*, 57 (1984), 230–7.

Fink, Zera S., *The Classical Republicans*, 2nd edn (Evanston, 1962).

Firth, C. H., '"The British Empire"', *Scottish Historical Review*, 15 (1918), 185–89.

Firth, Katherine R., *The Apocalyptic Tradition in Reformation Britain 1530–1645* (Oxford, 1979).

Fitzmaurice, Andrew, 'Classical Rhetoric and the Promotion of the New World', *Journal of the History of Ideas*, 58 (1997), 221–44.

'The Civic Solution to the Crisis of English Colonization, 1609–1625', *The Historical Journal*, 42 (1999), 25–51.

'Every Man That Prints Adventures: The Rhetoric of the Virginia Company Sermons', in Lori Anne Ferrell and Peter McCullough (eds.), *The English Sermon Revised: Religion, Literature and History 1600–1750* (Manchester, 2000), 24–42.

Flanagan, Thomas, 'The Agricultural Argument and Original Appropriation: Indian Lands and Political Philosophy', *Canadian Journal of Political Science*, 22 (1989), 589–602.

Folz, Robert, *The Concept of Empire in Western Europe from the Fifth to the Fourteenth Century*, trans. Sheila Ann Ogilvie (London, 1969).

Fowler, Elizabeth, 'The Failure of Moral Philosophy in the Work of Edmund Spenser', *Representations*, 51 (1995), 47–76.

Frost, Alan, 'New South Wales as *Terra Nullius*: The British Denial of Aboriginal Land Rights', *Historical Studies*, 19 (1981), 513–23.

Fulton, Thomas Wemyss, *The Sovereignty of the Sea* (Edinburgh, 1911).

Gerrard, Christine, *The Patriot Opposition to Walpole: History, Politics, and National Myth, 1720–1742* (Oxford, 1994).

Gilbert, Felix, 'Machiavelli e Venezia', *Lettere Italiane*, 21 (1969), 389–98.

Gillespie, Raymond, *Colonial Ulster: The Settlement of East Ulster 1600–1641* (Cork, 1985).

— *The Transformation of the Irish Economy 1550–1700*, Studies in Irish Economic and Social History, 6 (Dublin, 1991).

— 'The Ulster of Arthur Dobbs', in D. Helen Rankin and E. Charles Nelson (eds.), *Curious in Everything: The Career of Arthur Dobbs of Carrickfergus 1689–1765* (Carrickfergus, 1990), 1–5.

— 'Explorers, Exploiters and Entrepreneurs: Early Modern Ireland and its Context 1500–1700', in B. J. Graham and L. J. Proudfoot (eds.), *An Historical Geography of Ireland* (London, 1993), 123–57.

Gillingham, John, 'Images of Ireland 1170–1600: The Origins of English Imperialism', *History Today*, 37, 2 (Feb. 1987), 16–22.

— 'The Beginnings of English Imperialism', *Journal of Historical Sociology*, 5 (1992), 392–409.

— 'The English Invasion of Ireland', in Brendan Bradshaw, Andrew Hadfield and Willy Maley (eds.), *Representing Ireland: Literature and the Origins of Conflict, 1534–1660* (Cambridge, 1993), 24–42.

Ginzburg, Carlo, 'Killing a Chinese Mandarin: The Moral Implications of Distance', in Olwen Hufton (ed.), *Historical Change and Human Rights: The Oxford Amnesty Lectures 1994* (New York, 1995), 55–74.

Goebel, Jr, Julius, 'The Matrix of Empire', in Joseph Henry Smith, *Appeals from the Privy Council from the American Plantations* (New York, 1950), xiii–lxi.

Graham, Eric J., 'In Defence of the Scottish Maritime Interest, 1681–1713', *Scottish Historical Review*, 71 (1992), 88–109.

Grant, Alexander, and Keith Stringer (eds.), *Uniting the Kingdom? The Making of British History* (London, 1995).

Greene, Jack P., *Peripheries and Center: Constitutional Development in the Extended Polities of the British Empire and the United States 1607–1788* (Athens, Ga., 1986).

— 'The Glorious Revolution and the British Empire, 1688–1783', in Lois G. Schwoerer (ed.), *The Revolution of 1688–89: Changing Perspectives* (Cambridge, 1992), 260–71.

— 'Empire and Identity from the Glorious Revolution to the American Revolution', in P. J. Marshall (ed.), *The Oxford History of the British Empire*, II: *The Eighteenth Century* (Oxford, 1998), 208–30.

Greenfeld, Leah, *Nationalism: Five Roads to Modernity* (Cambridge, Mass., 1992).

Gregg, Robert, and Madhavi Kale, 'The Empire and Mr Thompson: Making of Indian Princes and English Working Class', *Economic and Political Weekly*, 33, 36 (6–12 September 1997), 2273–88.

Gregory, Donald, *The History of the Western Highlands and Isles of Scotland, From A.D. 1493 to A.D. 1625*, 2nd edn (London, 1881).

Grierson, Philip, 'The Origins of the English Sovereign and the Symbolism of the Closed Crown', *British Numismatic Journal*, 33 (1964), 118–34.

Guy, John, *Tudor England* (Oxford, 1988).

Guy, John (ed.), *The Reign of Elizabeth I: Court and Culture in the Last Decade* (Cambridge, 1995).

Hadfield, Andrew, 'Briton and Scythian: Tudor Representations of Irish Origins', *Irish Historical Studies*, 28 (1993), 390–408.

Hanford, James Holly, 'The Chronology of Milton's Private Studies', *Publications of the Modern Languages Association of America*, 36 (1921), 281–3.

Harding, R. W., *Amphibious Warfare in the Eighteenth Century: The British Expedition to the West Indies 1740–42* (Woodbridge, 1991).

Harlow, V. T., *The Founding of the Second British Empire, 1763–1793*, 2 vols. (London, 1952–64).

Harrison, John, and Peter Laslett, *The Library of John Locke*, 2nd edn (Oxford, 1971).

Harriss, G. L., 'Medieval Government and Statecraft', *Past and Present*, 25 (July 1963), 36–63.

'A Revolution in Tudor History?', *Past and Present*, 31 (July 1965), 87–94.

Hay, Denys, *Europe: The Emergence of an Idea*, 2nd edn (Edinburgh, 1968).

'The Use of the Term "Great Britain" in the Middle Ages', *Transactions of the Society of Antiquaries of Great Britain*, 89 (1955–56), 55–66.

Head, David M., 'Henry VIII's Scottish Policy: A Reassessment', *Scottish Historical Review*, 61 (1982), 1–24.

Hechter, Michael, *Internal Colonialism: The Celtic Fringe in British National Development* (London, 1975).

Helfers, James P., 'The Explorer or the Pilgrim? Modern Critical Opinion and the Editorial Methods of Richard Hakluyt and Samuel Purchas', *Studies in Philology*, 94 (1997), 160–86.

Helgerson, Richard, *Forms of Nationhood: The Elizabethan Writing of England* (Chicago, 1992).

Henretta, James A., *'Salutary Neglect': Colonial Administration under the Duke of Newcastle* (Princeton, 1972).

Henry, Bruce Ward, 'John Dee, Humphrey Llwyd, and the Name "British Empire"', *Huntington Library Quarterly*, 35 (1972), 189–90.

Hertz, Gerald Berkeley, *British Imperialism in the Eighteenth Century* (London, 1908).

Hill, Christopher, *The Experience of Defeat: Milton and Some Contemporaries* (London, 1984).

Liberty Against the Law: Some Seventeenth-Century Controversies (London, 1996).

Hill, George, *An Historical Account of the MacDonnells of Antrim* (Belfast, 1873).

An Historical Account of the Plantation in Ulster at the Commencement of the Seventeenth Century, 1608–1620 (Belfast, 1877).

Hoak, Dale, 'The Iconography of the Crown Imperial', in Hoak (ed.), *Tudor Political Culture* (Cambridge, 1995), 54–103.

Hont, Istvan, 'Free Trade and the Economic Limits to National Politics: Neo-Machiavellian Political Economy Reconsidered', in John Dunn (ed.), *The Economic Limits to Modern Politics* (Cambridge, 1990), 41–120.

'The Permanent Crisis of a Divided Mankind: "Contemporary Crisis of the Nation State" in Historical Perspective', *Political Studies*, 42 (1994), 166–231.

Hopkins, A. G., *The Future of the Imperial Past*, Inaugural Lecture, 12 March 1997 (Cambridge, 1997).

Howe, Stephen, 'Labour Patriotism, 1939–83', in Raphael Samuel (ed.), *Patriotism: The Making and Unmaking of British National Identity*, 3 vols. (London, 1989), I: *History and Politics*, 127–39.

Hudson, Winthrop S., *The Cambridge Connection and the Elizabethan Settlement of 1559* (Durham, NC, 1980).

Hutchison, Terence, *Before Adam Smith: The Emergence of Political Economy, 1662–1776* (Oxford, 1988).

Insh, G. P., *Scottish Colonial Schemes, 1620–1686* (Glasgow, 1922).

'The Founding of the Company of Scotland Trading to Africa and the Indies', *Scottish Historical Review*, 21 (1924), 288–95.

'The Founders of the Company of Scotland', *Scottish Historical Review*, 25 (1928), 241–54.

James, Lawrence, *The Rise and Fall of the British Empire* (London, 1994).

Jardine, Lisa, 'Mastering the Uncouth: Gabriel Harvey, Edmund Spenser and the English Experience in Ireland', in John Henry and Sarah Hutton (eds.), *New Perspectives on Renaissance Thought: Essays in the History of Science, Education and Philosophy in Memory of Charles B. Schmitt* (London, 1990), 68–82.

Jennings, Francis, *The Invasion of America: Indians, Colonialism, and the Cant of Conquest* (Chapel Hill, 1975).

Jones, Howard Mumford, 'Origins of the Colonial Idea in England', *Proceedings of the American Philosophical Society*, 85 (1942), 448–65.

Jordan, Gerald, and Nicholas Rogers, 'Admirals as Heroes: Patriotism and Liberty in Hanoverian England', *Journal of British Studies*, 28 (1989), 201–24.

Judd, Denis, *Empire: The British Imperial Experience, From 1765 to the Present* (London, 1996).

Juricek, John T., 'English Claims in North America to 1660: A Study in Legal and Constitutional History' (Ph.D. dissertation, University of Chicago, 1970).

Kammen, Michael, 'The Meaning of Colonization in American Revolutionary Thought', *Journal of the History of Ideas*, 31 (1976), 337–58.

Kearney, Hugh, 'The Political Background to English Mercantilism, 1695–1700', *Economic History Review*, 11 (1959), 484–96.

Kelley, Maurice, 'Milton and Machiavelli's *Discorsi*', *Studies in Bibliography*, 4 (1951–52), 123–7.

Kelly, James, 'The Origins of the Act of Union: An Examination of Unionist Opinion in Britain and Ireland, 1650–1800', *Irish Historical Studies*, 25 (1987), 236–63.

Kelly, Patrick, 'The Irish Woollen Export Prohibition Act of 1699: Kearney Revisited', *Irish Economic and Social History*, 7 (1980), 22–44.

'Ireland and the Glorious Revolution', in Robert Beddard (ed.), *The Revolutions of 1688: The Andrew Browning Lectures 1988* (Oxford, 1991), 163–90.

Kelsey, Harry, *Sir Francis Drake: The Queen's Pirate* (New Haven, 1998).

Kennedy, D. E., 'King James I's College of Controversial Divinity at Chelsea', in D. E. Kennedy, Diana Robertson and Alexandra Walsham, *Grounds of Controversy: Three Studies in Late 16th and Early 17th Century English Polemics* (Melbourne, 1989), 97–126.

Kennedy, Paul, *The Rise and Fall of British Naval Mastery* (London, 1976).

Kiernan, V. G., 'State and Nation in Western Europe', *Past and Present*, 31 (July 1965), 20–38.

Knapp, Jeffrey, *An Empire Nowhere: England, America, and Literature from Utopia to the Tempest* (Berkeley, 1992).

Knorr, Klaus E., *British Colonial Theories 1570–1850* (Toronto, 1944).

Koebner, Richard, '"The Imperial Crown of this Realm": Henry VIII, Constantine the Great, and Polydore Vergil', *Bulletin of the Institute of Historical Research*, 26 (1953), 29–52.

Koenigsberger, H. G., '*Dominium Regale* or *Dominium Politicum et Regale*: Monarchies and Parliaments in Early Modern Europe', in Koenigsberger, *Politicians and Virtuosi: Essays in Early Modern History* (London, 1986), 1–25.

'Composite States, Representative Institutions and the American Revolution', *Historical Research*, 62 (1989), 135–54.

Krynen, Jacques, *L'Empire du roi: idées et croyances politiques en France XIIIe–XVe siècle* (Paris, 1993).

Kupperman, Karen Ordahl, 'Errand to the Indies: Puritan Colonization from Providence Island through the Western Design', *William and Mary Quarterly*, 3rd ser., 45 (1988), 70–99.

Lake, Peter, *Anglicans and Puritans? Presbyterianism and English Conformist Thought from Whitgift to Hooker* (London, 1988).

'The Significance of the Elizabethan Identification of the Pope as Antichrist', *Journal of Ecclesiastical History*, 31 (1980), 161–78.

Lawson, Philip, *A Taste for Empire and Glory: Studies in British Overseas Expansion, 1660–1800* (Aldershot, 1997).

'The Missing Link: The Imperial Dimension in Understanding Hanoverian Britain', *The Historical Journal*, 29 (1986), 747–51.

Lee, Maurice, *Great Britain's Solomon: James VI and I in His Three Kingdoms* (Urbana, 1990).

Leranbaum, Miriam, *Alexander Pope's 'Opus Magnum' 1729–1744* (Oxford, 1977).

Lestringant, Frank, *Le Huguenot et le sauvage: l'Amérique et la controverse coloniale, en France, au temps des Guerres de Religion (1555–1589)* (Paris, 1990).

Levack, Brian P., *The Formation of the British State: England, Scotland, and the Union 1603–1707* (Oxford, 1987).

Linebaugh, Peter, *The London Hanged: Crime and Civil Society in the Eighteenth Century* (Cambridge, 1992).

Lintott, Andrew, 'What was the "Imperium Romanum"?', *Greece and Rome*, 28 (1981), 53–67.

Lloyd, T. O., *The British Empire 1558–1983* (Oxford, 1984).

Lokken, Roy N., 'Sir William Keith's Theory of the British Empire', *The Historian*, 25 (1963), 403–18.

Louis, Wm. Roger (gen. ed.), *The Oxford History of the British Empire*, 5 vols. (Oxford, 1998–99).

Lovejoy, David S., *Religious Enthusiasm in the New World* (Cambridge, Mass., 1985).

McConica, James B., 'Humanism and Aristotle in Tudor Oxford', *English Historical Review*, 94 (1979), 291–317.

McCullough, Peter E., *Sermons at Court: Politics and Religion in Elizabethan and Jacobean Preaching* (Cambridge, 1998).

Macdougall, Norman, *James III: A Political Study* (Edinburgh, 1982).

Macinnes, Allan I., *Charles I and the Making of the Covenanting Movement, 1625–1641* (Edinburgh, 1991).

Clanship, Commerce and the House of Stuart, 1603–1788 (East Linton, 1996).

Maclure, Millar, *The Paul's Cross Sermons 1534–1642* (Toronto, 1958).

McNeil, Kent, *Common Law Aboriginal Title* (Oxford, 1989).

MacQueen, John, 'Aspects of Humanism in Sixteenth and Seventeenth Century Literature', in MacQueen (ed.), *Humanism in Renaissance Scotland* (Edinburgh, 1990), 10–31.

Madden, A. F. McC., '1066, 1776 and All That: The Relevance of the English Medieval Experience of "Empire" to Later Imperial Constitutional Issues', in John E. Flint and Glyndwr Williams (eds.), *Perspectives of Empire: Essays Presented to Gerald S. Graham* (London, 1973), 9–26.

Mahan, A. T., *The Influence of Sea Power upon History 1660–1783* (Boston, 1890).

Maitland, F. W., 'The Anglican Settlement and the Scottish Reformation', in A. W. Ward, G. W. Prothero and Stanley Leathes (eds.), *The Cambridge Modern History*, ii: *The Reformation* (London, 1904), 550–98.

Maltby, William S., *The Black Legend in England: The Development of Anti-Spanish Sentiment, 1558–1660* (Durham, NC, 1971).

Marshall, P. J., '*A Free Though Conquering People': Britain and Asia in the Eighteenth Century*, Inaugural Lecture, King's College London, 5 March 1981 (London, 1981).

'Empire and Authority in the Later Eighteenth Century', *Journal of Imperial and Commonwealth History*, 15 (1987), 105–22.

'Imperial Britain', *Journal of Imperial and Commonwealth History*, 23 (1995), 379–94.

'Parliament and Property Rights in the Eighteenth-Century British Empire', in John Brewer and Susan Staves (eds.), *Early Modern Conceptions of Property* (London, 1996), 530–44.

'Britain and the World in the Eighteenth Century: I, Reshaping the Empire', *Transactions of the Royal Historical Society*, 6th ser., 8 (1998), 1–18.

Marshall, P. J. (ed.), *The Cambridge Illustrated History of the British Empire* (Cambridge, 1996).

(ed.), *The Oxford History of the British Empire*, II: *The Eighteenth Century* (Oxford, 1998).

Marshall, Peter, 'The First and Second British Empires: A Question of Demarcation', *History*, 49 (1964), 13–23.

Mason, Roger A., 'Scotching the Brute: Politics, History and National Myth in Sixteenth-Century Britain', in Mason (ed.), *Scotland and England 1286–1815* (Edinburgh, 1987), 60–84.

'The Scottish Reformation and the Origins of Anglo-British Imperialism', in Mason (ed.), *Scots and Britons: Scottish Political Thought and the Union of 1603* (Cambridge, 1994), 161–86.

'*Regnum et Imperium*: Humanism and the Political Culture of Renaissance Scotland', in Mason, *Kingship and the Commonweal: Political Thought in Renaissance and Reformation Scotland* (East Linton, 1998), 104–38.

Mayer, Thomas F., 'On the Road to 1534: The Occupation of Tournai and Henry VIII's Theory of Sovereignty', in Dale Hoak (ed.), *Tudor Political Culture* (Cambridge, 1995), 11–30.

Mehta, Uday Singh, *Liberalism and Empire: A Study in Nineteenth-Century British Liberal Thought* (Chicago, 1999).

Mendle, Michael, 'The Ship Money Case, *The Case of Shipmony*, and the Development of Henry Parker's Parliamentary Absolutism', *The Historical Journal*, 32 (1989), 513–36.

Menendez, Pidal Ramón, *El Idea Imperial de Carlos V* (Buenos Aires, 1941).

Merchant, W. Moelwyn, 'Donne's Sermon to the Virginia Company, 13 November 1622', in A. J. Smith (ed.), *John Donne: Essays in Celebration* (London, 1972), 437–52.

Merriman, Marcus, 'The Assured Scots: Scottish Collaborators with England during the Rough Wooing', *Scottish Historical Review*, 47 (1968), 10–35.

'War and Propaganda during the "Rough Wooing"', *Scottish Tradition*, 9/10 (1979–80), 20–30.

'James Henrisoun and "Great Britain": British Union and the Scottish Commonweal', in Roger A. Mason (ed.), *Scotland and England 1286–1815* (Edinburgh, 1987), 85–112.

Metcalf, Thomas R., *Ideologies of the Raj, The New Cambridge History of India*, III.4 (Cambridge, 1994).

Meyer, Arnold Oskar, 'Der Britische Kaisertitel zur Zeit des Stuarts', *Quellen und Forschungen aus italienischen Archiven und Bibliotheken*, 10 (1907), 231–7.

Miller, Leo, *John Milton and the Oldenburg Safeguard* (New York, 1985).

Miller, Peter N., *Defining the Common Good: Empire, Religion and Philosophy in Eighteenth-Century Britain* (Cambridge, 1994).

Milton, Anthony, *Catholic and Reformed: The Roman and Protestant Churches in English Protestant Thought, 1600–1640* (Cambridge, 1995).

Milton, John, 'John Locke and the Fundamental Constitutions of Carolina', *The Locke Newsletter*, 21 (1990), 111–33.

Moore, Stuart A., *The History of the Foreshore and the Law Relating Thereto* (London, 1888).

Morgan, Hiram, *Tyrone's Rebellion: The Outbreak of the Nine Years' War in Ireland* (Woodbridge, 1993).

'The Colonial Venture of Sir Thomas Smith in Ulster, 1571–1575', *The Historical Journal*, 28 (1985), 261–78.

'Mid–Atlantic Blues', *Irish Review*, 11 (1991–92), 50–5.

'British Policies Before the British State', in Brendan Bradshaw and John Morrill (eds.), *The British Problem, c. 1534–1707: State Formation in the Atlantic Archipelago* (Basingstoke, 1996), 66–88.

Morley, John, *The Life of Richard Cobden*, 2 vols. (London, 1881).

Moynihan, Ruth Baynes, 'The Patent and the Indians: The Problem of Jurisdiction in Seventeenth-Century New England', *American Indian Culture and Research Journal*, 2 (1977), 8–18.

Muldoon, James, 'Spritual Conquests Compared: *Laudabiliter* and the Conquest of the Americas', in Steven B. Bowman and Blanche E. Cody (eds.), *In Iure Veritas: Studies in Canon Law in Memory of Schafer Williams* (Cincinnati, 1991), 174–86.

Muller, Samuel, *Mare Clausum: Bijdrage tot de Geschiedenis der Rivaliteit van Engeland en Nederland in de Zeventiende Eeuw* (Amsterdam, 1872).

Nicholson, G. D., 'The Nature and Function of Historical Argument in the Henrician Reformation' (Ph.D. dissertation, University of Cambridge, 1977).

'The Act of Appeals and the English Reformation', in Claire Cross, David Loades and J. J. Scarisbrick (eds.), *Law and Government under the Tudors* (Cambridge, 1988), 19–30.

Norbrook, David, *Writing the English Republic: Poetry, Rhetoric and Politics, 1627–1660* (Cambridge, 1999).

Norton, David Fate, 'Francis Hutcheson in America', *Studies on Voltaire and the Eighteenth Century*, 154 (1976), 1547–68.

Novick, Peter, *That Noble Dream: The 'Objectivity Question' and the American Historical Profession* (Cambridge, 1988).

Ohlmeyer, Jane H., '"Civilizinge of Those Rude Partes": Colonization within Britain and Ireland, 1580s–1640s', in Nicholas Canny (ed.), *The Oxford History of the British Empire*, I: *The Origins of Empire* (Oxford, 1998), 124–47.

Olsen, Palle J., 'Was John Foxe a Millenarian?', *Journal of Ecclesiastical History*, 45 (1994), 600–24.

Osmond, Patricia, 'Sallust and Machiavelli: From Civic Humanism to Political Prudence', *Journal of Medieval and Renaissance Studies*, 23 (1993), 407–38.

Pagden, Anthony, *Lords of All the World: Ideologies of Empire in Spain, Britain and France c. 1500 – c. 1800* (New Haven, 1995).

'Dispossessing the Barbarian: The Language of Spanish Thomism and the Debate over the Property Rights of the American Indians', in Pagden (ed.), *The Languages of Political Theory in Early-Modern Europe* (Cambridge, 1986), 79–98.

'The Humanism of Vasco de Quiroga's "Información en Derecho"', in
  Wolfgang Reinhard (ed.), *Humanismus und Neue Welt* (Bonn, 1987), 133–42.
Parekh, Bhikhu, 'Liberalism and Colonialism: A Critique of Locke and Mill', in
  J. P. Nederveen Pieterse and Bhikhu Parekh (eds.), *The Decolonization of
  Imagination: Culture, Knowledge, and Power* (London, 1995), 81–98.
Parker, John, 'Religion and the Virginia Colony 1609–10', in K. R. Andrews,
  N. P. Canny and P. E. H. Hair (eds.), *The Westward Enterprise: English
  Activities in Ireland, the Atlantic, and America 1480–1650* (Liverpool, 1979),
  245–70.
  'Samuel Purchas, Spokesman for Empire', in Ton Croiset van Uchelen,
  Koerst van der Horst and Günter Schilder (eds.), *Theatrum Orbis Librorum:
  Liber Amicorum Presented to Nico Israel on the Occasion of his Seventieth Birthday*
  (Utrecht, 1989), 47–56.
Parker, William Riley, *Milton: A Biographical Commentary*, 2nd edn, ed. Gordon
  Campbell, 2 vols. (Oxford, 1996).
Parkhill, Trevor, 'Arthur Dobbs: Colonial Undertaker and Governor of North
  Carolina', in D. Helen Rankin and E. Charles Nelson (eds.), *Curious in
  Everything: The Career of Arthur Dobbs of Carrickfergus 1689–1765* (Carrickfergus,
  1990), 15–22.
Parks, George Bruner, *Richard Hakluyt and the English Voyages* (New York, 1928).
Peltonen, Markku, *Classical Humanism and Republicanism in English Political
  Thought, 1570–1640* (Cambridge, 1995).
  'Classical Republicanism in Tudor England: The Case of Richard Beacon's
  Solon His Follie', *History of Political Thought*, 15 (1994), 469–503.
Pennington, L. E., '*Hakluytus Posthumus*: Samuel Purchas and the Promotion of
  English Overseas Expansion', *Emporia State Research Studies*, 14, 3 (1966).
Pennington, L. E. (ed.), *The Purchas Handbook: Studies of the Life, Times and Writings
  of Samuel Purchas 1577–1626*, 2 vols. (London, 1997).
Perceval-Maxwell, Michael, *The Scottish Migration to Ulster in the Reign of James I*
  (London, 1973).
  'Ireland and the Monarchy in the Early Stuart Multiple Kingdom', *The
  Historical Journal*, 34 (1991), 279–95.
Pettit, Philip, *Republicanism: A Theory of Freedom and Government* (Oxford, 1997).
  'Liberalism and Republicanism', *Australian Journal of Political Science*, 28 (1993),
  Special Issue, 162–89.
Pincus, Steven C. A., *Protestantism and Patriotism: Ideologies and the Making of English
  Foreign Policy, 1650–1668* (Cambridge, 1996).
  'The English Debate over Universal Monarchy', in John Robertson (ed.), *A
  Union for Empire: Political Thought and the British Union of 1707* (Cambridge,
  1995), 37–62.
Pocock, J. G. A., *Virtue, Commerce and History: Essays on Political Thought and History,
  Chiefly in the Eighteenth Century* (Cambridge, 1985), 125–41.
  'British History: A Plea for a New Subject', *New Zealand Historical Journal*, 8
  (1974), 3–21, rptd in *Journal of Modern History*, 4 (1975), 601–24.
  'The Limits and Divisions of British History: In Search of the Unknown
  Subject', *American Historical Review*, 87 (1982), 311–36.

'History and Sovereignty: The Historiographic Response to Europeaniz-ation in Two British Cultures', *Journal of British Studies*, 31 (1991), 358–89.

Porter, Andrew, '"Cultural Imperialism" and Protestant Missionary Enter-prise, 1780–1914', *Journal of Imperial and Commonwealth History*, 25 (1997), 367–91.

Porter, H. C., *The Inconstant Savage: England and the North American Indian 1500–1660* (London, 1979).

Price, Jacob M., 'Who Cared About the Colonies? The Impact of the Thirteen Colonies on British Society and Politics, circa 1714–1775', in Bernard Bailyn and Philip D. Morgan (eds.), *Strangers within the Realm: Cultural Margins of the First British Empire* (Chapel Hill, 1991), 395–436.

Quinn, D. B., *The Elizabethans and the Irish* (Ithaca, 1966).

'Sir Thomas Smith (1513–1577) and the Beginnings of English Colonial Theory', *Proceedings of the American Philosophical Society*, 89 (1945), 543–60.

'Ireland and Sixteenth Century European Expansion', in T. Desmond Williams (ed.), *Historical Studies*, 1 (London, 1958), 21–32.

'The First Pilgrims', *William and Mary Quarterly*, 3rd ser., 23 (1966), 359–90.

'Renaissance Influences in English Colonization', *Transactions of the Royal Historical Society*, 5th ser., 26 (1976), 73–92.

Quinn, D. B. (ed.), *The Hakluyt Handbook*, 2 vols. (London, 1974).

Ramsay, G. D., 'Clothworkers, Merchant Adventurers, and Richard Hakluyt', *Economic History Review*, 2nd ser., 92 (1977), 504–21.

Ramsland, Clement, 'Britons Never Will Be Slaves: A Study in Whig Political Propaganda in the British Theatre, 1700–1742', *Quarterly Journal of Speech*, 28 (1942), 393–9.

Reid, John G., *Acadia, Maine, and New Scotland: Marginal Colonies in the Seventeenth Century* (Toronto, 1981).

Richardson, J. S., '*Imperium Romanum*: Empire and the Language of Power', *Journal of Roman Studies*, 81 (1991), 1–9.

Robbins, Caroline, '"When It Is That Colonies May Turn Independent": An Analysis of the Environment and Politics of Francis Hutcheson (1694–1746)', in Barbara Taft (ed.), *Absolute Liberty: A Selection from the Articles and Papers of Caroline Robbins* (Hamden, Conn., 1982), 133–67.

Roberts, Michael, *The Swedish Imperial Experience, 1560–1718* (Cambridge, 1979).

Roberts, Peter, 'Tudor Wales, National Identity and the British Inheritance', in Brendan Bradshaw and Peter Roberts (eds.), *British Consciousness and Ident-ity: The Making of Britain, 1533–1707* (Cambridge, 1998), 8–42.

Robertson, John, 'Universal Monarchy and the Liberties of Europe: David Hume's Critique of an English Whig Doctrine', in Nicholas Phillipson and Quentin Skinner (eds.), *Political Discourse in Early Modern Britain* (Cam-bridge, 1993), 349–73.

'Union, State and Empire: The Britain of 1707 in its European Setting', in Lawrence Stone (ed.), *An Imperial State at War: Britain from 1688 to 1815* (London, 1994), 224–57.

'The Scottish Enlightenment', *Rivista Storica Italiana*, 108 (1996), 792–829.

Rodger, N. A. M., *The Safeguard of the Sea: A Naval History of Britain, I: 660–1649* (London, 1997).

Roelofsen, C. G., 'Grotius and the International Politics of the Seventeenth Century', in Hedley Bull, Benedict Kingsbury and Adam Roberts (eds.), *Hugo Grotius and International Relations* (Oxford, 1990), 95–131.

'The Sources of *Mare Liberum*: The Contested Origins of the Doctrine of the Freedom of the Seas', in Wybo P. Heere (ed.), *International Law and its Sources: Liber Amicorum Maarten Bos* (The Hague, 1989), 93–124.

Rogers, Nicholas, *Whigs and Cities: Popular Politics in the Age of Walpole and Pitt* (Oxford, 1989).

Rose, J. Holland, A. P. Newton and E. A. Benians (gen. eds.), *The Cambridge History of the British Empire*, 9 vols. (Cambridge, 1929–61).

Rose-Troup, Frances, *John White, The Patriarch of Dorchester and the Founder of Massachusetts 1575–1648* (London, 1930).

Rosenthal, Earl, '*Plus Ultra, Non Plus Ultra*, and the Columnar Device of the Emperor Charles V', *Journal of the Warburg and Courtauld Institutes*, 34 (1971), 204–28.

Russell, Conrad, *The Fall of the British Monarchies 1637–1642* (Oxford, 1991).

Ryan, Lawrence V., 'Richard Hakluyt's Voyage into Aristotle', *Sixteenth Century Journal*, 12 (1981), 73–83.

Sacks, David Harris, *The Widening Gate: Bristol and the Atlantic Economy, 1450–1700* (Berkeley, 1991).

Said, Edward, *Culture and Imperialism* (London, 1993).

Sambrook, James, *James Thomson 1700–1748: A Life* (Oxford, 1991).

Sasso, Gennaro, *Studi su Machiavelli* (Naples, 1967).

Saville, Richard, *Bank of Scotland: A History 1695–1995* (Edinburgh, 1996).

Schama, Simon, *The Embarrassment of Riches: An Interpretation of Dutch Culture in the Golden Age* (London, 1987).

Schmitt, Carl, *Land and Sea*, trans. Simona Draghici (Washington, DC, 1997).

Schmitt, Charles B., *John Case and Aristotelianism in Renaissance England* (Kingston, Ont., 1983).

Scott, W. R., *Francis Hutcheson: His Life, Teaching and Position in the History of Philosophy* (Cambridge, 1900).

Seed, Patricia, *Ceremonies of Possession in Europe's Conquest of the New World 1492–1640* (Cambridge, 1995).

Sherman, William H., *John Dee: The Politics of Reading and Writing in the English Renaissance* (Amherst, Mass., 1995).

Shklar, Judith, 'Ideology-Hunting: The Case of James Harrington', *American Political Science Review*, 53 (1959), 662–92.

Skinner, Quentin, *The Foundations of Modern Political Thought*, 2 vols. (Cambridge, 1978).

Liberty Before Liberalism (Cambridge, 1998).

'Sir Thomas More's *Utopia* and the Language of Renaissance Humanism', in Anthony Pagden (ed.), *The Languages of Political Theory in Early Modern Europe* (Cambridge, 1987), 123–57.

'Language and Social Change', in James Tully (ed.), *Meaning and Context: Quentin Skinner and His Critics* (Princeton, 1988), 119–33.

Smith, G. C. Moore, 'Robert Hayman and the Plantation of Newfoundland', *English Historical Review*, 33 (1918), 21–36.

Smith, H. F. Russell, *Harrington and His Oceana* (Cambridge, 1914).

Smyth, Jim, '"No Remedy More Proper": Anglo-Irish Unionism before 1707', in Brendan Bradshaw and Peter Roberts (eds.), *British Consciousness and Identity: The Making of Britain, 1533–1707* (Cambridge, 1998), 301–20.

Spielman, M. H., *Millais and His Works* (Edinburgh, 1898).

Sreenivasan, Gopal, *The Limits of Lockean Rights in Property* (Oxford, 1995).

Steele, Ian K., *The English Atlantic: 1675–1740: An Exploration of Communication and Community* (New York, 1986).

Stevens, Paul, '"Leviticus Thinking" and the Rhetoric of Early Modern Colonialism', *Criticism*, 35 (1993), 441–61.

Stocker, Margarita, and Timothy Raylor, 'A New Marvell Manuscript: Cromwellian Patronage and Politics', *ELR*, 20 (1990), 106–62.

Stokes, Eric, *The Political Ideas of English Imperialism: An Inaugural Lecture Given in the University College of Rhodesia and Nyasaland* (Oxford, 1960).

Stone, Lawrence (ed.), *An Imperial State at War: Britain from 1689 to 1815* (London, 1994).

Strype, John, *The Life of the Learned Sir Thomas Smith, Kt. D.C.L. Principal Secretary of State to King Edward the Sixth, and Queen Elizabeth* (London, 1820).

Taylor, Miles, 'Imperium et Libertas? Rethinking the Radical Critique of Imperialism during the Nineteenth Century', *Journal of Imperial and Commonwealth History*, 19 (1991), 1–23.

Thompson, E. P., *'Alien Homage': Edward Thompson and Rabindranath Tagore* (Delhi, 1993).

Torchiana, Donald J., 'Brutus: Pope's Last Hero', in Maynard Mack (ed.), *Essential Articles for the Study of Alexander Pope* (Hamden, Conn., 1968), 705–23.

Trevor-Roper, Hugh, *From Counter-Reformation to Glorious Revolution* (London, 1992).

Truxes, Thomas M., *Irish-American Trade, 1660–1783* (Cambridge, 1988).

Tuck, Richard, *Natural Rights Theories: Their Origin and Development* (Cambridge, 1979).

Philosophy and Government, 1572–1651 (Cambridge, 1993).

Tully, James, *A Discourse on Property: John Locke and His Adversaries* (Cambridge, 1980).

Strange Multiplicity: Constitutionalism in an Age of Diversity (Cambridge, 1995).

'Rediscovering America: The *Two Treatises* and Aboriginal Rights', in Tully, *An Approach to Political Philosophy: Locke in Contexts* (Cambridge, 1993), 137–76.

Ullmann, Walter, 'The Development of the Medieval Idea of Sovereignty', *English Historical Review*, 64 (1949), 1–33.

'"This Realm of England is an Empire"', *Journal of Ecclesiastical History*, 30 (1979), 175–203.

Viner, Jacob, *The Role of Providence in the Social Order: An Essay in Intellectual History* (Princeton, 1972).

Viroli, Maurizio, *Machiavelli* (Oxford, 1998).

'Machiavelli and the Republican Idea of Politics', in Gisela Bock, Quentin Skinner and Maurizio Viroli (eds.), *Machiavelli and Republicanism* (Cambridge, 1990), 143–71.

von Maltzahn, Nicholas, *Milton's History of Britain: Republican Historiography in the English Revolution* (Oxford, 1991).

Walker, David M., *The Scottish Jurists* (Edinburgh, 1985).

Walvin, James, *Fruits of Empire: Exotic Produce and British Taste, 1660–1800* (Basingstoke, 1997).

Washburn, Wilcomb E., 'The Moral and Legal Justification for Dispossessing the Indians', in James Morton Smith (ed.), *Seventeenth-Century America: Essays in Colonial History* (Chapel Hill, 1959), 15–32.

Weslager, C. A., *New Sweden on the Delaware 1638–1655* (Wilmington, Del., 1988).

Williams, Gwyn A., *Welsh Wizard and British Empire: Dr. John Dee and Welsh Identity* (Cardiff, 1980).

Williamson, Arthur H., *Scottish National Consciousness in the Age of James VI* (Edinburgh, 1979).

'Scots, Indians and Empire: The Scottish Politics of Civilization, 1519–1609', *Past and Present*, 150 (Feb. 1996), 46–83.

Wilson, Kathleen, *The Sense of the People: Politics, Culture and Imperialism in England, 1715–1785* (Cambridge, 1995).

'Empire, Trade and Popular Politics in Mid-Hanoverian Britain: The Case of Admiral Vernon', *Past and Present*, 121 (Nov. 1988), 74–109.

Winch, Peter, *The Idea of a Social Science and its Relation to Philosophy*, 2nd edn (London, 1990).

Wirszubski, Chaim, *Libertas as a Political Idea at Rome during the Late Republic and Early Principate* (Cambridge, 1950).

Wood, Neal, *Foundations of Political Economy: Some Early Tudor Views on State and Society* (Berkeley, 1994).

Worden, Blair, 'Oliver Cromwell and the Sin of Achan', in Derek Beales and Geoffrey Best (eds.), *History, Society and the Churches* (Cambridge, 1985), 125–45.

'English Republicanism', in J. H. Burns and Mark Goldie (eds.), *The Cambridge History of Political Thought 1450–1700* (Cambridge, 1991), 443–75.

Worden, Blair, 'Milton and Marchamont Nedham', in David Armitage, Armand Himy and Quentin Skinner (eds.), *Milton and Republicanism* (Cambridge, 1995), 156–80.

Wormald, Jenny, 'The Creation of Britain: Multiple Kingdoms or Core and Colonies?', *Transactions of the Royal Historical Society*, 6th ser., 2 (1992), 175–94.

Wormell, Deborah, *Sir John Seeley and the Uses of History* (Cambridge, 1980).

Wright, Louis B., *Religion and Empire* (Chapel Hill, 1943).

Yates, Frances A., 'Charles V and the Idea of the Empire', in Yates, *Astraea: The Imperial Theme in the Sixteenth Century* (London, 1975), 1–28.

Zagorin, Perez, *A History of Political Thought in the English Revolution* (London, 1954).

Zakai, Avihu, *Exile and Kingdom: History and Apocalypse in the Puritan Migration to America* (Cambridge, 1992).

Zeller, Gaston, 'Les Rois de France, candidats à l'empire: essai sur l'idéologie impériale en France', *Revue Historique*, 173 (1934), 273–311, 497–543.

Index

Ideas in context